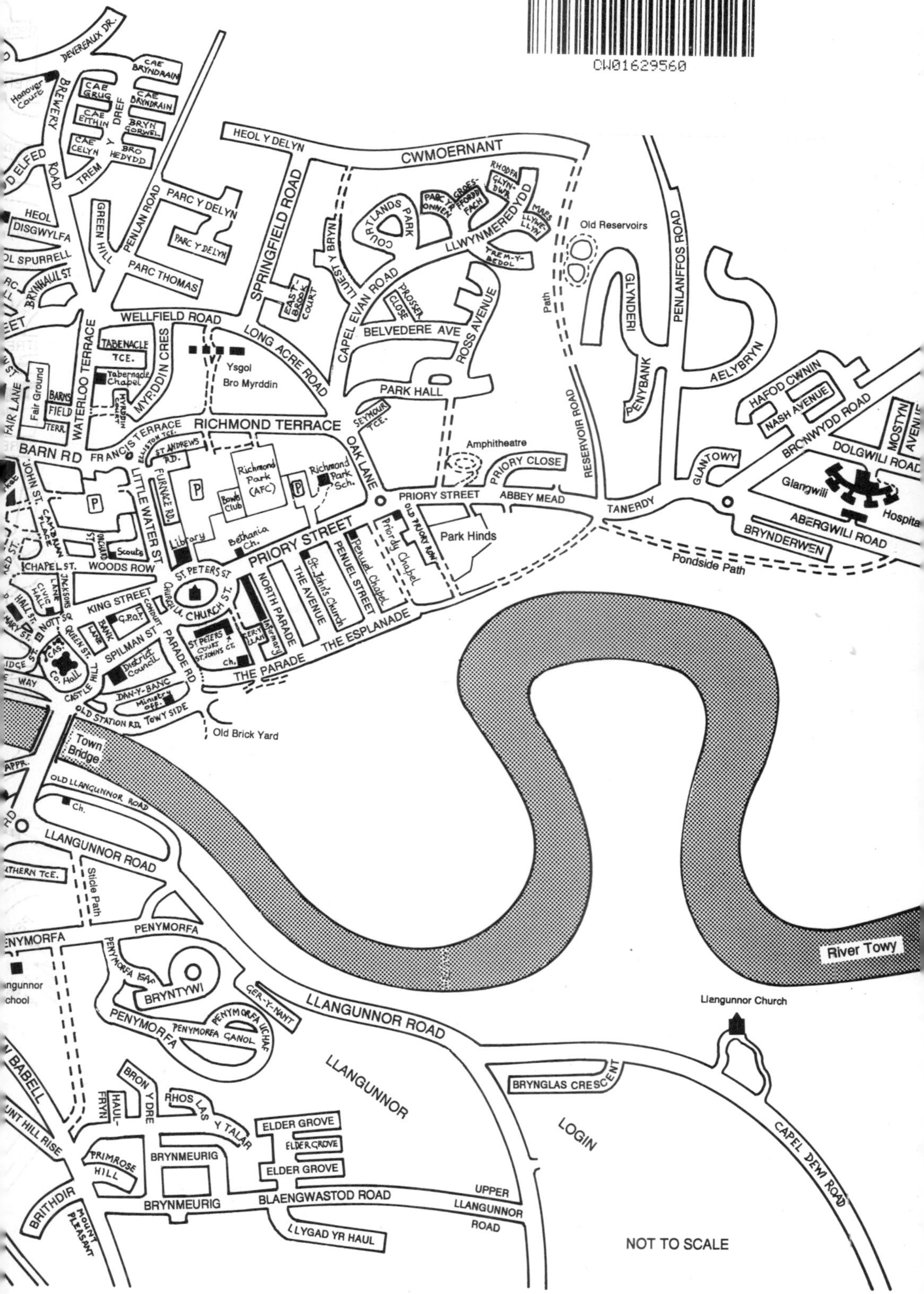
DEVEREAUX DR.
Hanover Court
BREWERY ROAD
CAE BRYNDRAIN
CAE GRUG
CAE BRYNDRAIN
CAE EITHIN
DREF
BRYN GORWEL
CAE CELYN
Y
BRO HEDYDD
TREM
ELFED
HEOL DISGWYLFA
SPURRELL
BRYNHAUL ST.
GREEN HILL
PENLAN ROAD
PARC Y DELYN
PARC Y DELYN
PARC THOMAS
HEOL Y DELYN
CWMOERNANT
SPRINGFIELD ROAD
EAST-BROOK COURT
LLUEST Y BRYN
COURTLANDS PARK
PARC YR ONNEN
GROES-FFORDD FACH
RHODFA GLYNDWR
LLWYNMEREDYDD
MAES LLYWELYN
TREM-Y-BEDOL
CAPEL EVAN ROAD
PROSSER CLOSE
BELVEDERE AVE
ROSS AVENUE
PARK HALL
Old Reservoirs
Path
GLYNDERI
PENLANFFOS ROAD
PENYBANK
AELYBRYN
HAFOD CWNIN
NASH AVENUE
BRONWYDD ROAD
MOSTYN AVENUE
DOLGWILI ROAD
Glangwili
Hospital
ABERGWILI ROAD
BRYNDERWEN
GLANTOWY
TANERDY
RESERVOIR ROAD
Pondside Path
WELLFIELD ROAD
LONG ACRE ROAD
Ysgol Bro Myrddin
TABERNACLE TCE.
Tabernacle Chapel
WATERLOO TERRACE
MYRDDIN CRES
MYRDDIN COURT
FAIR LANE
Fair Ground
BARNS FIELD TERR.
RICHMOND TERRACE
FRANCIS TERRACE
ELLISTON TCE.
ST ANDREWS RD.
SEYMOUR TCE.
OAK LANE
Amphitheatre
PRIORY CLOSE
PRIORY STREET
ABBEY MEAD
BARN RD
JOHN ST.
CAMBRIAN PLACE
LITTLE WATER ST
FURNACE RD.
Richmond Park (AFC)
Bowls Club
Richmond Park Sch.
Library
Bethania Ch.
PRIORY STREET
OLD PRIORY ROW
Priordy Chapel
Park Hinds
ORCHARD ST
Scouts
CHAPEL ST.
WOODS ROW
ST. PETERS ST
CIVIC HALL
JACKSONS LANE
KING STREET
G.P.O.
CHURCH LA.
CONDUIT
CHURCH ST.
NORTH PARADE
THE AVENUE
St. John's Church
PENUEL STREET
Penuel Chapel
THE ESPLANADE
NOTT SQ
QUEEN ST.
BANK LANE
SPILMAN ST
PARADE RD
ST PETERS COURT
ST. JOHNS CT.
Ch.
Infirmary
THE PARADE
CAS. Co. Hall
CASTLE HILL
District Council
DAN-Y-BANC
Ministry Off.
OLD STATION RD.
TOWY SIDE
Old Brick Yard
Town Bridge
OLD LLANGUNNOR ROAD
Ch.
LLANGUNNOR ROAD
Stiele Path
PENYMORFA
PENYMORFA ISAF
BRYNTYWI
GER-Y-NANT
PENYMORFA UCHAF
PENYMORFA GANOL
PENYMORFA
LLANGUNNOR ROAD
River Towy
Llangunnor Church
LLANGUNNOR
BRYNGLAS CRESCENT
LOGIN
CAPEL DEWI ROAD
BABELL
HILL RISE
BRON Y DRE
HAUL-FRYN
RHOS LAS
Y TALAR
ELDER GROVE
ELDER GROVE
ELDER GROVE
PRIMROSE HILL
BRYNMEURIG
BRYNMEURIG
BLAENGWASTOD ROAD
UPPER LLANGUNNOR ROAD
BRITHDIR
MOUNT PLEASANT
LLYGAD YR HAUL
NOT TO SCALE

THE STORY OF CARMARTHEN

Charter Rolls and Ancient Deeds

RELATING TO THE TOWN AND COUNTY OF CARMARTHEN.

ROTULI CHARTARUM. ANNO DOMINI 1201. 2ND KING JOHN. MEMB. 16.

Confirmatio hominum de Kaermerdin. } **Johannes** Dei, &c. Justiciarijs, &c. Precipimus vobis quod Burgenses nostri de Kaermerdin sint quieti de theolonio et passagio et pontagio et omnibus consuetudinibus per terram nostram totam: et prohibemus ne quis eos injuste disturbet super forisfacturam omnium catellor' suor', sicut carta Henrici Regis patris nostri rationabiliter testatur.

Teste R. Sancti Andree Episcopo. G. filio Petri Comitis Essexie. Willielmo de Braosa, &c. Datum per manum nostram apud Geytinton vj die Januarij regni nostri anno secundo.

Confirmation of the men of Kaermerdin. } **John**, by the Grace of God, &c. to his Justiciars, &c. We command you that our burgesses of Kaermerdin be quit of toll and passage and pontage, and all customs throughout our Kingdom, and we prohibit that any one unjustly disturb them upon forfeiture of all his chattels as the Charter of King Henry reasonably testifies.

Witness R.[2] Bishop of Saint Andrews. G.[3] the son of Peter, Earl of Essex. William de Braosa, and others. Dated by our hand at Geddington the 6th day of January in the second year of our reign.

[2] Roger de Bellomont

[3] Geoffrey Fitz Piers

Charter Roll of King John, 1201
(From *Royal Charters and Historical Documents relating to the Town and County of Carmarthen* .... by J. R. Daniel-Tyssen.)

THE STORY of CARMARTHEN

REVISED EDITION

Joyce and Victor Lodwick

Illustrated by
Edith Lodwick

ST. PETER'S PRESS, CARMARTHEN

First published 1953
Second edition 1972
This updated, expanded and reillustrated edition published 1994
Reprinted 1995

ISBN 0-9517962-0-8

Printed in Wales
and published by
St. Peter's Press,
8 & 9 Woods Row,
Carmarthen

Contents

THE SOUTH-EAST VIEW OF CARMARTHEN.

CARMARTHEN IN 1748

(As seen and described by Samuel and Nathaniel Buck)

Carmarthen, call'd by the Britains Kaer Vyrdhin, and by the Romans Maridunum, is a place of great Antiquity; famous, amongst other things for the birth of the Wise Merlin about 480. It is seated on the rising North bank of the fine River Towy or Tobius, which is Navigable to the Town for Vessels of 100 Tun; and here is a convenient Key for them to load, and unload; their Merchandizes. It is plentifully supplied with Salmon and other Fish; and with all other Provisions at an Easy rate. It is in itself very populous, and is much resorted to, by the neighbouring Gentry. It was formerly well fortified, as may be seen by the present remains of the Old Walls, and the ruins of a very Strong Castle. In the contests between the Britains and the Normans; this Place hath often felt the Severe Effects of War. When the Eldest Sons of our Kings became Princes of Wales, they here fixed their Chancery and Exchequer for the South part of their Principality. It hath now but one Church dedicated to St. Peter which is a very large one: Tho' it had formerly a free Chapel call'd the Rood Church dedicated to St. Mary, Standing where is now St. Mary's Street, & one call'd ye. King's free Chapel in ye. Castle. At the East end of the Town a Priory for 6. Black Canons was erected to the honour of St. Jno. the Evangelist before 1148. of wch. the Ruins are still Visible. It is a County Borough & is govern'd by a Mayor & other Officers. The Weekly Markets are on Wed. Frid. & Sat. ( ). The present Membr. in Parliament is Thos. Matthews Esqr.

Saml. & Nathl. Buck del. et Sculp, Publish'd according to Act of Parliamt. Septr. 8th 1748. Garden Court No. 1. Middle Temple London. 1. Friers Park. 2. The Castle. 3. The Road to Swansea. 4. The River Towy. 5. The Church. 6. The Free School. 7. The Priory.

Preface

The first edition of *The Story of Carmarthen*, by Malcolm and Edith Lodwick, appeared in 1953 and was designed to fill the need for a reference book on the town's history which was both informative and of general appeal. It was an attempt to gather together, in one volume, a wealth of data concerning Carmarthen which had been gleaned from historical records, books, periodicals and miscellaneous articles. In this the authors were following in the tradition of William Spurrell, local printer and historian, who produced his first edition of *Carmarthen and its Neighbourhood* in 1860 and his second, enlarged, edition in 1879.

The second edition of *The Story of Carmarthen*, by Joyce and Victor Lodwick, which appeared in 1972, necessitated much revision in the light of historical research and archaeological excavation but the format of the book remained largely unchanged.

With the production of this third edition we have taken the opportunity to adopt a different approach to the subject. Whilst retaining some of the features of the earlier editions, we have now adopted a chronological approach to the text, dealing in a consecutive manner with events in the town's history. At the same time, however, we have found it expedient for certain subjects to be considered separately in individual chapters. This has resulted in some unavoidable repetition and cross references, particularly where specific topics have been dealt with in greater detail. No special chapter has been devoted to the events of the 20th century but certain matters have been brought up to date under their own chapter headings. In attempting to trace Carmarthen's history from the first century A.D., we have also tried to show how local events were influenced by national affairs, thus putting local history into a wider perspective.

The illustrations are mainly by Mrs. Edith Lodwick and span a period of sixty years but we have also used the work of certain other artists of earlier periods where they illustrate the changes that have taken place in the town.

In the thirty-eight years that have now elapsed since the first edition, great advances have been made in local history research and archaeological excavation. What was once the realm of the amateur has now become a fully acknowledged subject of professional study. We are indebted to the *Dyfed Archaeological Trust* whose excavations and publications have added substantially to all previous knowledge of Carmarthen's past and whose work has provided much source material for this third edition.

No one can write a book of this kind without incurring a multitude of debts and we trust that what we owe to the published work of others is properly recorded in the foot-notes at the end of each chapter and in the bibliography. In this connection we must particularly mention the valuable material derived from the *Transactions of the Carmarthenshire Antiquarian Society, The Carmarthen Antiquary* and the *Carmarthen Journal.* We should especially like to thank Heather and Terrence James, of the Dyfed Archaeological Trust, whom we have consulted on several chapters, including those on Roman, post-Roman and medieval Carmarthen. Their advice and constructive suggestions have been invaluable and we are particularly grateful to them for allowing us to adapt some maps and illustrations from their publications. Our thanks are also due to the Revd. Towyn Jones for his helpful advice, especially on the translation of Welsh place-names, to the archivists of the County Record Office whom we have consulted on numerous occasions and to the staff of the Carmarthen Reference Library and the Carmarthen Museum for their invaluable assistance at all times. We repeat our thanks to those whose help in the two earlier editions was recorded previously. However, all opinions stated and conclusions drawn, together with all errors and deficiencies, are the responsibility of the authors alone.

Finally, we hope that this book will appeal to general readers, to those who love the town of their birth or adoption and to students of local history, bringing information and pleasure to all who open its pages.

Joyce and Victor Lodwick
Carmarthen
1994

- 1 -

HISTORICAL SURVEY

Carmarthen is the County town of Dyfed which comprises the three former counties of Carmarthen, Cardigan and Pembroke. Known as 'The Gateway to the West', and overlooking the beautiful Towy valley, Carmarthen is a thriving administrative, commercial, educational and agricultural centre serving an extensive hinterland. It is the headquarters of the three local authorities: Dyfed County Council, Carmarthen District Council and Carmarthen Town Council.

Under the Local Government Act of 1972, Carmarthen ceased to be a Borough, losing much of its local autonomy to the District Council. However, the authorities are very concerned to preserve Carmarthen's ancient heritage and traditions. Recent years have brought many changes to the old town, sweeping away some of its narrow, irregular streets, quaint alley-ways and courts, all whispering of a more leisured past. Modern shopping precincts, supermarkets and chainstores have replaced many of the small shops of individual character, although there are still parts of the town retaining something of its old-world charm, with buildings and memorials of historic interest.

Today's Carmarthen, with a population of just over 12,000 (1991 Census), has much to offer both residents and visitors - modern shopping facilities, sports and leisure activities, cultural pursuits, near-by beaches and unspoiled countryside.

The origins of the town go back almost 2,000 years, to the time of the Roman conquest of Wales, when a military fort was established here in about AD 75. To the east of the fort there grew up a civil settlement which eventually developed into a Romano-British town enclosed by rampart and ditch defences. Named *Moridunum*, its boundaries can still be traced today on the eastern side of Carmarthen. So too can the remains of its amphitheatre, one of only seven in Britain. With an estimated seating capacity of between four and five thousand, the amphitheatre reinforces the theory that Moridunum was the tribal capital of the Demetae - the name given to the Celtic tribe inhabiting this region. The only other known tribal or civitas capital in Wales is Caerwent.

The decline of Roman Carmarthen is linked with the decline of Roman power in Britain and the decline of the Roman Empire itself which was subjected to barbarian attacks from all directions. The fall of Rome in AD 410 was followed by the so-called Dark Ages, when for several centuries civilised urban living was extinguished throughout most of Europe. However, this period is traditionally known in Wales as the Age of the Celtic Saints when Christianity was established through the example and teaching of monks such as Saint David and Saint Teilo. The latter were active in this area in the sixth century. There is some historical evidence for the foundation of an early Christian church in a Celtic monastic community, referred to as Llandeulyddog, established just outside the eastern boundary of Roman Moridunum and on the site of the later medieval Priory.

When the Norman invaders reached this area in 1093, they built their first castle at Rhydygors, some distance away from Llandeulyddog but in 1109 they moved to the more strategic site on what is now known as Castle Hill. Under the protection of this new castle a market town was established for the followers of the Norman overlords; this was called New Carmarthen to distinguish it from Old Carmarthen, the native Welsh community which had grown up around the monastic settlement of Llandeulyddog. In 1125 the latter was absorbed into the newly-founded Norman Priory dedicated to St. John the Evangelist and to St. Teulyddog. While Old Carmarthen was under the jurisdiction of the Priory, New Carmarthen was under the authority of the royal castle. Throughout the Middle Ages there was constant friction between the two towns over market rights, fairs and the payment of tolls.

During the thirteenth century New Carmarthen enjoyed a period of commercial expansion, coupled with a great deal of building activity, including the rebuilding of the castle in stone, the construction of the first town wall, commenced in 1233, the building of St. Mary's Church and the probable rebuilding of St. Peter's on its earlier foundations. By the end of the century the castle was the administrative, financial and judicial seat of royal government in South Wales.

Although Old Carmarthen could not keep pace with New Carmarthen's commercial expansion, it was at the Priory that the famous Black Book of Carmarthen, the oldest surviving book of vernacular Welsh poetry, was produced in the late twelfth and early thirteenth centuries. Virtually nothing remains of the Priory today. After its dissolution in 1537 it was sold into private hands and two centuries later lead works were built on part of the site, only to be demolished in the mid nineteenth century to make way for the railway.

In addition to the Priory there was another religious House in medieval Carmarthen. This was the Franciscan Friary, also called Grey Friars, founded in the latter part of the thirteenth century on Lammas Fields in New Carmarthen. Recent excavations by the Dyfed Archaeological Trust have shown this to be one of the largest and most notable Franciscan establishments in Britain. Nothing can be seen of the original building today, however. Following its dissolution in the sixteenth century it became, for a short time (1543-47), Carmarthen's first grammar school but subsequently went into private ownership. Its site is now occupied by a supermarket where decorated wall panels describe and illustrate the Friary's history.

St. Peter's Church is the original parish church of Carmarthen and its oldest surviving building. The exact date of its foundation is unknown but its first known record appears in the early twelfth century in the *Chronicle of Battle Abbey.* St. Peter's Church was conferred on this Abbey, built to commemorate the battle of Hastings, early in the reign of Henry I (1100-1135). The main body of the present church probably dates from the thirteenth century with later additions but there were several restorations in the eighteenth and nineteenth centuries.

Following Owain Glyn Dŵr's rebellion in the early 1400's when the castle was captured and the town ravaged, new town walls were commenced in 1415 enclosing a larger area than that of the earlier walls, including King Street and Spilman Street. The legacy left by medieval Carmarthen can still be seen today in its narrow streets, lanes and alley-ways, such as Bridge Street, Quay Street, St. Mary Street and Conduit Lane, although some have disappeared over the years.

The accession of Henry VII in 1485 marked the end of the Middle Ages and the beginning of the Tudor dynasty which established strong government, security and prosperity. Henry VIII's reign saw the unification of England and Wales under the Acts of Union of 1536 and 1542. By the 1536 Act a new 'Carmarthenshire' was to be represented in Parliament at Westminster, for the first time, by one knight and the shire-town, Carmarthen, by one burgess. Henry's reign also saw the dissolution of the Priory and Friary which paved the way for the amalgamation of Old and New Carmarthen into a Corporate Borough, granted under a new Charter of 1546. At the same time the Mayor was made Admiral of the Port, his appointment indicating Carmarthen's continuing importance as a port from medieval into Tudor times.

By the middle of Elizabeth I's reign (1558-1603) records show that Carmarthen was the most populous town in the Principality, with a population of just over 2,000, twice that of Cardiff. Llanelli was then but a tiny hamlet of twelve houses! In 1576 the Queen Elizabeth Grammar School, one of the oldest and most celebrated grammar schools in Wales, was founded; it continued in existence for over four centuries until comprehensive education was introduced.

The accession of James I in 1603 marked the beginning of the Stuart dynasty and Carmarthen was given a new charter in 1604 raising its status from that of Borough into that of County Borough. However, the first map of the town, drawn by John Speed in 1610, shows that Carmarthen had changed little from late medieval times, being still mainly contained within the town walls. During the Civil War of 1642-48 'bulwarks' were constructed, consisting of ditch and earthen bank defences, to the west and north of the town. Nevertheless, Carmarthen was taken twice by Parliamentary forces in 1644 and 1645, the townspeople offering little resistance.

For the next hundred years few changes occurred but then from the middle of the eighteenth century there was a quickening rate of change which continued into the nineteenth century. Changes included a growing political awareness, economic and social unrest, religious revival and the growth of Nonconformity, the Welsh educational movement, town development and the growth of industry.

The mid eighteenth century brought several landed county families into the political arena to contest Parliamentary and municipal elections under the political banners of Whig and Tory. The struggle between the two parties to get their respective candidates elected frequently led to riots and bloodshed in the town's streets. Bribery and corruption were rife and both parties utilised mob violence for their own ends which even continued after the Parliamentary Reform Act of 1832. Growing economic and social grievances, particularly among the agricultural classes, caused discontent and distress which culminated in the Rebecca Riots of 1843. These were a protest, at least ostensibly, against the payment of tolls at the numerous toll-gates on turnpike roads.

The Welsh religious revival of the eighteenth century led to the growth of Nonconformity and the establishment of a large number of chapels which, by the end of the nineteenth century, had transformed Carmarthen's skyline and architecture. After the Dissolution of the Monasteries and Chantries, St. Peter's church was the sole religious establishment in town until 1726 when Heol Awst Independent Chapel was built, to be followed by many other Nonconformist chapels.

Hand-in-hand with the religious revival went the Welsh educational movement which began under the inspired leadership of Griffith Jones of Llanddowror, founder of the Circulating Schools. In Carmarthen the spread of education was assisted considerably by the numerous pamphlets and books which were printed, in both Welsh and English, at its many printing presses. Vicar Prichard's *Canwyll y Cymru* and Peter Williams' Welsh Bible of 1770 were printed here as were many of the inspiring hymns of William Williams *(Pantycelyn)* and David Charles.

An increasing interest in town development was shown in the completion of a new Guildhall in 1777, the removal of the narrow medieval gates in King Street and Spilman Street, paving of the main streets, removal of Dark Gate and the covering over of the Wynveth Stream to form a wagon road to the Quay (now Blue Street) and the construction of The Parade as a scenic amenity. A new purpose-built market was completed in 1846, its central feature being a picturesque clock-tower, now restored in the present market on the same site.

From the mid nineteenth century a new dimension was added to the townscape in the form of educational establishments. In 1848 the South

Wales Training College (Trinity College) was opened, the first teacher-training college in Wales. The ensuing years saw the building of many schools, including the Model, Pentrepoeth, Priory Street, St. Mary's Catholic in Mill Street, Quay Street and Johnstown schools. In Wellfield Road three secondary schools were established: the Diocesan High School for Girls, a new Queen Elizabeth Boys' Grammar School and the County Girls' School, later called the Girls' Grammar School.

To cope with the increasing social needs of an expanding community, a number of public institutions were opened, such as the Carmarthenshire Infirmary in 1858, St. David's Mental Hospital in 1865 and the Cemetery in 1856, while the need for leisure pursuits was met by the opening of the Park, complete with cycle-track and bandstand, in 1900.

Carmarthen continued to be the most populous town in Wales until about the middle of the nineteenth century when it was outstripped in size and population by the rapid industrial expansion of Llanelli and Swansea. The latter were affected by the Industrial Revolution to a far greater extent than was Carmarthen, whose industrial enterprises, with the exception of the iron and tinplate works, were chiefly service industries for agriculture. The Morgan family of 'ironmasters', who lived at Furnace House, were pioneers in the iron and tin industry from the 1740's. Although, subsequently, the tinplate works had a chequered career, with several owners, they played an important part in the industrial and economic life of the town, employing in the later nineteenth century a substantial number of men and women. The closure of the works in 1900 came as a severe blow to the community.

Whilst the first half of the twentieth century was dominated by the two World Wars, the second half has witnessed scientific and technological advances which have transformed modern living, in Carmarthen as elsewhere. The visible changes to the fabric of the town include the closure of the port, the closure of all except the main railway lines, with the demolition of the engine sheds, the closure of the milk processing factories and the demolition of many old streets and buildings to make way for motorways and shopping precincts. However, Carmarthen still remains 'The Gateway to the West'; it is still a market town with an agricultural hinterland and it is still a centre of commercial enterprise and educational prestige. Since 1974 it has been the capital of Dyfed for local government administration, it has many government departments located in the town and it is the headquarters of the police, the fire-brigade and the health authority.

In the 1991 Census Carmarthen's population stood at 12,240. If parts of the surrounding built-up areas are included this total rises to 14,610, as estimated by the County Planning Office. With recent new developments the town is now poised to enter the next millennium enriched by its heritage of two thousand years of history.

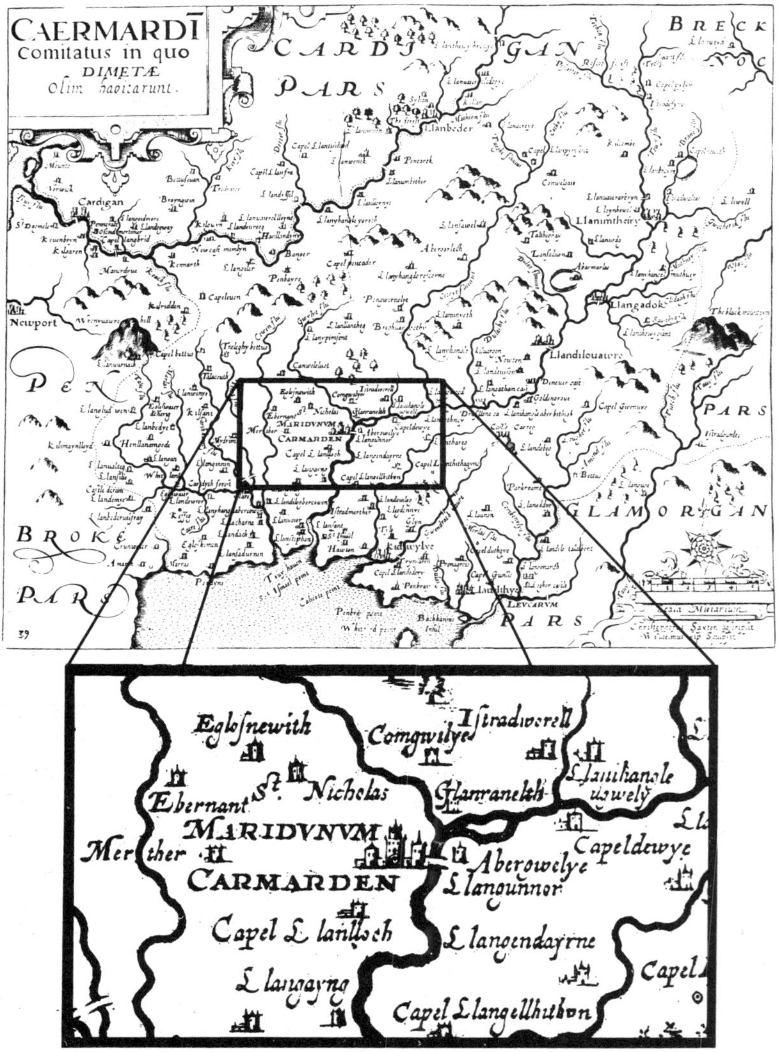

Caermardi comitatus in quo Dimetae olim habitarunt
Carmarthen county in which the Demetae once lived
A map of Carmarthenshire by Christopher Saxton, 1575-76
(with an enlargement of the district around Carmarthen)

Christopher Saxton: topographical draughtsman.
Travelling in Wales being a matter of difficulty, special injunctions were sent in 1576 to all justices of peace, mayors and others in Wales 'to see him conducted into any towre, castle, high place or hill to view that countrey, and that he may be accompanied with ij or iij honest men, such as do best know that countrey, for the better accomplishment of that service; and that at his departure from any towne or place that he hath taken the view of, the said towne do set forth a horseman that can speke both Welshe and Englishe to safe conduct him to the next market towne.'
Acts of the Privy Council, 1575-6.

- 2 -

ROMAN CARMARTHEN

THE CELTIC BACKGROUND

A study of Carmarthen's physical features and natural setting shows that its site could have been favourable for human settlement from early times. Commanding a strategic position overlooking a wide area to the south, the site lay on a comparatively level ridge of land at the tidal limit of the river and only seven miles from the sea. It was protected to the north and west by the valley of a stream and marshy ground and by hills further to the north.[1] Nevertheless, there is no positive evidence for human settlement prior to the arrival of Roman military forces in about AD 75. There are, however, the remains of Celtic Iron Age hillforts in the vicinity, such as on Merlin's Hill, Abergwili, and possibly on Penlan, Ystrad Hill at Johnstown and Llangunnor Hill. Evidence of a circular enclosure at Crispin Avenue, with an adjacent field called Castle Crispin, may indicate another possible settlement site. Although there is no evidence for a hillfort on Castle Hill, this may be the result of continuous occupation from Norman times.

From about 500 BC defended hillforts were the dominant form of Iron Age settlement and they were also the centres of Celtic tribal life. The Celts had originally entered Britain in successive waves from their homeland in central Europe, north of the Alps. The first Celtic people to arrive, the Gaels, had been pushed into the westernmost parts of the island by a later wave, known as the Britons. The latter spoke British, a language of the Brythonic (or Brittonic) group of Celtic speeches, now represented by Welsh, Cornish and Breton. The earlier Goidelic branch is now represented by Irish, Manx and Scots Gaelic.[2]

Although the Celts were one of the great peoples of central and western Europe 500 years or more before Christ, they were never able to unite because they were divided into many tribes who were continually fighting each other. It was this inability to unite which finally led to their defeat by the Romans and the inclusion of most of Celtic Europe within the Roman Empire. As far as Britain was concerned, she was never romanised to the same extent as Gaul or Spain, for instance, while the Celtic tribes in the north of Scotland and in Ireland were never brought within the Roman orbit.

THE ROMAN INVASION OF BRITAIN, AD 43

It was in AD 43 that the Roman Emperor Claudius invaded Britain from Gaul, nearly one hundred years after Julius Caesar's military expeditions of 55 and 54 BC. The Roman general Aulus Plautius was put in charge of the campaign backed by four complete legions, each legion comprising 5,000 to 6,000 highly-trained men, with a roughly equal force of auxiliaries. For about the next 350 years the Romans were to remain in Britain which, as *Britannia,* became the north-western frontier province of their Empire.

For many years prior to the actual invasion, however, south-eastern Britain had been in contact with the Roman world, mainly for trading purposes. Several tribes living in this area were closely related to Gallic tribes across the Channel and merchants were constantly travelling to and fro. Exports from Britain included corn, cattle, hides, slaves, hunting-dogs, iron, tin and silver. (After the conquest of Wales, large quantities of gold were exported from the Dolaucothi gold mines.) In return, pottery bowls, dishes and jars, jewellery, wine, olive oil and other luxury goods from the Mediterranean were imported. Several of the Celtic rulers of southern Britain were on very friendly terms with the Romans and enjoyed the benefits and comforts of the Romanised world. Within four years of the invasion, British resistance in the lowland areas of the island had been broken, but it took nearly forty years before the highland zone of what is now Wales was completely subdued.

THE CONQUEST OF WALES

The conquest of Wales, based on a network of military forts and roads, was not completed until about AD 80. The main conquest period c.AD 75-80 saw the final defeat of the fierce Silures, the Celtic tribe of south-east Wales, by the Roman governor of Britain, Julius Frontinus. This was followed by the defeat of the Ordovices of north Wales and the conquest of Anglesey by the new governor, Julius Agricola, who arrived in Britain probably during the late summer of AD 78. It is the *Biography of Agricola,* written by his son-in-law, the historian Tacitus, that provides the main source of information on the conquest of Britain, but it is unfortunate that his accounts of the geography, history and people of Britain do not provide more detailed and precise information. Thus, in his account of the military conquest, Tacitus mentions the stiff resistance of Celtic tribes such as the Silures and Ordovices, but he never mentions the tribe or tribes living in south-west Wales, the area now covered by Dyfed. However, according to the Greek geographer, Ptolemy of Alexandria, who produced a *Geography* of the known world in about AD 140, this area was the tribal territory of the Demetae. It is from this ancient tribal name that Dyfed is thought to be derived. There is no documentary evidence of the Demetae putting up any resistance to the Roman occupation and there have been few archaeological excavations of Iron Age sites in the area which might reveal concrete evidence of military resistance: so the reaction of the native population remains an unknown factor. However, the existence of Roman 'marching camps' at Y Pigwn on Mynydd Trecastell, between Brecon and Llandovery, and at Arosfa Garreg, close to the source of the Usk, shows that campaigns were waged across these uplands on the eastern fringes of Demetic territory. Also within the territory itself the existence of Roman forts has now been firmly established at Carmarthen, Llandovery, Pumpsaint, Llanio, Loughor and possibly Llandeilo suggesting the need for military conquest and control in at least parts of south-west Wales.[3]

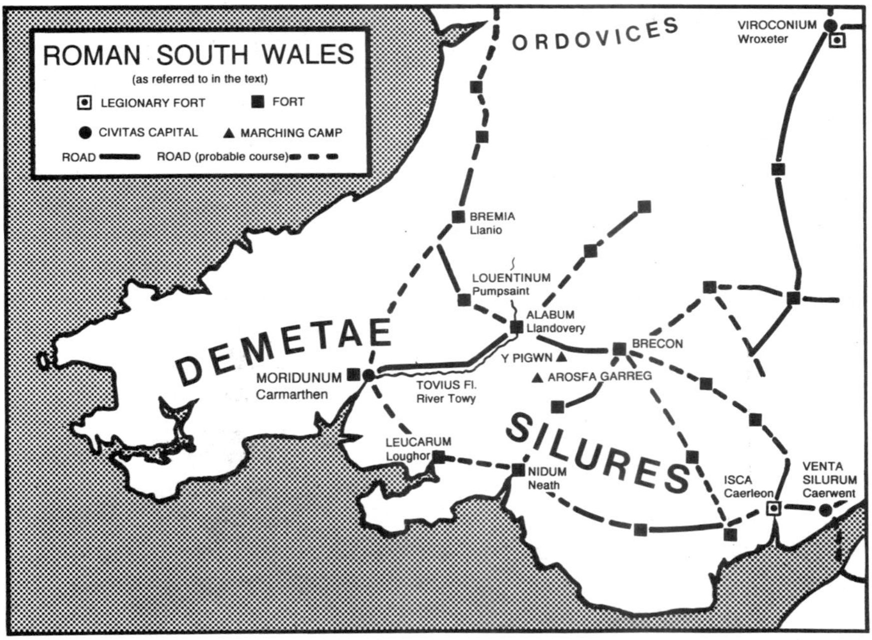

EXCAVATIONS AT CARMARTHEN

In recent years archaeological excavations, especially by the Dyfed Archaeological Trust, have greatly increased our knowledge of Roman Carmarthen. Prior to this time evidence was based on chance finds of Roman material which were often only casually recorded. Professor F. Haverfield in his book, *Military Aspects of Roman Wales,* written in 1910, considered that the archaeological evidence then available for Carmarthen indicated 'that the place was inhabited in some fashion from the first or second to the fourth century . . . These remains point to a country town, possibly the capital of the Demetae, if "capital" be not too grand a word. If ever a fort was set to guard the estuary of the Towy, no recognizable trace of it has been yet recorded.' Subsequently, Professor Sir John Lloyd, editor of *A History of Carmarthenshire,* 1935, assumed that there probably was a Roman fort at Carmarthen, basing his assumption on the findings of the *Royal Commission on Ancient Monuments in Wales, Carmarthenshire Inventory* 1917. At the same time he emphasised the need for chance finds to be preserved and recorded and for trial excavations to be carried out - but over thirty years had to elapse before any proper archaeological excavations were undertaken. The first of these commenced in 1968 under the direction of Professor G. D. Barri Jones of Manchester University, while from 1976 onwards the Dyfed Archaeological Trust has been responsible for undertaking carefully recorded excavations, together with aerial photography, which have added substantially to the previous meagre knowledge and thrown fresh light on Roman Carmarthen.

It is now generally accepted that Carmarthen was the *civitas* capital (tribal capital) of the local tribe, the Demetae. It evolved as a Romano-British town, known as Moridunum, from a civil settlement (or *vicus*) which grew up outside the Roman fort established about AD 75. Moridunum meant Sea-fort, derived from the Celtic Brythonic *mori* (sea) and *dunon* (fort). Subsequently Moridunum was formally recognised as the *civitas* capital, *Moridunum Demetarum*, Sea-fort of the Demetae, and as such acted as the administrative centre for local government. It was given a planned street layout in grid form and was later enclosed within a defensive rampart and ditches. The only other such Romano-British town in Wales was Caerwent or *Venta Silurum*, Venta of the Silures.

THE ROMAN MILITARY FORT

There is some doubt as to whether the first Roman forces to arrive here came overland, possibly down the Towy valley, from the legionary base at Caerleon *(Isca Silurum)*, headquarters of the Second Augustan Legion, or whether they came by sea to secure control of the western coasts and estuaries. In any case, their first priority would have been to establish a military fort, to form yet another link in the network of forts and roads being constructed through Wales, not only to secure the western frontier of the Roman Empire but also to exploit the economic wealth of this area which was rich in minerals - gold (from Dolaucothi), silver, lead and tin.

The location of the fort was a matter of conjecture for several years and was only finally resolved by the excavations undertaken by the Dyfed Archaeological Trust in 1989. These located a military fort in the Spilman Street/King Street area, probably covering some four or five acres. It is thought that the fort was established in about AD 75. The excavations were on the site of the demolished properties Nos. 5-8 Spilman Street, near to the District Council Offices. Traces were found of a pebbled street surface running around the inside perimeter of the fort, thus allowing speedy access to the palisaded fighting platform along the rampart bank. There was evidence of timber buildings, probably barrack blocks, which had been altered and rebuilt on several occasions. The evidence also pointed to a later, smaller fort built within the earlier, larger one when the garrison was presumably reduced in size. There was also evidence for systematic demolition and abandonment of the fort, probably around AD 120, when the bulk of the Roman army in Wales was sent north for the construction of Hadrian's Wall. The discovery of fragments of pottery and a coin of the Emperor Vespasian (AD 69-79) helped to date the site of the military fort to the first century AD.

The Spilman Street/King Street area had been the favoured site for the fort on the strength of earlier excavations by the Trust. Their 1985-86 excavations under the District Council car park in Spilman Street revealed traces of timber buildings and a tanning pit, all dated to about AD 75-95. Some fragments of first century Samian pottery and a worn coin of the Emperor Domitian (AD 81-96) were also found.

Earlier excavations between 1976 and 1978 to the rear of Church Street revealed a substantial quantity of first century coins and pottery in a series of palisaded enclosures and ditches, together with a leat. These features indicated to the excavators an initial occupation and settlement at Carmarthen around AD 75-80. The features also suggested an annexe to the military fort, although at that date its location still remained a mystery. The discovery of the fort in the Spilman Street/King Street area finally ended years of speculation.

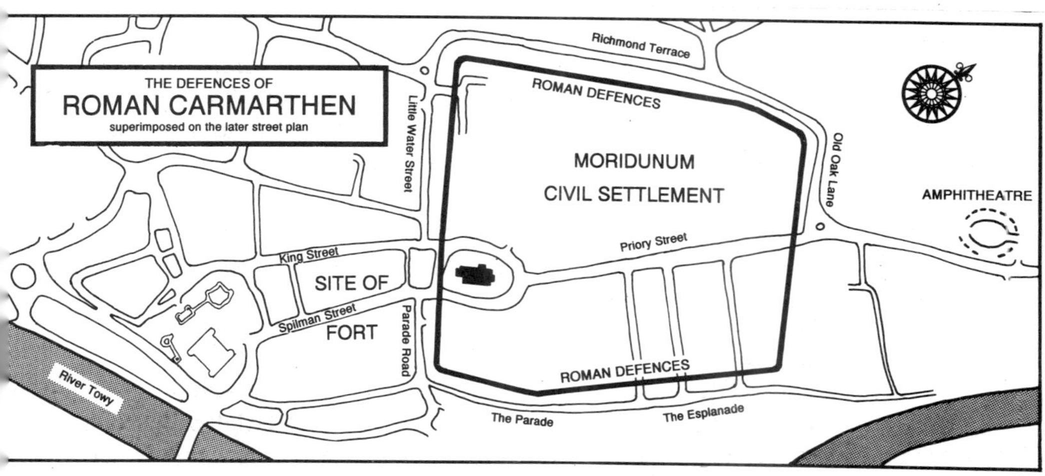

THE ROMAN TOWN OF MORIDUNUM

Once a fort was built and garrisoned, it was quite usual for a small civil settlement of traders, craftsmen, artisans and various other followers to grow up outside its gates. Such a settlement was called a *vicus* and many of the towns of Roman Britain originated in this way. At Carmarthen this civil settlement grew up outside the east gate of the military fort, catering for any additional needs of the garrison and increasingly enjoying the new goods which came in from the Roman Empire, initially as supplies for the military. Eventually the settlement expanded into an extensive Romano-British town which was enclosed by a strong defensive rampart and ditches. The town was known as Moridunum.

It was only in the late 1960's that the site of Roman Moridunum was recognised, although for nearly two-hundred years there had been 'chance' finds of Roman objects and traces of buildings, especially in the area around Priory Street. Excavations carried out in 1968 and 1969 by Professor G. D. B. Jones established that the settlement at Carmarthen was more than just military in nature; it was also a large civil settlement, the defences of which can still be traced today in the line of modern streets and property boundaries. Although little of these defences, consisting of rampart and ditches, now remain, their southern line is marked by The Esplanade and The Parade, their western line by Parade Road and Little Water Street, their northern line by Richmond Terrace and their eastern line by Old Oak Lane and the footpath called Llwybr-y-ardd leading down to The Esplanade. Thus the enclosed area of Moridunum was about 32 acres.

Excavations by the Dyfed Archaeological Trust to the rear of Church Street in 1978 revealed that Moridunum's defences were constructed in two phases. The first phase, dating from the latter part of the second century, consisted of a clay and turf rampart 4.6 metres wide and about 2.2 metres high fronted by two V-shaped ditches. The second phase, constructed after a lapse of time, during which the inner ditch became silted up and neglected, was a much wider rampart made across the infilled ditches and fronted by a stone wall about 3.2 metres thick, the total width of bank and revetment being about 16 metres. Outside this wall at least one other ditch was detected and it was conjectured[4] that yet another ditch might lie beyond this under the present Parade Road. The date of this second phase of town defences was put, tentatively, in the late third century. The Church Street excavations also showed that in this area the defences were built over previous buildings belonging to the mid to late second century.

It is interesting to note that when Giraldus Cambrensis visited the town in 1188 he wrote 'this ancient city is situated on the banks of the noble river Tywy, surrounded by woods and pastures, and was strongly inclosed with walls of brick, parts of which are still standing.' These walls of brick must have been the old Roman walls, since the medieval town walls, surrounding the Norman town centred on the castle, were not commenced until 1233 by order of Henry III.

No doubt many of the Roman 'bricks' were used in medieval building as coin evidence suggests that most of the stone robbing from the Roman walls took place in the thirteenth century. Nonetheless, the outlines of Moridunum could still be seen in the fourteenth century when its walls and towers are mentioned in the *Cartulary of the Priory.*

THE 'CIVITAS' CAPITAL

It is now generally accepted that Moridunum, having expanded from a *vicus* settlement outside the Roman fort, eventually developed into the *civitas* capital of the local tribe of Demetae. The tribal capitals were a feature of Roman Britain, for the Romans were careful to preserve the tribal system which they found and adapt it to their civil administration. They induced local tribal leaders - many of whom, especially in southern Britain, rapidly became Romanised - to adopt Roman ways, dress and town life. One town in an area served as the administrative centre for the tribe as a whole and was given a measure of self-government through its *ordo* or town council. Such a town was known as the *civitas* capital. Since Carmarthen (Moridunum) is the only known defended town in the tribal territory of the Demetae, it is now assumed that Moridunum achieved this status. This assumption is reinforced by the existence of an amphitheatre, with a large seating capacity, just outside the town. Hence the name *Moridunum Demetarum* or Moridunum of the Demetae. There is only one other such town known in Wales, namely Caerwent *(Venta Silurum),* the tribal or civitas capital of the Silures.

It was customary for such towns to be formally constituted as civitas capitals when a planned lay-out of the streets in grid form would be initiated and at a later stage the town enclosed within defensive walls and ditches. It is not known when Moridunum was thus formally constituted as civitas capital, but it has been suggested by J. Wacher[5] that this could have happened during the rule of the Emperor Hadrian (AD 117-138) when he visited Britain in AD 121 or 122. His visit stimulated building activity in towns especially since he withdrew large numbers of troops from Wales for the construction of his northern frontier Wall. To replace military control, dependable self-governing *civitas capitals* were necessary for local administration. Excavations by Dyfed Archaeological Trust have shown that Moridunum's military fort was abandoned by AD 120, thus strengthening the case for Moridunum being made a civitas capital while Hadrian was Emperor.

THE INTERIOR OF MORIDUNUM

For many years prior to the archaeological excavations, there had been several chance finds of Roman objects and traces of buildings especially in the area around Priory Street and The Parade.

In 1768 a curious twelve-sided hollow bronze object (dodecahedron) was found on the north side of St. Peter's Church at a depth of eight feet. Each side of approximately two inches diameter was pierced, in the centre, with a graduated opening, varying from about half-an-inch to one-and-a-half inches. At every angle a ball-foot was attached so that the dodecahedron could stand steadily in any one of the twelve possible positions. Its use remains a mystery, although several theories have been put forward, including a gauge for use in workshops and a twelve-sided candlestick. More recently it has been suggested that they were used as surveying instuments. Several such objects have been found, chiefly on Roman military sites in the northern provinces of the Empire.

The Roman altar or pedestal now in St. Peter's Church

Several finds were recorded by Edward Donovan in his *Descriptive Excursion through South Wales and Monmouthshire in the Year 1804.* These included the so-called Nato stone, the only Roman inscribed stone yet to be found, bearing the common official phrase *(bon)o r(ei) p(ublica) nato* which is thought to allude to a fourth century emperor. According to Donovan this was 'dug up with some others of a similar nature in the street near the vicar's house.' Donovan also recorded: 'In Priory street we observed two small Roman altars, placed at the entrance to the forecourt of one of the houses.' One of these altars or pedestals is now in the porch of St. Peter's Church, while the other is in the Museum, together with the *Nato* stone. Also in the Museum is a sculptured stone head, found in Priory Street, possibly part of a grave stone from the Roman cemetery. Another carved stone head, found in King Street, is dated c. 1st century AD.

In 1861 a châtelaine (a set of short chains for holding keys) was found at the site of Elm Lodge on The Parade; in 1871 part of a tessellated floor and portions of a wall were seen behind 136 Priory Street and in 1897 the foundations of a building, thought to be a Roman bath-house, were discovered on the site of a house now called Bryn Roma on The Esplanade. Other finds included a Roman lamp and stone foundations seen near St. John's Church in Priory Street about 1905.

In 1952, on Richmond Park football field, a Roman brooch and quantities of Samian pottery were found, while in the same year a trumpet brooch and a carved bone knife handle were discovered near St. Peter's church. In 1954 when part of St. Peter's churchyard was removed for road-widening, a large quantity of Flavian and later Samian ware was unearthed. A small excavation by the Carmarthenshire Antiquarian Society in 1961 to the rear of Dyffryn House, The Esplanade, unearthed a large stone drain, with a smaller one joining it, from the direction of the Bath-house site lying immediately to the east of Dyffryn. In addition there were two coins of the late third century and quantities of pottery dating from the first and fourth centuries, thus indicating a long-term period of occupation. Dyfed Archaeological Trust excavations have recovered considerable quantities of pottery, coins and brooches, all deposited in Carmarthen Museum. From the Church Street excavations came various pottery vessels dating from the late 1st to mid 3rd century, including Samian ware dishes, parts of decorated bowls, some stamped with the potter's name, cooking jars, a flagon and an amphora, used for the storage of wine and oil. Also displayed at the museum are many common jewellery articles including bracelets, glass beads and a selection of brooches including a trumpet brooch in silver gilt, a fine example of Romano-Celtic art dated AD 25-50, found in Priory Street.

All information about the lay-out of streets and buildings inside Moridunum has been obtained from the excavations of Professor G. D. B. Jones and of the Dyfed Archaeological Trust. Excavating on the north side of St. Peter's car-park and to the rear of Richmond Terrace in 1968-69, Professor Jones revealed the existence of a Roman east-west street or *decumanus* and of the foundations of buildings of both wood and stone. Pottery found in the earliest timber buildings belonged to the early second century and a coin of Emperor Marcus Aurelius (AD 161-180) was discovered in a layer of the street surfacing. The development of the areas to the north and south of the *decumanus* or east-west street took different lines. To the north, i.e. towards the rear of Richmond Terrace, the buildings were small, built of timber and associated with trade or industry; there was evidence of three small furnaces in these shops or workshops. South of the *decumanus* four buildings were located, of better quality, large and residential in character. One dating from the third century had a colonnaded portico along the edge of the street. In the largest building, measuring about 25 metres by 34 metres the rooms had been floored with tesserae of terracotta and Prescelly stone and one of the rooms contained a hypocaust with a furnace. The discovery in the building's foundation level of two fresh coins of Magnentius and Decentius (AD 350-353) implied that urban life in Moridunum continued into the late fourth century, if not longer. Significantly this was the time when many Romano-British towns were in decline.

Further excavations near Priory Street car park, in the gardens to the rear of 105-110 Priory Street, were undertaken by the Trust in the late 1970's and early 80's. These located the eastern end of the east-west aligned street mentioned above, the evidence suggesting an early second century date. Also a second street laid out at right-angles to the first one, i.e. in a north-south direction, was discovered, indicating that Moridunum followed the regular street lay-out in grid form common to Roman towns. Traces of rectangular timber buildings on the north side of the east-west aligned street were uncovered, some with hearths and furnaces for metal working, representing artisans' workshops and houses. On the south side the buildings were of better quality, just as in the St. Peter's Street car park excavations. One half-timbered building, located in the corner at the junction of the intersecting streets, was about 18 metres square and could have been two storeys high. It had stone and cobble floors and on either side of a central corridor were fireplaces set into walls. In the yard outside was a granary 3 metres by 4 metres with a raised floor supported by massive timber uprights to keep out rodents. Heather James suggests[6] that the house might have belonged to a corn merchant or maltster since the granary could hold more than was needed for domestic use and quantities of charred grains of spelt wheat were found around one of the burnt-out postholes, perhaps indicating that the wheat had been accidentally burnt while being roasted for malting.

Although only about 10% of the internal area of Moridunum has been excavated to date, the Priory Street site has revealed well-laid-out shops, workshops and houses fronting the two gravelled streets. The corner of a Roman temple has also been revealed. The main east-west street bisecting the Roman town must lie partly below present-day Priory Street, while much more of Moridunum must lie below modern buildings.

The Trust's excavations have shown that the Priory Street site was a busy artisan quarter for about 250 years. Remains of hearths, where bar iron was heated up, were found in association with nails, tools and weapons, providing evidence for blacksmiths' shops. A number of clay ovens were found which were used for baking bread and other ovens may have been used for malting grain for beer. Many broken fragments of hand-querns, used for grinding corn, were also found, as were numerous leather scraps and off-cuts, suggesting leather trades.

To quote from the Trust's review, *Archaeology in Dyfed:* 'There was a succession of different buildings, each built over the site of earlier ones, although by the late 300's the area was fairly run down - the latest timber buildings were more spread out, parts of the site lay vacant, or were given over to an unhealthy combination of rubbish pits and wells.' Nevertheless, 'the streets continued to be efficiently resurfaced and maintained - the latest resurfacing seems to have taken place when most of the site was abandoned, which argues for continuing urban life in most central areas of the town to a very late date in the Roman period. A coin of the Emperor Honorius (AD 398-423), a rare find in Wales, came from the latest Roman levels of the Priory Street site.'

Life in Roman Moridunum must have made a tremendous impact on the native Celtic population living in the immediate vicinity. Accustomed to small thatched huts of wattle and daub, huddled together in hillforts for protection, they now came into contact with sophisticated urban life, for towns were an essential feature of Roman civilization. Apart from shops and houses, the more luxurious with paved floors, plastered walls and under-floor heating, a whole new range of consumer goods became available. These included many varieties of pottery for cookery and table use, wine, olive oil and perhaps more exotic goods from the Mediterranean. Items of jewellery, especially bronze and colourfully enamelled brooches and glass beads were also widely produced and became readily available; Roman coins were also used in the shops and markets of the town. However, since Moridunum was the most westerly town in Roman Britain, it is unlikely that Roman manners, customs and dress were adopted to the same extent as they were in south-east Britain. Again, in the case of language, although Latin was used for military, administrative and commercial purposes, it is probable that Celtic speech remained dominant in the town and even more so in the rural areas.

THE AMPHITHEATRE

The status of Moridunum as a tribal capital is also indicated by its amphitheatre sited outside the town's eastern boundary behind the north

The Amphitheatre

side of Priory Street. It was a former Borough surveyor, George Ovens, who in the 1940's recognised the importance of the site and prevented housing development within the area.

According to John Little, former curator of Carmarthen Museum, who partially excavated the site in 1970, the amphitheatre was probably constructed in the second century AD by cutting into the natural hillslope to form the northern seating bank and using the spoil thus obtained to form the southern seating bank. This southern bank is now, however, largely eroded and the western half of the site is still built over. The oval arena, surrounded by a stone wall, was nearly 50 metres long by 25 metres wide and covered by a thick layer of sand and gravel. Only one entrance, at the east end, has been excavated showing three road surfaces: perhaps an interesting indication of a long period of use. Timber seating was provided in the form of timber revetted steps cut into the hillslopes and underpinned by heavy beams, but no evidence emerged to show how access was obtained to the seats. The estimated seating capacity was 4,500-5,000 which must be well in excess of the population of the town itself, showing that the amphitheatre was probably catering for the native populace of the surrounding tribal area. However, further excavation is needed to obtain more definite information on its date, seating capacity and function. Public entertainments probably took the form of bull fighting or bear baiting rather than gladiatorial shows which were very expensive to stage.

HISTORICAL REFERENCES TO MORIDUNUM

The first two historical references to Moridunum occur in the *Geography* of Ptolemy, produced in about AD 140, and in the *Antonine Itinerary*, a Roman 'road-book' giving routes and distances and thought to date to the early third century. Ptolemy (Claudius Ptolemaeus) was a geographer and astronomer of Greek origin who worked in Alexandria, Egypt. His *Geography*, written originally in Greek, consisted of eight books containing lists of places in the then known world together with their latitudes and longitudes, i.e. their positions on the map. Ptolemy based much of his information on the work of earlier geographers, travellers and on reports from the Roman legions. His original manuscripts are now lost but many copies survive in both Greek and Latin versions. None are earlier than the eleventh century, however. Owing to copying errors by scribes, many entries have a variety of spellings.

Ptolemy named the people of west Wales Δημῆται, the Demetae, and named two 'cities' in their territory - Μαρίδουνον (Maridunum) and Λουέντινον (Louentinum - i.e. Dolau Cothi, Pumpsaint). One manuscript has the variant Μορίδουνον (Moridunum). He also gave the name Tovius (variants Tobius and Tubius) to the river Towy or Tywi.

The other historical reference occurs in the *Antonine Itinerary*. Written in Latin, this was a collection of some 225 routes along the roads of the Roman Empire. The routes are not all of the same date and the Antoninus of the title is uncertain. There are many manuscripts of the *Itinerary* and derivative copies which have resulted in errors of transmission. Route XII (Iter XII) ran from Moridunum to Viroconium (Wroxeter) and listed mileages and stopping places en route. However, owing to miscopying, Moridunum is recorded as Muridunum.[7]

Although Roman Carmarthen has also been called Maridunum in recent times, most scholars now accept that the correct form is Moridunum, meaning Sea-fort, from the Celtic Brythonic (i.e. British) *mori* meaning sea and *dunon* meaning fort. Dunon was regularly represented in Latin as dunum.

THE DECLINE OF ROMAN CARMARTHEN

The decline of Moridunum is linked with the decline of Roman power in Britain and the decline of the Roman Empire itself, subjected as it was to barbarian attacks on all its frontiers and finally on Rome itself. In the late third century AD Saxon raids on the south-east coast of Britain began while the western coasts were attacked by sea raiders from Ireland. In the mid fourth century a destructive incursion of Picts and Scots swamped all the defences of the north and west and brought disaster in its wake. Attempts to usurp the Imperial throne by various governors and army commanders only increased Britain's troubles and when in AD 383 Magnus Maximus, an army officer in Britain, assumed the title of Emperor and crossed to the continent to lay claim to the Imperial throne, taking large numbers of troops with him, the island was left open to further invasions. Magnus Maximus, the Macsen Wledig of the *Mabinogion*, was a Spaniard whose wife was Elen, reputed daughter of a Welsh chief. Although Maximus was defeated and killed in 388 by the Emperor Theodosius, the seal was set on the ruin of Britain. By AD 410 when Rome fell to the barbarians, all Imperial troops had been withdrawn from Britain and this island was left to defend itself as best it could. In the wake of attacks from all directions crops failed, agricultural productivity declined, as did imported food-stuffs and other goods, all contributing to the disintegration of society. Added to this, outbreaks of major epidemics swept through Europe between the third and sixth centuries, drastically reducing populations, especially in towns. Since Roman Britain was in direct contact with the Mediterranean world, virulent diseases could be readily spread by trading activities. It was this combination of hostile attacks, famine and pestilence which resulted in the general decline of Roman towns in Britain.

As far as Moridunum is concerned, there is evidence from recent excavations that urban life continued into the late fourth century at least, but, in common with other towns in Britain, and particularly as it lay on the westernmost fringe of the Roman Empire, Moridunum probably deteriorated politically, economically and socially until it became shrouded in the obscurity of the Dark Ages. But its name was to live on!

DERIVATION OF THE NAME CARMARTHEN

The present-day name of Carmarthen is derived from the Celtic Brythonic place-name *Moridunon,* meaning sea-fort, with the Welsh prefix *caer,* denoting a Roman fort, attached. According to Professor A. O. H. Jarman,[8] the Brythonic form *mori* meant 'sea' while *dunon* meant 'fort'. The Latin form of the name was Moridunum.

During the post-Roman period, in the fifth and sixth centuries, the Brythonic language developed into Early Welsh by a regular process of phonetic change. The terminations *-i* and *-on* were dropped from *mori* and *dunon* and these two forms became *mer* and *ddin* respectively, so that Moridunon became Merddin or its variant Myrddin. Merddin or Myrddin was now a place-name and its original meaning of sea-fort became obscure because speakers of Early Welsh in the sixth century were not familiar with (probably having forgotten) the original Brythonic constituent elements of *Mori* and *dunon.* Subsequently the word *caer* was attached, since during this period caer was commonly used as the first element in the names of places which had been Roman forts or towns. With the passage of time *Caer-merddin* or *Caer-myrddin* became associated in people's minds with an imaginary personage thought to have been the founder of the fortress in the distant past. In this way *Myrddin* was created by popular imagination out of a mere place-name. Furthermore, by the process of Welsh linguistic mutation, *Caer-myrddin* then became *Caer-fyrddin.* Thus *Caerfyrddin* was interpreted as the 'Fortress of Myrddin', whereas in fact *caer* simply denoted the former Roman fort, while *fyrddin* or *myrddin* was derived from Moridounon

To this shadowy. local figure of Myrddin, mystical founder of the town, was later attached the popular Celtic legend of 'a wild man of the woods' who was also a wizard, prophet and magician. In the Middle Ages this Welsh legend of Myrddin was used by Geoffrey of Monmouth in his book *History of the Kings of Britain,* which was written in Latin in about 1136. Geoffrey's book was intended to be read as a history book but much of the material was pseudo-historical and a product of the author's imagination. Geoffrey was the first to use the name *Merlinus,* which he Latinised from the Welsh Merddin or Myrddin. He then associated Merlinus (English *Merlin*) with King Arthur, attributed to him a whole series of prophecies, and first linked Merlin and Carmarthen in European literature. Geoffrey's book, which was translated into French, gave rise to a vast crop of legends about Merlin until he became a famous character in European literature, far removed from the original

Welsh Myrddin.

Such then is the origin of Merlin - not a historical person but a name derived from the Welsh Caermyrddin/Caerfyrddin which was itself derived from the Celtic Moridunon (sea-fort).[9]

The various Medieval spellings such as Kaermerdyn, Kaermerdin and Kermerdin and the seventeenth century Caermarden show the link between the original and present-day names.

1 Terrence James, *Carmarthen: An Archaeological and Topographical Survey,* 1980.
2 A. L. F. Rivet and Colin Smith, *The Place-names of Roman Britain,* 1979.
3 Terrence James, *Carmarthen: An Archaeological and Topographical Survey,* 1980 and Heather James, *Roman West-Wales,* 1982.
4 Terrence James, *Carmarthen: An Archaeological and Topographical Survey,* 1980.
5 J. S. Wacher, *The Towns of Roman Britain,* 1975.
6 Heather James, *Roman West-Wales,* 1982.
7 A. L. F. Rivet and Colin Smith, *The Place-names of Roman Britain,* 1979.
8 A. O. H. Jarman, *The Legend of Merlin and its associations with Carmarthen* in *The Carmarthenshire Antiquary,* Vol. XXII, 1986 and *The Legend of Merlin,* 1970.
9 See *Folk-lore and Customs - The Legend of Merlin.*

The Parade in 1874
The Parade marks the southern boundary of Roman Moridunum

(As seen and described by Samuel and Nathaniel Buck in 1740)

- 3 -

THE AGE OF CELTIC SAINTS AND PRINCES

Apart from the archaeological evidence of urban life continuing in Moridunum into the late fourth century, there is no positive evidence for continuous settlement in the town beyond this date and into the post-Roman period and the so-called Dark Ages. Nevertheless, there may have been some form of continuity since the town's present name is derived from Moridunum with the prefix caer, denoting a Roman fort, attached.

It is known that during the third century Irish sea-raiders were attacking the Welsh coast and that towards the end of the Roman period the area that is now roughly Dyfed was subjected to waves of immigration and subsequent settlement by Irish invaders, known as the *Deisi*. By the later fifth century an Irish dynasty was ruling in west Wales. Evidence for this is provided by the number of place-names of Irish derivation and by the number of memorial stones bearing inscriptions in both Latin and Ogam found in the area. Ogam was an archaic Irish script of strokes and notches cut into the edges of stones. However, no such stones have been found in or near Carmarthen town.

The so-called *Voteporix Stone*, inscribed in Ogam and Latin, and now preserved at Carmarthen museum, originally stood outside the entrance to Castell Dwyran churchyard, in the south-west corner of former Carmarthenshire. It is a memorial stone to Voteporix, a sixth century ruler of Demetia (Dyfed), who was of Irish descent and was given the Roman title of Protector on the monument. Such a title was bestowed in the later days of the Roman Empire and had perhaps become hereditary in the Irish dynasty. A recent theory suggests that Irish settlers may have been encouraged officially to settle in west Wales as allies of Rome. The inscription in Latin reads: MEMORIA VOTEPORIGIS PROTICTORIS (Memorial of Voteporix Protector). The Ogam inscription is round the edge of the stone. Above the Latin is a small cross within a circle indicating, perhaps, that

The Voteporix Stone

Voteporix received a Christian burial. Nevertheless, he was denounced in the mid sixth century by the chronicler Gildas as the 'tyrant of the Demetae' and 'the bad son of a good king'.

It is not known when Christianity first came to Wales but it was probably brought into Britain during the Roman occupation by soldiers and traders and survived the end of Roman rule. During the 5th and 6th centuries Christianity was spreading through Wales following the paths of missionary monks, for this was the Age of the Celtic Saints, as is attested by the number and distribution of early Christian memorial stones. Among missionaries in this area were St. David (reputedly died in 589) and his contemporary, St. Teilo, who founded Llandeilo Fawr. Both are thought to have been pupils of St. Paulinus whose monastery may have been at Llanddeusant. A memorial stone commemorating Paulinus, found at Caio, is now in Carmarthen museum, together with other Christian memorial stones from the parish of Newchurch.

LLANDEULYDDOG

Although no early Christian memorial stones have been found in Carmarthen, there are several historical references suggesting that a Celtic monastic church was founded here well before the Norman conquest. In the *Liber Landavensis,* the Book of Llandaff, which was compiled in the twelfth century and contains the Llandaff charters, there are four references to a certain Llandeulyddog, which is now generally accepted as a church founded at Carmarthen and dedicated to Teulyddog, a mysterious person about whom there is much debate. The references, of which the earliest dates to c.1025, are in a series of charters listing many Teilo churches. The four references are: *Lanntoulidauc i cair* (dated about 1025 and thought to be the only one dating from before the Norman Conquest); *Lann Toulidauc ig Cair Mirdin; Lann Toulidauc i cair* and *Lanteuledauc in Ggair uyrdin.*[1]

Llandeulyddog is also referred to (as *Llan Teulydawc*) in a list of seven Bishop Houses of Dyfed in the *Welsh Laws of Hywel Dda.* The list also includes a reference to an Abbot there. A reference to an Abbot at Carmarthen was noted by Leland in a 'charter' which is now lost.

The intriguing question is where this Celtic monastic church was located in Carmarthen. For a possible answer we must turn to the *Chronicle of Battle Abbey*[2] - the Abbey built near Hastings by William the Conqueror to commemorate his victory over Harold in 1066. The Chronicle records 'that in the time of Abbot Ralph (1107-1124) the King (i.e. Henry I) conferred upon the Abbey a certain church dedicated to St. Peter the Apostle, in the city of Chaermedi (Carmarthen) in Wales and also another church in the same place *founded in very ancient times* in honour of St. Theodore the Martyr.' The name Theodore was probably written by a Norman scribe unfamiliar with the Welsh name Teulyddog.

This church, according to the Chronicle, was of a much earlier foundation than that of St. Peter. In 1125 these same two churches were transferred from Battle Abbey to Bernard, the first Norman Bishop of St. Davids, who then proceeded to confer them on his newly-founded Priory at Carmarthen.

The Priory was dedicated jointly, and significantly, to St. John the Evangelist and to St. Theulacus. *The Cartulary of the Priory,* a collection of charters and land-holdings relating to the Priory, has many references to Sancti Theulaci (the genitive case in Latin). It would seem probable that the church of St. Theulacus was none other than the church of St. Theodore, which was a misnomer for the original Celtic church of Teulyddog. The fact that the newly-formed Priory received a joint dedication would seem to indicate that it absorbed and incorporated the church of Teulyddog. At the same time, by dedicating the Priory to this Celtic saint as well as to St. John the Evangelist, an attempt was made to soothe local feelings.

The identity of the enigmatic Teulyddog has always been open to debate: whether he was a follower of St. Teilo or whether he and Teilo were the same person. According to Baring-Gould and Fisher (*Lives of the British Saints,* 1907) Teulyddog was a contemporary and follower of St. Teilo who was a contemporary of St. David. Other suggestions have been made that the name Teulyddog may refer to Teilo himself, the name being derived from Teilo's original name, Eliud, as a hypocoristic form i.e. a pet name (Ty+Eliud+auc/og). The subject has been dealt with in scholarly detail by the Revd. Canon J. Wyn Evans in an article entitled *Aspects of the Early Church in Carmarthenshire.*[3] It would appear that the giving of hypocoristic or pet names to Welsh Saints was a regular practice in the pre-Norman Church. The name Teilo itself is thought to be a hypocoristic form of Eliud and it would seem that the St. Davids tradition was to name him Eliud whilst that of Llandeilo Fawr was to name him Teilo.

Having stated the arguments for and against Teulyddog and Teilo being one and the same person, Canon Evans then speculates on the implications which could arise from the hypothesis that they were identical. Such implications include the following: that the chief site of Teilo's cult may have been centred on the 'bishop-house' at Llandeulyddog; that the former Roman Moridunum may have been granted to Teilo in which to exercise a communal monastic or collegiate life, with the walled town forming the monastic enclosure in which were a number of churches, of which St. Peter's is the sole survivor; that the dynasty to which Voteporix belonged may have granted the abandoned Roman town to Teilo so he might exercise an episcopate from there, perhaps in the knowledge that there had once been an episcopate there in late Roman times and that finally, on account of dynastic changes, the cult of the saint was forced to move further up the Towy to Llandeilo Fawr.

Canon Evans emphasises that the above conjectures are all highly speculative but they raise many interesting questions regarding the early Church in Carmarthenshire.

The following two references may also strengthen the view that Llandeulyddog was dedicated to St. Teilo: a charter roll of Edward I, dated 1290, refers to the Church of St. John the Evangelist and *Sancti Teulaci*, whilst the 16th century Augmentation Records refer to a well in the Priory precincts dedicated to *St. Teulot*.

Although little remains of the Priory today its site is a fascinating one, for it lies immediately to the south-east of Roman Moridunum, just outside the Roman walls and to the south of Priory Street which probably follows the line of the Roman road entering the town's east gate. It has been suggested by Terrence James[4] that this area could well have been the site of a cemetery in the Roman period, for Roman cemeteries were always located along the roads just outside towns. Subsequently the cemetery could have continued as a Christian burial-ground in the post-Roman/early Christian period, which could explain the location of the Celtic monastic settlement of Llandeulyddog.

Excavations in 1979 by the Dyfed Archaeological Trust, on part of the Priory site, revealed some remains of medieval buildings and the medieval cemetery but no positive evidence of the pre-Conquest church and monastic settlement. Traces of ditches underneath the medieval cemetery were revealed and were radio-carbon dated to the mid-eighth century, thus giving them a Dark Age origin and indicating human activity in this area. The site of Llandeulyddog may thus provide a link, albeit a tenuous link, for some form of continuity with Roman Moridunum.

As suggested previously, Moridunum may have been the base for an early Christian episcopate but, as yet, there is no positive evidence for the existence of Christianity there at this early date. Nor is there any evidence for any link between Moridunum and the Irish dynasty (e.g. Voteporix) ruling in south-west Wales at this period.

THE AGE OF PRINCES

Nothing is known of Carmarthen's part, if any, in the dynastic struggles between the Welsh princes. During the seventh and eighth centuries Wales was broken up into various small kingdoms owing allegiance only to their own local rulers, who were constantly at war with each other. In the ninth century Rhodri Mawr conquered a large part of Wales but on his death his territories were divided between his six sons. Cadell inherited Seisyllwg - i.e. Ystrad Tywi (roughly Carmarthenshire) and Ceredigion (Cardiganshire). On his death Cadell was succeeded by his famous son, Hywel Dda (Hywel the Good). By

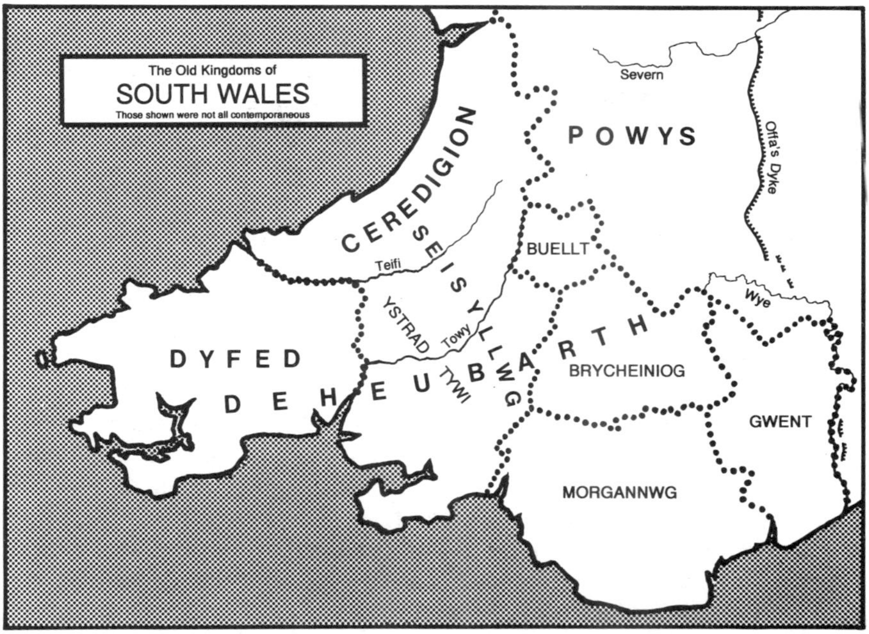

marriage Hywel acquired the kingdom of Dyfed which he subsequently united with Seisyllwg, becoming the ruler of the united Kingdom of Deheubarth.

The long reign of Hywel Dda (c.910-949) is a distinctive one in Welsh history. Besides ruling Deheubarth, Hywel gradually brought most of Wales under his control and during his reign Wales enjoyed a period of exceptional peace. According to tradition, however, his greatest achievement was in drawing up a uniform code of laws for all the Welsh territory under his rule. This body of Welsh law is one of the most valuable sources of Welsh social history in existence. It is reputed that the laws were drawn up at a representative assembly meeting at *Y Ty Gwyn ar Dâf* (The White House on the Tâf), Hywel's hunting lodge near Whitland. Hywel is the only ruler in Welsh history described as 'The Good' and 'the head and glory of all the Britons'.

On his death, Wales again became a country of strife and disorder, and although nothing is known of Carmarthen's part in the various struggles for power, there were battles fought at Abergwili in 1022 and at Pencader some years later.

After the victory of William the Conqueror at Hastings in 1066, the shadow of Norman power overhung the whole of Wales. Nevertheless, a descendent of Hywel Dda, namely Rhys ap Tewdwr ap Cadell ap Einion obtained recognition as the ruler of Deheubarth in 1081, a right acknowledged by William. Rhys ap Tewdwr was the last Welsh prince to hold, by hereditary right, the whole of Carmarthenshire. Although he had to contend with attacks from Welsh rivals, Rhys ap Tewdwr ruled without interference during the life of William the Conqueror, probably on condition of the payment of tribute. It seems likely that Rhys met William when the latter made a pilgrimage to St. Davids in 1081 and, for an annual payment of £40 recorded in Domesday Book, Rhys was allowed to keep his domains intact.

With the accession of William Rufus in 1087, however, conditions changed and the Normans made deeper advances into south-west Wales so that Rhys ap Tewdwr found his kingdom of Deheubarth being increasingly surrounded. In 1093 he was killed on the banks of the Usk near Brecon resisting the Norman invaders.

1 Dr. Wendy Davies, *An Early Welsh Microcosm, Studies in the Llandaff Charters* (Roy. Hist. Soc. 1978) and *The Llandaff Charters* (N.L.W. Aberystwyth 1979). See also Terrence James, *Carmarthen: An Archaeological and Topographical Survey,* 1980.

2 M. A. Lower, *Chronicle of Battle Abbey, 1060-1176,* 1851.

3 J. Wyn Evans, *Aspects of the Early Church in Carmarthenshire* in *Sir Gar: Studies in Carmarthenshire History,* ed. Heather James, Carmarthenshire Antiquarian Society, 1991.

4 Terrence James, *Carmarthen: An Archaeological and Topographical Survey,* 1980.

An excellent background source for this period is Professor Wendy Davies's book *Wales in the Early Middle Ages,* Leicester University Press, 1982.

Carmarthen Castle in 1748
(detail from Samuel and Nathaniel Buck's engraving of the town)

- 4 -

THE CASTLE

Just over a thousand years elapsed between the arrival of the Romans at Carmarthen and the arrival of the Normans around the year 1093. The first priority of the Normans, as in the case of the Romans, was to establish a stronghold which would act as a base for the conquest of the surrounding area.

RHYDYGORS CASTLE

The first reference to a Norman castle occurs in 1093 when *Brut y Tywysogion* (Welsh Chronicle of the Princes) refers to the construction of a castle at Rhydygors (ford-of-the-marsh). It was erected by William fitz Baldwin, a Devonshire knight, probably at the command of William Rufus. The precise location of this original castle at Rhydygors cannot be fixed with any certainty, although it is thought to have stood near Myrtle Hill, Pensarn. There, a *motte* (earth mound) is marked as Banc-y-castell on the 1830 Ordnance Survey map. Today there are no remains at all since they were apparently destroyed by the construction of the railway in the mid nineteenth century. Just across the river, however, the name of Rhydygors still survives in that of a late medieval residence, now demolished, and in the name of the general area. It is thought that in Norman times Rhydygors was the site of a ford, as the name implies.

The castle was presumably a wooden fortified tower upon the *motte,* but since it was very short-lived, it is unlikely that it ever had a *bailey,* i.e. an adjoining fortified enclosure for provisions, armoury and stables.

In 1096 William fitz Baldwin died, the garrison withdrew and the castle was abandoned. However, in 1102 Henry I gave Ystrad Tywi with Rhydygors castle to Hywel ap Gronw, who had supported him in putting down a rebellion by the powerful Montgomery family. Three years later Richard fitz Baldwin, William's brother, occupied and rebuilt the castle. *Brut y Tywysogion* records that in 1106 Hywel ap Gronw was treacherously betrayed by his friend and fellow-countryman and was killed by men from the castle. This is the last reference to Rhydygors castle, after which it appears to have been abandoned in favour of the more strategic site at Carmarthen.

HENRY I's CASTLE AT CARMARTHEN

In 1109 Henry I sent Walter, Sheriff of Gloucester, to Carmarthen 'for the protection of those parts', presumably to superintend the erection of a royal castle which was necessary for establishing more royal control in the area. This castle was probably a motte and bailey structure; the motte surviving today as The Mount at the top of Castle Hill while the bailey was in the area now partly occupied by County Hall. The site was a strategic one, commanding the river crossing, at the normal tidal limit and navigable from the sea. It overlooked the Towy valley and a wide area to the south, while to the north and west it was protected by a stream (the Wynveth, now covered over by Red Street and Blue Street) and to the north-east by marshy ground.

We have no record of how the native Welsh settlement around Llandeulyddog reacted to the coming of the Normans, but it has been suggested that the sites of Rhydygors and Castle Hill were chosen at some distance from the native community in order to avoid antagonising the local inhabitants.

However, in 1116 Gruffydd, son of the Rhys ap Tewdwr killed by the Normans in 1093, returned from exile in Ireland, raised a band of followers in his father's domain of Ystrad Tywi and attacked Carmarthen castle. He succeeded in capturing the outworks (the bailey?) but the Keep (*twr*) resisted capture. He set fire to the small civil settlement growing up outside the gate of the castle and retreated with much plunder into Cantref Mawr - an upland area north-east of Carmarthen. It is an interesting commentary on the times that the castle was being defended for Henry I by three Welsh chieftains of Ystrad Tywi who took it in turns to do garrison duty. One of them, a minor lord of Cantref Mawr, was killed in Gruffydd's attack on the castle.

Gruffydd ap Rhys ap Tewdwr was the brother of the famous Nest, the beautiful 'Helen of Wales', who had married Gerald de Windsor of Pembroke castle. The descendants of Nest became some of the most ambitious Norman-Welsh barons of Pembrokeshire and one of her grandsons was the famous Gerald of Wales (Giraldus Cambrensis). Intermarriages between members of aristocratic Welsh and Norman families became quite commonplace as time went by and Welsh princes built castles for themselves in the Norman mould. Moreover, the various Welsh princes just as often fought against each other as they fought against the Normans, which only served to advance the gradual conquest of Wales. Loyalties were by no means rigid and clear-cut but merely reflected the unsettled times.

BATTLES FOR THE CASTLE [1]

The strong rule of Henry I (1100-1135) was followed by the civil war of Stephen's reign (1135-1154), giving the Welsh an opportunity to rise against the invaders. Carmarthen castle was captured on several occasions. Following the death of Gruffydd ap Rhys ap Tewdwr and also in revenge for the defeat and slaughter of Gruffydd's wife, Gwenllian, near Kidwelly in 1136, an expedition led by Owain of Gwynedd captured and destroyed Carmarthen castle in 1137. It was rebuilt by Gilbert fitz Gilbert, Earl of Pembroke, in 1145.

In 1146 Gruffydd ap Rhys's sons, Cadell, Maredudd and Rhys, who were now the leaders of Welsh resistance in Ystrad Tywi and eastern Dyfed, captured Carmarthen castle and slaughtered the garrison. A large force of Normans and Flemings under William and Maurice fitz Gerald and William fitz Hay attempted to recapture the castle, which was heroically defended by Maredudd against superior numbers. Allowing the enemy to scale halfway up the walls, the defenders threw down the ladders and routed the foe. The sons of Gruffydd ap Rhys subsequently dominated Ystrad Tywi with the chief Welsh castle being at Carmarthen.

THE LORD RHYS

In 1150 Cadell strengthened the castle, now the key to the whole region. He was later seriously wounded and his leadership passed to his younger brothers. Maredudd died in 1155 at the age of twenty four. He left his extensive possessions covering Ystrad Tywi, Ceredigion and most of Dyfed to his younger brother Rhys, the last survivor of the sons of Gruffydd ap Rhys. The young Rhys ap Gruffydd came to be acknowledged as the leading Welsh prince in south-west Wales. After twenty years' conflict with Henry II (1154-89), the two became reconciled and Henry appointed The Lord Rhys (as he came to be called) royal Justiciar over South Wales in return for Rhys' assistance in Henry's domestic and continental exploits. The Lord Rhys acted as the King's deputy in all Welsh matters relating to the area, his chief seat being at Dinefwr castle, although he had another home at Cardigan castle. Dinefwr was described as 'built on a lofty summit above the Tywi, the royal seat of the princes of South Wales', by Giraldus Cambrensis (Gerald of Wales), when he accompanied Baldwin, Archbishop of Canterbury, on his journey through Wales in 1188.

The Lord Rhys
(Effigy in
St. Davids Cathedral)

With the accession of Richard I in 1189, the Lord Rhys renewed hostilities against the Crown. He unsuccessfully attacked Carmarthen castle, the siege being raised by Prince John, brother of King Richard, and a strong English army. In 1196 the Lord Rhys again attacked and burnt the town to the ground but failed to conquer the royal castle, possibly because it had been strengthened with stone. Rhys ap Gruffydd died in 1197, having been a dominant figure and outstanding leader in south-west Wales for forty years. On his death his sons quarrelled among themselves, having been in conflict with their father for several years previously, and his dominions were split up and torn asunder by years of family feuds.

In December 1215 Llywelyn the Great of North Wales (Llywelyn ap Iorwerth) captured Carmarthen castle after five days' resistance and placed a garrison in the town. He gave the castle to Maelgwn, a son of the Lord Rhys, who kept it until 1223, although in 1218 Llywelyn paid homage to the young Henry III and promised to restore it to the King's use when he came of age.

In 1223 the castle garrison surrendered to William Marshall, the new Earl of Pembroke, acting on his own initiative with no authority from the King. Llywelyn then sent his son to retake the castle, the opposing armies meeting on Carmarthen bridge which was then a timber structure. After an indecisive battle both sides retired, William Marshall returning to the castle 'which he repaired' and in 1226 handed back to the Crown.

CASTLE REBUILT IN STONE

The ten year period 1223-1233 is thought to be the time when the castle was rebuilt totally in stone for in 1233 it withstood a siege lasting three months. Carmarthen castle was now a key fortress of west Wales and with its growing town was a centre of increasing royal influence. In 1233 ten wooden cross-bows were sent from the Tower of London for the defence of the castle. In March 1233 Carmarthen was the first Welsh town to be granted *murage* for the building of a stone town wall. *Murage* was a tax levied on a wide range of goods coming into or going out of a town for the purpose of building and maintaining a town wall. Many grants were subsequently made to Carmarthen.

It was in late winter 1233 that Llywelyn, with the son and grandsons of the Lord Rhys, i.e. Rhys Gryg, Maelgwn Fychan and Owain ap Gruffydd, together with Richard Marshall, who had recently succeeded as Earl of Pembroke but then revolted against the King, besieged the castle for three months but failed to capture it. They built a temporary bridge below the town to prevent supplies and reinforcements being brought up to the castle by sea. However, in March 1234, Henry de Turberville sailed up the Towy on a high tide with a fleet from Bristol, crashed through the bridge, killing many of its defenders (Rhys Gryg was fatally wounded) and relieved the castle garrison.

A record of 1234 states: 'The good men of Carmarthen to be paid their expenses incurred in defending the castle and town.' Subsequently a new town bridge was built in stone. The next twenty years saw a power struggle between English and Welsh with the town being burnt in 1244 by David, Llywelyn's heir, and pillaged in 1246 by Maredudd ap Rhys Gryg. The castle, however, resisted capture and in 1248 was given into the custody of Robert Waleran who built a hall and chamber there. In 1254 Henry III bestowed the castle, together with all royal lands in Wales, upon his eldest son, then aged fifteen, later to become Edward I.

THE BATTLE OF COED LLATHEN

The year 1257 brought a crushing defeat in the Towy valley for an English force sent out from Carmarthen castle. Since royal power was at a low ebb, Henry III sent Stephen Bauzan to restore order in Ystrad Tywi and to restore Dinefwr castle and its lands to Rhys Fychan, a descendant of the Lord Rhys. Dinefwr had been taken by Llywelyn Prince of Gwynedd and then granted to Maredudd ap Rhys Gryg. Stephen Bauzan set out from Carmarthen with a large and formidable force. Harried in the Towy valley by the Welsh under Maredudd ap Rhys Gryg and Maredudd ap Owain, they were treacherously deserted by their ally and guide, Rhys Fychan, who fled to Dinefwr, leaving them to be slaughtered as they attempted to return to Carmarthen. In the words of a Welsh chronicler, possibly a monk at Talyllychau: 'At Coed Llathen the English lost all their provisions and all their horses carrying all their arms and other requisites. About mid-day, when the fighting had reached Cymerau, the Welsh, with the help of God, fell upon the armed English and thrust the noble Saxons valiantly from their warhorses, so that they were trodden under the feet of their steeds, their knights and their footmen in the ditches and marshes and dingles. More than three thousand Saxons fell that day; few, if any, of the armed knights escaped from that encounter.'

Although neither the site of Coed Llathen (Llangathen?) nor of Cymerau can be fixed with certainty, the *Black Book of Carmarthen* speaks of 'the battle of the Confluences' (probably the confluence of the Towy and the Cothi). It is now thought that the fighting took place in the vicinity of Broad Oak where several fields around an old farmhouse called Cadfan (place of battle) bear names suggestive of fighting: e.g. *field of vengeance, field of groans, field of death, field of Normans and corner of shouting.* This was the greatest disaster which an English army had suffered in Wales for many years. Carmarthen castle, however, was too strongly held for the Welsh forces to capture it. In 1265 Prince Edward granted the castle to his brother, Edmund, but it was returned to the Crown in 1279.

EDWARD I's ROYAL CASTLE

After the accession of Edward I in 1272 power gradually slipped from the grasp of the Welsh princes and by the time of the death of Llywelyn, the last Welsh Prince of Wales who was killed near Builth in 1282, royal

The Keep

authority in the Towy valley was firmly established and centred on the royal castle at Carmarthen.

In 1275 the castle was described in an official document (Extent of the Manor of Kermerdin) as being in need of repair: it contained a great tower (the Keep?), five small towers, a hall, chapel, stable and kitchen - all surrounded by a stone wall with one castle gate. The cost of repair was put at 100 marks. Subsequently the castle became the principal seat of royal government in south-west Wales, for in 1280 Edward I appointed Bogo de Knovill Justiciar of South Wales. (The title must not be confused with the present geographical area.) The Justiciar was the political and judicial head of royal government, responsible only to the King. (The two 'royal shires' of Carmarthen and Cardigan came to be known together, for convenience, as the Principality of South Wales.) The Justiciar was responsible for the appointment of other royal officials in the two counties, especially the Constables of the royal castles and the Sheriffs. In 1281 Robert de Tibetot succeeded Knovill as Justiciar of South Wales with headquarters at Carmarthen castle.

The Statute of Wales, drawn up in 1284, brought in the Edwardian Settlement which lasted until the Act of Union, 1536. The 'county' of Carmarthen, originally the land governed directly from the castle, was regarded as a double county, Welsh and English. The 'Welshry' consisted of the upland *commotes* of Elfed and Widigada (the latter lay between the Gwili and the Cothi), while the 'Englishry' consisted of the castle, the borough (Old and New Carmarthen), the demesne lands of Llanllwch and, after the rebellion of Rhys ap Maredudd in 1287, Cantref Mawr with the castles of Dinefwr and Dryslwyn.[2]

The chief royal officer for the double county of Carmarthen and also for Cardigan was known as the Justiciar (Justice) of South Wales. His headquarters were at Carmarthen castle, where he presided over the courts of justice. The 'county' of Carmarthen also had the Sheriff, who presided at a court dealing with disputed possessions of freehold land.

In 1299 a Chamberlain or Treasurer, with an office in Carmarthen castle called the Exchequer, was appointed to be responsible for supervising the collection of revenue and the payment of fees and wages to those employed in governing the Principality of South Wales.

Meanwhile, in 1286, Rhys ap Maredudd, grandson of Rhys Gryg and a descendant of the Lord Rhys of Dinefwr, broke into revolt against Robert de Tibetot, the King's Justiciar. During Edward's wars against Llywelyn, Prince of Gwynedd, Rhys ap Maredudd had remained consistently loyal to the Crown and so, in addition to his Lordship of Ystrad Tywi, with Dryslwyn as its castle, he now held the whole of Cantref Mawr and lands on the other side of the Teifi. However, he came into conflict with de Tibetot who tried to compel Rhys to attend the County Court at Carmarthen castle to answer some charges brought against him. This, Rhys refused to do as being contrary to the privileges granted to him by King Edward. Tibetot asked the King to declare Rhys an outlaw but Edward declined to do this and ordered an enquiry into the dispute. Before this could take place and while the King was abroad in Gascony, Rhys rose in revolt, capturing several castles including Dinefwr, Carreg Cennen and Llandovery but failing to take Carmarthen. In 1287 Rhys pillaged and burnt the town. (In 1288 the castle was restored at a cost of £169 15s. 3d. while in 1289 Robert de Tibetot was commanded to 'roof with stones the houses of the King's castle of Kermerdyn now covered with straw . . to the amount of Thirty Pounds.')

Rhys ap Maredudd was now declared a rebel and outlaw and his castle at Dryslwyn, which was the headquarters of his territory, was besieged by a very large army. After three weeks Dryslwyn fell, as did the other castles captured by Rhys, but Rhys himself escaped to become a fugitive for several years. Eventually he was captured and taken to the King at York, where he was executed in 1291.

The only recorded son of Rhys ap Maredudd, another Rhys, was imprisoned in Norwich castle. Numerous entries in the *Calendars of Close Rolls* refer to the payment of allowances to Rhys, the last dated October 16th, 1340. So ended the renowned dynasty of *Dinefwr,* dating back to the rulers of Deheubarth, with their principal seat at *Dinefwr Castle,* now in ruins. (The later dynasty of *Dynevor* founded by Gruffydd ap Nicholas [1425-56], a descendant of the Lord Rhys, was based on the 15th century manor house of Newton, Llandeilo. This was rebuilt in the 17th century, enlarged in the 18th and from 1782 was known as *Dynevor Castle,* the seat of the Barony of Dynevor. It still stands today in close proximity to the late 12th and 13th century ruins of *Dinefwr.*)

The rebellion of Rhys ap Maredudd had only served to strengthen the political and administrative power of the Crown, centred at Carmarthen, which remained unchallenged until Owain Glyn Dŵr's

The Chamberlain's room over the gateway

rebellion in the early fifteenth century - except for one episode in 1294. In that year Maelgwn Fychan, a descendant of the Lord Rhys, from Cardiganshire, raided Carmarthenshire but was slain 'in a field between the mill-dam and the pool of the Prior of Carmarthen.'

The era of the Welsh Princes finally came to an end in 1301 when King Edward I bestowed the title of Prince of Wales upon his infant son and heir at Caernarfon castle.

FOURTEENTH CENTURY EXTENSIONS TO CASTLE

During the fourteenth century frequent renovations and extensions were made to the castle so that the accommodation was extensive. It included the King's Hall and chambers, the King's chapel, the Queen's apartment, chambers for the Justiciar and Constable, the Chamberlain's Hall, a chapel for the knights and esquires, Exchequer offices, a bakehouse and kitchens, a granary and wine cellar, an armoury, a well and stables. In 1340 the Chamberlain's Hall was ordered to be repaired 'with timber at the top and the gutters with lead' and in 1355 a wine cellar was made under the hall. By 1370 another reception hall had been added and by 1394 a newly-made gate and crenellated chamber between the inner and outer wards had been constructed.

To pay for such extensions and repairs, orders were frequently given to the Chamberlain who was the chief fiscal officer and head of the Exchequer where all dues were received on the King's behalf.

THE BLACK PRINCE

In 1343 the Black Prince, warrior son of Edward III (1327-77) was granted Lordship of Carmarthen and its surrounding Crown lands. These were administered by the Prince's council. In the Hundred Years' War against France, which began in 1338, many Carmarthenshire men took part. About 1,200 Carmarthenshire infantry, half of them armed with bows and arrows and half with long light spears (lances) and long knives fought at the battle of Crécy in 1346. They were led to France by Rhys ap Gruffydd, who was subsequently knighted, and who was originally Lord of Llansadwrn but by the time of his death had become a magnate holding vast estates in Wales and England.

For the siege of Calais, 1347, Sir Rhys returned to Carmarthen to collect more reinforcements and on the instructions of the Black Prince, the Chamberlain at the castle clothed them 'in short coats and hats of green and white cloth, green to the right.' Their pay was twopence a day. Sir Rhys ap Gruffydd died in 1356 shortly before the Black Prince's victory at Poitiers. According to the Welsh bard, Iolo Goch, he was buried at Carmarthen.

The Black Prince visited Carmarthen in 1351, 1362 and 1370, when several grants to the Priory were signed by him. His son, Richard II, stayed at the castle in 1399. Shortly afterwards he was deposed by his cousin, Henry Bolingbroke, Duke of Lancaster. Henry IV was the first Lancastrian monarch and as Duke of Lancaster held the Lordships of Kidwelly with Carnwyllion and Iscennen. On Henry's becoming King these Lordships passed directly to the Crown, thus increasing the Crown lands of the county of Carmarthen. In 1400 Henry IV sent twenty men-at-arms and forty archers to garrison the castle.

OWAIN GLYN DWR'S REBELLION

The year 1400 was a momentous one in Welsh history for it saw the beginning of Owain Glyn Dŵr's rebellion. A descendant of the Princes of North Wales and also, through his mother, of the old dynasty of Dinefwr, Glyn Dŵr had received some of his education in England, had served as a knight under Richard II and Henry of Lancaster and subsequently lived the life of a country nobleman at Sycharth. The immediate cause of revolt was a quarrel with his neighbour, Lord Grey of Ruthin, a great friend of Henry IV; but there were far deeper causes which wafted the flames of rebellion. Social and economic unrest caused by misgovernment and oppression by alien lords and greedy officials, unjust taxation, restrictions on trade, the cost of the French wars and the devastating effects of the Black Death all took their toll. In England the Peasants' Revolt of 1381 was caused by these same underlying factors.

In September 1400 Owain Glyn Dŵr was proclaimed Prince of Wales by his supporters, and the fight was now for independence. In July 1403 Owain Glyn Dŵr arrived in Carmarthenshire and was acknowledged as Prince of Wales by the local leaders of the rebellion, namely Henry

Dwnn or Don of Kidwelly, William Gwyn of Llansteffan and Rhys ap Gruffydd of Dryslwyn.

On July 5th he besieged Carmarthen castle and burned the town, slaying more than fifty of the townsmen. He destroyed the title deeds and documents of the Priory as well as others deposited in the town. The next day the town was surrendered to him by Wigmore, the Constable. Glyn Dwr and his army then moved on but, in September, Henry IV brought an expedition to Carmarthenshire to break the rebel-hold and without any real opposition he entered Carmarthen on September 24th, staying for five days. He rewarded those who had stayed loyal to him and compensated them for losses sustained. He left a small garrison at the castle under the Earl of Somerset but they soon begged to be allowed to leave, fearing their fate, saying they would not stay 'for anything in the world.'

The Castle Gateway

At the end of October the Duke of York took charge at Carmarthen in command of 250 men-at-arms and 780 archers and he was appointed Lieutenant of South Wales.

In 1404 a letter was sent to Sir Thomas Carew (and £200 for costs) to summon men-at-arms and archers to defend the castle and town of Carmarthen and also Newcastle Emlyn.

In 1405 Owain came again to west Wales with 10,000 men to meet a French force which had landed at Milford Haven. The combined armies recaptured Carmarthen town and castle, the garrison surrendering on condition that their lives were spared. However, the rebellion was losing momentum and in 1406 Carmarthenshire yielded to royal authority and by 1408 the rebellion had died down.

In 1409 over £380 was spent on repairing the castle and nearly £100 on reconstructing the gateway flanked by its drum towers. Although modified by time, this is the best preserved portion to be seen today.

On 25th October 1415, Carmarthenshire men fought at the battle of Agincourt under Henry V.

In 1424 the debt owed by Lewis or Lodwig Peyntour, reeve of Newcastle Emlyn, was cancelled 'by consideration of the Chamberlain of Carmarthen and the auditor for divers paintings done and to be done by him in the chapel within the castle of Carmarthen and in the king's exchequer there.'

1455-1485: THE WARS OF THE ROSES

The events of this conflict, in so far as they are related to Carmarthen, are summarised as follows:

Carmarthenshire was predominantly Lancastrian in sympathy. The reason was that when Henry Bolingbroke, Duke of Lancaster, became Henry IV in 1399 he combined the crown lands of Carmarthen and its neighbourhood with the Lancaster lordships of Kidwelly, Carnwyllion and Iscennen. Lancastrian power was further strengthened in south-west Wales in 1452 when Jasper, son of Owain Tudor, was made Earl of

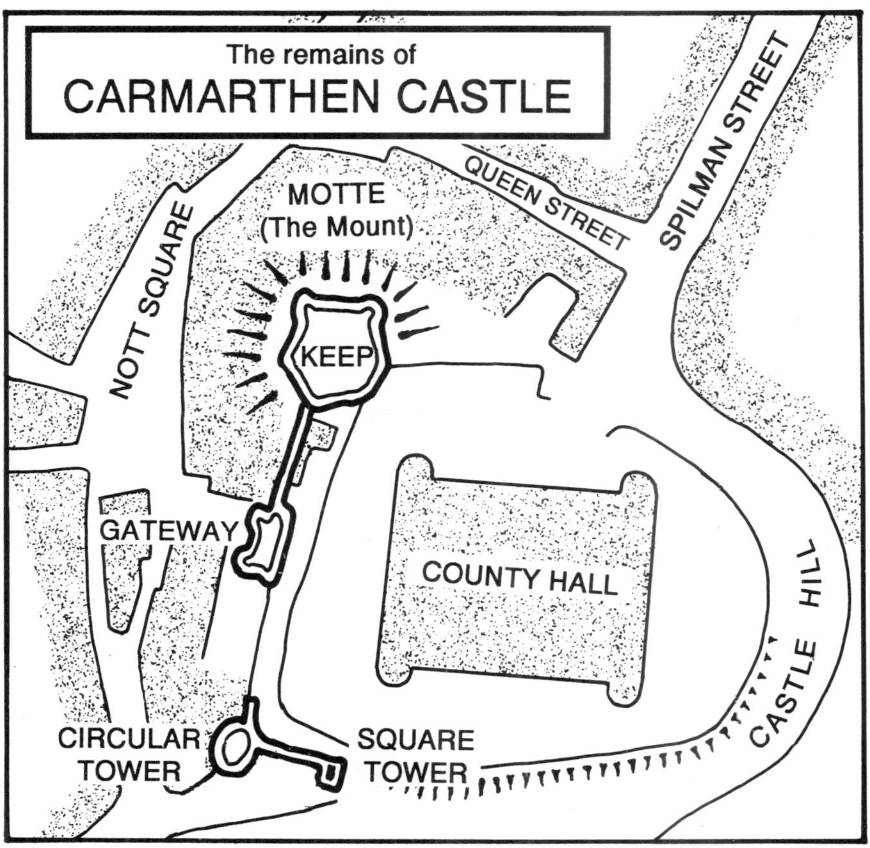

Pembroke. Owain, who was Owain Glyn Dŵr's godson and originated from Anglesey, served in Henry V's household and fought at Agincourt. He later married Henry V's widow, Katherine, and his two sons, Edmund and Jasper, were brought up under the protection of their half-brother, King Henry VI. In 1452 Jasper was created Earl of Pembroke, while Edmund was created Earl of Richmond. Edmund married Margaret Beaufort, a descendant of John of Gaunt, son of Edward III, and their son, Henry Tudor, was born at Pembroke castle in 1456.

1457: Jasper, Earl of Pembroke and lord of Llansteffan was Constable at Carmarthen castle.

1461: Jasper, accompanied by his father Owain Tudor, and the two sons of Gruffydd ap Nicholas of Dynevor (Newton, Llandeilo), the most influential Carmarthenshire magnate at this period, together with troops from Carmarthenshire and Pembrokeshire, were defeated at Mortimer's Cross by Edward, Duke of York. Owain was beheaded but Jasper and the two sons of Gruffydd escaped.

1461: Edward of York proclaimed King Edward IV.

1461: The Yorkist Sir William Herbert of Raglan made Chief Justice and Chamberlain of South Wales at Carmarthen castle. The Yorkist John Dwnn of Kidwelly made Constable and Sheriff of Carmarthen.

1468: Baron Herbert given Jasper Tudor's Earldom of Pembroke. The young Henry Tudor, later Henry VII, was well treated by Lady Herbert and brought up with her family.

1471: After the final defeat of the Lancastrians at Tewkesbury and the subsequent murder of Henry VI in the Tower, Henry Tudor was now the Lancastrian heir to the throne. Jasper and Henry Tudor fled to Brittany where they remained for fourteen years.

1483: Edward IV died: his son Edward, the young Prince of Wales, and his younger brother were imprisoned by their uncle, Richard of Gloucester, in the Tower of London where, as tradition has it, the young princes were murdered.

1483: Richard III proclaimed King. His chief supporter the Duke of Buckingham, was made Justice and Chamberlain of Carmarthen and custodian of the castle.

1483: Buckingham executed for conspiring to put Henry Tudor on the throne. Rhys ap Thomas of Dynevor, grandson of Gruffydd ap Nicholas and a descendant of the Lord Rhys, was granted an annuity of 40 marks for inactivity during Buckingham's rising, payable at Carmarthen Exchequer. There can be little doubt, however, that he was already secretly negotiating with Henry Tudor and had promised him assistance.

1485: The Battle of Bosworth Field. Rhys ap Thomas joined Henry Tudor at Welshpool, having led thousands of Carmarthenshire men up the Towy valley and through Breconshire under his standard of the

Black Ravens. With this substantial support, which was further increased by other contingents from Monmouthshire and North Wales, Henry met Richard III at Bosworth in Leicestershire. After a fierce struggle Richard was killed and Henry Tudor, who had fought under the standard of the Red Dragon, was crowned King Henry VII on the battlefield.

Rhys ap Thomas was knighted for his services and was made Chamberlain of Carmarthen castle. In 1495 he was made Chief Justice of South Wales and until his death in 1525 he virtually ruled south-west Wales in the name of the King. Appointed a Privy Councillor, he was also Mayor of Carmarthen on three occasions and owned such extensive estates that there was a popular saying: 'the King owns the whole island except that part which belongs to Sir Rhys'. He was the last of the great medieval landed magnates. His tomb can be seen in St. Peter's Church.[3]

After the death of Sir Rhys ap Thomas in 1525, Walter Devereux, Lord Ferrers, was appointed Chief Justice and Chamberlain at Carmarthen castle. In 1534 Henry VIII appointed Justices of the Peace in the 'county' of Carmarthen. More Welshmen were now entrusted with the duties and responsibilities of local government and with maintaining law and order in their districts - they were Officers of the Crown.

THE ACTS OF UNION, 1536 and 1542

It was in the reign of Henry VIII (1509-1547) that England and Wales were united under the Acts of Union of 1536 and 1542. The old 'county' of Carmarthen was increased in size and given Parliamentary representation, as was the county town. Justices of the Peace and Sheriffs were appointed and a new system of courts was established. Although the castle was still the centre of political and judicial administration, the Tudor settlement encouraged the rise of a new class of landed gentry, the squirearchy, who served the Tudor monarchs loyally and obediently as officials of the government.[4]

THE CIVIL WAR, 1642-48

During the Civil War (1642-48) the castle and town were captured twice by Parliamentary forces without much resistance. However, in 1660 the royal auditor reported that the castle was 'quite demolished'. It may well be that Oliver Cromwell ordered the dismantling or demolition of the castle's defences when he stopped at Carmarthen in 1648 on his way to besiege Pembroke Castle.[5] Nevertheless, in the eighteenth century the castle's prison cells and part of the gate-house were in use as a gaol.

THE COUNTY GAOL AND COUNTY HALL

In 1789 the building of a new County Gaol was commenced on the castle site by John Nash. This remained in use until 1922 and was eventually demolished in 1938 to make way for the building of

Carmarthenshire County Hall, which was not completed until after the 1939-45 war. Built to a 'chateau' design by Percy Thomas (later knighted for his services to architecture), County Hall is now the headquarters of Dyfed County Council.

For nearly nine hundred years the castle site has been the scene of much of Carmarthen's history but its continued occupation has resulted in the destruction of much of its fabric. All that can be seen today are the motte (The Mount) with the remains of a shell-keep, the Nott Square gate-house dating from 1409 and portions of the curtain wall incorporating a circular 13th century tower and a small square tower, both of which can be seen from Coracle Way.

1 Sir John E. Lloyd, *A History of Carmarthenshire,* Vol. 1, 1935 and A. G. Prys-Jones, *The Sory of Carmarthenshire,* Vol. 1, 1959.
2 A. G. Prys-Jones, *The Sory of Carmarthenshire,* Vol. 1, 1959.
3 See *Some Carmarthen Personalities: Sir Rhys ap Thomas*
4 See *The Sixteenth Century* for the Tudor Settlement.
5 See *The Seventeenth Century.*

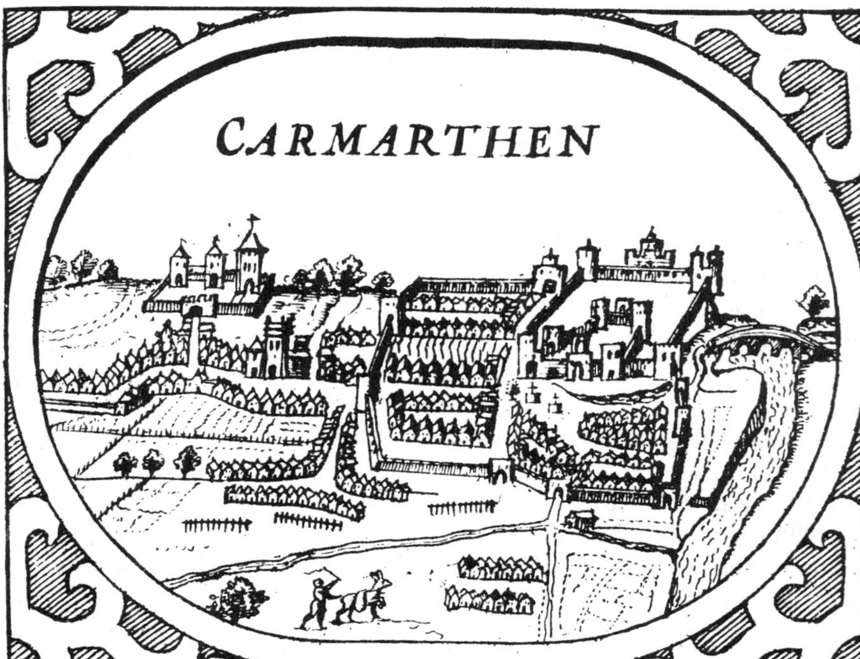

A map of Carmarthen in 1610 by John Speed, taken from his map of Wales.

This version is not as well known as the one reproduced on page 118 which shows more detail.

- 5 -

CARMARTHEN IN THE MIDDLE AGES

A distinctive feature of Carmarthen's history in the Middle Ages was the development of two separate towns which came to be known as Old and New Carmarthen. This distinction continued until 1546 when Henry VIII amalgamated them into a corporate borough under a new charter.

Old Carmarthen comprised the native Welsh community which, prior to the Norman conquest, had grown up around the monastic settlement of Llandeulyddog. Llandeulyddog was centred on the Celtic church of St. Teulyddog who is thought to have been either a disciple of St. Teilo or possibly even St. Teilo himself. When the Normans built their castle in 1109 on what is now Castle Hill, they built it some distance to the west of Llandeulyddog, perhaps to avoid antagonising the local community. However, in 1125, Bernard, first Norman Bishop of St. Davids, founded a Priory at Llandeulyddog which was dedicated to St. John the Evangelist and to St. Theulacus. In the Latin text of the *Cartulary of the Priory* (medieval documents relating to the Priory), there are many references to the church of St. Theulacus, in the genitive form 'Sancti Theulaci'. This is thought to be an attempt to Latinise the Welsh Teulyddog and the joint dedication may have been a means of placating local Welsh feeling. The Priory now ruled over Old Carmarthen which was administered by the Prior's reeve or bailiff.[1]

In contrast to Old Carmarthen, New Carmarthen was essentially a medieval planted town which grew up outside the gates of the Norman Castle. Under the protection of the castle the followers of the Norman conquerors first established a market outside the castle's main gate (now Nott Square) and from this small civil settlement of traders and artisans, described in 1116 as 'villa', there gradually evolved a town which was essentially a trading community based upon the market place.

While Old Carmarthen was under the authority of the Priory, New Carmarthen was under the authority of the royal castle which, from the time of Edward I (1272-1307), became the centre for the judicial and financial administration of south-west Wales. During the Middle Ages there was constant friction between Old and New Carmarthen over market rights, tolls, fairs and other privileges. Separate charters were granted to both by succeeding monarchs until the amalgamation, or to be more precise, the annexation of Old Carmarthen to the borough of New Carmarthen in 1546.

OLD CARMARTHEN

Little is known about the lay-out or extent of this native Welsh settlement around the Priory of St. John. When Giraldus Cambrensis wrote in 1188 'this ancient city is situated on the banks of the noble river Tywy, surrounded by woods and pastures and was strongly inclosed with walls of brick, part of which are still standing', he was referring to the ruins of Roman Moridunum. The Priory lay just outside the walls of Moridunum, to the south-east and near the river.

Sometime during the reign of Henry II (1154-1189), possibly around 1180, the King confirmed, by charter, the Priory's jurisdiction over Old Carmarthen, St. Peter's church and the castle chapel. This jurisdiction had been granted originally in 1125 when the Augustinian Priory of St. John was established. The charter also confirmed to the Priory earlier grants of arable plough-land outside the town in Newchurch, Llangain, Pentowyn (near Llansteffan) and Cwmau (the name Maes-y-Prior still survives in the area west of Llanllwch). In addition, the Priory was granted other plough-lands at Trebersed (north of the present St. Clears road near Llanllwch). Trebersed and Cwmau subsequently grew into the neighbouring Granges (farms) of the Priory. This charter of Henry II was confirmed by Henry III in 1247. (*Royal Charters and Historical Documents of Carmarthen*, J. R. Daniel-Tyssen, 1878)

Arable cultivation was also carried on nearer the Priory at Longacre and neighbouring Crug Gwenllian, north of present Priory Street. (An 'acre of land' was given to Prior John Edrich c.1280-1290.) There may also have been the cultivation of crops in the ruins of Moridunum itself.

The Commons of Old Carmarthen (common land which could be used for growing hay, grazing cattle, etc.) were at Waun Dew, Cwmoernant and Morfa Moch Ucha. The latter was below the town near the river and was used for feeding swine. The Priory also rented various

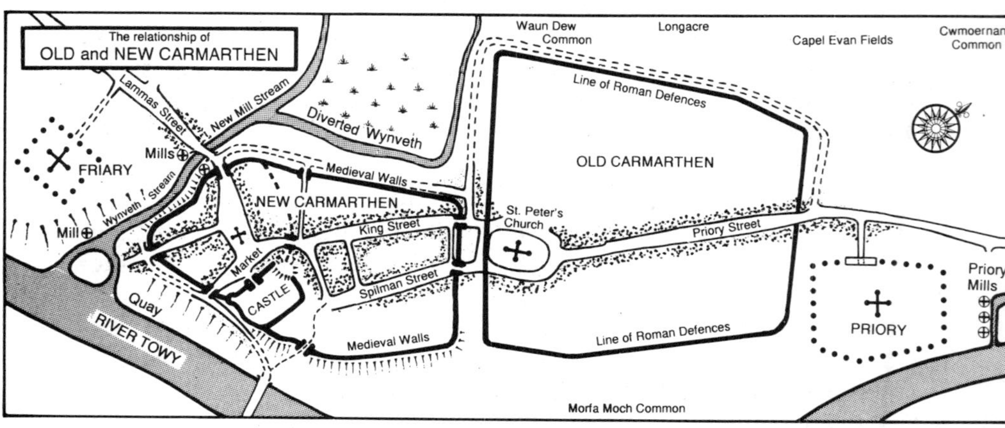

The relationship of OLD and NEW CARMARTHEN

acres of arable land belonging to New Carmarthen at Cillefwr and on the Archdeacon's Land (an area south of the present Picton Terrace and Monument Hill).

Much of the documentary evidence for Old Carmarthen comes from the *Cartulary of the Priory* - a collection of grants, charters and land-holdings relating to the Priory. Unfortunately, this does not give much exact information about the lay-out and extent of the town itself, and although there are many references to burgages (plots of land held for rent), these are difficult to locate. Burgages also differed in area and in the amount of rent paid. It would appear that in the fourteenth century there were burgage plots running off the north wall of the Priory precincts, others along the south side of Priory Street and an entry dated to 1350 refers to tenements adjoining the Vicarage near the burial ground of St. Peter's.[2] (According to the *History of Carmarthenshire, Vol. I,* a certain tenement near St. Peter's Church in 1350 was 44ft. long and 40ft. broad.) The Priory also owned a number of land-holdings in the area of what is now King Street and Spilman Street. In 1355 these holdings were claimed as 'suburbs' of New Carmarthen by the Black Prince; he said that they had been annexed by Edward I and did not belong to the Priory. His claim was successfully rejected by the Prior who referred to Spylmanstret and Sutternistreet (probably King Street) - the first recorded reference to these streets. (*Carm. Cartulary,* 119a) Even when this area was enclosed within the new walls of New Carmarthen (commenced in 1415) the Prior continued to keep these holdings.

The Priors administered Old Carmarthen through their reeves or bailiffs just as the Crown administered New Carmarthen, from the castle, through royal reeves. More is known about the burgesses (inhabitants enjoying certain privileges) of New Carmarthen and their burgages (land holdings) than is known about the burgesses of Old Carmarthen, since the 'Extents' or surveys of 1275 and 1280 give details of land-holdings only in the royal borough. (*Royal Charters,* J. R. Daniel-Tyssen.) *The Cartulary of the Priory* gives many names of witnesses to land transactions of the Priory but of these names some were burgesses of New Carmarthen, such as the families of Chapman, Kyng, Spilman, Laurence and Louring. Some names, however, appear only in the Cartulary and not in the Extents; names such as Bertelot, Boly and Broun and these may have been burgesses of Old Carmarthen.[3]

The Priors were very keen to preserve their rights and privileges and one constant cause of friction with New Carmarthen was that of market rights which were a source of profit. In about 1315 the burgesses of New Carmarthen complained to Edward II that the Prior and his tenants bought and sold all manner of goods in Old Carmarthen contrary to an Ordinance of Edward I made in 1305 which made it illegal to trade within five leagues (15 miles) of the King's borough of New Carmarthen.

The Prior was ordered to produce the royal charter or warrant proving his right to trade in Old Carmarthen but this he failed to do. The burgesses of New Carmarthen again petitioned the King and again the Prior was ordered to produce the royal warrant. Again he failed to do so, claiming that he and his predecessors were accustomed 'from time out of memory' to trade in 'all manner of merchandise' in Old Carmarthen (*Transactions of Carmarthenshire Antiquarian Society,* Vol. 17). In 1318 Edward II finally acknowledged the Prior's right to hold a market in Old Carmarthen. Nevertheless, friction continued and on one occasion in 1353, the Prior sent the royal reeve, Thomas Japhes, to prison for coming into the Old Town to collect tolls. In 1394 Richard II confirmed the Prior's right to hold, and therefore to profit from, a weekly market (Monday) and a yearly fair (29th August).

Some of the Prior's reeves in the fourteenth century are recorded as Adam le Skynner, John Hopkyn, John le Scriveyn (scribe), Walter Lloyd and John Hugon Raulyn.

During Owain Glyn Dŵr's rebellion the Priory was pillaged in 1403 and many of its old documents and charters looted; consequently Henry IV ratified all its privileges and rights in 1404. The famous Carmarthen Eisteddfod of 1450, held under the patronage of Gruffydd ap Nicholas of Dynevor, was probably held in the precincts of the Priory. On the accession of Henry Tudor as Henry VII in 1485 the King granted to all residents of Old Carmarthen 'full use of the Quay in New Kermerdyn: and enjoyment of all liberties as enjoyed by residents of New Kermerdyn.'

At the time of its Dissolution in 1537 the Priory held 29 tenements, 15 pieces of land and 6 burgages in Old Carmarthen.[4] There were probably other burgage tenements which were by this time privately owned. The town comprised Lake Street (Little Water Street), Priory Street and Gutternistret (Old Oak Lane?) and was probably settled along the eastern end of the present Priory Street.[5]

In 1541 the Mayor of New Carmarthen contemptuously described the old town as 'no Town' but only 'a street adjoining the town of New Carmarthen without (outside) the walls.' These were the medieval walls of New Carmarthen.

However, it must be remembered that St. Peter's Church, the oldest building still standing and still in use, also stood 'without the walls' in Old Carmarthen. The exact date of its foundation is unknown but its recorded history dates from early in the reign of Henry I (1100-1135). Sited midway between Llandeulyddog, subsequently the Priory, and the Norman castle, St. Peter's Church served both Old and New Carmarthen and was the original parish church.[6]

Old Carmarthen also had three water mills owned by the Priory, two being corn mills and the third a fulling mill. They were situated to the east of the Priory and were fed by a leat over two miles long starting at the River Gwili near Bronwydd. Parts of the leat's watercourse can still be seen at Pond Side although the mills have gone.

Resulting from the dissolution of the Priory, Old Carmarthen was amalgamated with new Carmarthen, forming a Corporate Borough. By a new Charter of 1546 the terms Old and New were abolished and all the rights, liberties and franchises of Old Carmarthen 'heretofore belonging to the late dissolved Priory' were henceforth to be under the government of the Corporate Borough.

NEW CARMARTHEN

As we have seen, New Carmarthen evolved from a small settlement of traders and artisans outside the main gate of the Norman castle. In 1116 it was burnt, together with the outworks of the castle, by Gruffydd ap Rhys ap Tewdwr. The first half of the twelfth century saw the emerging new town suffer the same fate as the royal castle which was captured by the Welsh on several occasions. Later, during the strong rule of Henry II (1154-1189), the King granted certain privileges to the townsmen, such as freedom from 'toll, passage, pontage and all customs throughout our kingdom': an indication that the original settlement had

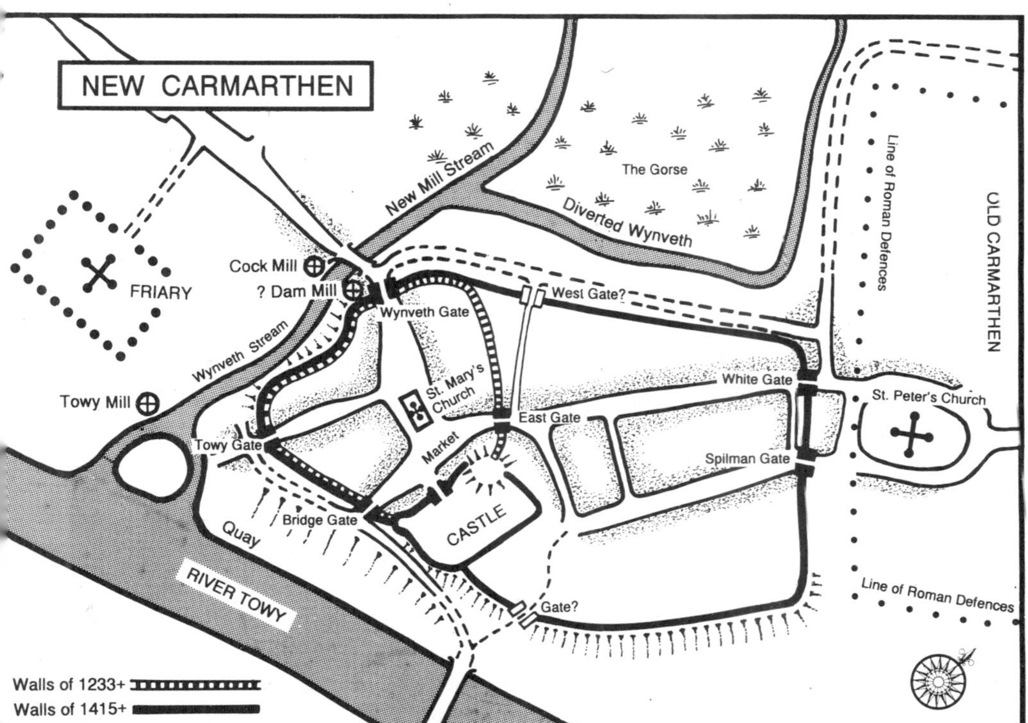

expanded into a trading town. In 1201 King John confirmed Henry II's privileges in a new royal charter.

There was a set-back in 1214, however, when the townspeople under attack from the Welsh, set fire to the settlement themselves and in the following year Llywelyn the Great of North Wales captured the castle which remained in Welsh hands under Maelgwn, son of the Lord Rhys, until 1223. With the return of English influence, Henry III granted a charter in 1227 confirming all former privileges to the townsmen.

Nevertheless, the town was sacked again by the Welsh in 1231. Two years later the castle withstood a siege of three months but the town succumbed to the Welsh attack and the town bridge, a timber structure, was destroyed. Subsequently a new town bridge was built in stone.

In 1233 Henry III granted *murage* to New Carmarthen for the purpose of enclosing the town with a stone defensive wall. (*T.C.A.S.* Vol. 17.) *Murage* was a tax levied for building or repairing a town wall and took the form of customs dues on a wide range of goods coming into or going out of the town and on the sale of goods. The 1233 grant of murage to Carmarthen was the first murage grant for any Welsh town.

Although the first town wall was begun in 1233, building and repairs continued for years afterwards with many grants of murage being made. The area of New Carmarthen enclosed by the first wall was relatively small with four gates: the Bridge Gate, the Towy Gate, the Wynveth Gate (later called Dark Gate), and the East Gate (later called Prisoners' Gate). Probably much of the stone used was robbed from the ruins of Roman Moridunum.

Little Bridge Street, c. 1910
showing town wall on right

The wall ran from the south-west tower of the castle (overlooking the present Coracle Way) westwards to the Bridge Gate (bottom of Bridge Street) and westwards again for 100 metres to the Towy Gate in Quay Street, which section of wall, up to a maximum height of 5 metres, can still be seen above what remains of Little Bridge Street. From the Towy Gate the wall ran between the rear of the present-day properties in Quay Street and Blue Street, where it can still be seen in some places, to join the Wynveth Gate (later called Dark Gate). The Wynveth Gate was demolished in 1796; at the same time the Wynveth stream was covered over to make a new 'waggon road' to the Quay - now Blue Street. The present Dark Gate does not exactly mark the site of the Wynveth Gate, for the latter was located further into what is now Guildhall Square. From the Wynveth Gate the town wall ran behind the present properties on the east side of Guildhall Square and Hall Street, although its exact line is unknown, to the East Gate (also later called the Prisoners' Gate) which stood between the present King Street and Nott Square, where, even today, the road narrows to a bottle-neck. The Prisoners' Gate, demolished in 1792 had a watch-house over it, reached by a flight of thirteen steps from the street. In its last days it was used as a gaol and naughty children were often threatened with the punishment of being sent 'up the thirteen steps'.

From this East Gate the town wall of 1233+ ran to the castle Keep on the north side of the castle, i.e. the motte, now called The Mount, behind Queen Street. So, roughly, the area enclosed by the first town wall included the present-day Nott Square, Guildhall Square, Bridge Street, Quay Street and the castle site.

Bridge Street

COMMERCIAL GROWTH OF NEW CARMARTHEN

During the thirteenth century there is evidence of commercial expansion within New Carmarthen. In 1252 Henry III directed that shops be built 'in the midst of our town of Kermerdyn, to wit, to the west of the Church of St. Mary.' Obviously St. Mary's Church was in existence before 1252 and it is known that it stood on the north side of the market place near the medieval market cross; indeed, it was often referred to as the Church of the Rood - *rood* meaning cross. Sited between the present Nott Square and Guildhall Square and alongside St. Mary Street and St. Mary's Lane, it was built to cater for the spiritual needs of the townspeople. It was probably built during the 1240's when the medieval town expanded. Like St. Peter's church in Old Carmarthen, St Mary's was a Chantry church where masses were sung for the souls of those who had endowed the chantry. St. Mary's was endowed with a considerable amount of property in New Carmarthen.

By the middle of the thirteenth century commercial contacts with ports, especially Bristol, were flourishing, for the importance of the river to the trade of the town must not be underestimated. From the construction of the castle in the early twelfth century ships had sailed up the Towy bringing supplies of men, armaments, food and wine and from this initial contact with the outside world commercial expansion followed. In 1242 Carmarthen merchants were trading in Bristol when the King granted them freedom from the wool tax of Bristol city; other records show trade with other ports, especially in the west country, such as Barnstaple and Bideford. Further afield there was a growing wine trade with Gascony (France) and Portugal.

Further evidence for an expanding prosperous town is provided by the Charter granted by the Lord Edward, eldest son of Henry III, who later became the famous Edward I. This Charter, dated about 1254-55, made New Carmarthen a chartered Borough. Edward modelled Carmarthen's new privileges on those of Hereford. The Borough charter confirmed all former privileges and also extended them to include the right of burgesses to judge all trespasses committed within their free borough; exoneration from charges of theft perpetrated by servants or others without the knowledge of the burgesses; security against imprisonment, where the accused was able to pay bail; immunity from responsibility for the debts of fellow townsmen and the rights of heirs to receive the property of deceased burgesses without fear of confiscation. Thus the burgesses of New Carmarthen were in a much more favourable position than the inhabitants of the surrounding countryside. Edward's charter was subsequently confirmed by his father King Henry III in 1257. There is a record of a Portreeve for the Borough 'who collects the King's monies there' in either the reign of Henry III (1216-1272) or of Edward I (1272-1307). The Portreeve was nominated by the Constable of the castle from among four burgesses chosen by their fellow burgesses. (*T.C.A.S.* Vol. 17.)

Some indication of New Carmarthen's inhabitants in the second half of the thirteenth century can be obtained from so-called *Extents* or surveys. An *Extent* of 1268 [7] shows that there were 123 burgesses (inhabitants enjoying certain rights and privileges) holding 168 burgage plots (burgages). Over a quarter of these plots were outside the town wall: 21 were sited along the road leading from the Wynveth Gate (i.e. the present Lammas Street); 12 lay outside the Bridge Gate; 11 outside the Towy Gate; but only 6 were outside the East Gate in the area between New and Old Carmarthen. Another survey of 1275 called *The Extent of the Manor of Kermerdin* shows that there were then 181 burgesses paying 12d each annually for their burgages and an unspecified number of burgesses *de vento* (literally 'of the wind') who did not hold burgages but paid a rent for enjoying the same privileges as burgesses. A later *Extent* of the Manor dated 1280 states that there were 169 burgesses and 86 burgesses *de vento*, while in 1300 there were 281 burgesses and 87 *de vento*. The 1275 *Extent* also states that 'The Toll of the Market is valued yearly at 66s. 8d.' The toll of the Fairs was the same. In 1280 the tolls were £8 and £5. 6s. 8d. respectively. (*Royal Charters*, J. R.Daniel-Tyssen.)

Bull Lane
(view from Quay Street)

Bull Lane
(from Blue Street)

Manorial records show that while most burgesses held one or two burgage plots (although increasing population led to the subdivision of some holdings), there were several burgesses who managed to acquire a considerable number of land-holdings. Their families accumulated more burgages and so increased their prosperity. The 1268 survey shows that the most prominent land-holding families included those of Laurence, Louring, Chapman, Young, Kyng, Michael, Wyte, Spilman and Baret. These names indicate that Carmarthen's burgesses originated mainly from England, especially the south-west; they were English pioneers settling in a planted borough in the shadow of the royal castle. Nevertheless, the survey also shows that there were about 11 Welsh burgesses holding burgage plots, but only seven actually lived within the town walls. The most outstanding Welsh burgess was Meylor Vachan or Meilyr Vychan who held four burgages; he also held a substantial amount of land outside the town. He became reeve of Carmarthen sometime between 1280 and 1300 and it is possible that he gave his name to Trevaughan which was first recorded about 1270-1280.[8]

Two notable burgess families were those of Kyng (or le Kyng) and Spilman who gave their names to two of Carmarthen's main streets. They are the earliest recorded burgess families. A certain William Kyng is first recorded in about 1197 when, together with Robert Spilman, he was witness to a document giving Abernant Church to the Priory. In the 1268 *Extent* Nicholas Kyng held seven burgages (one shared); he was a juror in the 1275 *Extent* and reeve of New Carmarthen about 1280. The first Spilman to be mentioned was Richard, in the twelfth century, while his son, Robert, was a witness to the document giving Abernant Church to the Priory as previously mentioned. Other Spilmans were Nicholas and Andrew, recorded as witnesses to documents in the *Cartulary of the Priory*. In one entry dated 1270 Andrew is named as witness to an exchange of land, while later in the century his name occurs as a juror and as a witness to grants of land to the Priory. A later member of the family, John Andrew Spilman, is referred to as *maiore eiusdem ville* (mayor of the said town) when he was a witness to a land transaction recorded in the Cartulary between Prior William and Robert de Penres, Lord of Llanstephan: but no definite date is given on this document. In 1352 John Andrew is recorded as holding meadows at Rhydygors which had been leased to his older relative, Andrew Spilman, from about 1280.

The Wynter family also figure prominently in medieval records: John Wynter held a substantial amount of land in the early 14th century and was reeve c.1312-1313. The family provided a number of canons, priors and an Archdeacon of Carmarthen, namely Walter Wynter, who gave land to the Priory in 1329 and in 1331 leased 22 acres of arable known as the Archdeacon's Land. The Chapman family also held considerable property in both New and Old Carmarthen from the late 13th century.

MEDIEVAL WATER MILLS

Located outside the walls of the new town were several water mills for grinding corn. The earliest reference occurs in 1233 when Henry III granted a charter to 'Daniel the Miller of Kaermerdin, that he and his heirs for ever shall have and hold that Mill situate without the walls of Kaermerdin upon the water of Wynveth, which the same Daniel by Our licence, erected at his own cost: Rendering therefor to Us and Our Heirs each year five shillings by the hands of Our Bailiffs of Kermerdin for all service . . .' It is probable that this mill stood between the Wynveth (Dark) Gate and the river Towy and was known as the Towy Mill in subsequent surveys.

In 1251 Henry III granted an application by three millers, Henry le Arblaster, Falco Boneker and John Luringer (or Louring), to divert the waters of the Tawelan brook, coming from the Trevaughan area, into the Wynveth stream for the benefit of their mills outside the walls of Carmarthen. He also granted their further application to divert water from the Wynveth stream to run along what is now Little Water Street and then to turn to run parallel to Woods Row, finally joining the new mill stream (the original Wynveth) just before it came to Dark Gate. Thus a kind of defensive moat was provided to protect the northern and western sides of the growing town. In return for having the water diverted to their mills, Henry le Arblaster gave the King a third share of his mill, while the other two millers gave the King half shares of their mills (*T.C.A.S.* Vol. 17).

Among the mills named in the survey of 1268 (*Longleat MS.* 624) and in the *Extents* of 1275 and 1280, were the Towy Mill (1268, 1275 and 1280), the Dam Mill (1268 and 1275), the Cog or Cock Mill (1275) and the mill of Redcors or Redgors (1275) - Rhydygors? There are references to other mills but they are un-named. The precise location of the above mills is not known but it is thought that the Dam and Cock Mills stood close to each other on the Wynveth stream. The mill shown on Speed's map of 1610 is not named. According to Spurrell, the Cock (or Cog) Mill was removed when Dark Gate was taken down in 1796 and the Wynveth stream covered over. The mill stood on the corner of present Blue Street and Dark Gate, while the mill pond or dam was near the upper end of Dam Street (now Mill Street). The medieval Dam Mill may have stood just outside the Wynveth Gate or between the Cock and Towy Mills.

A mill is also recorded at Llanllwch in 1300.

'EXTENT OF THE MANOR OF KERMERDIN', 1275 and 1280

Although little is known about the open fields and commons of New Carmarthen, some details of the *demesne lands*, i.e. the lands belonging to the Royal castle, are given in the surveys or *Extents of the Manor of Kermerdin* of 1275 and 1280. In later accounts the Manor is also referred to as the Manor of Llanllwch which appears to cover the same demesne lands. The arable lands of the demesne were apparently at Cillefwr, Llanllwch, the Archdeacon's Land (roughly land south of Picton Terrace and Monument Hill), Redcors and Dothoc (Docket land). There were also hay meadows at Redcors and Dothoc. These were extensive lands adjacent to one another lying broadly in the present area of Rhydygors, Johnstown and extending down to the Towy. The *Extent* of 1280 states that there were other meadows on the other side of the Towy opposite the castle. Some snippets from the 1280 *Extent* make interesting reading:

> *They say that* - There are 20 acres of land in demesne, which land is called The Archdeacon's each acre of which is worth yearly 12d. There are 12 acres of land in demesne in a certain place which is called Kilelevor (Cillefwr) each acre of which is worth yearly 8d. There are 78 acres of land in demesne, which the farmers hold at the will of the Lord, and each acre is worth yearly 8d.
>
> Thomas Bolpen renders for a certain meadow at Redcors half a pound of pepper, value 4d . . . John Luring renders for a certain meadow in the aforesaid place, yearly, half a pound of pepper, value 4d.
>
> There are 6 streams in the water of Towy . . . worth with the fishery yearly 60s. There is a certain fishery on the upper side of the bridge, and it is worth yearly 8s.

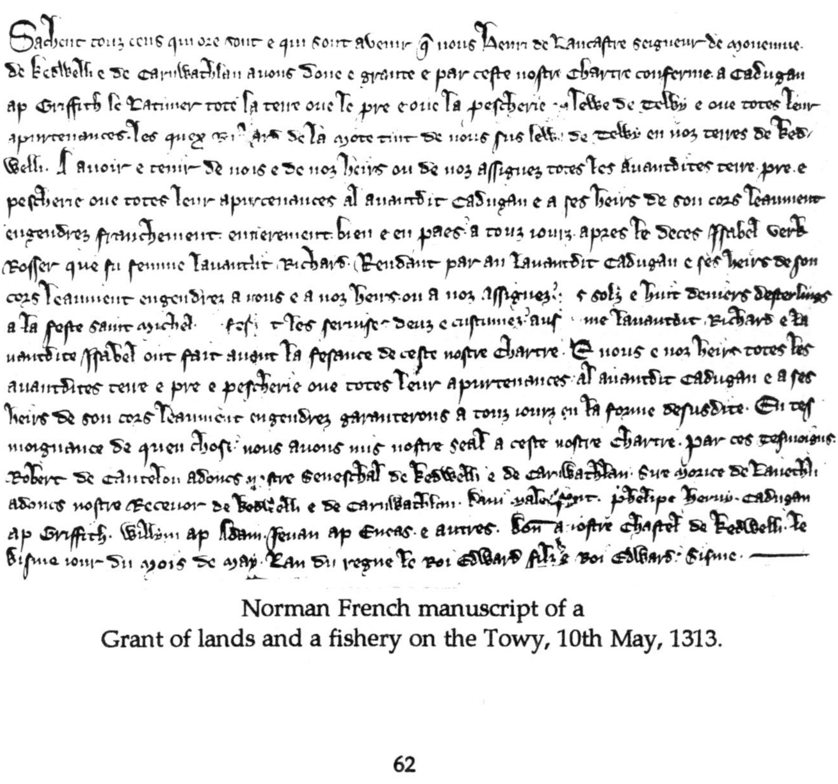

Norman French manuscript of a
Grant of lands and a fishery on the Towy, 10th May, 1313.

Since the demesne lands lay so far to the west of New Carmarthen, it is possible that the town's open fields for strip cultivation lay on either side of the trackway (now Lammas Street) emerging from the town at the Wynveth (Dark) Gate and leading to the demesne lands. By the time of the survey of 1268, however, there were 21 burgage plots sited along this road and more were to come with the foundation of the Friary several years later. The Friary stood on the site of the Lammas fields, probably part of the town's open fields, which were thrown open for common pasture on August 1st, Lammas Day, i.e. 'loaf-mass' Day. (The 1st of August, in the early church, was a harvest festival at which loaves of bread, made from the first ripe corn, were consecrated.) According to Terrence James there is also some evidence for open-field strip cultivation on the north-west of Lammas Street, in the Parcmaen Street area.

Around New Carmarthen were various commons, the nearest being at The Gorse (the area north of Woods Row). At Gwaun Iago common (Wauniago) there is evidence of open-field arable cultivation and there were other common lands at Royal Oak common in Johnstown and Gweyn Ellis, north of Job's Well. It would appear that Morfa Moch Issa (lower pig sea-marsh), near where the Tawelan flows into the Towy at Johnstown, was used for feeding swine; while Horsemoor, across the bridge, is self-explanatory.

NEW CARMARTHEN IN THE FOURTEENTH CENTURY

It is likely that New Carmarthen continued to grow in the early years of this century, at least until the Black Death took its toll in the late 1340's. One constant source of friction was Old Carmarthen's claim to equality of treatment. The burgesses of New Carmarthen complained to Edward II, in about 1315, that the Prior and his tenants were buying and selling all manner of merchandise in Old Carmarthen contrary to Edward I's Ordinance of 1305. They were conducting unfair trading in wool, leather, skins, wax, honey and other goods, which of right ought to be sold only in New Carmarthen, and were thus evading the payment of tolls, which was costing New Carmarthen a great loss in revenue. Moreover, the Prior and his tenants had weights and measures of their own and they kept a market and fair in Old Carmarthen without the King's warrant.

The Prior was ordered by the Justiciar of South Wales to produce the royal warrant: but he failed to do so, whereupon the burgesses of New Carmarthen again petitioned the King in 1315. Once more the Prior was ordered to produce the royal warrant, but again failed to do so, protesting that 'his predecessors were accustomed, from time out of memory, to buy, sell and offer for sale all manner of merchandise in the old Town of Carmarthen.' In spite of the protests of New Carmarthen that the Prior could not substantiate his claim, Edward II in 1318 acknowledged the Prior's right to hold a market in Old Carmarthen. Nevertheless, in 1330 the burgesses of New Carmarthen again complained and in 1353 their reeve, Thomas Japhes, went into Old Carmarthen to collect tolls. He was put in prison by the Prior!

THE RIVER AND PORT

The importance of the river to the trade of the town during this period must not be forgotten. Ships such as *Le Nicholas de Kermerdyn* and *Le Julien de Kermerdyn* sailed up the Towy bringing provisions, initially for the castle, including large quantities of wine from Gascony and Portugal. In 1244 the bailiffs of Bristol were ordered to put 40 tuns of wine, 200 quarters of wheat and 200 pigs on board one or two good ships and convey half to Carmarthen castle and half to Cardigan castle. Between 1302 and 1324 forty-four vessels brought cargoes of wine up the Towy and by 1335 this number had risen to fifty-two. The river was the main highway of transport in the Middle Ages, the quay being at Island Wharf (now demolished), where the Wynveth stream ran into the Towy. At high tide this area became an island.

Exports included wool, hides, woolfells (skins with the fleece still on), leather and tin. In 1326 Carmarthen was selected as a 'staple' town for the export of wool, hides and woolfells. It had long been the custom for a tax to be levied on all exported wool, and in order to make it easier for the King's officials to collect the tax ('the custom'), it was decreed that all wool had to be exported through selected towns, known as 'staple' towns. Here the quality of goods was scrutinised and fair trading under royal supervision guaranteed. By the Ordinance of the Staple, 1353, Carmarthen became the only staple town in Wales. This monopoly gave Carmarthen a big advantage over other west Wales ports.

By 1326 the stone bridge was in great need of repair. It was 'broken and destroyed' and so Edward II allowed *pontage* (a bridge toll) to be levied for three years. The burgesses were to have a boat for the passage of those who wished to cross and to collect tolls for the reparation of the bridge. (*T.C.A.S.* Vol. 18.)

In medieval times the town's ships were often commandeered by the Crown to transport fighting men for the King's service. In 1319 the Prior, who was at that time Chamberlain of Carmarthen, was ordered to provide 'a great ship' and man it for war against the Scots. In 1324 there was an order 'to cause all ships of that port of Kermerdyn capable of carrying 40 tuns of wine and upwards to be prepared and made ready to set out in the King's service.' In the following year a ship loaded with arms by order of the Prior, for the King's castles in Wales, was captured by 'Scotch rebels'. A certain ship-owner and merchant of Carmarthen, named Bernard Saundre, who was described as reeve c.1340-41 and also

Quay Street
(Engraving by William Jones, 1921)

1349-50, provided and fitted out *Le Neweshyp* of 100 tuns for coastal defence. He was also joint owner of the cog *Seynte Marie* which was appropriated for the King's French expedition on 31st July, 1342. In the following year two of his ships were ordered to be seized for plundering a *tarite* at Falmouth.[9]

During the Hundred Years War with France about 1,200 Carmarthenshire men, led by Rhys ap Gruffydd fought at Crécy (1346) and a similar number were summoned as reinforcements for the siege of Calais (1347). Their uniform, provided by the Chamberlain at the castle, on the instructions of the Black Prince, comprised 'short coats and hats of green and white cloth, green to the right' - a uniform of national significance.[10] Moreover, these Welshmen had their own chaplain and surgeon. For the siege of Calais, Carmarthen also provided one ship with 16 marines.

In 1370 Edward III ordered the mayor and bailiffs

> 'as they love the King and his honour and desire the salvation of the realm, to cause all ships of 100 tuns burden and upwards with sufficient gear which are in the port of that town to be arrested without delay, furnished with seamen, men-at-arms, armed men and archers, and brought to the port of Plymouth . . . ready to resist the malice of the King's enemies of France, who are now at sea, and with God's help to destroy them.' (*T.C.A.S.* Vol. 18.)

Three years later Edward III ordered ships from Carmarthen to be commandeered 'with sufficient equipment of sea-men' and to sail for Ireland and the King's service.[11]

THE EFFECTS OF THE BLACK DEATH

The mid fourteenth century saw a decline in Carmarthen's expansion and a drastic reduction in its population caused by the devastating effects of the Black Death. Being a trading port, Carmarthen was particularly vulnerable to the plague; the officials of the Staple were among its first victims in 1349. In that same year no returns were made for the Cock Mill 'because of the pestilence' while the demesne lands at Llanllwch were left without tenants, all except one having died, and the lands lay waste and uncultivated. The Prior, who held twelve acres of land at Kythlefour (Cillefwr), gave up the tenancy because no profits were being made. Similarly the rents paid by the burgesses in the town to the Crown dropped sharply and took a good many years to recover.

EARLY STREETS

References to Carmarthen in the second half of the fourteenth century include the first references to Spilman Street and what was later King Street in 1355 (Cartulary 119a). In this year the Black Prince claimed that the area between 'Halogyn (possibly Little Water Street) which is a certain lane and pool unto the Walls of the New Town' (i.e. the area of King Street and Spilman Street) were suburbs of New Carmarthen annexed by Edward I and did not belong to the Priory. This could indicate that there had been some development in this area between Old and New Carmarthen. In his reply, the Prior referred to 'Spylmanstret' and 'Sutternistreet' (probably King Street) and successfully rejected the Black Prince's claim. The 'pool' could be the Wynveth Stream which had been diverted in the previous century to run along what is now Little Water Street and then to run parallel to the present Woods Row for the protection of the northern side of the growing new town. These activities could indicate the development of settlements along King Street and Spilman Street which lay outside the walls of New Carmarthen.

It is at this period that certain burgesses are named as 'mayors' of the town, such as John Laurence in 1356 and 1382, John Andrew Coubrigge (1368-9) and John Andrew Spilman, probably 1369. The mayors were not yet elected - this had to wait until Richard II's charter of 1386 - they were more in the nature of royal agents. In 1363 John Laurence was nominated by the Black Prince to deliver the patronage of Llanfihangel-ar-Arth Church to Carmarthen Priory and in 1364 to do the same with regard to Llanybydder Church. In April 1380 he was ordered to arrest William Wyriot and to transport him to Pembroke Castle. As mayor in 1382 he was nominated to take Talley Abbey into the King's hands. But in 1384 and 1385 he had to be pardoned formally for an array of treasons and felonies. He was murdered on 5th October, 1385, on the road between Carmarthen and Cardigan, by Morgan ap Dafydd ap Llywelyn Foel.

In 1386 Richard II granted the town a new charter which, in addition to confirming all previous charters, also granted to the burgesses the right of freely electing a Mayor, two Bailiffs and a Coroner every year, on the first Monday after Michaelmas. The 1386 charter also confirmed the holding of the County Court and the Great and Petty Sessions at the castle. This charter was subsequently confirmed by Henry IV in 1400, Henry V in 1413, Henry VI in 1422 and Edward IV in 1464.

Dark Gate before redevelopment in 1973

NEW CARMARTHEN IN THE FIFTEENTH CENTURY

The early years of this century were dominated by Owain Glyn Dŵr's Rebellion which devastated the town and halted further expansion. In 1403 Carmarthenshire rose in revolt, threatening all the castles. The Sheriff of Somerset was ordered 'to leave all else and without excuse to load ships with wine, ale, floure, salt, fish and convey them to Carmarthen for victualling of the army there.' Records show that Thomas Chaucer, son of poet Geoffrey Chaucer, was actively engaged in conveying these stores from Bridgwater, Somerset.

On July 5th, 1403 Owain Glyn Dŵr besieged the town and castle, burning the town and slaying fifty townsmen. The Priory was ransacked and its archives of old documents and title deeds destroyed. Houses in Spilman Street were also burnt down and in the new town the burgesses suffered 'burnings, robberies and destructions' to their properties. The castle surrendered but subsequently Glyn Dŵr withdrew. In September Henry IV himself conducted an expedition to Carmarthen where he stayed for five days and the castle garrison was strengthened.

In 1405, however, Owain Glyn Dŵr again captured the town and castle. Llanllwch too was totally destroyed and devastated. The following year royal authority was restored as the rebellion gradually petered out, but the effects were felt for many years afterwards, including a decline in the fortunes of the port.

THE SECOND TOWN WALLS FROM 1415

After the rebellion large sums of money were spent on repairing the castle, while in 1415 Henry V made a new grant of murage of £20 yearly to the town, 'as the King understands that the walls have been razed by the Welsh rebels and the inhabitants are being robbed at night for the lack of enclosure, and the mayor and commonwealth are too poor to enclose the town without aid.' The new walls begun in 1415 enclosed a much larger area than previously, including Spilman Street and King Street, although Lammas Street still remained excluded.

The new wall ran along the same course as the first wall of 1233 i.e. from the south-west tower of the castle to the Bridge Gate, to the Towy Gate (Quay Street) then up between Quay Street and Blue Street to the Wynveth Gate (Dark Gate). From here there is no above-ground evidence of the wall's line but it is conjectured that it ran to a gateway, traditionally known as the West Gate, which has now disappeared. Speed's map of 1610 shows a gateway at the end of a lane which is often thought to be Jackson's Lane, but which in fact ran a little to the west of Jackson's Lane and which was probably closed up in the seventeenth century. This lane led from King Street to The Gorse (town commons to the north and west of Woods Row). From this West Gate the wall ran parallel to Woods Row, then it turned to run behind Little Water Street to a new gateway at the eastern end of King Street. This was called the White Gate which was subsequently demolished in 1792. From the White Gate the wall ran along the east side of Conduit Lane to the Spilman Gate which was demolished in 1768. Continuing along the rear of the properties in Parade Road, the wall turned south-west to run above Dan-y-Banc. A stretch of wall can still be seen to the rear of the Ivy Bush Hotel and another stretch behind the District Council offices, although these have been subject to much re-building.

From Dan-y-Banc the new wall joined up with the south-east of the castle, possibly with another gateway, but all remains of this were swept

Waterloo Steps
or Love Lane
(demolished 1963)

Conduit Lane
(follows the line of the
medieval wall of 1415)

away when Castle Hill was constructed in 1804. Nothing of the original castle or town walls is incorporated in the walls on Castle Hill today - they are of modern construction.

With King Street, Spilman Street and Queen Street, which follows the line of the castle ditch, now enclosed within the new wall, the area of New Carmarthen was greatly enlarged and the two towns were now adjacent to each other. The medieval lay-out of street patterns, incorporating various lanes and alleyways, has remained unchanged within the town's boundaries until the present time. Although there was later expansion it was always outside Carmarthen's medieval walls.

BURGESSES AND MERCHANTS

Not a lot is known of Carmarthen in the fifteenth century but some activities of her burgesses and merchants, some of whom were mayors, have been recorded:

In 1405 a grant for life was given to *'Thomas Frauncéis,* burgess and clerk of the town of Kermerdyn, in consideration of the great losses sustained by him through the Welsh rebels by the burning of his houses and otherwise, of a tenement with a garden adjoining in Spilman Street.'

Thomas Dier claimed to have lost £1,000 in goods during Glyn Dŵr's rebellion on account of remaining loyal to Henry IV. He was handsomely rewarded by gifts of estates, especially in Kidwelly.

Thomas Hugon (Higon) who had hurriedly repaired the bridge when Richard II visited Carmarthen in 1394 was engaged in shipping leather and hides from the port early in the next century.

John More, too, was engaged in shipping hides while in 1422-26 he leased 8 acres of land at Llanllwch and in 1434-36 he leased the royal barge kept at Carmarthen.

John Willy Fisher, a merchant engaged in trading ventures, bought a pipe (a large cask) of honey in 1403 from a Welshman's goods captured at sea and sold by the garrison of Carmarthen castle. In 1424-25 he was leasing the royal barge kept at Carmarthen for 8s. 4d. per annum and he frequently sold materials for repairing royal buildings in South Wales.

Nicholas Bluet sold wine coming into the port in 1433-35 and also sold carpentry and building materials.

Philip Banov held 5 acres of arable land, 2 tofts and 5 messuages (dwelling houses with adjoining land) in King Street in 1428 but on 30th December he was outlawed for debt![12]

At the close of the Middle Ages Carmarthen's skyline must have been pierced by the towers and walls of the castle, the walls and gateways of New Carmarthen borough, the ruinous Roman ramparts of Old Carmarthen with the Priory to the east of them and St. Peter's Church on the western edge, while St. Mary's Church stood in the middle of New Carmarthen and the Friary stood outside the town walls on its western outskirts.

The medieval street pattern can still be seen today in the layout of narrow streets and lanes which lay within the walled town.

The thirty years of dynastic struggles, known as the Wars of the Roses, 1455-1485, (see *The Castle*) ended in Henry Tudor's victory at Bosworth Field and the establishment of the Tudor dynasty, bringing sweeping changes in both national and local government administration. The Middle Ages were now over. The next century saw Old and New Carmarthen amalgamated into a Corporate Borough under a new charter of 1546.

1 See *The Age of Celtic Saints and Princes* and *The Priory.*
2 Terrence James, *Carmarthen: An Archaeological and Topographical Survey,* 1980.
3 Terrence James, *Medieval Carmarthen and its burgesses* in *The Carmarthenshire Antiquary,* Vol. XXV, 1989.
4 G. Dyfnallt-Owen, *Extent and distribution of lands of the Priory of St. John* in *The Carmarthen Antiquary,* 1941.
5 Terrence James, Carmarthen: *An Archaeological and Topographical Survey,* 1980.
6 See *St. Peter's Parish Church.*
7 Terrence James, *Carmarthen: An Archaeological and Topographical Survey,* 1980.
8 Terrence James, *Medieval Carmarthen and its Burgesses* in *The Carmarthenshire Antiquary,* Vol. XXV, 1989.
9 R. A. Griffiths, *The Principality of Wales in the Later Middle Ages,* 1972.
10 Sir John E. Lloyd, *A History of Carmarthenshire, Vol.1,* 1935.
11 See *Trade and Industry* for further details of the Port.
12 R. A. Griffiths, *The Principality of Wales in the Later Middle Ages,* 1972.

St. Mary Street, 1937

St. Peter's Church, mid nineteenth century.

Originally engraved for and published by H. White and Sons.

- 6 -

ST. PETER'S PARISH CHURCH

(including MEDIEVAL CHURCHES and CHAPELS which have disappeared)

St. Peter's Church is the original parish church of Carmarthen and is the oldest building still surviving and still used for its original purpose. Although the exact date of its foundation is unknown, its recorded history dates from the reign of Henry I (1100-1135). The earliest known record of St. Peter's Church is found in the *Chronicle of Battle Abbey*[1] - the abbey built near Hastings by William the Conqueror to commemorate his victory over Harold in 1066. *The Chronicle* records: 'that in the time of Abbot Ralph (1107-1124) the King, cherishing a great affection for the Abbey, freely and of his own proper gift, conferred upon it a certain church dedicated to St. Peter the Apostol, in the city of Chaermedi (Carmarthen) in Wales, with all its appendages for ever.'

The question must be asked whether St. Peter's Church was founded by the Normans or whether it was a pre-Conquest foundation. The fact that it is dedicated to St. Peter and not to a Celtic saint may indicate a Norman foundation and it is possible that it was founded soon after the Norman castle was constructed. Moreover, the *Chronicle of Battle Abbey* further records that not only was St. Peter's Church given to the Abbey but *'also another church in the same place founded in very ancient times in honour of St. Theodore the Martyr.'* This could imply that St. Peter's Church was a later foundation than that of St. Theodore which is thought to be the Celtic church of St. Teulyddog in the monastic settlement of Llandeulyddog and which was in existence before the Norman Conquest.[2]

If St. Peter's Church was founded soon after the construction of the Norman castle, its position midway between Llandeulyddog and the castle may have been determined by the fact that it could then serve the spiritual needs of both Old Carmarthen, with its Welsh community, and New Carmarthen growing up in the shadow of the castle.

Nevertheless, the question still remains of whether a pre-Norman church originally stood on the site, for St. Peter's Church lies within Old Carmarthen which is on the site of Roman Moridunum. The church is sited just inside the presumed west gate of the Roman walls. Moreover, the churchyard appears to have been curvilinear in origin, a characteristic of Celtic practice, which may indicate a Dark Age foundation.

The two churches of St. Peter and St. Teulyddog must have been given to Battle Abbey before 1115 because in that year, Bernard, the first Norman bishop of St. Davids, was elected to the See, whereupon he made continuous representations to the King to have the churches transferred into his own authority. Apparently 'the Bishop was allured by the pleasantness of the place.' Eventually in 1125 St. Peter's Church and Llandeulyddog were transferred back and Bishop Bernard then founded the Augustinian Priory of St. John at Llandeulyddog. St. Peter's Church, with its tithes and benefits, was conferred on the new Priory which was sited to the east of St. Peter's between the Towy and present-day Priory Street.

Since St. Peter's Church belonged to the Priory, the Prior claimed the right of nominating the vicars, although this nomination was often claimed in later years by both the Pope and the King. The first recorded vicar was Richard ap John in 1278, when in consequence of a dispute between the Vicar and the Prior, an agreement was drawn up by Richard de Carew, Bishop of St. Davids and sealed at Lamphey Palace in April 1278. By this agreement the Prior agreed to pay the Vicar 10 marks yearly with certain vicarial fees. In 1291 the 'Church of Kermerdyn' was valued at £9. 6s. 8d. in the taxation of church benefices under Pope Nicholas IV.

THE CHURCH BUILDING

St. Peter's Church is one of the largest churches in the Diocese of St. Davids, being 52 metres long from inside the west porch to the east window and 15 metres wide across the nave and south aisle. It consists of a west tower, nave, chancel, south aisle with a Consistory Court at its east end, south porch which is now a Chapel of Rest and a north transept, now called the Lady Chapel.

Owing to the lack of decorative architectural detail and also to the fact that the church has undergone several restorations during the eighteenth and nineteenth centuries, it is difficult to date the various parts of the church accurately, but it is thought that the tower, nave and chancel belong to the thirteenth century on the foundations of the earlier church. Traces of the latter can be detected about one metre above ground in the north wall of the nave. The nave is divided from the south aisle by a row of arches resting on massive pillars. The south aisle and porch were probably added in the late fourteenth century after the

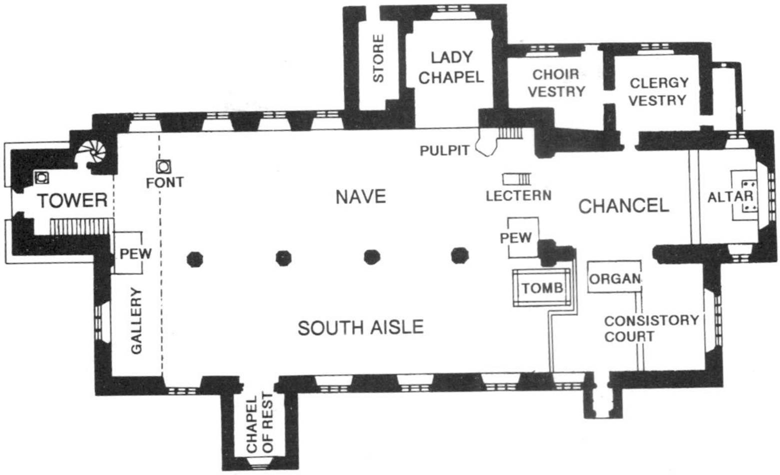

endowment of a Chantry chapel to the Blessed Mary in 1394. Richard II in 1394 permitted Thomas Rede of Carmarthen to endow 'a certain Chaplain to celebrate divine service daily to the honour of the blessed Mary, in a certain Chantry *anciently founded* within the church of the blessed Peter of Kermerdyn.' From this it would appear that there was already a Chantry, which was possibly absorbed by the later Chantry.

In the north wall of the nave are four sepulchral recesses, one of which contains a stone coffin lid unearthed in 1855. Possibly of the thirteenth century, the lid shows a figure with fleur-de-lys cross and round the edge is an inscription in Norman French which is thought to read: RICAR. ROSB(U)R. GIT. ICI. DEU. DE. LALME. EIT. MERCI.

A possible translation could be: Richard Rosb(u)r lies here, may God have mercy on his soul.

Under the slab is a piece of masonry reputed to be a carved boss from the Priory. It has also been suggested that it may be a fragment of a Romanesque capital of possibly 12th century date. Another recess contains part of a recumbent effigy without any inscription. On the north side of the chancel wall beneath a memorial to the men of St. Peter's who fell in the 1914-18 war, and just above floor level, is a fascinating broken stone slab with a crudely carved figure above heraldic devices.

During restoration work in the early nineteenth century steps leading to a rood loft were revealed in the wall behind the pulpit.

The tower and battlements have undergone several restorations, and the earliest surviving window now remaining is to be found on the south side of the tower; it is a single lancet window with trefoiled head of thirteenth century date. The windows on the north (older) side of the church are narrower than those on the south. The stained glass is mostly Victorian apart from some recently donated memorial windows.

Choir Stalls and Organ

An interesting feature in the west porch is a Roman altar or pedestal found near the church, recalling Carmarthen's ancient past as Roman Moridunum. Also of interest is a board inscribed with the names of the Bishops of St. Davids - taking us back to the time of St. David himself. There is also a list of Vicars of St. Peter's from 1278.

The south porch, dating from the late fourteenth century and originally containing a vaulted roof, a holy water stoup and a niche for the figure of the patron saint, has been converted into a Chapel of Rest by the Queen Elizabeth Grammar School Old Maridunians' Association. It is in memory of former pupils who gave their lives in the two world wars and succeeding conflicts.

The organ was built by George Pyke England and was erected in 1796 as the result of a public subscription. According to tradition, it was originally built for George III for St. George's Chapel, Windsor.

A new roof and plaster ceiling were constructed by the famous architect John Nash in 1785, when several tombs in the church, together with relics from the Friary ruins, were ground down to provide materials for the work. However, since part of the ceiling fell down in 1860, the rest was removed and was replaced by the present wooden beams.

At the east end of the south aisle, formerly known as the Town Chancel, is the Consistory Court of the Diocese. Here, when necessary, ecclesiastical law is administered and the Bishop's chair can be seen on a raised dais

The tower contains eight bells, variously inscribed, four of which are the original bells cast by Abraham Rudhall of Gloucester in 1722.

COMMUNION VESSELS AND REGISTERS

The oldest Communion vessels are an Elizabethan silver Chalice and Paten Cover dated 1573 and inscribed:

POCVLVM ECCLESIE SANTI PETRI CARMARTHEN 1573.

Other pieces date from the eighteenth century. The old Communion Table, dated 1716, is placed at the entrance to the Lady Chapel. On the table stands the Poor Box, dated 1710, which was used until about the middle of the last century.

The first recorded Vicar was Richard ap John in 1278. The registers of baptisms, marriages and burials date from 1671. They are written in Latin at first and then change to English in 1742. The earliest Vestry Book recording the accounts and presentments of the Churchwardens dates from 1751 and gives interesting accounts of the state of repair of the church, of the administration of parish relief and of tax assessments made on the inhabitants of the Borough.

MEMORIALS

Lining the walls of the nave and chancel are many intriguing memorial tablets, bearing witness to the host of parishioners buried in the vaults beneath. In the chancel, in 1576, was buried Walter Devereux, 1st Earl of Essex, who was born at the castle and who was one of the founders of the Queen Elizabeth Grammar School.

Near the chancel stands the tomb of Sir Rhys ap Thomas and his wife. Sir Rhys, who died in 1525, was instrumental in the accession of Henry Tudor to the throne of England in 1485. Leading his tenantry and followers, Rhys ap Thomas joined Henry at Welshpool, and from there they proceeded to Bosworth Field. King Richard III was killed and Henry was crowned Henry VII on the battlefield. Shakespeare in *Richard III* speaks of 'Rice ap Thomas with a valiant crew'.

Rhys was knighted for his services and rewarded with vast estates. He was buried originally in the church of the Grey Friars but after the Dissolution of the Friary his tomb was removed to St. Peter's Church. It was originally placed in the north-east angle of the chancel. In September 1865 it was dismantled and removed prior to its restoration by Lord Dynevor, a descendant. In April 1866, after heavy restoration, it was placed under the arch between the Chancel and the Consistory Court. In 1886 it was finally moved to its present site.

On the south wall of the Consistory Court is a brass tablet commemorating Sir Richard Steele (1671-1729), the celebrated essayist and contributor to *The Tatler, The Spectator* and *The Guardian,* 'The first chief promoter of the Periodical Press of England', i.e. he was the first publisher of the modern periodical - the magazine. He was associated with Carmarthen by his marriage in 1707 to Mary Scurlock of Ty Gwyn, Llangunnor, and here he lived until his last days which were spent in a

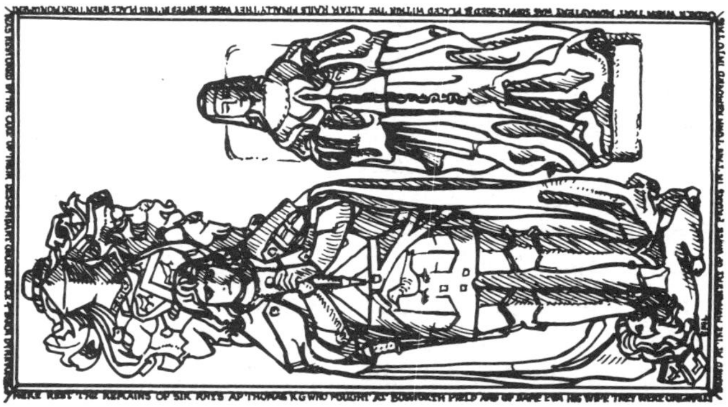

The tomb of Sir Rhys ap Thomas and his wife

house in King Street, later to become the Ivy Bush Inn. He was buried in the Scurlock vault under the Consistory Court. The vault was accidentally uncovered in 1876 when the tessellated flooring was being laid and the decayed coffin and remains were seen.

Below Steele's memorial is a stone tablet depicting an heraldic shield with the arms of England and France. When discovered in 1878 it was serving as a hearth stone, face down, in a cottage near the Priory Gateway.

Near to the shield is a tablet to the memory of Dr. Robert Ferrar, Bishop of St. Davids, who was burnt at the stake in Carmarthen's old market place (now Nott Square) on Saturday, 30th March, 1555, during Queen Mary's reign. The Protestant martyr was brought into St. Peter's Church on several occasions during his trial for heresy and stated that he had preached in St. Peter's 'rite often'.

Yet another tablet nearby on the south wall commemorates General Sir William Nott, Carmarthen's most famous soldier, who was buried in 1845 in the churchyard on the north side of the church.

The churchyard has been closed for burials since 1856, except for cremated remains.

In 1684 Thomas Dineley, Secretary to the Duke of Beaufort, who made a tour of Wales in that year, drew a sketch in the *Beaufort Progress* of 'a charnel for the bones of men in the angle of the south porch.' The present boiler-house on the north side of the church was described as a Charnel House in 1783 and was called 'the bone hole' until quite recently.

CUSTOMS

For many years it has been customary for the Mayor and Corporation to attend St. Peter's in their official capacity on Christmas Day, when the old Tudor sword-of-state and the maces are carried before the Mayor. In Corporation records the north transept, now called the Lady Chapel, is called the Mayor's Chapel, for the Mayor and Corporation occupied this transept until 1836, when their seating was removed to the nave. Here the finely carved Mayor's chair with the town coat-of-arms and iron rest for sword and maces may be seen.

It was also customary for the Assize service to be held in St. Peter's when the Assize Judge, the High Sheriff, the Borough Sheriff and their retinue attended. The famous Archbishop Laud, when he was Bishop of St. Davids, wrote in his diary 'that on September 11th 1625 he had preached at St. Peter's, the judges being present.' John Wesley also records that on August 22nd, 1764 he was present at St. Peter's and heard the assize sermon.

The following dates record just a few events in the life of the church:

Early 12th Century - St. Peter's Church conferred upon Battle Abbey.

1125 The church with its tithes and benefits placed under the authority of Bernard, Bishop of St. Davids, who then conferred St. Peter's on his newly-founded Priory of St. John the Evangelist at Carmarthen.

1278 Richard ap John, the first recorded vicar.

1291 The Church of Kermerdyn valued at £9. 6s. 8d. in the taxation of church benefices.

1329 The Prior of St. John's accepted 2 acres of land in Llanllwni from Walter Wynter, Archdeacon of Carmarthen, in return for employing a Chaplain to celebrate Mass daily in St. Peter's. The Chaplain was to receive four marks yearly together with his food and was to be provided with a suitable chamber, vestments, vases, lights, etc.

1340 A thief, Thomas Sathavas, successfully claimed sanctuary in the church when fleeing from justice in the town.

1394 Richard II permitted Thomas Rede of Carmarthen to endow 'a certain Chaplain to celebrate divine service daily to the honour of the blessed Mary in a certain Chantry anciently founded within the church of the blessed Peter of Kermerdyn.'

1557 It was stated that the church had grown into such decay for want of care to provide a stock of money and materials requisite for the repair thereof that . . . the inhabitants are forced to bear a rate of £50 to preserve the same from utter ruin and decay. Ordered that an annual rate of £20 be levied on the inhabitants by the church wardens who are to account to the Mayor and Council.

1569 A charter granted to the Company of Cordwainers (shoemakers) states that the 'ffraternitie cordiners do bynde themselves and their successors to pay yearlie XXs. towards the fyndinge of a preeste to mentayne Divine Service in St. Peter's Church in Carmarthen.'

1634 Thomas Wood, being Mayor, bestowed one great Bible upon St.Peter's Church.

1637 'The Church was newly paved and the geates newly made.'

1658 Tennis and Fives were played in the church and churchyard; the offenders were put in the stocks.

1672 The churchwardens reported the church windows to be out of repair; the absence of a Welsh Bible and the English Bible to be in bad condition.

1693 The Council agreed to pay the Minister, Revd. Philip Jones, £10 per annum.

1701 Richard Vaughan, Recorder of the Borough, gave £100 which the Town Council thought 'fitt to apply the sd. money for the buying and purchase of an Organ, to be sett up in the Parish church.' The yearly sum of 20 nobles (£6. 13s. 4d.) was to be paid to the organist.

1710 The Archdeacon, Revd. Edward Tenison, noted that the floor and roof needed repairing and 'on some Sundays the minister does not preach.' He also noted the survival of the custom of ringing a hand-bell before a corpse to the church door.

1720 The churchwardens reported 'We do not know of any within our Parish that do follow their ordinary labour on Sundays (except barbers), that there are no shops kept open, and as for vintners, inn-keepers or victualers, we shall present as many as shall come to our knowledge that suffer tipling (boozing) or gameing in their houses upon Sundays.'

St. Peter's Church in 1858

1785 A new roof and plaster ceiling were constructed by the famous architect John Nash. However, in 1860 a portion of the ceiling fell down and the whole plaster ceiling was removed. The present wooden beams and roofing were constructed in 1861.

1788 'Griffith Williams, Esq., used to come to church in a coach with 8 liveried servants dressed in green and gold - made such a figure in a country church!' (From a contemporary diary.)

1789 New seats installed, gallery erected and aisles flagged.

1796 The present organ was built and placed in the gallery.

1817 The tower struck by lightning which demolished the belfrey window, forced out a panel of the door and did other damage.

1849 The old colours of the 23rd Royal Welsh Fusiliers lodged in church with military honours. (These are still to be seen in the chancel.)

1851 The fine arch at the entrance to the north transept was pulled down to enable the organ to be removed from the gallery to the north transept (now the Lady Chapel).

1855 Church given new pews, but two original box pews still remain dating from 1709.

1858 A clock was fixed in front of the tower. The present clock dates from 1905.

1865 Organ put back in the gallery. Repaired by Mr.Walker of London for £225. Sir Rhys ap Thomas's tomb in the chancel removed for restoration and resited.

1876 Present tessellated pavement was laid down.

1886 The organ moved to its present position. Sir Rhys ap Thomas's tomb moved to its present site.

1886 The choir was provided with surplices for the first time.

The Lych Gate
erected by parishioners
in 1879 in memory of the
Rev. Latimer Maurice Jones,
Vicar 1863-1877.

During the last century St. Peter's has been blessed by many benefactors and more recently much restoration work has been undertaken to preserve its historic fabric.

St. Peter's Church is something more than a denominational religious institution in the town; it is the original parish church and, in one sense, the very soul of Carmarthen. For nearly nine centuries it has been linked with Carmarthen's history and each generation has left its mark. Despite the ravages of time, this venerable church stands today as a link between the past and the future - a noble and spiritual heritage which deserves to be preserved for future generations.

MEDIEVAL CHURCHES AND CHAPELS WHICH HAVE DISAPPEARED

In medieval times there were other churches and chapels in Carmarthen which have now disappeared.

ST. MARY'S CHURCH - the Church of the Rood.

St. Mary's Church stood in the centre of the medieval market place and its position is marked today by the names of St. Mary Street and St. Mary's Lane between Nott Square and Guildhall Square. First mentioned in 1252, when Henry III directed that shops be built 'in the midst of our town of Kermerdyn, to wit, to the west of the Church of St. Mary,' it was probably constructed in the 1240's when the medieval town expanded. It was founded for the townspeople and was probably called the Church of the 'Rood' (Cross) because of the market-cross which stood nearby. Whilst St. Peter's Church was in Old Carmarthen, St. Mary's was in New Carmarthen and was a Chantry Church where masses were sung for the souls of those who had endowed the Chantry. St. Mary's was endowed with a considerable amount of property in New Carmarthen.

Sculptured stone arcading found on the site of St. Mary's (The Rood) Church

In Edward VI's reign (1547-1553) the Church is referred to as 'one ffree chappell of Our Ladie comonly callyd the Roode Churche.' It possessed one silver chalice, one set of vestments of blue satin, two altar cloths and two small bells; Nicholas Byford was chantry priest. St. Mary's was closed at the Dissolution of the Chantries in the reign of Edward VI and subsequently appears to have become part of Corporation property.

A lease of 1652 indicates the church's location: 'that messuage and tenement situate in St. Mari-Streete, on the south side of the Dissolved church called the Rood Church and right opposite to the north end of ye streete called Keye Streete . . .' In 1655 a lease was granted by the corporation of a house 'lying and being over against the east side of the Towne Hall, the wall of the Rood Church on the south side, and the streete called St. Marie's Streete on the north side.'

By the nineteenth century St. Mary's Church had become incorporated into the houses in Lower Market Street, now called Hall Street. In 1957 when Nos. 11 and 12 Hall Street were demolished prior to rebuilding, parts of the south-east end of the church were revealed, showing a doorway, part of a window and a piscina, thought to be late thirteenth century.

In 1862 when the court and county offices adjoining the Guildhall were being erected (on the site of a cook-shop) and when St. Mary's Lane was being made, remains of two winding staircases were traceable in the walls, along with portions of a Rood Loft and west gable. In 1830 a length of carved stone arcading, thought to be from the side of a tomb, and dated to about 1350, was dug up on the site. This interesting piece of sculpture is now in the Carmarthen Museum.

In the 1957 demolitions in Hall Street, fragments of mouldings from the church's windows were discovered incorporated in cellar walls, indicating that the cellars had been built after the church had been demolished.

ST. CATHERINE'S CHAPEL

No trace remains today of St. Catherine's Chantry Chapel which is supposed to have given its name to St. Catherine Street. It is believed to have been situated near the cattle market, where later stood St. Catherine's Mill. It is mentioned by Lhuyd (c.1700) as being 'one of the four chantries in the town.' At one period six hermits and chaplains lived there 'at the cost of the town.' Although nothing is known of the original foundation, the chapel in mentioned in the will of Sir Rhys ap Thomas, dated 1524, when he bequeathed to it 'a vestment'.

Further information can be gleaned from two documents, dated 1539, during the reign of Henry VIII, containing interrogatories and replies by witnesses relating to a dispute between Gruffith Tucker and Moris Rynolde *'co'cerning one park or close lyeing ov'r ageinst the hermytage called Seint Caterynis chaple.'* (*T.C.A.S.* Vol. 12, part XXXI)

Such information includes:

'The said chapel was made and founded upon part of the commons apperteyning to New Carmarthen.'

'Knew six hermits and chaplains, and that when any of them died the mayor and burgesses of New Carmarthen would give the chaplain(ship) aforesaid to any other whom they pleased, which hermits so appointed lived upon the almshouse of the town.' (i.e. The chapel or hermitage, founded on common land, was financed by the town in return for which the hermits were to pray for the town's prosperity.)

'When any offering of candles was made in the said chapel to the image of St. Catherine, the prior of Carmarthen claimed to have the same because it was within his parish whereof he was parson.'

'The said park was never part or parcel of the lands belonging to the suppressed house of Old Carmarthen.' (i.e. the Priory).

In Henry VIII's day the chapel was still known as The Hermitage of St. Catherine, but it was eventually suppressed at the Dissolution of the Chantries.

In 1655 we hear of 'one lease, granted by Robert Birtt, Mayor, unto Edmund Harries, on St. Katherin's Chappell and Close thereto belonging, and a garden on the backside of his house in the Gorse containing 20 yards in length, and 4 yards in breadth . . .' The map of 1786 shows 'houses on the Gors' (marsh) between part of Woods Row and Orchard Street on the present John Street car-park. This area was originally marshy land extending as far as St. Catherine's Mill.

ST. BARBARA'S CHAPEL

The earliest reference to this chantry chapel occurs in the will of Sir Rhys ap Thomas, 1524, when he bequeathed to it a vestment. It is later mentioned in 1585 (Elizabeth's reign) as being leased, with its four acres of arable land, to Edward Middleton, former mayor, at 10 shillings a year for 21 years. In Edward Middleton's will of 1587 'the lease of the Chapel of St. Barbara which I hold of the Queen' was bequeathed to his nephew.

A seventeenth century reference states 'that tenement called St. Barbara, alias St. Barbara's Chappell, and now called the Royal Oak'; while a Rental of the Corporation (1633) states that Wauniago Common stood to the north of it. This could imply that the Chapel stood somewhere near the junction of Monument Hill and Job's Well Road, but its exact location is still unknown. In 1656 a lease was granted 'upon the pinfold and piece of ground thereto belonging betweene St. Barbaraes Chappell and Lammas Street.' (Borough Order Book.)

THE CASTLE CHAPEL

A castle chapel is referred to in a charter of Henry II (possibly c. 1180) which confirmed an earlier grant of 1125, whereby the castle chapel was given to the Priory of St. John the Evangelist. Since the castle was captured and destroyed on several occasions, the chapel probably suffered the same fate. When the castle was rebuilt in stone c. 1223 - 33 and enlarged, references are made to both a King's chapel and to a chapel for the knights and esquires. Nothing remains of the castle chapel (or chapels) today.

ST. JOHN'S CHAPEL

A chapel dedicated to St. John is recorded at 'Canon Hill' now recalled by the name Capel Ewan (Evan). By the will of Sir Rhys ap Thomas it was left a vestment, as in the case of St. Catherine's and St. Barbara's Chapels

1 M. A. Lower, *Chronicle of Battle Abbey, 1060-1176,* 1851.
2 See *The Age of Celtic Saints and Princes* and also *The Priory.*

Church Street, 1972

Church Street, 1972

- 7 -

THE PRIORY

A great deal of the early history of Carmarthen is connected with the Priory of St. John the Evangelist, which once stood near the river below the site of the houses now known as Old Priory Road, off Priory Street. Few traces of the Priory now remain, for the ruins were demolished in the late eighteenth century to make way for lead smelting works which were themselves demolished in the mid nineteenth century to make way for the railway line laid through the area.

In dealing with the post-Roman, early Christian period, we have already seen that a native Celtic monastic settlement, Llandeulyddog, existed at Carmarthen before the Norman Conquest.[1] Llandeulyddog is referred to in the Llandaff Charters on four occasions and it is also generally accepted that Llandeulyddog is the 'Bishop-house' referred to in the Welsh Laws where reference is also made to an Abbot there. After the Norman Conquest Llandeulyddog was incorporated into the Priory.

In the early twelfth century, after the arrival of the Normans at Carmarthen and the establishment of the royal castle in 1109, Henry I conferred upon Battle Abbey both St. Peter's Church and 'also another church founded in very ancient times in honour of St. Theodore the Martyr.' It is now thought that Theodore was probably a Norman scribe's version of the Welsh name Teulyddog, the patron saint of Llandeulyddog and reputed disciple of St. Teilo. Since nothing is known of Teulyddog, it has been suggested that the name may even refer to St. Teilo himself.[2] The reference to these two Carmarthen churches occurs in the *Chronicle of Battle Abbey*, the Benedictine Abbey built by William the Conqueror to commemorate his victory at Hastings in 1066.

In 1125, however, these same two churches were transferred from Battle Abbey and put under the authority of Bernard, Bishop of St. Davids, who had made repeated requests to the King for their return (i.e. to obtain their tithes and other benefits). He then established an Augustinian Priory at Llandeulyddog. The newly-founded Priory was dedicated jointly to St. John the Evangelist and to St. Theulacus. The actual words in the Latin text of the *Cartulary of the Priory* are Sancti Theulaci (genitive case), probably a Latinised form of Teulyddog. *The Cartulary of the Priory* is the main documentary evidence for the Priory and consists of a collection of grants, charters and land-holdings.[3] That the newly-founded Priory received a joint dedication would seem to indicate that it absorbed and incorporated the old Welsh church of Teulyddog. Moreover, by dedicating the Priory to a Celtic saint as well as to St. John the Evangelist, the Norman Bishop was probably trying to reconcile the native populace to the new Norman foundation.

For a short period prior to 1125, when Llandeulyddog was attached to Battle Abbey, a community of Benedictine monks was established at Llandeulyddog, but after its transfer to Bishop Bernard and the See of St. Davids a community of Augustinian Canons was installed at the newly founded Priory. The Order of Augustinian or Black Canons, founded in the eleventh century, followed the example of the early Christian Church, the Canons being concerned with the world outside their Priory and concentrating on parochial work. They had more in common with Celtic monasticism and therefore were probably more acceptable to the native populace than the Benedictine monks. Augustinian or Austin Canons were often called Black Canons from the sombre colour of their habits.

PRIORY'S JURISDICTION OVER OLD CARMARTHEN

Although the Priory of St. John was a Norman foundation, incorporating the earlier Llandeulyddog, it still had jurisdiction over the native Welsh community. The Prior ruled and administered this community, which became known as Old Carmarthen, through his bailiff or reeve. The Priory was also given jurisdiction over St. Peter's Church and the castle chapel. In addition it was given certain ploughlands: a ploughland was originally the amount of land that could be ploughed by a single plough in one year; which on average, roughly equalled 100 acres.

Early grants were two ploughlands at Cwmau (the name Maes-y-Prior, 'Prior's field', still survives in the area west of Llanllwch) given by Bishop Bernard; four ploughlands in Newchurch given by the Welshman Bledri 'Latimer' *(The Interpreter);* one ploughland in Llangain, with its chapel, given by Alfred Drue (or Dryue); and one ploughland at Pentowyn, Llansteffan, which had been held by Llandeulyddog before the Conquest. It was customary for grants of land to be given to monastic houses in return for which the monks were expected to pray regularly for the souls of their benefactors.

A charter granted by Henry II, possibly about 1180, confirmed to the Priory its jurisdiction over Old Carmarthen, St. Peter's Church and the castle chapel, all of which had been originally granted in 1125. It also confirmed to the Priory the early grants of ploughlands previously mentioned. In addition other arable ploughlands were given at Trebersed; later Trebersed and Cwmau grew into neighbouring granges (farms) of the Priory. Henry II's charter was later confirmed by Henry III in 1247.

It is unlikely that Carmarthen Priory was originally a daughter house of the Augustinian Llanthony Priory, near Abergavenny, although the latter sought to establish a claim to it. Consequently, in 1208 King John ordered that Carmarthen Priory be restored to the Priory of Llanthony. Later in the same year, however, he revoked the order and the Bishop of St. Davids was told to remove from Carmarthen Priory the canons of Llanthony, whom the King had sent there, and to maintain 'Kadmor' or Cadifor, the Welsh Prior, in his possessions. For this favour Cadifor paid the King ten marks and achieved independence.

THE BLACK BOOK OF CARMARTHEN

To what extent the Priory was inhabited by Welshmen at this time is unknown, but there must have been a Welsh presence in the late twelfth and early thirteenth centuries because it was at this period that the famous *Black Book of Carmarthen* was transcribed at the Priory. *Llyfr Du Caerfyrddin* is the earliest complete manuscript of Welsh verse; it contains a collection of poems connected with traditional history, mythology, religion and nature. It is partly a transcription of older poems and partly the production of contemporary scribes in the late twelfth and early thirteenth centuries. As the oldest surviving book of vernacular Welsh poetry, the Black Book is one of the most precious treasures of Welsh literature and is now kept in the National Library at Aberystwyth. Fortunately, it was saved for posterity when the Priory was dissolved in 1537 in Henry VIII's reign.

From about the middle of the thirteenth century it would appear that English influence was predominant at the Priory since from 1247 onwards the Priors had English names. Moreover, royal assent was necessary for all elections for new Priors and letters of licence had to be procured; for this the canons or their representatives had to journey to the King. The Priory does not appear to have been very wealthy, however, for in 1265, during the election of a new Prior, the Bishop of St. Davids petitioned the King begging that the canons be excused the journey on account of the poverty and devastation of the Priory. In the *Taxatio Ecclesiastica* of 1291 the Priory was valued at £29. 16s. 3d., a low valuation in comparison to other South Wales monasteries, although the Taxatio did not include all of the Priory's land-holdings. In the late 13th century the *Cartulary of the Priory* records several gifts of land to John Edrich who was Prior at that time.

FOURTEENTH CENTURY

During the fourteenth century the Priory acquired a large number of churches and chapels, in addition to those already held, which increased its income. Included in the total were St. Peter's with the castle chapel, Llangain, Newchurch, Abernant, with the chapel of Cynwyl (Elfed), Abergwili, Llanllawddog, Llanllwch, Llandeilo Abercywyn, Llanfihangel-ar-Arth, Llanfihangel Ioreth, with a chapel at Pencader, and

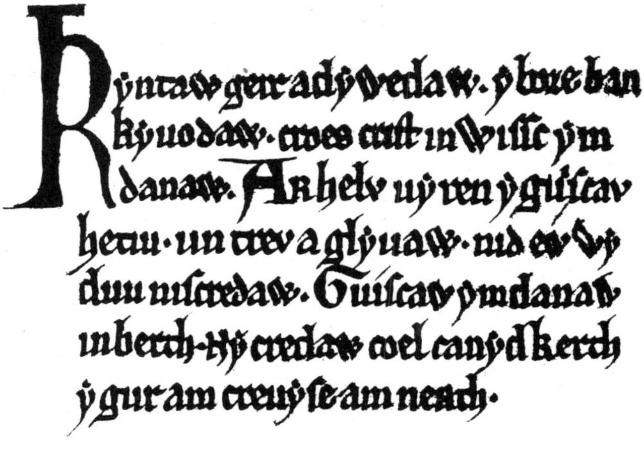

Kẏntaw geir adẏwedaw. ẏ boze ban
kẏuodaw. croes criſt inwiſſc ẏm
danaw. ARhelv uẏ ren ẏguiſcav
hetiu. un trev a glẏuaw. nid ew wẏ
duu niſcredaw. Guiſcaw ẏmdanaw
inberth. Nẏ credaw coel canẏd kerth
ẏ gur am creuẏſe am nerth.

The first word I will say
When I arise at break of day:
'The Cross of Christ be my array.'

My Lord's livery I will wear this morning,
Hark! One sneeze my ears hear!
That's not my God, I will not fear.

Rich in that Robe I can endure;
No portent will I trust one hour:
He who made me will grant me power.

Top: A photographic reproduction of a stanza from the *Black Book of Carmarthen,* page 41b.
Centre: A transcription of the same text into modern type.
Bottom: A free translation into English by D. M. Lloyd.

Llanllwni with Rhosycorn.

In addition to its spiritualities, the Priory continued to be given land by the burgesses of both Old and New Carmarthen, including burgage plots within both towns. The *Cartulary of the Priory* refers to tenements and burgage plots belonging to the Priory and running off the north wall of the Priory precincts and also running along what is now Priory Street. An entry dated to 1350 refers to tenements adjoining the Vicarage near the burial ground of St. Peter's. The Priory also owned land-holdings in New Carmarthen in the area of King Street and Spilman Street.[4]

Outside the town were the Priory's granges of Trebersed and Cwmau and its arable ploughlands in Newchurch, Llangain and Pentowyn. It also owned or rented various acres of land at Cwmoernant, Cillefwr, Archdeacon's Land (roughly an area south of the present Picton Terrace and Monument Hill), Capel Evan fields and Long Acre. The Priory owned three water mills situated immediately to the east of the Priory; the watercourse for these mills can still be seen at Pond Side. Two were corn mills, the third being a fulling mill and all may date from the establishment of the Priory.

In the early fourteenth century we hear of the burgesses of New Carmarthen complaining that the Prior and his tenants of Old Carmarthen were conducting unfair trading in wool, leather, skins, wax, honey and other goods; that they had weights and measures of their own and that they kept a fair and market in Old Carmarthen without the King's warrant. Moreover, evasion of tolls by the Prior and his tenants had cost the royal borough of New Carmarthen £1,000 in revenue. The King ordered the Prior to produce the royal warrant; this the Prior failed to do, protesting that Old Carmarthen had enjoyed an independent status before the New Town had been founded. In spite of the protests of New Carmarthen, the Priory appears to have maintained its claimed privileges, for in 1318 Edward II acknowledged the Prior's right to hold a market in Old Carmarthen.[5]

In 1394 Richard II confirmed the Prior's right to hold a weekly market on Monday (probably near the site of the later Old Oak, being just outside the former east gate of Roman Moridunum and at the top of the road leading to the Priory). A yearly fair was also confirmed.

From the mid fourteenth century the Priory, in common with other monastic houses, must have suffered from the burden of greatly increased taxes (to pay for the Hundred Years war with France), from the effects of the Black Death and from the widespread economic depression which followed. Its numbers declined so that by 1377 there were only six canons in residence.

FIFTEENTH CENTURY

However, at the beginning of the fifteenth century the Priory could have been quite a wealthy establishment, for it held twenty-two churches and chapels, and it has been estimated that its total annual income could have exceeded £200. Nevertheless, records show that it was continually in financial difficulties, indicating inefficient management. When Bishop Guy de Mone conducted a visitation of the Priory in 1401 he found its finances to be in a highly irregular condition and had to give strict instructions for better management in the future.[6] The fact was that Carmarthen Priory, like other religious houses, was faced with acute labour shortages and economic decline, arising from the set-backs of the previous century and from the breaking up of the medieval manorial system. To cope with this economic depression the Priory was forced to lease out some of its lands and even churches for a fixed rent, thus losing direct control of its possessions. The leases were usually to laymen which further weakened ecclesiastical authority. The situation was made worse by the Owain Glyn Dŵr rebellion. In 1403 the Priory was pillaged and many of its charters and documents looted; consequently, in 1404 Henry IV ratified its privileges and ancient rights granted by former kings.

Financial difficulties continued to plague the Priory, however, and in 1421 the King put it under the guardianship of Llanthony Priory for two years. But the Priory's troubles were not only financial - it suffered too from a decline in moral discipline. Examples of moral laxity, misbehaviour, quarrels and rivalries were quite common among the religious community, resulting in lack of respect for the monastic rule. In 1427 the Prior, John Mathew, was dismissed for misrule, whilst a later Prior, Maurice Winter, handed over the Priory in 1472 to his own illegitimate son, Thomas, who continued as Prior for several years.

Towards the end of the fifteenth century, however, the Priory appears to have made quite a good recovery, for a picture of life there at this time is given in one of the poems of the Carmarthenshire bard Lewis Glyn Cothi. He tells us that those under its pastoral charge numbered five hundred; the choir numbered sixty, the singing of which 'surpassed even that of the birds'; the organ made fine music, 'sweet as the honey of bees', and there were 'vessels of yellow gold', silver chalices, white silken vestments and ornamented books.

PRIORY'S DISSOLUTION, 1537

In the sixteenth century the Priory seems to have flourished until it was dissolved and taken over by royal commissioners in February 1537. Before its dissolution a favourable report by royal agents showed that the Priory was well built and in good repair; a 'new Lodging' had been built in the reign of Henry VII which was still fit to receive royalty and open hospitality was offered to rich and poor alike. Alms were distributed weekly to the poor and needy and about 80 persons were to be found within its precincts daily. Strangers and merchants were so warmly received and entertained that even the King of Portugal had expressed his thanks for the kind treatment received by his merchants at the Priory.[7] Nevertheless, this favourable report could not save the Priory and its possessions from being taken over by Henry VIII's commissioners. At its dissolution there were eight canons in residence in addition to the Prior, Griffith Williams, who apparently co-operated fully with the royal agents, namely Dr. John Vaughan, Sir John Price and Edward Gostwyk. These agents reported that they received excellent hospitality and that the Prior behaved 'like a worshipful man concerning the plate and jewels. He concealed nothing.'

In the *Valor Ecclesiasticus* of 1535 (a report of the value of all the possessions of monastic houses in England and Wales) the Priory's possessions were valued at £164, although an earlier survey returned a value of £209, making it one of the richest monastic houses in Wales. At £164 the Priory was undervalued, which brought it within the 1536 Act for dissolving minor houses of £200 and under.

At the Dissolution the Priory owned a considerable number of properties in both Old and New Carmarthen. In Old Carmarthen they extended from St. Peter's Church to the eastern end of Priory Street and comprised 29 tenements, 15 pieces of land and 6 burgages.[8] In New Carmarthen the Priory owned holdings in the area of Spilman Street and King Street.

There appears to have been no public outcry at the dissolution of the Priory. By this time monastic life had lost its appeal; people had become more secular in outlook and there was no enthusiasm for preserving the religious houses as being necessary for the survival of the Church. Moreover, according to Professor Glanmor Williams: [9]

> 'an important part of the explanation may lie in the fact that a majority of leading men in Carmarthen saw in the extinction of the monastery a long-awaited opportunity finally to rid themselves of a greatly-resented source of privileged commercial competition . . . It is a reminder that merchants, as well as landed gentry, hoped to benefit from the disappearance of the monasteries.'

Subsequently the Priory was sold by the King to Richard Andrew and Nicholas Temple; later it was sold to Griffith Leyshon or Leyson, who was High Sheriff at the execution of Bishop Ferrar in 1555. In his will dated 18th June, 1555, Griffith Leyshon bequeathed the Priory, described as his 'mansion house', to his second wife, Lady Joyce Gamage and after her decease to Edward Croft, eldest son of Sir James Croft. (Sir James was the brother of Lady Joyce Gamage, neé Joyce Croft, who retained her first husband's surname and rank on marrying Griffith Leyshon.) Under the will of Lady Joyce Gamage, 1586, the Priory was bequeathed to 'James Croft, the third son of my brother, Sir James Croft.'

Incidentally, Sir James Croft (or Crofte) was one of the founders of the Queen Elizabeth Grammar School in 1576. In the Letters Patent dated

The Priory ruins in 1748
(detail from Samuel and Nathaniel Buck's engraving of the town)

July 1576 founding the Free Grammar School of Queen Elizabeth, Sir James Croft is described as 'our beloved and trusty councellor, Controller of our Household.'

Both John Speed's map of Carmarthen of 1610 and Samuel and Nathaniel Buck's engravings of 1740 and 1748 show the Priory buildings still standing and set within a walled enclosure, but they are too stylised to give an accurate description. However, from the Buck engraving of 1748 it would appear that some of the buildings were in a ruinous state.

THE PRIORY POORHOUSE

St. Peter's Church Vestry Books dating from 1751 indicate that there was a Poorhouse at the Priory from about 1758 although they are not clear as to when exactly this Poorhouse ceased to function. The Vestry Books, which were kept as administrative records of the parish, (St. Peter's was the only parish at this time) deal not only with church matters but also with the administration of parish relief to the poor, sick and orphans. Many poor families were given weekly payments as out-door relief but the old and infirm had to go to the Poorhouse. Orphans were often apprenticed to tradesmen and were clothed by the parish. The books record vestry meetings dealing with such matters and with the assessment and collection of the Poor Rate which was levied on the members of the parish to pay for poor relief.

The Vestry Books contain entries such as:

Oct. 20, 1758: At a Vestry meeting agreed that the sum of £15 be paid out of the Poor Rate for the rent of the Priory for the present year which was taken by Mr. George James for a workhouse for the use of the poor of this parish.

Dec. 1, 1758: Overseers of the Poor of this parish to bring the poor pensioners of their respective wards to the Priory House for their further settlement.

Jan. 26, 1759: George James to purchase certain articles for the use of the workhouse . . . iron pot and kettle for kitchen; 2 washing tubs; tables and benches in the Common Room . . . and other utensils.

May 11, 1759: David Jones, Master of the Workhouse. Vestry meeting agreed that a Church Rate of 1s. 9d. in the £ be assessed on the inhabitants for each year.

July 8, 1773: Mark Roch was paid 3 guineas for his care and trouble in attending the sick of the Poorhouse and for medicine given to them.

Oct. 1784: Parish meeting held at the Poorhouse. William Morgan to buy books for the use of poor children.

March 1785: Thomas Evans to be relieved with 10s. 6d. together with 4s. 6d. to buy him a pair of shoes that he may go to look for work; his wife and children to come to the Poorhouse.

Oct. 1785: Ordered that all ye paupers within ye poorhouse are to eat all their victuals at the table at all meal times, and no provisions will be allowed to be carried off from the table. If any of the paupers should fall sick, the opinion of the Apothecary belonging to the poorhouse must be had first before any of the paupers be allowed to have their provisions in their lodging rooms.

Further entries continue well into the next century but whether they relate to the Priory Poorhouse is doubtful. The 1786 street plan of the town, drawn by Thomas Lewis, marks a Poor House in what was then called Water Street, but is now St. Catherine Street, near to Morley Street. The Priory Poor House is not marked as such on the plan. In 1803 the Water Street Poor House was given up and premises in King Street (formerly the Ivy Bush Inn) were used as temporary accommodation for paupers until a new purpose-built Poor House was erected in 1805 at the foot of Penlan Hill.

PRIORY RUINS IN 19th CENTURY

Edward Donovan in his *Descriptive Excursion through South Wales and Monmouthshire* (1804) noted:

> 'one wing, including a handsome gate-way yet standing, some few of the apartments are inhabited by poor people who have converted the remainder into carthouses, pigsties, and other such receptacles . . . There are still remains of carved work in stone above the gateway, ornamented with the red and white rose.'

In the latter part of the nineteenth century this arched gateway was incorporated into the row of cottages now called Old Priory Road, and can still be seen, although nothing now remains of the carved stonework mentioned by Donovan. However, in 1878 a stone slab displaying a shield of arms of England and France was found being used as a hearth stone, face downwards, in one of the gateway cottages and is now preserved by being fixed in the wall of the Consistory Court in St. Peter's Church. There is also a record of a small Tudor mullioned window, now blocked and concealed, in an interior wall above the gateway.

According to Donovan in 1804:

> 'the ruins of the Priory Church were considerable till within a few years past, when the ground on which they stood became the property of Lord Cawdor, who ordered the ruins to be demolished, and the area of the church dug up, for the convenience of establishing a lead works upon the spot. Pits were therefore dug, furnaces erected and railroads constructed upon the old church . . .'

Priory ruins in 1875, showing remains of cottages as recorded by Donovan in 1804

The smelting houses can be seen in Thomas Lewis's map of 1786 standing in the south-eastern part of the Priory enclosure. The lead works appear to have flourished during the last quarter of the eighteenth century but in the mid-nineteenth century the lead works were demolished to make way for the railway.

The remains of what is thought to be the Prior's house (or the guest-house) were demolished in 1855, for William Spurrell writing in 1879 states that:

> 'an ivy-covered ruin, inhabited not many years ago, the remains of the prior's house (or guest-house) was removed in August 1855, and the stones were used in building the cottages, called Priory-row, then erected between the site of the old church and the school.'

(The latter is the old Grammar School.) It was probably the Prior's House which was retained as a secular residence at the Dissolution.

EXCAVATIONS BY DYFED ARCHAEOLOGICAL TRUST

In 1979 the first archaeological excavation was undertaken on part of the site of the Priory by the Dyfed Archaeological Trust. Before these excavations very little was known about the position of the Priory buildings for practically nothing survives above ground today, apart from the arched gateway, mentioned above, and certain stretches of precinct wall. The 1979 excavations in the southern area of the precinct located part of the Priory Church, Chapter-house and Prior's House, revealing portions of standing walls and wall footings, stained window glass, a large quantity of inlaid floor-tiles and green and yellow glazed tiles dating to the fifteenth/sixteenth century. Among other finds were imported pottery, bronze metalwork and glazed ridge-tiles. Beneath the Priory Church numerous burials were discovered, one grave containing a lead Papal *bulla* or seal of Benedict XII (1334-1342). Until further excavations can be undertaken, it is conjectured that more buildings lie under the allotment gardens and under the houses in Priory Row, near the Old Grammar School, behind which a large number of skulls have been unearthed in the past.

The 1979 excavations also investigated the medieval lay cemetery to the east of the church. Underneath the cemetery a number of ditches were discovered which were radio-carbon dated to the mid eighth century, thus giving them a Dark Age origin and indicating human activity in the area. However, there was no evidence to indicate the position of the pre-Norman church of Llandeulyddog.

The Papal Bulla or seal

1 See *The Age of Celtic Saints and Princes.*
2 Ibid.
3 T. Phillips, *Cartularium S. Johannis de Caermarthen,* Chelt. 1865.
4 Terrence James, *Carmarthen: An Archaeological and Topographical Survey,* 1980
5 See *Carmarthen in the Middle Ages.*
6 Glanmor Williams, *Carmarthenshire Monasteries in the 14th and 15th centuries* in *The Carmarthen Antiquary,* 1961.
7 Glanmor Williams, *Carmarthen and the Reformation,* to be found in *Carmarthenshire Studies, 1974 - Essays presented to Major Francis Jones.*
8 G. Dyfnallt-Owen, *Extent and distribution of lands of the Priory of St. John* in *The Carmarthen Antiquary,* 1941.
9 Glanmor Williams, *Carmarthen and the Reformation,* to be found in *Carmarthenshire Studies, 1974 - Essays presented to Major Francis Jones.*

An artist's impression and reconstruction of the Friary
based on excavated evidence published by Dyfed Archaeological Trust
(after *Archaeology in Dyfed* published by the Trust in 1986, with additions)

- 8 -

THE FRIARY

The Franciscan Friary or Grey Friars stood on the site now known as Friars Park, to the west of the medieval walled town and to the south of present-day Lammas Street. Described as 'of the King's foundation', the earliest documentary reference to it is in 1282 when William de Valence, son of the Earl of Pembroke, was buried in its church. Evidence from recent excavations by the Dyfed Archaeological Trust indicates that the Friary was founded sometime between the middle to third quarter of the thirteenth century, either in the reign of Henry III or Edward I. Although nothing remains above ground today (the site now being occupied by Tesco's superstore), excavations prior to redevelopment of the site revealed an extensive range of buildings of exceptionally high quality, including part of the Friary church, much larger than originally envisaged, two cloisters and substantial domestic quarters.

The Franciscans were founded in 1209 by St. Francis of Assisi and were an order of mendicant, preaching friars (brothers) vowed to poverty, who went out into the world to preach and to tend the sick, poor and needy, administering not only to the soul but also to the body. They wore coarse grey habits, hence the name of Grey Friars. Their evangelical and social work among the ordinary people made them well liked and they became a dominant religious influence. Their work could be likened to that of the social services of today. Unlike the older monastic Orders, the friars never acquired great landed estates as they preferred to use any gifts for the adornment of their churches. They became renowned for theological learning, exerting a powerful influence at medieval universities. Their popularity, however, eventually declined.

Carmarthen Friary was one of the largest Franciscan Friaries in Britain. There were only three houses of Grey Friars established in Wales: one in Anglesey, one at Cardiff and one at Carmarthen - and of these, Carmarthen Friary was the largest and most important. The Friary stood on the site of the Lammas fields, probably part of the town's open fields, which were thrown open for common pasture on August 1st, Lammas Day, i.e. 'loaf-mass' Day. (The 1st of August, in the early church, was a harvest festival at which loaves of bread, made from the first ripe corn, were consecrated.) The Welsh name for Lammas Street is Heol Awst - August Street.

The Friary was built around two cloisters, with the church on the north side of the main cloister and the chapter house on the east. An infirmary with its own kitchen and privy lay on the south side of the second cloister. Other buildings contained dormitories, a refectory, wash-house, bakehouse and a brewhouse. The cloister alleys were paved in polished limestone (oolite), while the interior floors were colourfully tiled with decorated inlaid floor-tiles.

Evidence from the Dyfed Archaeological Trust's excavations showed that the infirmary range of buildings had been destroyed by fire shortly after the Dissolution of the Friary in 1538. The fire was probably started accidentally when lead from the roof was being melted down. From this site a nearly complete stained glass window was recovered. It had fallen inwards during the fire and been saved by the roof collapsing and smothering the flames. The glass of red, blue, yellow, green and clear colours was made up in a geometrical pattern of oblongs, circles and lozenges around a central armorial shield depicting a chevron and three eagles. Its age has been estimated as 1250-1280, the time when the Friary was founded, which makes it extremely important as there is very little medieval stained glass in Wales, especially from such an early period.

The excavations also unearthed an intricate drainage system which provided the Friary with fresh running water. The conduit bringing the water ran down from Trevaughan through what is now Water Street. Other finds included numerous decorated floor-tiles, pieces of pottery from France, Germany, Spain and Portugal, glazed ridge-tiles, water pipes and dressed stonework. Part of a clay mould, used in the production of small metal flasks which were sold to pilgrims as souvenirs, two 14th century seal matrices, used for sealing documents, and the remains of a press used in the brewhouse were other interesting finds. Many skeletons, probably of medieval friars, were also unearthed from unmarked graves beneath interior floors and the cloister alleyway.

THE EARLY HISTORY OF THE FRIARY

As previously stated, the precise date of the foundation is not known, the earliest documentary reference being in 1282. In 1284, when Edward I visited Carmarthen, the friars petitioned the King for permission to divert a watercourse - possibly the mill stream running to the Cock Mill near Dark Gate - to their Friary in Lammas fields. Edward granted them the right to draw water through a conduit to their house. In 1295 the same Edward granted the friars a croft in Carmarthen and the right to bring a watercourse across it. Another grant of land was given them in about 1330 by Edward III, while in June 1331 the King confirmed the gift of a spring of water 'on the slope of Mount Berwyn' so that the friars could use it to make an aqueduct or conduit for their benefit. It is thought that this aqueduct may have been somewhere near Trevaughan and that it then ran down what later came to be known as Water Street. At the same time the friars were allowed to dig and search for the 'veins of water' of such springs and conduct these by underground passages for the purpose of erecting 'a little house of stone, either round or square, ten feet long and as many broad' (possibly a latrine?). It would seem that the friars were very concerned about water supply and drainage and devoted much attention to the construction of conduits and stone built drains, as has been revealed by the recent excavations.

BURIALS

Although little is known about the Friary's history there are a few references in the medieval period which throw some light on the relationship between the friars and the local populace. In 1340 three felons successfully sought sanctuary in the Friary church. In 1391 a settlement was finally reached between the Priory of St. John and the Friary over the question of burial rights and mortuary fees, indicating the increasing demand for burial within the Friary precincts, either in the church or in the adjoining cemetery. The popularity of the Friary as a last resting place, together with numerous testimentary bequests and endowments, provide evidence of the affection and respect in which the Grey Friars were held. In 1394 they were granted a licence by Richard II to acquire three roods of land adjacent to their House, for the purpose of enlarging their 'close' which was probably their burial ground. It is thought that the Friary cemetery lay between the principal buildings and what is now Lammas Street.

The most important building was the church, which was impressive and beautiful, containing valuable treasures. Many men of distinction were buried within its walls, including Edmund Tudor, father of Henry VII, who died in 1456. After the dissolution of the Friary his remains were reinterred in St. David's Cathedral. Sir Rhys ap Thomas and several members of his family were also buried in the Friary church. Sir Rhys spent the last days of his life in the Friary, desiring in his will to be buried 'in the chauncell of the gray freres of Kermerdyn whereas my mother lyeth, and whansoever it please God to call my wife out of this transitory lyfe my will is that she be buried by me.' Sir Rhys ap Thomas died in February 1525 and his wife Janet died ten years later. Some time after the Dissolution their tomb was removed to St. Peter's Church where it can still be seen, although much restored.

Others buried at the Friary were William de Valence, son of the Earl of Pembroke, who was killed in 1282, Sir Rhys ap Gruffydd, who died in 1356 and the Welsh bard, Tudur Aled, who died at the Friary in 1526.

THE DISSOLUTION

When Henry VIII broke with Rome and was made Supreme Head of the Church in England by the Act of Supremacy of 1534, the dissolution of the religious houses followed, since these were the last bastions of Papal authority in the realm and sources of great wealth. Carmarthen Friary, like the Priory, did not escape Henry's commissioners. The Friary, with all its goods,was finally surrendered in 1538 to Richard Ingworth, the King's Visitor. The Inventory 'of all the stuffe of the Grey Freeris of Karmardein' was signed by the Bishop of St. Davids; Thomas Prichard, Vicar of St. Peter's and Martyn Davy (David), Mayor of the town. The fourteen friars were given 'twelve pence each and their own stuffe' and then turned adrift into the world. However, the King's Visitor showed some compassion for a poor friar who lay sick - he was left the food in the house together with a small sum of money.

The Inventory is interesting in that it tells us of the composition and contents of the Friary at the time of dissolution.[1] The Friary comprised the church with *quire* (choir) and steeple, a *sacristy* (a room attached to the church in which sacred vessels and vestments were preserved), a king's chamber, an inner chamber, a chamber next to the *lavery* (washing place), a chamber next to the parlour door, a kitchen, brewhouse, hall (refectory) and buttery. The *quire* of the church (i.e. the chancel) contained a selection of candle-sticks, mass books, crosses, 'a goodly peyer of orgaynis,' and 'a goodly tumbe of Sir Ryse ap Thomas, with a grate of yron abowthe him, a stremer banner of his armys with his cote armor and helmit,' and other items. The nave contained five altar tables of alabaster and a frame of iron before the altars for tapers. The steeple contained a clock and two bells; after the dissolution one of the bells was sold at Carmarthen for twenty shillings and the other was conveyed to Bristol. In the *sacristy* were many beautiful 'sutes' (vestments) and copes of 'blacke and redde welwit' and of 'white silke and damaske,' decorated with flowers as well as altar cloths and other items.

The roof of the *quire* and part of the church were covered with lead, as were the chapel, gutters and conduits. As for the domestic quarters, the king's chamber contained a featherbed, bolster, a pair of blankets and a pair of sheets, coverings, a cupboard, chair and coffer. The other chambers contained similar bedroom furniture. In the 'kechin' was 'a gret range of iron, to make in fyer,' brass pots and pans and pewter plates. The 'halle' (refectory) contained two trestle tables and two forms for the friars and 'a gret chayer of timber' for the Warden. Nevertheless, it would seem that the Friary was in financial difficulties at the time of its dissolution because the King's Visitor noted that some of its plate, including the Cross and the best chalice, were in pledge at the time.

The real estate of the Friary, as shown by the rent returns for 1539 - the rents now going to the Crown - comprised the Friary and demesne, garden, cemetery, stable and other buildings, the Great Park (about three acres), a small close called Park Cyrill (about one acre), a small close called the Little Park (about half an acre), a burgage in Quay Street (outside the walls of New Carmarthen) and a tenement next door to the Friary. Thus the real property belonging to the Friary was by no means as extensive as that of the Priory, its land extending to no more than five acres.

The house of the Grey Friars was left vacant for several years after its dissolution. Bishop William Barlow of St. Davids had long cherished a wish to remove the seat of his diocese from St. Davids to Carmarthen. He was convinced that the Friary would be an ideal site for a new cathedral since Carmarthen was the most frequented place in the middle of the diocese and an appropriate centre for administration and communication. As early as March 1536 Bishop Barlow wrote to Thomas Cromwell, Henry VIII's 'Vicar-General', who was reponsible for sending the royal commissioners round the monasteries, asking that a grant be made to him for the Grey Friars and pointing out the advantages. He also stated that he was prepared to maintain at Carmarthen a free grammar school and a daily lecture of Holy Scripture 'which would civilize the Welsh rudeness'. Bishop Barlow was aware of the need for better education in his diocese and he was also motivated by his desire to spread the reformed religious doctrine among both clergy and laity. However, the Bishop's schemes came to nought, partly because of opposition from some of his own cathedral canons with whom he had an uneasy relationship. Eventually, he established a grammar school at Brecon, in 1541, which came to be known as Christ College. He also managed to move the Bishop's place of residence from St. Davids to Abergwili, where it has remained ever since.

THOMAS LLOYD'S SCHOOL, 1543-47

Prior to Bishop Barlow's letter of March 1536, royal permission had been granted in January 1536 to Thomas Lloyd, the Precentor of St. David's Cathedral (i.e. the head of the Cathedral Chapter), to found a grammar school in 'New Karmarden' to be called 'Thomas Lloyd his skole'.[2] But nothing appears to have been done in the matter at this time, possibly because Lloyd became engaged in a bitter quarrel with his bishop. However, after the dissolution of the Friary, the mayor and aldermen of Carmarthen sent a petition in 1539 to Thomas Cromwell urging him to persuade the King to grant the Friary and its adjoining land (three meadows, a garden and an orchard) at an annual rent of 18 shillings 'so that they may have a Grammer scoole at the coste and charge of Mayster Thomas Lloyd, chauntier of Sainte David'. The petition stated that the Friary had fallen into ruin and decay, there was no lead upon any part of it and it was a pity that such a building should not be put to some convenient use for the common good. They offered Henry VIII £40 for the property and Thomas Cromwell £20 for using his influence with the King! Eventually, in February 1543, the King issued new Letters Patent for the school which was to be known as 'the King's

Scole of Carmarden of Thomas Lloyd's fundacion'. Lloyd was granted the site of the former Friary, together with gardens and closes called Great Park (3 acres), Park hill or Pentre Cyrill (half acre) and Little Park (half acre) and also some property in Quay Street at an annual rent of 3 shillings and 4 pence. All the profits were to be applied to the upkeep of the school. A master and an usher (assistant master) were appointed and the educational benefits of the King's School were not to be confined to the inhabitants of the town only but were also available to those 'of the country theretoe adjoining'. The school, apparently, brought 'virtue and learning' to Carmarthen.

Unfortunately, the school did not last long after Lloyd's death in 1547. In his will he left 'the situation of the late Gray Fryers' together with other property in Dewsland, Pembrokeshire, for the maintenance of the school. However, the Friary properties were appropriated by William and John Parry (or ap Harry) and the Pembrokeshire property by John Davies (or David) of Tre-fin in Dewsland, thus causing the school to be closed. The mayor, aldermen and inhabitants of Carmarthen brought a Bill of Complaint against the three offenders, with the object of reviving the school, but the lawsuit was not heard until early in the reign of Elizabeth I. Then William Parry claimed that he had legally taken a lease of the premises and his claim was successfully upheld. John Parry denied ever having entered the Friary premises at all.

LATER DEVELOPMENTS

In the late sixteenth century Thomas Parry, son and heir of the William Parry already mentioned, was in possession of the Friary House and its other buildings, yards and property. In the early seventeenth century the Friary, together with its adjoining properties and land, passed from the hands of the Parry family and in November 1632 was sold to Lord Richard Vaughan of Golden Grove. It remained part of the vast Golden Grove estate until 1912 when it was sold to a local doctor and subsequently in 1936 it was sold to Mr. D. H. Lloyd, a Carmarthen surgeon. Part of the land was sold in 1954 to Carmarthenshire County Council for building their Police Headquarters and in 1965 Friars Park House and the surrounding land was sold to Carmarthen Borough Council for use as the Mayor's Parlour and administrative offices. With the reorganisation of local government in 1974 Park House became the Parlour of the Chairman of Carmarthen District Council. Since then a further chapter has been added to the story of Friars Park: a supermarket has been built on this historic site, together with an extensive carpark, thus adding a late twentieth century dimension to seven hundred years of history.

Although nothing of the Friary remains above ground today, the Friary church, or part of it, was still standing in the early eighteenth century when Archdeacon Yardley described it as 'tho but a small Building of a single Isle, and without a Steeple or Pillars, it is in length about 70 or 80 feet and in breadth 30 feet.' Obviously the steeple mentioned in the Inventory of 1538 must have been taken down by the time of Archdeacon Yardley's visit. According to Spurrell, writing in 1879, the remains of the Friary 'are to be seen in Friars'-park. The tower of the church was pulled down within the memory of some of the inhabitants of the town. Part of the walls are incorporated with houses in the neighbourhood.'

Prior to recent excavations undertaken by the Dyfed Archaeological Trust, a few finds had been recovered from the Friary site. These included a section of early English mullion from a window, part of a fourteenth century moulded door jamb and fragments of late medieval green glazed floor-tiles - all now preserved in the Museum. In the late nineteenth century 'a beautiful square of tessellated pavement' thought to be part of the church or chapter house was discovered, but it was subsequently covered over and its location forgotten. In 1978 several lay burials were unearthed behind Friars Park cottages and near the site of a 'Burial Ground' marked on the 1890 Ordnance Survey map. According to Terrence James[3] this implies that burials may have been discovered there in the nineteenth century and this area may have been the Friary's graveyard for townspeople which fell into disuse after the Dissolution.

As we have already seen, more recent excavations by the Dyfed Archaeological Trust have established that Carmarthen's Friary was one of the largest in Britain, the only other Friary known to have a double cloister being Walsingham in Norfolk, hitherto regarded as the largest of the provincial Grey Friars.

1 Francis Jones, *The Grey Friars of Carmarthen* in *The Carmarthenshire Historian,* Vol. III, 1966

2 Glanmor Williams, *Thomas Lloyd his Skole* in *The Carmarthenshire Antiquary,* Vol. X, 1974

3 Terrence James, *Carmarthen: An Archaeological and Topographical Survey,* 1980

Quay Buildings in 1939

The Quay before the building of Coracle Way

- 9 -

THE SIXTEENTH CENTURY

THE TUDOR DYNASTY

The accession of Henry Tudor as Henry VII in 1485 marked the end of the Middle Ages in general and the Wars of the Roses in particular, and established the Tudor dynasty which lasted until the death of Queen Elizabeth I in 1603. Henry VII's reign (1485-1509) ushered in a period of strong, central government bringing much-needed peace, security and prosperity to both England and Wales. Henry, who was born at Pembroke castle in 1456, publicly acknowledged his Welsh ancestry, being the grandson of Owain Tudor who had originated from Anglesey and who had married Henry V's widow. Henry's father, Edmund Tudor, married Margaret Beaufort, a descendant of Edward III.

During the Wars of the Roses, after the final defeat of the Lancastrians, Henry Tudor, the Lancastrian heir to the throne, had been forced to flee to Brittany where he remained in exile for fourteen years. During this time he became aware of Welsh bardic prophecies hailing him as the long-awaited deliverer from English dominance and when he landed at Dale on Milford Haven in 1485 to challenge Richard III of York for the throne of England, he used his Welsh ancestry to gain Welsh support for his cause. After defeating Richard at Bosworth, Henry was crowned King on the battlefield. He rewarded his Welsh supporters liberally for their services and many obtained royal posts. One such supporter was Rhys ap Thomas of Dynevor who was knighted and rewarded with estates and offices, including Chief Justice of South Wales. He ruled with a firm, though often unscrupulous, iron hand and brooked no opposition. He was Mayor of Carmarthen three times and the town experienced a long period of peace under his powerful authority. He died in 1525 and was buried at the Friary, his tomb being later removed to St. Peter's Church. However, Henry's policy of reducing the power of the barons, in the interest of strong, central government, ensured that Sir Rhys ap Thomas was the last of the local landed

Henry VII
Founder of the
Tudor Dynasty

magnates to exercise such wide authority.

THE ACTS OF UNION

Henry VIII's reign (1509-1547) saw the unification of England and Wales under the Acts of Union of 1536 and 1542, the most momentous of all enactments relating to Wales.

As far as Carmarthen was concerned, the new County or Shire became the unit of local government in both legal and administrative affairs. The new 'Carmarthenshire' consisted of the old 'county' of Carmarthen established by Edward I, i.e. the royal castle, Old and New Carmarthen with the lands attached to them, Cantref Mawr (all known as 'the Englishry') , together with the upland commotes of Elfed and Widigada (known as 'the Welshry'), plus the addition of the former independent marcher lordships of Kidwelly, Carnwyllion, Is Cennen, Llandovery, St. Clears, Emlyn, Meidrim, Llansteffan and Laugharne. This Carmarthenshire remained unchanged until it was incorporated into Dyfed in 1974 under local government reorganisation.

The new 'Shire' under the 1536 Act was to be represented in Parliament at Westminster, for the first time, by one knight while the shire-town, Carmarthen, was to be represented by one burgess.

Carmarthenshire, Cardiganshire and Pembrokeshire were to form a Judicial circuit under a new Justice to be appointed by the King. More Justices of the Peace were also to be appointed for the new counties, the first J.Ps. having been appointed in 1534.

One system of law was now to operate throughout the united countries of England and Wales and all men were equal before the law (at least in theory if not in practice).

This Tudor Settlement was welcomed for the most part by leading Welshmen for it brought new opportunities for advancement in government and administration, combined with material benefits, and heralded a period of peace and prosperity.

THE DISSOLUTION OF THE MONASTERIES

Henry VIII's reign also saw the Dissolution of the Monasteries, which in Carmarthen meant the dissolution of the Priory in 1537 and of the Friary in 1538. This was followed by the dissolution of the Chantry chapels and of St. Mary's Church in Edward VI's reign (1547-1553). The Priory was sold into private hands whilst Carmarthen's first grammar school was founded at the Friary in 1543. When Thomas Lloyd, the founder, died in 1547 the school closed and the Friary property was appropriated into private hands. St. Mary's Church or the Church of the Rood was closed and the building eventually became incorporated into the houses in Lower Market Street (Hall Street).[1]

THE BOROUGH CHARTER OF 1546

Since the dissolved Priory no longer had jurisdiction over Old Carmarthen, the latter was amalgamated with New Carmarthen by Henry VIII's Charter of 1546 and the names 'old' and 'new' abolished. The charter made Carmarthen a corporate Borough to which new privileges were given. The corporation was to be called 'The Mayor, Burgesses and Commonalty of the Borough of Carmarthen.' The Charter appointed certain persons to be the Mayor and Burgesses (inhabitants possessing certain property rights and other privileges) who were to chose a 'Common Council' of twenty members. Two of the burgesses were to be chosen annually to be Bailiffs of the Borough. The amalgamation was intended to end the old rivalry between the two towns. Under the Charter the Mayor was also appointed Admiral of the Port of Carmarthen, his authority extending from the bridge to the bar of the Towy. This appointment reflects Carmarthen's continuing importance as a port during Tudor times for both coastal and overseas trade, although the silting up of the river was causing some difficulty. In the mid 1530's the traveller Leland reported that because of sand banks the larger ships had to anchor at Green Castle while 'small balinggers' were used to carry cargo to and from the quay. In those days the quay was located at Island Wharf, a tract of land which became an island at high tide, with the Wynveth stream running on either side of it and wharfs probably surrounding it. (The present quay reaching up to the bridge was not constructed until 1808-09.)[2]

Island Wharf

As for the town itself, in 1548 it was described as 'a fayre Market Towne, having a fare haven, and the ffarest Towne in all South Waills, and of most Scevillytie.'[3]

QUEEN ELIZABETH I's REIGN (1558-1603)

One of the earliest preserved records of Carmarthen Borough is a leather-bound volume entitled *A Booke of Ordinaunces made in the Tyme of Griffith ap Ievan, Maior Anno Dom. 1581.* It contains entries, backdated to 1569, and continues until 1600 when a new Borough or Corporation Order Book (i.e. Minute Book) was used. The 1569 entry records that the Mayor, Recorder and Common Council assembled in the 'gwyld' (guild) hall on 4th May to make orders for the public good of the town, including the annual appointment of two Chamberlains to levy and collect the town rents, fines, dues and fees.

In Queen Elizabeth's reign records show that Carmarthen was the largest town in the Principality; in 1566 it had 328 households compared with Kidwelly 101, Tenby 200, Caernarfon 120 and Llanelli only 12. In 1577 Carmarthen had 4 or 5 inns, 2 taverns and 31 ale-houses! Sources available for estimating population suggest that Carmarthen was the only town in Wales with a population of just over 2000, compared with Brecon at 1,750, Wrexham 1,515, Haverfordwest 1,490, and Cardiff at 1,100.[4]

As in the Middle Ages, Carmarthen's market place was still outside the castle gateway (now Nott Square) and it was there in 1555, in Queen Mary's reign, that Bishop Robert Ferrar was burnt at the stake at 'the south side of the market cross'. There were also shops in what is now Guildhall Square and it was here that the Guild Hall or Shire Hall was situated. There is a reference to a 'Shirehall' in 1540 in a dispute between Old and New Carmarthen over rights of jurisdiction, when the Mayor of New Carmarthen called out 300 armed men whom he had 'laid in a bushment (ambush) and hid in the Shirehall'.[5]

The Borough Order Book Volume I also contains several references to a Guild Hall, such as the 'gwyld' hall recorded in 1569, while in 1576 it was ordered that all wool bought and sold within the town was to be brought to the Guild Hall to be weighed 'at the commom beam and by the common balances and weights there appointed by the Mayor'. (This was because of complaints about diversity and deceit in weights and weighing of wool.) On January 4th, 1579, the Mayor and Common Council 'assembled themselves in the Guyld-hall' and agreed that 'all the high waies throughout the town shall be paved . . . at the proper cost and charge of the inhabitants . . . everyone of the inhabitants to be taxed according to their abilitie.'

In 1580 Robert Toy (or Toye) paid a rent 'for the shop under the Shire Hall' and so too did the 'Buchers for the Arches under the Shire Hall'. In

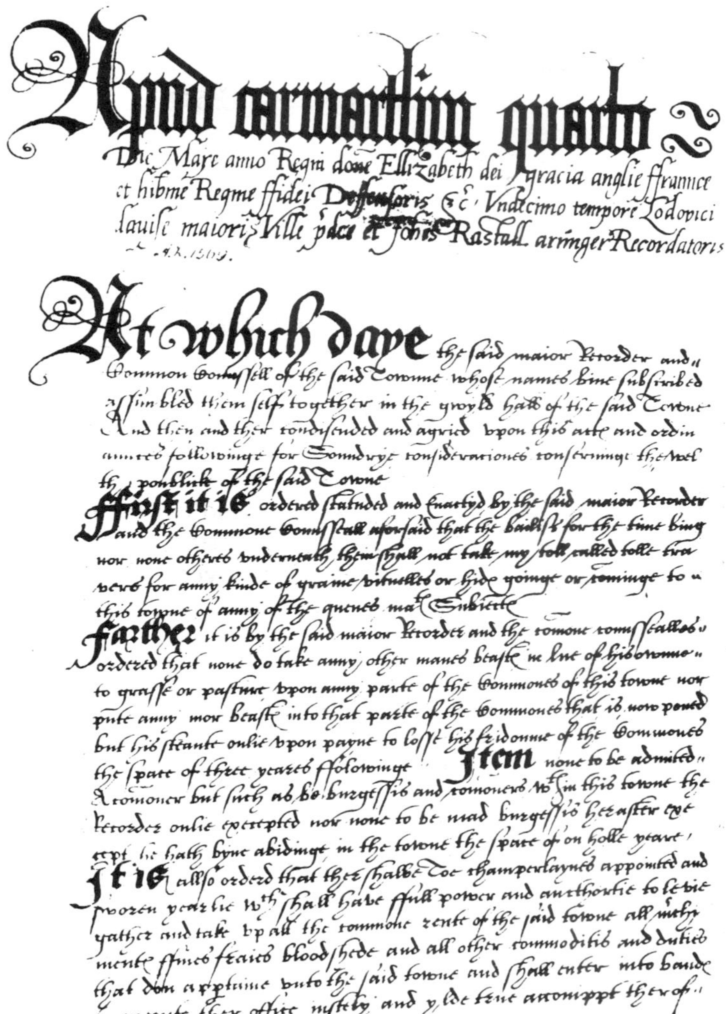

Apud carmarthin quarto Die Maii anno Regni dne Elizabeth dei gracia anglie ffrancie et hibnie Regine ffidei Defensoris &c. Undecimo tempore Lodovici Davise maioris Ville pdce et Johis Rastall armiger Recordatoris

At which daye the said maior Recorder and Common Counsell of the said Towne whose names bine subscribed assembled them self togither in the yelde hall of the said Towne And then and ther concluded and agried upon this acte and ordinaunce followinge for Somdrye consideraciones concerninge the weal the publik of the said Towne

ffirst it is ordered statuted and enacted by the said maior Recorder and the Common Counsell aforsaid that the baillifs for the time being nor none others underneath them shall not take any toll called toll corn for any kinde of graine vitualls or hide goinge or cominge to this towne of any of the quenes ma[tie]s Subiects

ffarther it is by the said maior Recorder and the Common Counsellors ordered that none do take any other mannes beastes in lue of hisowne to grasse or pasture upon any parte of the Commones of this towne nor pute any mor beastes into that parte of the Commones that is now pounded but his stante onlie upon payne to lose his fredome of the Commones the space of three yeares ffolowinge Item none to be admitted a Commoner but such as be burgesses and commoners wthin this towne the Recorder onlie excepted nor none to be mad burgesses hereafter excepte he hath byne abidinge in the towne the space of on holle yeare

It is allso ordered that ther shalbe too chamberlaynes appointed and [illegible] yearlie wth shall have full power and authoritie to lebie gather and take up all the common rents of the said towne all [illegible] ffines feaies bloodshede and all other commodities and duties that doth apperteine unto the said towne and shall enter into bande to execute ther office [illegible] and ylde true accompt therof

Entry dated 4th May, 1569 from Carmarthen Borough Order Book

1582 the Order Book records a 'Shambles (meat market) under the Shirehall'.

Other references to orders and decrees being made by the Mayor and Common Council assembled in the Guild Hall occur in 1581, 1582 and 1585. (This Tudor hall was pulled down in 1766 and a new one, the present Guildhall, was finally completed in 1777.[5])

THE TRADE GUILDS

The Borough Order Book shows that there were many Trade Guilds in Carmarthen, indicating a flourishing commercial community. There were guilds of tanners, glovers, weavers, tailors, shoemakers, saddlers, tuckers (cloth finishers) and hambermen or hammermen (goldsmiths, silversmiths, ironsmiths, cutlers, pewterers, plumbers and tinkers). However, little is known of the Trade Guilds apart from the dates of their charters and their annual payments to the Corporation, in return for which they were given an absolute monopoly in their trades. Thus the 'Ffraternitie Tanners' (Charter granted 1569) paid 50s. yearly 'at everie feast of Saint Michaell the Archangel' to the Corporation. Payment to the Corporation was in return for the Fraternity being able to elect a Master, make rules, decide on the admission of craftsmen and determine questions of apprenticeship.

The 'Gold Smithes, Iron Smithes, Cutlers, Pewterers, Metellers and Tynkers,' known as the 'fraternities hambermen', whose charter was also granted in 1569 paid 13s. 4d. yearly to the Corporation. Among the Hammermen were: Lewis ap Owen, John Salsbury, John Cotton, David ap Ievan and Rice ap Ithell.

The Tailors paid 13s. while the Saddlers paid 6s. 8d. yearly 'to the common coffer'.

However, the Charter granted by Carmarthen Corporation to the 'Company of Cordiners' (cordwainers or shoemakers) on 8th February, 1569, states that the 'ffraternitie cordiners do bynde themselves and their successors to pay yearlie XXs. towards fyndinge of a preeste to mentayne Divine Service in St. Peter's Church.'

In April 1574 the Fraternity of Weavers was incorporated, paying 13s. 4d. yearly, and in May 1574 we find that the 'Tuckers, Clothworkers, Fullers and Shearmen within this Towne being manie and not incorporated' - 'geveth and graunteth to the Maior of Carmarthen towards the comon coffer 40s. yerely.'

'The fraternitie of white taners or Glovers' agreed to pay 30s. yearly for their Charter but in 1575 only 20s. was paid.

It was not until 1651, however, that the last of the Guilds, the 'Hatters and Feltmakers', were incorporated, paying the 'some of Twenty shillinges of good and lawful money of England.'

Masters and Wardens were chosen to supervise the Guilds and to see that the rules for their trades were carried out.

In the sixteenth century the medieval corn and fulling mills dependent upon water power continued to operate, both on the Wynveth Stream (e.g. Towy and Cock Mills) and at Pondside (Priory Mills).

TOWN MERCHANTS

Carmarthen's Port Books show that there were at least 63 merchants and about 28 registered ships in Elizabethan times. The merchants lived in the more fashionable quarter, mainly St. Mary Street, Quay Street and King Street but none of their houses has survived. However, some of their names have survived, for several merchants appear as foundation governors in the Charter of the Queen Elizabeth Grammar School which was founded in July 1576. Among those named are Robert Toy (Toye), Edward Middleton (Myddleton), Richard Lewis Hopkyn, Griffith ap Ievan, Nicholas Roache and Richard Nash. These governors are named in the Charter in addition to the original founders who had petitioned the Queen. Robert Toy, however, called 'benefactor and councillor', is named as an original founder of the free grammar school as well as a governor. The school continued in existence for the next four centuries until it became the Queen Elizabeth Maridunum Comprehensive School in September 1978.[6]

Robert Toy's father, Humphrey, came from a family of printers in business in London but he had Carmarthen connections through marriage. Humphrey Toy, who became Mayor of Carmarthen in 1557, was a prosperous merchant who lived in St. Mary Street. He is described as supplying cloths, holland, linen and fustian to customers in Llangeler, Trelech and Eglwys Cymmin and he was also engaged in the tanning business. In his will proved in 1575 he left 'towards a free school and for the use thereof, once yearly rent of three pounds out of the great close called Friar's Park.' He also gave 10 shillings towards the reparation of Carmarthen bridge and 20 shillings to St. Peter's church as well as money for the poor and the prisoners in gaol. He left houses in St. Mary Street, Quay Street and the Market Place, a fulling mill by the Priory and former ecclesiastical property at 'Pencarreg', 'Llanvairarybryn' and Llandingat. Humphrey and his wife are buried in St. Peter's churchyard. They had thirteen sons of whom Robert, Mayor in 1582-83, was one. (Another Robert Toy was Sheriff of the Borough in 1645 and appears as a signatory to the surrender to Gen. Laugharne in 1645 in the Civil War.)

CORPORATION PROPERTY AND INCOME

From the mid sixteenth century it would appear that some of the town's medieval 'common lands' were enclosed, as is shown by the rents recorded in the Borough Order Book. Thus in 1575 rents were collected for parcels of common land, which had been enclosed, between Spilman Street and the river, at *Morva Moch, Morva Mawr, Morva Bach,* on parts of *The Gorse* and in the area of St. Mary Street and the Castle.

In 1575 the Corporation also received income from the following rents:

Item, of Mr. Toy (probably Humphrey) for his newe bylding in the back side of his Mansion Howse and an entry to the comons . . . 20d.

Item, of the same Mr. Toy, for a tanne howse with a garden and a store howse without the walls, under Wirriot's Tower (on the Wynveth stream, now covered by Blue Street.) . . . . 2s.

Item, of the same Mr. Toy, for the course of water coming upon the comon ground toward his mille (near the Priory) . . . . 4d.

Item, of Griffith Morgan, Gent, for one pcell (parcel) of the town wall of 60 foote of length and 14 foote of breadth adjoyninge on the North Side of Dark Gate, demised to the said Gr. by Jenkin D'd ap Ieu'n . . . for 4 score and 19 years . . . 12 pence

Item, a lease granted to Margaret Reade, widowe, during her natural life upon the towlle (toll) of the market, so that she keep the market cleane, the rent of . . . . . 4 pounds

Item, of Gwenllian Morgan for her howse abounding upon the Towne Wall in Bridg Streete . . . . 2 pence

Item, of John Morgan ap David for the Shop adjoyninge to the White Gate . . . . 2 shillings

Item, of the Receavers of the Shire Hall 13s 4d

Item, the yearly rent for the common beame for wayeinge of Woll. Granted for life to Richard Jenyns 5s

Item, a lease demised and graunted in the time of Griffith ap Ieu'n, maior, to my lady Joys Gammage of 6 score foote in length and 6 foote in breadth, in King Streete, of the common lane that is betwixt the house of Ieu'n Hoell and R's ap Rhudderch paying yearly for 99 yeares 6d

Item, of Richard ap Harry for the byldinge of his parlour and his kitchen, his stable and his garden, nigh to his house . . . 4s

An attempt was made in 1575 to keep swine off the town streets by levying a fine of 4 pence on the owner of every straying pig. Nor were swine allowed onto the town commons unless each was ringed and yoked. In 1585 David Edwards, the Mayor, ordered a fish market to be erected 'nighe the conduit in the markett-place' (i.e. Nott Square).

Another entry in the Corporation Order Book, dated 1582, recalls how one Thomas, a tyler, was called before Griffith ap Ievan, Mayor, and the Common Council, 'the said Mayor objecting against the said Thomas that he abused the Mayor by speaking of certain words as the Mayor was about the performing of his office, viz., that Thomas spoke to the Mayor - "Yt is but an office for a yeare, and when you are out of office I will talke with you." ' Thomas was fined and put in gaol for eight days!

During the Mayoralty of Robert Toy (1582-83), the Mayor and Common Council ordered on 5th February, 1583, that the Bailiff should not take any greater sum than the tolls fixed by the Council for goods bought and sold at the town's fairs and markets: namely, for every horse, 4 pence; for every bull or ox 2 pence; for every piece of frieze (coarse woollen cloth with a nap) 1 penny, etc. The penalty for disobeying the order was a fine of 20 shillings to be paid to the Chamberlain while double the sum taken was to be paid to the aggrieved party. At a meeting of the Common Council on 9th June, 1583, it was ordered that fines be imposed on persons walking and talking in the churchyard (i.e. of St. Peter's Church) 'when the minister is in reading of divine service.' Fines were also imposed on the keepers of taverns who allowed persons to frequent their houses and to sit 'tippling' (boozing) during divine service. The frequenters of such taverns were also fined and were to remain in the town gaol until payment was made. Moreover, it was the duty of the church wardens to see that the above orders were carried out; failure to do so resulted in a fine 'to the use of the town.'

It was also ordered that fines be imposed on any councillors who behaved in a disorderly manner in the council chamber, such as continuing to speak after the Mayor had decreed silence by knocking on the table with a mallet. Fines could also be imposed on councillors and bailiffs for not accompanying the Mayor, Recorder and Justices of the Peace to the General Sessions and other courts 'in their scarlet gowns'.

On 10th November, 1583, the Mayor and Common Council ordered that standard weights and measures for wool, woollen yarn, wheat, malt and other grain be stamped or sealed with a mark and kept in the 'Shirehall' under the custody of a person whose duty was to weigh goods brought to be sold. Any persons using their own unsealed weights and measures for wool or grain could be fined 20 shillings.

THE PORT BOOKS

A study of the Welsh Port Books 1550-1603 shows that Carmarthen was the commercial and maritime centre of the shire at this time, her merchants having a virtual monopoly over certain trade routes, especially the Carmarthen-Bristol trade. Imports included salt (for preserving meat), barley, household goods such as pewter cups, coffers, bedsteads and stools, oil, wine and luxury velvets and silks. Exports were mainly cloth to Bristol and coal to France, La Rochelle being the chief centre. However, imports of wine and salt decreased later in the century as did exports of cloth. Trade with Ireland and Scotland was negligible, while foreign trade was chiefly with France. It was the coastal trade with Bristol, and to a lesser degree with Barnstaple and Bideford, which was the mainstay of Carmarthen's commerce.

The Port Books reveal the names of at least 63 Carmarthen merchants, but the majority of these were traders on a small scale. Of the 28 vessels registered at Carmarthen none was very large or of heavy tonnage for the silting up of the Towy was a growing problem. The names of some ships recorded include: *Le Trinitie, Le Nightingale, Le Lyon, The Grace of God* and *The Wheele of Fortune.*

Apparently the Quay was kept in good repair at this time for the Borough Order Book records in September 1580 that a certain Richard Nash, to whom the Quay was leased, 'doth covenant to keepe the Key in reparacions both with lyme and stone and beames of timber bound about in the number of 30.'

In Elizabethan times pirates and smugglers were frequently a menace to shipping in the Bristol Channel and evidently some Carmarthen worthies were not averse to conducting business with them, for in 1587 a French ship laden with salt was seized by pirates and brought to Carmarthen. It was sold to Robert Toy, Edward Middleton (both former Mayors) and other merchants. On the other hand, in 1592, the town's merchants complained to the Court of Admiralty that they had been despoiled by pirates of '4 barkes laden with silks, velvets, wine and oil to the value of £10,000.'

With the end of the century came the closing years of the Elizabethan era and, on Elizabeth's death in 1603, the end of the Tudor dynasty.

1 See *The Priory* and *The Friary*. Also *St. Mary's Church* in chapter on *St. Peter's Church*.

2 See *Trade and Industry - The Port of Carmarthen.*

3 J. R. Daniel-Tyssen, *Royal Charters*, p. 40, 1878.

4 Glanmor Williams, *Carmarthen and the Reformation* in *Carmarthenshire Studies*, 1974.

5 See *Civic Dignity - The Guildhall.*

6 See *Education - Queen Elizabeth Grammar School.*

St. Mary Street

- 10 -

THE SEVENTEENTH CENTURY

THE STUART DYNASTY

The accession of James I in 1603 marked the end of the Tudor dynasty and the beginning of the Stuart. Carmarthen was given a new Charter in 1604 raising the status of the Borough to that of a County Borough. This meant that Carmarthen became a county of itself and its formal title was 'The County of the Borough of Carmarthen'. The burgesses were to choose a Mayor and twenty others to be called the 'Common Council'. The Charter replaced the two bailiffs with two Sheriffs and it confirmed all the Borough's previous possessions, privileges, jurisdictions and exemptions. This original Charter of 1604, written in Latin, with the Great Seal attached, still hangs in the Mayor's Parlour. The new County Borough of Carmarthen returned its own Member of Parliament, not to be confused with the M.P. representing the County of Carmarthenshire.

Throughout the seventeenth century Carmarthen was still the largest town in the Principality but its population was periodically reduced by the ravages of plague. In 1604, 1606, 1611 and 1651 the plague raged through the town and in 1657 the Mayor was 'sworne at Ridgorst by reason that the sickness not ended at Carmarthen.'

We can get a good idea of the extent and lay-out of Carmarthen in the early seventeenth century from the first map of the town, drawn by John Speed in 1610, although it cannot be regarded as completely accurate. It is not drawn to scale and is aligned with the south-east at the top of the page instead of the more usual north. However, it shows that Carmarthen had changed little from late medieval times and there had been no major expansion outside the town walls. The latter appear to be in quite good condition, although the gates in Bridge Street (Bridge Gate) and Quay Street (Towy Gate) are missing. Probably they had been removed because they impeded the increasing trade at the Quay and were no longer essential in the more peaceful and settled times. Within the walls, the map shows the medieval street pattern of King Street and Spilman Street, the Castle with its main gateway facing the market cross, where Nott's monument now stands, and the stocks close by. This area is called High Street while the present Guildhall Square is called St. Maries (Mary's) Street. The Friary is not shown, nor is the Queen Elizabeth Grammar School. A preaching cross is shown in Lammas Street and another in Priory Street, both of which have disappeared.

The map shows the Priory within its precinct wall, and also St. Peter's Church and 'The Key', which stops short of the bridge. Outside the

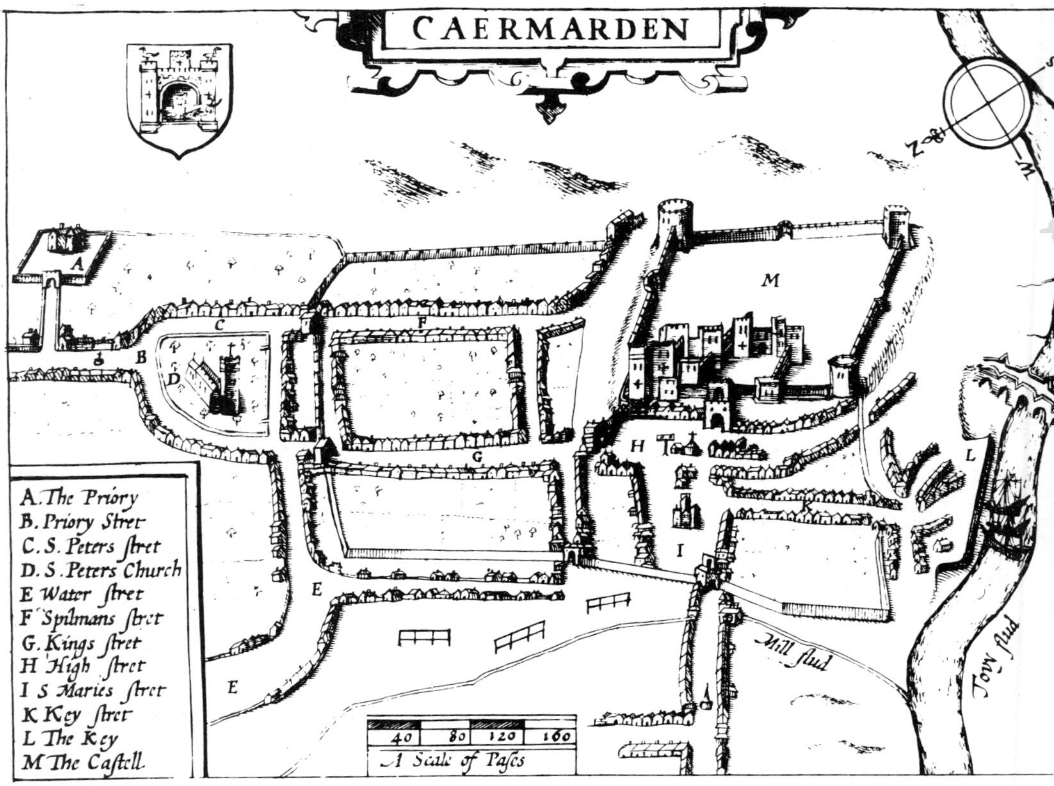

John Speed's map of Carmarthen, 1610
(detail from the county map of Carmarthenshire)

Wynveth Gate (Dark Gate) is shown a mill, which could be the Cock Mill or the Dam Mill, which gave its name to Dam Street, later Mill Street. Development is shown up Lammas Street and into what is now Water Street. The name Water Street, however, is given on the map to what is now Little Water Street and Elliston Terrace.

The danger of fire must have been a constant hazard in the densely packed narrow streets within the town walls for, in 1633, the Corporation Order Book records that 'Thomas Atkyns, being then Mayor, bestowed on the town 12 buckets, with 2 hooks with iron heads (for pulling off burning thatch) and iron chains for fire'. The Order Book also records the Mayor's Inventory of 1633: '1 green carpet, 1 pair of scales, 1 sword and 2 scabbards, 1 seal of office, 1 chest in the Counsell chamber and 3 velvet hats.'

THE CIVIL WAR 1642-1648

Little enthusiasm was shown in Carmarthen, as in Wales as a whole, for the constitutional and religious principles which were at stake in

Parliament's struggle with the King, Charles I. Initially Carmarthen was royalist in sympathy, stemming from the tradition of loyalty to the Crown established under the Tudors. Parliament drew its support generally from London and south-east England with their prosperous commercial and trading classes, the sea-ports and the navy. While most of Wales supported the King, south Pembrokeshire was Parliamentarian, for Tenby and Pembroke had a flourishing sea-trade with Bristol and relied upon commerce for their livelihood.

The leader of the Royalists in Carmarthenshire was Richard Vaughan of Golden Grove, 2nd Earl of Carbery, supported by most of the County squires. The leader of Parliamentary forces in Pembrokeshire was General Rowland Laugharne, supported by Col. John Poyer, a merchant of Pembroke and Col. Rice Powell, a professional soldier. After some early successes in Pembrokeshire in 1643, the Royalists under Carbery were forced to withdraw and in April 1644 Carmarthen surrendered to General Laugharne after only weak resistance. A record states: 'The towne of Carmarthen was gotten by the sword by Pembrokeshire men in April 1644.'[1] The same reference also states: 'The towne of Carmarthen was fortified with a mudd wall round about it.'

This record must refer to Carmarthen's Bulwarks - the Civil War defences consisting of a ditch and bank linking earthen bastions. These earthwork defences were thrown up apparently to defend the west and north of the town which lay outside the medieval town walls, for by the mid seventeenth century Carmarthen had expanded especially in the

The Bulwarks

Lammas Street / Water Street area. Parts of these Bulwarks can be seen today behind Christ Church and Morfa Lane and behind the Police Headquarters at Friars Park, where a length of bank and ditch connects with the remains of a bastion to the rear of Christ Church. Another portion was sited to the north of Francis Terrace where a dyke and ditch stood in a field called Park-y-Bulwark. This was levelled about 1860 when Francis Terrace was built. The line of the earthworks between Friars Park and Francis Terrace can only be conjectured but it is thought to lie to the north of St. Catherine Street and Barn Road; a line which could explain their origin as being routes following along the inside of the defences. At Francis Terrace the Bulwarks could have linked up with the old Roman rampart behind present-day Richmond Terrace.[2]

Whether these defences on the north of the town were ever completed in unknown, but it was a very large area to defend and this may explain why Carmarthen was taken without much opposition. Following the town's surrender, Lord Carbery resigned his command and his place was taken by Col. Charles Gerard, an experienced professional soldier and cavalry leader.

Gerard rapidly retook Carmarthen in June 1644 and made advances into Pembrokeshire. However, after Royalist defeats at the battles of Marston Moor, 1644 and Naseby, 1645, Gerard was recalled from Wales and General Laugharne was able to take Pembrokeshire into Parliamentary hands and then advance towards Carmarthen. Here, and in the County, support for the Royalist cause was evaporating because of its heavy demands on men and money and when, on 10th October 1645, General Laugharne again marched on Carmarthen, he had the support of many former Royalists and entered the town without opposition. Officials of the borough negotiated with him, records stating: 'Carmarthen was gott by Pembrokeshire forces upon condicion' and 'Carmarthen taken by Parliamentarian Major-General Laugharne. Public thanksgiving for same, 2 Nov.'[3] A member of the Toy family, named Robert, was Sheriff of the Borough in 1645 and appears as a signatory to the surrender of Carmarthen to General Laugharne.

CROMWELL AT CARMARTHEN

The second phase of the war in 1648 was marked by General Laugharne changing sides to support the King, together with the other two Parliamentary leaders in south Pembrokeshire, namely Colonels Poyer and Powell. So serious was the threat to the Parliamentary cause posed by these Pembrokeshire rebels, that Oliver Cromwell himself led his troops to besiege Pembroke castle and on the way halted at Carmarthen. A letter from Cromwell to *'my noble Friends the Committee of Carmarthen',* when he was encamped before Pembroke, throws some light on the situation at that time. Cromwell asks for assistance

> "in procuring some necessities to be cast in the iron-furnaces in your county of Carmarthen. The principal things are: shells for our mortarpiece . . . . some demi cannon-shot and some culverin-shot, may with all possible speed be cast for us and hastened to us also. We give thanks for your care in helping us with bread and water etc. You do herein a very special service to the state; and I do most earnestly desire you to continue herein, according to our desires in the late letters. . . . Your affectionate servant,
>
> O. Cromwell" 9th June, 1648.

It may be that the following undated entry, on a slip of paper fastened into the Borough Order Book for the Civil War period, refers to the quartering of troops at this time:

> "I doe heareby engage my seulfe unto the Constables of the Towne of Carmarthen to discharge the quarters of eight score men one night in the sayd Towne, witness my hande, Jo: Mathewes."

(The Order Book is significantly lacking in entries for the Civil War Years.)

The siege of Pembroke lasted for seven weeks during which time Cromwell's army suffered greatly from lack of food and supplies.

When Pembroke finally fell the three defectors were tried by court-martial and sentenced to death; but they were then allowed to

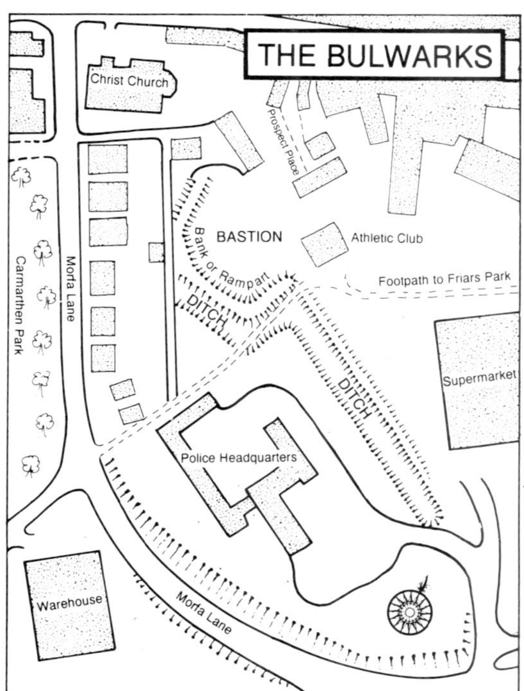

Oliver Cromwell

draw lots for their lives. The fatal lot, drawn by a child, was given to Poyer who was shot. Laugharne and Powell were later pardoned.

In July 1649 Cromwell was in Carmarthen again on his way to Ireland. He is said to have lodged at the 'Nagg's Head, St. Mary Street'.

Oliver Cromwell (1599-1658) came of Welsh ancestry in that his great, great grandfather was a certain Morgan Williams who had married Katherine, sister of Thomas Cromwell, Henry VIII's Chancellor and Vicar-General. Morgan's son, Richard Williams, i.e. Oliver Cromwell's great grandfather adopted the name of Cromwell after his uncle Thomas who was also his patron. When Oliver Cromwell married on 22nd August 1620 a settlement was drawn up in which the bridegroom was described as "Oliver Cromwell, alias Williams" (Noble's Memoirs of the Protectoral House of Cromwell, ed. 1787. Noble, i 123-4). According to local tradition, Morgan Williams had connections with Cwmcastell farm in the parish of Newchurch.

THE COMMONWEALTH

During the Commonwealth, which followed the execution of Charles I in 1649, fines were imposed on many Royalist supporters for their 'delinqency'. The list of Carmarthen's delinquents contained many corporation officials including several mayors, e.g. George Oakley, Thomas Griffith, George Jeanes and Dawkin Gove, and a number of aldermen. Lodowick Jones, recorder of the borough from 1637 to 1657, had been 'very violent and active in promoting the King's cause'.

In May 1651 Carmarthen suffered a severe outbreak of the plague which continued until the following April. A contemporary wrote: 'The town and market have been forsaken of all commerce and the inhabitants loathsome to their nearest friends.' The plague swept away whole families in the town and neighbouring parishes. Nevertheless, when John Taylor visited the town in 1652 he observed: 'It is one of the plentifulest towns that I ever set foot in for very fair eggs are cheaper than small pears. Butter as good as the world affords, two-pence halfpenny or three-pence a pound. A salmon two-foot and-a-half long, twelve pence; oysters, a penny a hundred; beef, three half-pence a pound; eggs, twelve for a penny and pears, six for a penny.' It would appear that Carmarthen was not doing too badly under the Commonwealth! However, by 1660 the country had experienced eleven years of Republican government, marked by iron military rule, oppressive Puritan domination, heavy taxation and bitter sectarian squabbles. Cromwell 'The Protector' had died in 1658 and the ensuing quarrels between Parliament and the Army prompted the Convention Parliament to invite Charles II to return from exile as King.

THE RESTORATION, 1660

Everywhere the Restoration of the King was welcomed with relief and rejoicing. 'Charles II returned and his health was drank in wine, drank from the Cunditts in Carmarthen.' Nevertheless, in fairness to Cromwell and the Puritans, Parliamentary institutions would not have survived but for their persistent stand against the Divine Right of Kings.

There is a local story, which cannot be verified, that Carmarthen's Old Oak grew from an acorn planted in 1659, by a schoolmaster named Adams, of the Queen Elizabeth Grammar School. The acorn was planted, supposedly, to mark the town's proclamation of Charles II; this proclamation took place a year before Charles actually landed in England. However, no reference can be found to a master of the Grammar School named Adams.

One casualty of the Civil War in Carmarthen was the castle. In 1660 the royal auditor reported the castle to be 'quite demolished'. Although the castle had changed hands twice during the war, there had only been weak resistance on the first occasion and none on the second. It may well be that Cromwell ordered the dismantling or demolition of the castle's defences, as a discretionary measure, when on his way to besiege Pembroke castle.

With the restoration of Charles II in 1660 came the restoration of monarchy, Parliament, landed gentry and the Anglican church. While former Anglican clergy, who had lost their livings under the Commonwealth, were reinstated, Puritan ministers who refused to 'conform' were ejected from their livings. Several penal acts, embodied in the Clarendon Code, were passed against Nonconformists and Roman Catholics alike, virtually outlawing them from all public office. As far as Carmarthen was concerned, however, the Code had little impact, for, according to a census return of 1676, there were in Carmarthen only nine Nonconformists and three Roman Catholics.

Personally, Charles would have liked to restore Roman Catholicism as the national religion but he was shrewd enough to realise the strength of opposition, both in Parliament and in the country, and he did not want 'to go on his travels again', referring to his years of exile during the Commonwealth.

CORPORATION PROPERTY IN 1675

An entry in the Borough Order Book on 31st August, 1675, gives some indication of property leased by the Corporation and of the town's common land. There were houses and shops clustered round the town gates and adjoining the town walls, shops and chambers under the Shire

Thomas Dineley's drawing of the Quay and river made in 1684

Hall and rooms over the town gates. There was the Prisoners' Gate between King Street and the present Nott Square, with stairs outside leading to two rooms above the gate and with a 'dungeon' (prison) underneath; there was the Cock Mill near Dark Gate and a newly erected dye-house on the commons between the Quay and the Cock Mill. The 'oven' (bakery?) of Dawkin Gove (Mayor in 1677) was in the Great Close (Clos Mawr) 'over against the Shire Hall,' while 'a high way was to go from the Great Close with horses and carts to the Gorse.' Parcels of common land lay near the Market Cross, the Castle, the Rood Church, St. Catherine's Chapel, in Gell Street (lower end of Lammas Street), between Gell Street and the Gorse and in Priory Street. Spilman Street Gate, together with the garden belonging to it, and a lane leading from the gate towards Morfa-moch-ucha were also Corporation property.

Some of the people occupying the above properties make interesting reading: Bonaventura Dyer, Jane Stedman, John Read, William Rees, mercer, Robert Callow, bookbinder, Robert Evan, dyer, Richard Jenkins, saddler, Edmund Harry, Thomas Awbrey and James Penry.

During the seventeenth century certain references occur relating to the Free School (i.e. the Queen Elizabeth Grammar School founded in 1576). According to the minutes of the Common Council, a school house was built in 1622 after much delay caused by financial difficulties. Its location is not given but subsequent references show that it stood on what is now the forecourt of Priory Street Infirmary and that it was a low single-storey building of limestone. From 1686 the administration of the Free Grammar School became the responsibility of the Common Council when the latter took over the appointment and payment of the school's Masters.[4]

THOMAS DINELEY'S DIARY, 1684

In August 1684 the Duke of Beaufort, as Lord President of the Council in Wales, visited Carmarthen in the course of his Progress through the Principality. Among his entourage was Thomas Dineley, who recorded and illustrated places of interest in his Diary, now known as 'The Beaufort Progress'. Since only hasty notes could be taken, Dineley was not always accurate in his facts and descriptions, but his pen-sketches of the Carmarthen bridge, quay, St. Peter's Church and the 'ffree schoole' (i.e. Queen Elizabeth Grammar School) are most intriguing.

He describes the tumultuous reception accorded to the Duke in Carmarthen:

> 'ringing of bells, bonfires, shouts of the people, the publick Conduit running with Wine . . . and the aforemenconed necessary Healths (i.e. of the royal family) were so often repeated at ye publick Fountain stream that severall of the Carmartheners repair'd the Fires there by their Hatts, Cravats and Canes.'

WHIGS AND TORIES

Party politics began with the Whigs and Tories. These originated as political parties in Charles II's reign (1660-1685) when a *Country party* was formed in opposition to the *Court party.* The *Court party* supported the King and the Anglican Church and was opposed to toleration for Protestant dissenters. The *Country party* advocated toleration for Protestant dissenters and attacked Charles' attempts to restore absolute royal power and the restoration of the Roman Catholic Church. They also wished to exclude Charles' brother, James, a Roman Catholic, from succeeding to the throne. The Exclusionists were nicknamed *Whigs* after fanatical Scottish Presbyterian Covenanters, while the royalists were nicknamed *Tories* after some Irish Catholic bandits; both names were derogatory, being given to each other by the opposing factions.

Lower Quay Street, 1909

Engraving by William Jones, from a drawing by his son Harold Jones.

The lettering over the door on the left reads ZB 1698. The Corporation Order Books contain an entry in 1738 of a lease renewed to Arthur Bevan, the Recorder, for 'a piece of Common on which Zachary Bevan, deceased, heretofore erected a stair-case, paying the usual reserved rent and fine.' Zachary Bevan of Laugharne was High Sheriff in 1703 and father of Arthur Bevan, husband of the distinguished Madam Bevan. The house was demolished for the construction of Coracle Way.

Another 17th century house recently demolished in Nott Square, by the castle, had an inscribed stone: 'John Davis and Jane his wife bildeth: Mar 1682.'

JAMES II AND THE GLORIOUS REVOLUTION

When Charles II died in 1685 he was succeeded by his brother James II, an ardent Catholic and a firm believer in absolute monarchy, both of which, in the climate of the times, aroused widespread opposition. In order to gain control of elections and therefore Parliament, James 'remodelled' borough charters. Carmarthen surrendered its charter late in 1685 and was granted a new remodelled one in the following year, with officials selected from families who had been strong Royalists during the Civil War. According to a Carmarthen record 'the towne clerke and most of the old Counsell were turned out.' Two years later, in another bid by James to secure Corporations favourable to his policy of restoring absolute monarchy and papal authority, Carmarthen Common Council was forced to expel eleven members and to elect others favourable to the King. But a few weeks later, in the face of mounting opposition, James had to make concessions and restore the old Borough charters. Carmarthen's 1604 charter was restored, changes made in the Common Council and on 29th October, 1688, a new mayor, Martin Beynon, replaced Sir Rice Williams who had supported, at least to some extent, James' policy. Eventually James II was deposed and in February 1689 William of Orange and his wife Mary, Protestant daughter of James, became joint sovereigns. By this so-called Glorious or Bloodless Revolution civil war had been avoided and Protestant constitutional monarchy established.

'PIOUS BENEFACTORS' OF THE TOWN

At the end of the seventeenth century Carmarthen was still the largest town in the Principality, a prosperous port, a commercial centre for the surrounding area and a centre for administrative and judicial authority. Records show that mercers' shops sold a wide range of goods, including tobacco boxes, sealing wax, looking glasses, spectacles, combs, buttons, thimbles, knives, razors, scissors, gloves, fans, lace and satin. The well-to-do classes lived in their own town houses in the fashionable area of St. Mary Street, Quay Street and King Street. But on the other side of the coin there were, as always, the poor and deserving of the town. In earlier days the poor had been catered for by the Priory and the Friary, but on their dissolution in the sixteenth century, their charitable work was gradually taken over by caring individuals with a strong religious and social conscience. Termed 'pious benefactors' in their day and age, they made charitable bequests to the poor and other deserving causes of the town. Some of these bequests are recorded on boards kept in St. Peter's church, while others appear in Corporation records.

RUDD'S ALMSHOUSES

Anthony Rudd, Bishop of St. Davids, by his will dated 25th January,

1614, directed that a place should be purchased on which a house 'divided into four partitions' should be built in which four poor men might dwell. His widow and son bought a plot of ground on the north side of St. Peter's Church and erected a 'hospital-house' there. The Bishop's widow also erected another dwelling for a fifth poor man. The five men each received a pension of £5 per annum and were called 'Brethren of Bishop Rudd's Hospital and Almshouse.' (Rudd's Cottage now stands on the site.)

Among other benefactors were the following:

David Edwards, Mayor in 1615, gave 6 shillings yearly 'to ye poor in bread.'

Dawkin Gove (corruption of Goch = red or gof = smith?), Mayor in 1648, gave '40 pounds for repairing ye three conduits in this county borough and for ye making 2 clocks with dyals, one in ye Church and ye other in ye Guild-hall of this Corporation; and also in his 2nd Mayoralty in the year 1677 he bestowed a pulpit cloth and a cushion of purple velvet with suitable fringe and Tassells.' Possibly a descendant of John Goch who had extensive land holdings in 1341.[5]

'The Lady Ann Vaughan of Terra Coed (Torcoed, Llangendeirne) gave by her will Augt ye 1st 1672 five pounds to ye poore of this Towne.'

'The Lady Elizabeth Morgan of Inniswen (Ynyswen) gave by her will Augt. ye 30th 1674 fifty pound to purchase Lands, ye rent to be distributed among ye prisoners of this County Borough of Carmarthen for ever.'

William Jones, Archdeacon of Carmarthen, 'gave by his will May ye 2nd 1676, 40 pounds 10 shillgs of ye Interest for a Sermon upon the Sunday after ye Mayor is sworne and ye remainder of ye Interest being 38 shillgs to be disposed by ye Mayor and Common Counsell for ye glory of God and ye Publick Benefit of ye Towne. As also ye house and Lands Next to ye Free Schoole to ye Mastr of ye said Free Schoole for Ever.'

Jonathan Oakley gave by his will of 1677 nine shillings yearly 'for ye Poore in Bread', while Thomas Edwardes of Rhydygors gave by his will of 1678 '7 shills to ye poore in bread ye 1st Monday after Michaelmass and 7 shills in bread ye 21st of December, yearly for Ever.' He also left money for Welsh books and for 'an Exhibition to a poore Schollar of ye Schoole of ye Towne, in Queen's College in Cambridge, for Ever.'

Thomas Beynon, Alderman, by his will of 13th December, 1685 'charged a House in upper water-street with 20 shillings to be payd to ye Minister of this Church (St. Peter's) for 2 sermons on 29th May and 5th November and 5 pounds ye use of it to ye Poor upon ye 25th November yearly for Ever.'

Charles Powell by his will of 1687 gave a house, stable and close to be converted into six rooms and six gardens 'for ye habitation of 6 Poor Men unmaryed, and 300 Pounds to be layed out for Lands ye rent to be thus distributed: To each Poor Man annually 15 shillings, for 20 load of coale yearly 10 shillings; for shoos and stokings yearly £1. 4 shillings; for blew gowns and hatts every 2nd yeare £2. 5 shillings.'

The money from these and other benefactions now forms part of the Welsh Church Fund.

PARLIAMENTARY REPRESENTATION

For most of the seventeenth century, apart from the Commonwealth period, both Carmarthen County Borough and Carmarthen County had been represented in Parliament by the Vaughans of Golden Grove, a politically ambitious, talented and numerous family who also had seats at Derwydd and Derllys. The Vaughans represented the County almost continuously from 1571 to 1689 and the Borough almost continuously from 1621 to 1725. At first they supported the King's party but later they disapproved of James II's politics and after the 1688 Revolution they became supporters of the Whigs. Members of the Vaughan family also filled the posts of County High Sheriffs, Deputy Lieutenants, Mayors and Sheriffs of the Borough and members of the Common Council. Five of the family were knighted and in 1628 Lord John Vaughan was created the first Earl of Carbery. His son, the second Earl, was made President of the Council of Wales in 1661, the highest office in the Principality, with great powers of patronage. In the following century, however, other county families were to challenge this monopoly of power and patronage, leading to political strife in the streets of Carmarthen.

1 Alcwyn C. Evans, *A History of the Town and County of Carmarthen,* 1867, unpublished M.S., N.L.W. and W. Spurrell, *Carmarthen and its Neighbourhood,* 1860 and 1879.

2 Terrence James, *Carmarthen: An Archaeological and Topographical Survey,* 1980

3 Alcwyn C. Evans, *A History of the Town and County of Carmarthen* and William Spurrell, *Carmarthen and its Neighbourhood.*

4 See *Education - The Queen Elizabeth Grammar School.*

5 *Transactions of The Carmarthenshire Antiquarian Society,* Vol. 18, part 45.

CHURCH STREET CORNER
DEMOLISHED 1951

Lammas Street about 1950

Dark Gate about 1950

- 11 -

THE EIGHTEENTH AND NINETEENTH CENTURIES:

POLITICAL STRIFE

Until about the middle of the eighteenth century Carmarthen had changed little for several hundred years, but the second half of the century saw changes in many directions which continued into the nineteenth century. Such changes included a growing political awareness, economic and social unrest, religious revival and the growth of nonconformity, the Welsh educational movement, town development and the growth of industry. Being so inextricably linked, the two centuries cannot be taken in isolation for nineteenth century Carmarthen was moulded and shaped in the previous century.

The Vaughan family of Golden Grove, who also had seats at Derwydd and Derllys, had represented both Carmarthen Borough and Carmarthen County in Parliament for most of the seventeenth century and even until 1724 Richard Vaughan of Derllys was M.P. for the Borough, having held the seat for nearly forty years. But the political predominance of the Vaughans was then challenged by other landed county families: the Philipps of Picton Castle (Pembs.) and the Philipps of Cwmgwili; the Rices of Dynevor and the Williams of Edwinsford. Although these families contested Parliamentary elections under the political banners of Whig and Tory, at first there was little political principle involved; it was chiefly a struggle for power between rival family groups. A seat in Parliament, whether it was the Borough seat or the County seat, was the usual way of obtaining lucrative offices and honours under the Crown and appointments in the civil service, army and navy. Having been elected, an M.P. was then expected to reward his supporters in his constituency accordingly. With the prospect of such gains, Parliamentary elections were often bitter struggles between rival factions sometimes accompanied by scenes of great violence.

The franchise (i.e. the right to vote) for the Borough M.P. was vested in the burgesses (or freemen) of the Borough. Burgess-ship could be acquired by birth or inheritance, by apprenticeship to a burgess, by marriage to a daughter of a burgess, by possession of property within the borough or by gift of the Corporation. Since there was no secret ballot, votes were given in public at the 'hustings' which encouraged bribery and corruption. Both Tories and Whigs utilised mob violence to intimidate their opponents and to further their own ends. Moreover, since residence within the borough was not a necessary qualification, it became a Tory practice to swell the list of burgesses eligible to vote by appointing freemen, from as far away as Pembrokeshire, who would rally to the polling booth at the given order. Thus in 1818 there were 700 burgesses - but of these only 250 resided in the borough and Pembrokeshire names figured prominently among the total.

To some extent the possession of the County seat over that of the Borough was considered a mark of social superiority, for the County franchise was vested in freeholders with land of an annual value of forty shillings. Holders of similar leases for one or more lives were also regarded as freeholders for voting purposes and so the greater the landowner the greater the power he possessed. Nevertheless, there was still keen competition for the Borough seat because of Carmarthen's status in the Principality, deriving from its trade and wealth and from the fact that many of the landed gentry maintained residences in the town.

BOROUGH POLITICS AND ELECTIONS

For nearly forty years, from 1685 until his death in 1724, Richard Vaughan of Derllys was the Member of Parliament for Carmarthen Borough. He was succeeded by James Philipps of Pentyparc who was defeated in 1727 by Arthur Bevan, Recorder of Carmarthen and husband of Bridget Vaughan, 'Madam Bevan'. This election of 1727 appears to have been the first contested election in the history of the town. Arthur Bevan held the seat until 1741 when the Tory and Jacobite, John Philipps of Kilgetty, later Sir John Philipps of Picton Castle (Pembs.), defeated the Whig candidate, Griffith Philipps of Cwmgwili, by 208 votes to 172.

Although the terms Whig and Tory can be somewhat misleading with regard to local politics, by the early years of the eighteenth century Carmarthenshire was predominantly Whig in politics; the Vaughans, the Philippses of Cwmgwili and the Rices of Dynevor all being Whig supporters. On the death of Queen Anne in 1714 without heirs, the Whigs supported George I and the Hanoverian Succession, whilst the Tories attempted a Stuart restoration. Consequently, for nearly half a century they were labelled as Jacobite sympathisers which kept them out of power and office.

The 1741 election for the Borough M.P., resulting in the return of John Philipps of Kilgetty, provides a good example of how corrupt practices were used by an outsider to control the Borough for his own purposes. John Philipps was admitted a burgess of Carmarthen in 1737 and elected to the Common Council in 1738. From this time he proceeded to manipulate the Council and about 200 new 'outside' burgesses were admitted, most of them coming from Pembrokeshire and being his own

Tory supporters. Such corrupt practices were later to become commonplace in the borough. Having won the Parliamentary seat in May 1741, John Philipps was appointed Recorder of the borough in August 1741, in place of Arthur Bevan who was discharged for alleged neglect of duty.

The Tories now had a majority on the Borough Common Council. However, in the Borough Council elections the Whig opposition enlisted the support of the mass of inhabitants who were dissatisfied at having no real voice in the administration of the town. They rejected the Mayor and the two Sheriffs elected by the Tory Council and proceeded to elect their own Mayor and Sheriffs. Three years later the Whigs induced the Common Council to disfranchise six of its Tory members which resulted in Sir John Philipps being deprived of the Recordership. This post was then given to Griffith Philipps who had the support of the local residents. Nevertheless John Philipps and his Tory supporters continued to act as the Common Council, side-by-side with the Whig Common Council, so that for several years, until the granting of the new 1764 Charter, Carmarthen found itself with two Mayors on some occasions and even three when the mob took a hand!

In the Parliamentary elections of 1751 and 1754 the Whig Griffith Philipps of Cwmgwili was returned for Carmarthen Borough, his support coming from the local resident burgesses. The election of 1754 was a General Election and the Tories did all they could to regain the seat but failed.

WHIG AND TORY RIOTS

In the following year, 1755, Carmarthen was the scene of political rioting and mob violence. There were three contemporary versions given of the rioting: one version, from the Whig standpoint, was given in letters from the Whig Mayor to Griffith Philipps, M.P.; a second version, from the Tory standpoint, was given in the *Gentleman's Magazine* of 1755 and a third version was given in a draft petition of 'the Inhabitants, Merchants and Tradesmen of Carmarthen' to the Crown.

The Whig Mayor, Evan Davies, wrote in November to Griffith Philipps, then in London:

> 'Five hundred separate fellows came from Pembrokeshire and other places armed with firearms and quarter-pieces . . . . . at present the lives and properties of the inhabitants are in the greatest danger, as the mob and rioters are publicly supported and espoused by a lot of gentlemen some of whom are of the Sea Serjeants Club and I am positive disaffected to the Government.'

(The *Sea Serjeants Club,* which existed from about 1725 to 1764, was a Jacobite club whose members were mainly Tory squires who met annually for one week in West Wales ports or tidal towns. Ostensibly their meetings were social gatherings for feasting and entertainment, although their private meetings were conducted in secret. However, there is no evidence of the Sea Serjeants participating in any Jacobite plots. But the Society's secretary was the Jacobite John Philipps of Picton, who in 1752 became its president. Moreover thirty-two Sea Serjeants were Tory burgesses of Carmarthen, all of whom were admitted when John Philipps was creating new burgesses to secure political control of the borough and many of whom were imported from Pembrokeshire.)

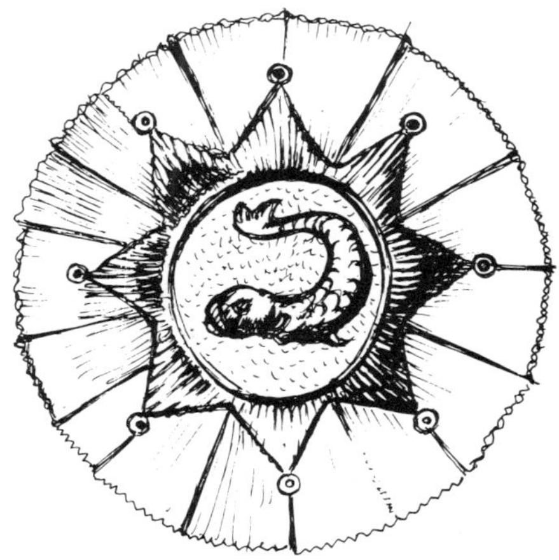

The Sea Serjeants Society Badge

In December 1755 the Whig Mayor again wrote to Griffith Philipps stating that several people had been seriously wounded and that more armed intruders were coming into the town. He feared for his life and the lives of the Whig inhabitants.

The Tory version of the rioting appeared in the *Gentleman's Magazine* which stated that:

> 'the mob had for a long time with impunity maimed several persons, beat out the brains of the barber at the Red Lion (the Tory headquarters), broke open and attempted to pull down the Red Lion so that it was necessary to send for guards . . . . . and a strong party arrived from Pembrokeshire who were quartered at the Red Lion and elsewhere.'

(The Tory headquarters were at the Red Lion Inn in Guildhall Square where number 6 now stands, and the Whig headquarters were at the Greyhound Inn in Bridge Street.) The account in the *Gentleman's Magazine* goes on to say that:

> 'the mob (presumably the local people who were mainly Whig supporters) reinforced themselves with men from the country and having fortified the Castle and upper house, made port-holes and supplied themselves with great guns and small arms. The Upper Gate (i.e. between King Street and Nott Square) is fortified by the Red Lion people and called Newgate, where the prisoners taken by the Sheriffs on one side are put. Mr. Lewis the bookseller, Newland the lawyer and Nicholls, a shopkeeper, are wounded, as are two women dangerously. In short the town is full of fire, smoke and tumult.'

The editor of the magazine added a further note that

> 'the true cause of all this is the violence of party and a dislike to the Jacobites.'

The third version of the rioting given in the petition to the Crown by 'the Inhabitants, Merchants and Tradesmen' stated that the riots were caused by people

> 'unlawfully assembled . . . . . armed with guns, swords and other

> offensive weapons threatening . . . . . wounding and maiming, shooting at and killing several'

of the King's subjects. The petition added that in November people armed with

> 'guns, hangers, pitchforks, spits, pokers and clubs'

had pursued a number of inhabitants into the town hall which was then attacked. A Sea Serjeant, by the name of Essex Jones, fired a gun through one of the windows and wounded Jacob Morgan. In December the rioters again assembled in the town

> 'firing guns loaded with ball and shot in the open streets, and from the stables of the Red Lion Inn, the chief place of their rendezvous . . . . whereby many were wounded and several killed. Joseph Thomas was shot through the head with a musket ball and killed, and John Lewis was also shot and killed.'

The Upper Gatehouse (also called Newgate, between King Street and Nott Square) continued to be garrisoned by an armed body of the Red

Lion people who apparently fired at everyone they disliked. In March 1756 they were still in occupation, for Griffith Philipps was informed by one of the Whig Sheriffs that 'the Newgate mob still continues tyrannical, outrageous and rebellious in opposition to justice and law.'

Subsequently, both the Whigs and the Tories began legal proceedings against each other's supporters but there is no evidence to show that anyone was punished for the rioting. The two parties continued to intrigue against each other and to elect two lots of corporation officials, including rival Mayors.

In 1757 there was a further outbreak of violence when rioters broke into a corn store. On their refusal to disperse, even after the Whig Mayor had read the Riot Act, five of their number were killed. The following extract from the *Gentleman's Magazine* gives a picture of the trial and acquittal of the Mayor of Carmarthen for alleged murder:

> 'Friday, 2 September, 1757. At the assizes for Carmarthen came on the trial of John Evans, Esq., Mayor, on five several indictments for the supposed murder of five colliers, concerned with about 100 others in a late riot, in breaking open a storehouse and stealing corn, when it appeared to the jury, from the prosecutor's own witness, that Mr. Evans had read the Proclamation and several times desired the rioters to disperse; that he offered them corn at a reasonable rate; that he had done all in his power as a prudent Magistrate to suppress the riot, but that the colliers continued the same, and with pickaxes and other weapons in their hands, had obliged the Mayor to retreat, and that self-preservation laid him under the necessity of commanding the military to fire, and whereby these five unfortunate wretches received their death. They *(the jury)* without going out of court, honourably acquitted him with the entire approbation of the judges and the whole Court.'

The Gentleman's Magazine then adds that

> 'The real mob are only the tools of those who are led by either principle or interest to wish for a general confusion, in order to overturn the government . . . . they are no friends to the present royal family (George II of Hanover) and the protestant interest . . . . . Those who supplied the prosecutors (of the Mayor) with money, had something more in view by encouraging these rioters than the ruin of a few private families.'

THE NEW BOROUGH CHARTER, 1764

A remedy was urgently needed to put an end to the chaotic maladministration resulting from the duplication of corporation officials, which was itself due to rival Whig and Tory political factions. In 1763 two petitions asking for a new charter were presented to the Crown, one from the Whig faction and the other from the Tory. Both parties tried to secure a new charter which would favour their own interest but in June 1764 Sir John Philipps, leader of the Tory faction, died and the Whigs were able to claim credit for the 1764 Charter of King George III.

This Charter confirmed all the customs and privileges of former charters and declared that there should be forty burgesses (who were actually named in the Charter), that the burgesses should choose one of their number to be called the Mayor and twenty others to be called the Common Council. This Common Council should advise, aid and assist the Mayor in all matters concerning the Borough. Various property and financial qualifications were laid down for the burgesses. Burgesses *de iure*, who could claim their freedom by right, were freeholders of three years' standing who owned property to the annual value of £4, and apprentices who had served for seven years under a burgess. Burgesses *ex gratia*, who could be admitted as an act of grace at the discretion of the Mayor and Common Council, were those who rented or occupied land to the annual value of £10 in the Borough.

The Mayor and burgesses were to be responsible for the election, in Common Hall, of all corporate officials. The Charter named Albert Davids to be Mayor for the ensuing year. The Mayor and two Sheriffs, 'discreet and lawful men' were to be chosen annually from among the burgesses. A penalty of £100 was imposed for refusing to be Mayor or Sheriff. All writs, summonses and warrants were to be directed to the two Sheriffs and to be executed by them. (By the Municipal Corporations Act of 1835 the two Sheriffs were reduced to one.)

The purpose of the 1764 Charter was to give more power to the burgesses, 'in Common Hall assembled', by curtailing the previous domination of the Common Council. This succeeded for a time, with the burgesses making decisions and initiating policy which the Council then carried out.

The Charter was brought to Carmarthen from London by George Rice of Dynevor on August 6th of that year. The *County History* records that the populace turned out in force

> 'in coaches and chariots and near 1000 horses and men on foot innumerable . . . The Charter being delivered to Albert Davids *(Mayor)*, at the town end of Abergwili Bridge, he brought it to town with great joy in his coach, which was dressed with laurel gilted with silver . . . An ox was roasted near the conduit in Lammas Street and a feast provided in the long storehouse near the Quay, to which nearly 1,500 tradesmen and gentlemen sat down; several hogsheads of ale and cider were brought into the streets for the public. At night there were fireworks and bell ringing, and the grand climax came with a ball.'

Unfortunately this Charter was very costly to the town and several pieces of Corporation land had to be mortgaged in order to pay off the debt of over £2,000 incurred.[1] Copies of the Charter were printed by John Ross in Carmarthen in 1765 and by J. P. Davies of King Street in the early nineteenth century.

For a few years Carmarthen enjoyed a period of improvement but by the end of the century the new corporation was corrupted by political intrigues and party rivalries stemming from a clash of county factions with vested interests. Politics in Carmarthen, both in borough and county, had become nothing more than repeated clashes between the *Blues*, represented by the Whig House of Golden Grove allied to Cwmgwili, and the *Reds* represented by the Tory House of Dynevor. (The Rices of Dynevor originally supported the Whigs).

The rivalry between the parties extended to the hunting-field, and two packs of hounds, known as the *Red Coat Hunt* (Tory) and the *Blue Coat Hunt* (Whig), were maintained. The kennels of the Red Coat Hunt were situated on the corner of present John Street and St. Catherine Street, and those of the Blue Coat Hunt in Fountain Hall Terrace.

In the Borough elections of 1784 and 1790 John George Philipps of Cwmgwili (Whig) was returned to Parliament without any difficulty but in the election of 1796 he was opposed by Magens Dorrien Magens, a London banker who was married to Lord Dynevor's sister and who stood as the Tory candidate. During this election pistols were fired in the streets, the inhabitants had to barricade their houses and at least one man was shot during a disturbance in Lower Market Street (Hall Street). Magens was declared the victor with a majority of five votes but subsequently, after a petition to Parliament by J. G. Philipps, a committee of the House appointed to deal with the dispute declared that the latter ought to have been returned. Accordingly, J. G. Philipps of Cwmgwili, representing the Whig interest and the 'Blues', and supported by the House of Golden Grove, took his seat for the third time. He was to be returned again for the Borough in 1802, although he resigned in the following year. On his resignation, the Whig Sir William Paxton of Middleton Hall, Llanarthney, who had been Mayor of Carmarthen in 1802 was elected in his stead. Paxton had made his fortune in Calcutta, India, and bought Middleton Hall Estate in 1776. He built a new Middleton Hall about 1785, described as 'the most splendid mansion in South Wales'. The Borough seat was some consolation for Paxton who had failed to win the County seat in the bitterly-contested election known as *Y Lecsiwn Fawr* (The Big Election) in 1802. His opponent was Sir James Hamlyn Williams, Tory, of Edwinsford supported by the Dynevor faction. Polling lasted fifteen days and was accompanied with much violence. Williams was declared the victor with a majority of 117 votes.

However, *Y Lecsiwn Fawr* is notable for Sir William Paxton's lavish expenditure which amounted to well over £15,000, a very large sum in those days. Among the items included in his expenses were 11,070 breakfasts, 36,901 dinners, 684 suppers, 25,275 gallons of ale, 11,068 bottles of whisky, 8,879 bottles of port, 460 bottles of sherry, 509 bottles of cider and election ribbons costing £ 786. Paxton had plenty of money left, however, because he built *Paxton's Tower*, overlooking the Towy valley at Llanarthney, in honour of Lord Nelson. It is sometimes called *Paxton's Folly* because it served no utilitarian purpose. Nevertheless, Sir William Paxton was a public-spirited man prepared to spend his money on local improvements. During his mayoralty of Carmarthen in 1802-03, the Corporation adopted his plan for supplying the town with piped water. He also offered to build a new bridge over the Towy but the townspeople of Carmarthen refused the offer. He represented the Borough in Parliament, as a Whig, from 1803 until 1806 when he was returned for the County seat.

Paxton's Tower

The new Borough M.P. was George Campbell, brother of Lord Cawdor, the latter having recently inherited the vast Golden Grove estates of the Vaughan family. George Campbell remained Whig M.P. until 1813 when he was succeeded by his nephew, J. F. Campbell, who held the seat until 1821, when he himself succeeded to the peerage becoming the second Lord Cawdor.

But then came a Tory reaction against the long period of Whig representation and John Jones of Ystrad, after whom Johnstown is supposed to be named, represented the Borough from 1821-1832. A successful barrister, born in Carmarthen, he enjoyed the utmost popularity with the general public on account of his charm and generosity, although all his election expenses were met by the subscriptions of his supporters.

Prior to becoming Tory M.P. in 1821, John Jones was nominated as Mayor of Carmarthen in 1809 by the Whig Lord Cawdor but three years later Jones changed sides and became leader of the opposition to the Whig Cawdor dominance. He stood against George Campbell for the Borough seat 'to prevent Carmarthen becoming a Family Borough', but he was unsuccessful. Again he failed to take the seat in 1818 but in 1821 he defeated the Whig candidate, Sir William Paxton. Tory John Jones was subsequently returned unopposed at the elections of 1826 and 1830.

Ystrad Mansion

THE PARLIAMENTARY REFORM ACT, 1832

The movement for Parliamentary reform was now growing apace and in March 1831 the Parliamentary Reform Bill was introduced in the House of Commons by Whig Lord John Russell. John Jones voted against it, subsequently losing the popular support he had enjoyed for ten years. In the Parliamentary election of April 1831 he was opposed by Captain John George Philipps of Cwmgwili, the Whig champion of Parliamentary reform. John Jones claimed to approve of reform in principle, but to be dissatisfied with certain sections of the Bill.[2] However, local feeling was in favour of Philipps. Once again Carmarthen was the scene of political rioting.

The Carmarthen 'mob', consisting largely of the so-called 'lower orders', packed the Guildhall and threatened any who dared to vote for the Tory John Jones. (The Secret Ballot was not introduced until 1872. Supporters of Parliamentary candidates had to openly declare their vote in public and so were subject to inducement at best or intimidation at worst.) The election had to be adjourned until the next day but once again the mob trooped in and intimidated any would-be voters for John Jones. In the end the election had to be called off and Carmarthen had made history. It had never happened in Wales before that a Parliamentary election had been prevented by public disorder.

The Mayor and magistrates appealed to the Home Secretary for military help and troops were soon dispatched from Brecon. Fearing the worst, the ringleaders of the mob gave themselves up and were promptly locked in jail by the Tory magistrates. The town became quiet, the troops returned to Brecon and the rioters were released on bail. Immediately the mob took over Carmarthen again and rampaged through the streets. An appeal for troops failed but a date was fixed for a new Parliamentary election - August 20th 1831 - and in anticipation of this, six policemen from the newly formed London Metropolitan Police Force were sent to Carmarthen.

The election duly took place and John Jones, the Tory candidate, was elected. His success, however, was largely due to the corrupt practices against which the mob was protesting: namely the large number of non-resident Tory burgesses whose claims to owning land within the Borough were largely fictitious. (Only burgesses had the vote.) The mob expressed their disapproval of his election in their usual manner. While John Jones was being chaired in triumph by his supporters through Guildhall Square 'he was pelted with stones and was severely wounded on the forehead . . . upon which several persons were taken into custody by the constables, who were wounded and beaten most severely by the rioters.' More violence followed for a few more days but then gradually petered out.

The second Reform Bill was passed by the Commons in September

1831 with John Jones voting in favour of the Bill this time, probably to placate the Carmarthen reformers. However, this Bill was rejected by the Lords, causing a national uproar.

The third Parliamentary Reform Bill was eventually passed in June 1832. As far as Carmarthen was concerned, the Borough franchise was given to all resident householders or occupiers of premises worth £10 annually, which brought in a substantial number of new voters, most of whom were Whig reformers. Non-resident burgesses were disfranchised, while Llanelli was added to the Carmarthen Constituency. At the General Election for the reformed Parliament held in December 1832, John Jones lost his seat to the Whig candidate, W. H. Yelverton, who had replaced John George Philipps of Cwmgwili.

The Corporation or Council elections of 1831 and 1832 were also marked by violence. In 1831 the election had to be postponed to the following day when extra special constables were pressed into service to maintain law and order. In 1832 the 'Blue' Whig mob attacked the 'Red' Star and Garter public house in Spilman Street, to be met by repeated shots from the landlord's pistols. Several were wounded and the enraged mob started to pull down the Star and Garter. The Mayor called out the troops and read the Riot Act to the mob. Several of the latter were arrested, and so too was the landlord of the pub.

That the violence continued is shown by a report in the *Carmarthen Journal* that the north and west galleries of the Guildhall were removed in 1833 because they were used as vantage points for hurling missiles on the Sheriffs and others employed in conducting election proceedings.

From 1837 until 1864 Carmarthen Borough was represented in Parliament by the Whig Carmarthen banker, David Morris of Coomb.

THE MUNICIPAL CORPORATIONS ACT, 1835

Following on Parliamentary reform came the Municipal Corporations Act of 1835, which sought to reform the government of towns. Town Councils, elected by all male adult ratepayers of three years' standing, displaced the old burgesses and closed bodies which previously constituted town corporations. Evidence given to the Municipal Corporations Commissioners prior to the Act revealed that 'the government of Carmarthen borough was mainly carried on for political purposes' and 'even the administration of justice was tainted, for justices and juries were of one political party.' For many years the affairs of the Borough had been conducted with inefficiency, negligence and corruption. As a result of financial mismanagement, Carmarthen had lost much of its former inheritance so that by 1834 the Corporation owed over £2,000 to the bank. This was in contrast to the Corporation's income as shown in the Borough Order Books recording the annual rents collected for Corporation property in the sixteenth and seventeenth centuries. Even in

1769 the Mayor was paid £10 for the annual perambulation of the corporation estates - the ancient custom of 'beating the bounds'. Moreover, a map of the town, drawn by Thomas Lewis in 1786, shows that at that time the Corporation still owned land and property in and around Carmarthen. But within a period of about fifty years the bulk of this property had disappeared, sold in periodical sales to pay the mounting debts of the Borough treasury. The estates were administered by the Common Council who acted as their own agents and auditors. There was a good deal of speculation carried on, chiefly by the granting of leases of the land to members of the Corporation. Apparently, no copies of the leases were kept and no surveys made of the property. Rents were hopelessly in arrears and few efforts made to collect them. A large proportion of the proceeds from the sale of Borough property never reached the Borough treasury. The extent to which the Corporation had frittered away its inheritance can only point to the irresponsibility and corruption of the Common Council of the period. Nevertheless, when the unreformed Common Council met for the last time on 5th December, 1835, the Mayor, David Davies, appended the following to his signature in the Borough Order Book: 'May the new Corporation act as zealously for the Prosperity of the town of Carmarthen as the old.'

When the new Council, elected by the newly appointed ratepayers, tried to get some information from the last Mayor regarding the 'most extraordinary account' which had been submitted to them, his flippant reply concluded with the lines:

'Do what you may, say what you will,
Asses will be but asses still.'

Neither the 1832 Reform Act nor the 1835 Municipal Corporations Act brought about any sweeping changes in the political system. Although the franchise was extended to the towns, it did not give the vote to the lower classes, while in the counties political power was still vested in the landed gentry. Such political disappointment, coupled with economic and social grievances, caused discontent and distress which found expression in this area in the *Rebecca Riots*.

THE REBECCA RIOTS [3]

In 1843 Carmarthen was hit by the Rebecca Riots, which were ostensibly a protest against the payment of tolls at the numerous toll-gates on the turnpike roads and took the form of attacks at night on the unpopular toll-gates. From the middle of the eighteenth century Carmarthenshire had been slowly covered with a network of roads administered by Turnpike Trusts, usually companies of landowners, who levied tolls for their upkeep. While the new roads brought benefits in transportation, the frequency of the toll-gates increased the costs considerably. The trouble lay in the number of Turnpike Trusts, with

Johnstown Toll-gate House

their roads often interlacing, and the very large number of toll-gates at which separate tolls were demanded. As early as 1786 a tourist reported: 'A traveller must stand reconciled to paying twice within a few hundred yards.' In 1848 it was reported: 'Taking the whole County of Carmarthen, on average there are not three miles of road without a toll bar.'

But there were deeper underlying social and economic causes leading to the Rebecca Riots. Thus a witness at the Royal Commissions' Inquiry into the riots stated: 'I think the commissioners are taking for granted that the gates have been the origin of this disturbance. It is no such thing; it is merely the means by which the feeling of the people has become apparent.' The deeper economic causes lay in the poverty and distress of the agricultural classes. Farmers had been hit by a succession of bad harvests which had reduced their capital, prices for stock were low and money was scarce. At the same time their rents remained high - most small farmers being tenants of the landed gentry - while their tithe payments, for the upkeep of churches and clergy, had been increased by an excessive amount. The farmers needed to use the turnpike roads frequently for transporting goods to market, lime from the kilns to their fields and coal for fuel. Therefore the tolls to be paid at the numerous toll-gates were a constant source of irritation. Moreover, changes in Poor Law administration, arising from the Poor Law Amendment Act of 1834, were also deeply resented. Under the Act parishes were grouped together to form Unions and each Union was to support a Workhouse by means of the Poor Rate levied on the inhabitants of the parishes in the Union. Relief for the poor was now only obtainable in the Union workhouses and not, as previously, as out-door relief in their own parishes. Conditions in Union workhouses were made as harsh and unattractive as possible in order to deter people from seeking admission. Husbands, wives and children were separated from each other, overcrowding was commonplace and food inadequate. Poor agricultural workers preferred to live with their families on the verge of starvation rather than give up their small cottages and enter the workhouse. Once they were in the workhouse their cottages were liable to be seized by their landlords and their furniture sold to pay the rent. Thus the Union workhouses soon became objects of hatred and fear.

These various grievances widened the gap between landlords and their tenants, the former showing little sympathy or understanding of their tenants' case, while the latter came to regard all landlords, gentry and magistrates, who were often one and the same, as symbols of hatred and oppression. By the 1840's the gap between the upper and lower classes was sufficiently wide to produce violent demonstrations, with the rioting spreading from west Wales and culminating in the drafting of police and troops into the area.

The first toll-gate to be attacked and destroyed was that of Efailwen, Llandysilio, near Whitland in May 1839. This was an additional gate put up by the Whitland Trust, in the spring of that year, in order to catch the farmers as they began to cart lime from the kilns to their fields. There was then a lull for over three years until, at the end of 1842, a new toll-gate erected at St. Clears was attacked and pulled down. This was followed by the destruction of other toll-gates in the surrounding area, the local magistrates and police seemingly helpless in their attempts to stop the rioting from spreading.

Attacks on toll-gates usually followed a set pattern: they were made at night and were carried out by large bodies of men, usually on horseback, dressed in women's clothing and with their faces blackened. They were led by *Rebecca,* their appointed leader, who was seated upon a large white horse and also disguised in female clothes, with a wig of horse-hair ringlets. To the accompaniment of horns, bugles, flutes and drums Rebecca and her *daughters* attacked the toll-gates and toll-houses with axes and sledge-hammers and then, often having set them alight, quickly dispersed into the darkness firing their guns as a parting shot. Attacks were also made on the property of some of the landowners and magistrates who had displeased them in actions or opinions. It would appear that there was no co-ordinated plan of campaign, each area carrying out its attacks on local toll-gates and each area having its own Rebecca.

It is thought that the name Rebecca referred to the blessing pronounced on Rebecca, Isaac's wife: 'Be thou the mother of thousands of millions, and let thy seed possess the gates of those which hate them.' *Genesis XXIV, v.60.* Considering the tremendous influence of the Bible on the rural communities at this time, the Bible being the chief, if not the only, source of literacy for the country-people, who learned its texts and passages by heart and took them literally, it is not surprising that such a passage from Genesis was taken as a vindication, indeed an encouragement, for them to 'possess' the hated toll-gates.

Carmarthen was surrounded by the toll-gates of five Turnpike Trusts whose roads converged on the town, but it was the Water Street toll-gate which apparently caused the greatest irritation. Bestriding the turnpike road from Carmarthen to Cardigan and being very near to the town centre, it effectively trapped many would-be market traders and farmers living to the north of the town, for there was no other way around it. The Water Street gate was kept by a certain Henry Thomas who lived with his wife and child in the toll-house alongside. In the early hours of Saturday, 27th May, 1843 he was rudely awakened by a noisy crowd of about three hundred rioters, most of whom were on horse back and carried axes, sledge-hammers and guns. They proceeded to demolish the gate, Rebecca having ordered her followers to do no harm to the gatekeeper and his family. Only the roof of the house was destroyed, although there was a great deal of noise and shouting together with gun-fire. The latter effectively deterred the town's five policemen from interfering with the rioters, let alone pursuing them! Having thanked the gatekeeper for his lack of resistance, Rebecca and her children then mounted their horses and made their retreat through Fountain Hall and Trevaughan into the hills of north Carmarthen.

The police were severely reprimanded by the Mayor and magistrates for not attempting to put a stop to the rioting and for failing to capture any of the gang. Within a few days the Water Street toll-gate was re-erected, but when three men from Talog refused to pay the tolls summonses were issued against them and they were each fined a considerable sum. They refused to pay the fines, probably because Rebecca had threatened that their goods would be burned and their lives taken from them if they paid. Consequently the magistrates issued warrants for the seizure of goods to the value of the unpaid fines and sent four special constables to Talog to execute the warrants. Before they could reach Talog, however, they were surrounded by forty or more black-faced men armed with sticks, scythes and pitchforks. The four constables hastily returned to Carmarthen! The borough magistrates then sent to Talog a larger force of forty, including armed regular police, special constables and elderly army pensioners. They were suddenly surrounded by Rebecca in full regalia, mounted on a large white horse and accompanied by about four hundred followers with blackened faces, some of whom carried shotguns. The policemen were overpowered and disarmed and then forced to march to Trawsmawr, the home of Captain Davies, a leading county magistrate, where they were compelled to demolish his boundary wall, part of which had been pulled down by Rebecca's followers on the previous day.

Such defiance of civil authority could not be tolerated, so the Mayor wrote to the Home Secretary appealing for troops to be sent to

Carmarthen as quickly as possible. This was followed by an even more urgent request for troops when it was discovered that Rebecca had held a meeting of all the farmers of the Hundred of Elfed on the 14th June. At this meeting the farmers had resolved to present their grievances and demands to the Mayor and magistrates of Carmarthen. For this purpose all the farmers and their tenants were ordered to assemble at the Plough and Harrow public house, two miles outside the town, at 11 o'clock on Monday morning 19th June, 1843, in order to march on Carmarthen. They were warned that failure to do so would result in their houses and barns being pulled down and burned.

In his second request for troops, the Mayor asked that a company of infantry be sent, as well as the cavalry promised in answer to his first appeal.

On the Monday morning a crowd of more than a thousand people assembled around the Plough and Harrow. Rebecca, wearing a horsehair wig of golden ringlets and mounted on a large white horse, led a procession of three hundred horsemen, followed by the rest of the crowd, behind a band playing the popular airs of the day and a large banner bearing the inscription:

CYFIAWNDER A CHARWYR CYFIAWNDER YDYM NI OLL
(Justice, and lovers of justice are we all)

The noisy procession marched down through the Water Street gate and then made its way through the streets of the town. The Mayor and magistrates were waiting among the crowds in Guildhall Square for the list of grievances and demands to be presented to them. However, Rebecca never got as far as the Mayor, for suddenly the procession turned from Guildhall Square into Red Street and proceeded to make its way towards the workhouse on Penlan Hill. Rebecca had lost control of her followers to the notorious Carmarthen mob, for whom the workhouse was a symbol of hatred and repression. The rioting mob forced the workhouse master, Ray Evans, to open the gates and then proceeded to take possession of the building and ransack it. The borough police and special constables were hurriedly sent by the Mayor to the Workhouse and fought with the mob.

Just as some of Rebecca's supporters, disillusioned with the outcome of their march, were about to depart, they were confronted by a troop of cavalry charging up Waterloo Terrace and Penlan Hill with sabres drawn. The 4th Light Dragoons had been on their way to Carmarthen when a message was received that the town was being invaded by thousands of insurrectionists. They dashed to Carmarthen where magistrates were waiting and one of them led the Dragoons up Waterloo Terrace. Many rioters were trapped in the workhouse, others were rounded up outside, making a total of about one hundred prisoners. However, of these, only five were committed in custody for trial at the next Carmarthenshire Assizes, the rest being released by the magistrates.

As for Rebecca herself, she was never positively identified. One theory, based on local historian Alcwyn Evans' account, is that Rebecca was a Trelech farmer named Michael Bowen, while another theory, which probably carries greater weight, is that given in *The History and Antiquities of the Parish of Newchurch* by the Revd. T. M. Morgan, Vicar, in 1910. According to the Vicar, Rebecca and her sister Charlotte were the Rees brothers of Rhydymarchog farm in the Parish of Newchurch. It was they who led the attack on the Water Street toll-gate and also led the march on Carmarthen. The vicar had been given this information by an old man named Thomas who had himself taken part in both incidents. Moreover, Rhydymarchog farm is very close to Trawsmawr, the home of the County magistrate whose boundary wall had been demolished on Rebecca's orders.

A few days after the attack on the workhouse, Colonel James Love, with a detachment of infantry, was sent to Carmarthen to take charge of all the troops employed in the area and to consult with the civil authorities upon all matters relating to the public peace. The Rebecca riots in west Wales, which were now spreading eastwards from Carmarthen, were becoming a matter of public concern, and since the civil power was unable to contain them, firm military measures were needed. Colonel Love was wise enough to realise that the smashing of toll-gates was but a symbol of far deeper grievances, the causes of which he proceeded to investigate. In a succession of letters to the Home Secretary he gave a lucid analysis of the situation, outlining the distress caused to local farmers already burdened with high rents and tithes and now exorbitant turnpike tolls. He also stressed the need for an efficient civil force to put down rioting, rather than relying on the military alone. To this end he asked for some policemen to be sent from London and one hundred and fifty Metropolitan Police officers were quickly sent. From this small beginning there grew the Carmarthenshire Constabulary.

One of Colonel Love's most important recommendations to the Home Secretary was that 'the whole affair of the Trusts demands a strict enquiry.' Accordingly, in October, the government set up a Royal Commission whose report appeared in 1844. Nevertheless, toll-gates continued to be attacked and demolished throughout the autumn and winter of 1843.

The third occasion on which Carmarthen encountered Rebecca occurred in the early hours of 25th August, 1843, when the Glangwili toll-gate and house were destroyed by about 200 of Rebecca's followers. David Joshua, a Carmarthen bookbinder, was the toll-gate keeper and although a committed Chartist, he was an outspoken opponent of the Rebecca movement. Joshua's furniture and the tools of his trade were buried beneath the ruins of his toll-house, his books burnt, and he was attacked with a hatchet. When the dragoons arrived from Carmarthen Rebecca and her children had all vanished into the night!

As the year wore on the original enthusiasm for the Rebecca movement began to wane, not only because of the public enquiry into its causes but also because the anonymous cloak of Rebecca was being used increasingly by unscrupulous and violent characters to further their own ends. Two such characters who terrorised the Gwendraeth valley in the name of Rebecca were colliers John Jones, known as *Shoni 'Sgubor Fawr* (John big barn) and David Davies, known as *Dai'r Cantwr* (David the singer). Having been enlisted by the farmers to break down the toll-gates, for which they were generously paid, they then proceeded to blackmail, terrorise and rob these same farmers. When one nocturnal raid resulted in the killing of a woman, albeit accidentally, and another in a near-miss, an informer went to the police. *Shoni 'Scubor Fawr* and *Dai'r Cantwr* were taken to Carmarthen gaol. About the same time Queen Victoria issued a proclamation offering generous rewards for information leading to the arrest and conviction of participants in the recent disturbances and also the Queen's pardon for informers who had themselves taken part in the disturbances. The result was the end of rioting in south-east Carmarthenshire, although the campaign continued in mid Wales.

In December 1843 the trials of Shoni, Dai and thirty-six others took place at the Carmarthenshire Assizes held in Carmarthen's Guildhall. Shoni and Dai both pleaded guilty to a whole host of charges and Mr. Justice Cresswell sentenced Shoni (John Jones) to be transported for life and Dai (David Davies) to transportation for twenty years. Of the others, several had the charges against them withdrawn for turning Queen's evidence and informing on their former colleagues, some were released on the promise of good behaviour, some were found not guilty, and of those found guilty, all received lenient sentences.

In view of the harsh penal code of the times, the Government's policy was obviously one of leniency and conciliation; only the ringleaders were given sentences sufficiently harsh to act as a deterrent. The government had no wish to make martyrs and thereby prolong the disturbances. The trial of those involved in the attack on the Carmarthen workhouse took place at the Spring Assizes held in the Guildhall in March 1844. All were found guilty but their sentences were very lenient. John Harries, a miller of Talog, who was also involved in the ambush of the police at Talog and was one of the ring-leaders, was given twelve months' hard labour, while five others were each given eight months' imprisonment.

THE AFTERMATH OF REBECCA

The Report of the Commission of Inquiry recognised the people's grievances as valid and completely vindicated the people's discontent with their 'most obnoxious burthens'.

Their demands for justice resulted in new legislation which was passed in 1845 and which remedied the grievance relating to the Turnpike Trusts and toll-gates. However, the deeper economic and social grievances could not be removed so easily by legislation but only by the gradual reforms which came into being as the nineteenth century progressed.

The Rebecca Riots took place during the Conservative ministry of Sir Robert Peel who was Prime Minister from 1841 to 1846, a period of economic slump and appalling social conditions, often referred to as the 'Hungry Forties'. In the face of much opposition Peel pushed through economic and social reforms which paved the way for later legislation. He was also responsible for reviving the old Tory party and giving it a new programme and a new image as the Conservative party. The Conservatives stood for a programme of moderate, cautious reform wherever there was a genuine need for it, while at the same time preserving all that was good in the British system. Coming from a middle-class background himself, he gained wider support for the new Conservatives from moderate people of all classes, particularly from middle-class manufacturers and businessmen who felt neglected by the wealthy, aristocratic Whig landowners.

During the middle years of the nineteenth century Britain enjoyed a period of industrial and agricultural prosperity which lasted until the last quarter of the century, a period marked by the Great Exhibition of 1851 and by the railway mania which covered the country with a network of railways. The latter created large-scale employment and brought cheap, fast transport both for manufactured goods and for perishable farming produce for sale in the cities.

REFORMS OF THE LATER NINETEENTH CENTURY

As economic and social reforms relating to factories, mines and public health were being undertaken, the need for further Parliamentary reform was also increasingly recognised. The Reform Act of 1867, usually known as the Second Reform Act, gave the vote in the boroughs to all householders who paid rates; in the counties the vote was given to all ratepayers paying £12 a year in rates and to lease-holders holding land valued at £5 a year. This voting qualification was high enough to keep agricultural labourers (the majority of the rural population) without the vote, so that the power of the wealthy landowners was preserved. This undemocratic feature was removed by the Parliamentary Reform Act of 1884 which gave the vote to all householders in the counties. The Secret Ballot Act of 1872 ensured that landlords and employers could no longer control the way their tenants and workers voted and so elections became

W. E. Gladstone

Benjamin Disraeli

more orderly, while bribery and corruption were reduced.

Although the 1867 Reform Act was passed in the Conservative government of Benjamin Disraeli, the general election of 1868 resulted in a large majority for the Liberal party (made up of former Whigs with some Peelites and Radicals) led by W. E. Gladstone. For the next twenty years politics at Westminster became a struggle between the Liberals and Conservatives with Gladstone and Disraeli dominating both their respective parties and Parliament.

As far as Carmarthen Borough politics were concerned, the general election of 1868 resulted in an overwhelming victory for the Liberal candidate, J. S. Cowell-Stepney of Llanelli, who had the support of the Nonconformist vote. The Carmarthen Liberals had favoured Lewis Morris as their candidate but the latter conveniently retired, allowing the Llanelli candidate to go forward, thus avoiding a split in the Liberal ranks. Under the 1832 Reform Act Llanelli was added to the County Borough of Carmarthen for electoral purposes. In 1918, however, they were split up, Carmarthen being incorporated into West Carmarthenshire and Llanelli into East Carmarthenshire.

By the middle of the nineteenth century Llanelli was an important industrial town and port; her population had exceeded that of Carmarthen and was continuing to increase. However, although out-stripped by her industrial neighbours, the County town was still the administrative centre of a wide agricultural region and still retained something of its old-world character.

1 M. C. S. Evans, *Expenses incurred by the Borough of Carmarthen, 1764-1775, in relation to the obtaining of a new Charter* in *The Carmarthen Antiquary,* Vol. IV, 1962.

2 David A. Wager, *Carmarthenshire Politics and the Reform Act of 1832* in *The Carmarthenshire Antiquary,* Vol. X, 1974.

3 Pat Molloy, *And They Blessed Rebecca - An account of the Welsh Toll-gate Riots 1839-1844,* 1983.

- 12 -

THE EIGHTEENTH AND NINETEENTH CENTURIES:

RELIGIOUS REVIVAL

The eighteenth century saw the beginning of a religious revival which led to the growth of Nonconformity and the establishment of a large number of Chapels in Carmarthen during the eighteenth and nineteenth centuries. For over six hundred years St. Peter's Church had been the Parish church and on the dissolution of the Priory, Friary and the Chantry chapels, the sole religious establishment in the town. The Civil War of the seventeenth century led to the emergence of the Commonwealth Puritans who, as far as Carmarthenshire was concerned, were mainly Independents and Baptists. These became the Dissenting Nonconformists of the Restoration period of persecution. They survived such persecution to lay down the foundations of Welsh Nonconformity which blossomed in the eighteenth century. Religious revival was also inspired by the growth of the Methodist movement.

THE METHODIST REVIVAL

The religious awakening, known as the Methodist Revival, began as an evangelising force within the Established Anglican Church. At this stage there was no intention to separate from the Established Church; all the leaders of the revival were Anglicans who were inspired by an evangelical zeal to bring a religious awakening into the apathy of the Church. The name *Methodist* originated from a small group of young students at Oxford in 1729, who were led by John Wesley, and later by George Whitefield, and who practised strict personal discipline to study Christianity in a *methodical* way. They set out to follow the example of the early apostles, to proclaim the Gospel, to save souls and to give practical help to the poor, sick and oppressed. Their mission was essentially evangelical and itinerant, with fervent public preaching which appealed to the emotions and swayed great crowds of people who usually congregated in the open air.

The early Welsh leaders of the Methodist revival were Howel Harris and Daniel Rowland who had commenced to evangelise in this area before the arrival of George Whitefield and John Wesley. From the 1740's Carmarthen was visited on many occasions by the revivalist leaders who preached to large crowds with tremendous influence and effect. In 1743 George Whitefield noted in his diary: 'Carmarthen, one of the greatest and most polite places in Wales.'

In the beginning there was no wish to change the Methodist movement into a Nonconformist sect or to make common cause with the Dissenters who traced their origin to the Commonwealth Puritans and who had survived the persecution of Nonconformists during the Restoration period. These Dissenters, composed of Independents and Baptists, were now more concerned with intellectual, doctrinal teaching, as emphasised in the importance of the sermon, rather than with evangelisation, having lost some of their former crusading zeal. At first they supported the Methodist revivalists but subsequently they disapproved of the emotional, disorderly scenes which often accompanied revivalist meetings.

In 1741 the Methodists themselves split into two camps: George Whitefield followed the narrow Calvinistic doctrine of predestination, whereby salvation was open only to the elect, whereas John and Charles Wesley rejected this doctrine in favour of salvation being open to all. The Welsh Methodist leaders decided to follow Whitefield and so became Welsh Calvinistic Methodists rather than Wesleyan Methodists, although their friendship with the Wesleys still continued. It was they who had the greatest impact on the Welsh-speaking areas, so that although John Wesley preached in Carmarthen on several occasions, Wesleyanism failed to take root until the early years of the nineteenth century.

John Wesley

Throughout the eighteenth century the Methodist movement remained part of the Established Anglican Church but in 1811 at Llandeilo Fawr the Welsh Cavinistic Methodists ordained their own ministers, and then in the 1820's the final and formal Separation took place so that the Methodists became a Nonconformist denomination. Thus there were now four main Nonconformist denominations: Independents and Baptists (the older Dissenters), Calvinistic Methodists and Wesleyan Methodists. This religious revival led to the establishment of a large number of Chapels in Carmarthen.

NONCONFORMIST CHAPELS:

HEOL AWST CHAPEL
(Lammas Street Chapel)

Heol Awst Independent Chapel was the first Nonconformist chapel to be built in 1726, although the present chapel building dates from 1826. It owes its origin to the work and influence of Stephen Hughes, the Nonconformist 'Apostle of Carmarthenshire'.[1] Stephen Hughes, born in Carmarthen in 1622, was appointed to the livings of Merthyr in 1650 and

Meidrim in 1655 during the Commonwealth period and played an important part in the Puritan movement in Wales. In 1661, after the Restoration of the Monarchy, he was ejected from his living at Meidrim, but, having made his home in Swansea, he continued to preach and teach secretly in Carmarthenshire during the period of religious persecution, visiting and encouraging the scattered Independent congregations. He was deeply concerned to teach the Welsh peasantry the Scriptures in their own language and he devoted many years to publishing Welsh books, including a cheap edition of the Welsh New Testament and selections of the verses of Vicar Prichard. He encouraged and trained young ministers including William Evans of Pencader, the new leader of Dissent after Stephen Hughes' death in 1688.

William Evans moved from Pencader to Carmarthen in 1702-03 to superintend the Independent congregations in the district. He became tutor of the dissenting *Welsh Academy,* later known as the *Presbyterian College,* when it moved to Carmarthen in about 1704. At this time it was located in Priory Street 'where five or six persons are instructed under him for preachers for the Dissenters.' He also taught a few poor children under the auspices of the S.P.C.K. until this Anglican Trust withdrew its support from him because he was thought to be too pronounced a Dissenter. Before the Toleration Act of 1689 Dissenting congregations met in secret places, often private dwellings, but subsequent to the Act meeting-houses were set up. It would seem that William Evans was also minister to a small congregation of Independents meeting in Priory Street at *Yr hen dŷ cwrdd* (The old meeting house), possibly established by Stephen Hughes. (J. Dyfnallt Owen: *Hanes Eglwys Heol Awst,* 1926)

The Independent Dissenters, originating from the Puritans of the Civil War, at first believed in the absolute independence and autonomy of the single congregation in matters of doctrine and discipline, but during the years of repression following the Restoration of 1660, they came closer to, and co-operated with, the Presbyterian Dissenters whose policy was to organise groups of 'churches' into synods and assemblies, bound by a system of representation. As a result of the 1689 Toleration Act, marking the end of religious persecution, a Happy Union was founded in London by the two sects and a Common Fund was established. Although the Union came to an end in 1695, the Common Fund, now managed by the Presbyterians, still continued to help the Independents.

William Evans, leader of the Independents, whose work earned him the title 'God's gift to His People', died in 1718 and was succeeded by the Revd. Thomas Perrot (or Perrott) of Llanybri. Perrot moved with his growing congregation to worship in premises in Lammas Street, where Heol Awst Sunday School now stands. In 1725 John Corrie, a silk merchant, gave the land on which the present chapel stands for a new

Meeting House and this was built in 1726. Through Perrot's efforts it was enlarged before he died in 1733. Thomas Perrot, like William Evans, was also tutor of the Welsh Academy and ran the school which was conducted side-by-side with the Academy. The close association between Lammas Street Chapel and the Academy (Presbyterian College) continued throughout the eighteenth century, for the ministers of the chapel, such as Revd. Samuel Thomas, Dr. Jenkin Jenkins and Revd. David Peter, were also senior tutors of the Academy. At this time there were only two tutors, the senior (often called the Principal) and the junior.

In 1792 David Peter accepted the pastorate of Heol Awst Chapel and under his ministry the chapel was rebuilt and enlarged in 1802 and again rebuilt and enlarged in 1826. He retired in 1835 and died in 1837, having also been the senior tutor of the Presbyterian Academy and head of the attached school from 1795 until his retirement in 1835.[2]

Heol Awst

In 1840 the Academy was separated from the Chapel since the Principal, a Unitarian who had his own small Unitarian congregation, was no longer the minister of Lammas Street chapel. The Academy was moved to premises on the Parade and about this time became known as the Presbyterian College. (*see* Education)

David Peter's successors at Heol Awst Chapel were the Revd. John Breese in 1835 and then Revd. Hugh Jones in 1845. Following a controversy, part of the Lammas Street congregation broke away to form the chapel in Union Street, Heol Undeb, which was built in 1846.

Heol Awst's spacious new Sunday School was built in 1888-9.

HEOL DWR CHAPEL
(Water Street Chapel)

Carmarthen has played an important part in the history of Welsh Calvinistic Methodism, the seat of influence being Heol Dŵr, Water Street Chapel. The early story of this chapel is linked with the life of Peter Williams, Methodist revivalist and publisher of the Welsh Family Bible, known as *Beibl Peter Williams,* in 1770.[3] While still a senior pupil at Carmarthen Grammar School, he was converted to Methodism when listening to George Whitefield preaching in Lammas Street at a meeting of the Methodist Assembly in 1743.

Heol Dŵr

But before this date the early Welsh leaders of the revival, Howel Harris and Daniel Rowland, visited the town on several occasions and by 1740 a Methodist Society had been established in the charge of William John of Glancothi. However, from the latter's reports it would appear that the Society was not a very flourishing one, consisting of twelve weak members in 1743, while in 1747 there were only three or four who were 'lukewarm and torpid'. In the following year there were 'no accessions but three expulsions'. At this time the Society had a meeting room in Goose Street (St. Catherine Street).

In December 1768 Howel Harris preached 'at the New House' while John Wesley wrote on 11th August, 1769, that Peter Williams offered him his 'preaching house', which was apparently called the 'Tabernacle'. In 1770 Howel Harris preached for the third and last time in this chapel, which, he tells us, was in Water Street. From these references it would appear that the chapel building was the property of Peter Williams, who came to live in the town in about 1765 prior to the printing of his Bible by John Ross in 1770. In 1771 a second 'Tabernacle' was built behind the first one, this building again being the property of Peter Williams, who then occupied the first building as a dwelling-house.

Although he had worked for the Methodist cause for many years, Peter Williams was expelled from the Calvinistic Methodist Association in 1791 on the grounds of heresy, his alleged heresy being 'denying the

Water Street Chapel, interior view, 1813

eternal sonship of Christ.'

The Methodist Society now met in Friars' Park but, on Peter Williams' death in 1796, the Society bought the Tabernacle from his widow and in 1797 resumed their services there, the name Tabernacle now being abandoned.

In 1813 a third chapel was built, on the same site as the second, and in 1815 the house and ground of the first Tabernacle (Peter Williams' dwelling house) was bought by the connexion. This house was demolished in 1833 to expose the front of the Chapel which was rebuilt again in 1891. The baptismal register begins in 1798.

All the great preachers of the Calvinistic Methodist Connexion, the present Presbyterian Church of Wales, have officiated at Heol Dŵr, which served as a rendezvous for the Calvinistic Methodists of south-west Wales.

THE WELSH BAPTIST CHAPELS

The history of the Baptists in Carmarthen goes back to Cromwell's time when itinerant preachers, inspired by John Miles, an ardent Baptist who had established a 'mother church' at Ilston in the Gower, visited the town. Early in 1651 several followers were baptised in Carmarthen and a few months later the General Meeting of all the Baptist Churches in South Wales was held in the town. Arrangements were made for the future care of the Carmarthen Baptists - 'the brethren of the Church at Carmarthen . . . . be desired to provide a chamber furnished, together with fire and candles, for the use of our brethren that are to come thither to minister.' However, in the persecution which followed the restoration of Charles II in 1660, Carmarthen Baptists were suppressed and scattered, many being imprisoned. There is no record of their existence for nearly another hundred years, though a tradition says that a number met secretly in a storehouse on the Quay and in small isolated groups in the country. In 1688, however, a Baptist Church was established at Rhydwilym, followed by one at Ffynonhenri near Llanpumpsaint.

PENUEL WELSH BAPTIST CHAPEL

Penuel Chapel is the oldest place of Baptist worship in the town. In 1757 Stephen Davies of Ffynonhenri took a house in Carmarthen as a meeting-place and preached there for three years, but with only limited success. In 1763 he leased the house again with much greater success. The meeting-house was in Old Chapel Yard, Priory Street (opposite the present Chapel). A baptismal service was held in the Towy in 1763 before a large crowd. However, in 1775, differences in personal and theological opinions became apparent among the congregation which resulted in the forming of two sections. The more orthodox section under the recognised and ordained minister, the Revd. David Evans, went to

Penuel Chapel

another place of worship nearby in Priory Street, leaving the other section, under their leader Stephen Davies, to remain in Old Chapel Yard. It was this latter group which purchased, in 1785, a plot of ground, opposite Old Chapel Yard, known as 'Park y Siop', from John Morgan, owner of the Tin Works. Here in 1786 was built Penuel Chapel.

A notable figure in the history of Penuel Chapel was the Revd. Joshua Watkins, minister for forty-seven years. A native of Llanwenarth, he came to Carmarthen in 1793 to assist his friend, the Rev. Morgan John Rhys, to produce his *Cylchgrawn Cymraeg* (Welsh Magazine). Rhys, a young Baptist minister who held advanced views on theological, political and educational matters, had resigned his pastorate at Penygarn, Pontypool, and settled in Carmarthen, where he kept a stationer's shop. His published views, particularly his sympathies with the ideals of the French revolutionaries, got him into trouble and in 1794 he emigrated to America, being accompanied as far as Liverpool by Joshua Watkins. Rhys is reputed to have crossed the American continent ten years previous to Lewis and Clark whose names are recorded as the first to achieve this journey. He also founded the Welsh Emigration Society in the Alleghany mountains.

Joshua Watkins became pastor of Penuel Chapel in 1794 and remained there until his death in 1841, aged 72 years. He is buried in the Chapel yard. For some years he also carried on business as a printer, running a printing press mainly for religious purposes.

As pastor of Penuel Chapel, he enlarged the building in 1797 to double its capacity. At this time, however, the Baptists were undergoing a period of doctrinal crisis, some followers departing from orthodox Calvinism, with the result that in 1799 the Baptist Association of south-west Wales meeting at Salem, Meidrim, expelled Joshua Watkins from the Association for refusing to assent to the 1689 'Confession of Faith'. Other Baptist Chapels in the neighbourhood, in addition to Penuel, were also expelled. These congregations were known as 'General Baptists' and were associated with Unitarian beliefs but, within a few years, the majority returned to orthodox Calvinism. In 1805 Joshua Watkins and Penuel Chapel returned to the fold. From this time onwards, until his death in 1841, Joshua Watkins rendered long and distinguished service to the Baptist cause.

Penuel Chapel was rebuilt in 1851 and again in 1910.

TABERNACLE WELSH BAPTIST CHAPEL

We have already seen that the Baptists had a meeting-place in Old Chapel Yard, Priory Street, as early as 1757 but by 1775 certain theological differences resulted in the more orthodox section of the congregation, under the ordained minister, the Revd. David Evans, departing to another place of worship in Priory Street. In 1782 they moved to *Eglwys y Porthtywyll* (Dark Gate Church) in Dark Gate. Records show that this was an old mercantile house before 1782 and was then leased by the owner, David Morris, to the Baptists who remained there until 1812, when Tabernacle Chapel in Waterloo Terrace was built. This was the result of the efforts of their gifted minister, Titus Lewis, who had come to the Baptist Chapel in Dark Gate in 1800. He was not only a popular preacher and indefatigable worker but was also a prolific writer on theology and published, among other things, a Welsh-English Dictionary, A History of the State and Religion of Great Britain, *(Hanes Wladol a Chrefyddol Prydain Fawr)* and a translation of Dr. Gill's Commentary on the New Testament. Unfortunately, he never lived to see the Tabernacle in Waterloo Terrace, for he died in 1811 at the age of thirty-eight. He was buried in the field on which Tabernacle Chapel was built in the following year. The chapel was rebuilt in 1842 and the schoolroom rebuilt and enlarged in 1878.

(The old mercantile house, mentioned above, which in 1782 became the Baptists' chapel, was used as a monumental workshop for many years during this century. In 1949 it was reconstructed as offices and finally demolished in 1969 to make way for the modern shopping-centre. It stood near Dark Gate in Red Street opposite the entrance to Chapel Street.)

Tabernacle Chapel

Eglwys y Porthtywyll
(Dark Gate Church)
in the early 1900's

WESLEY METHODIST CHURCH

Wesleyan Methodism in Carmarthen can trace its origin to the visits of John Wesley who preached in the town on several occasions. It was at Oxford that John Wesley gathered around him a group of devout scholarly Christians who became known as the *Holy Club* or *Methodists* since they studied Christianity in a methodical way. After experiencing conversion in 1738, his object was to proclaim the Gospel, to promote vital, practical Christianity and to bring God into the souls of men. His evangelical work, covering thousands of miles annually, was undertaken on horseback. While John was a born leader and organiser, his brother Charles was a gifted and indefatigable hymn-writer and both realised the value of hymns for missionary purposes. The Methodist Revival began as an evangelising force within the established Anglican Church and originally there was no intention to separate from this Church.

Although John Wesley visited Carmarthenshire on at least fourteen occasions, Wesleyan Methodism made only limited progress compared with that made by the Welsh Calvinistic Methodists. The latter, under their leaders Howel Harris and Daniel Rowland, followed George Whitefield and the Calvinistic doctrine of predestination, whereby only the elect few were chosen for salvation, whereas the Wesleyan Methodists rejected this doctrine in favour of salvation being open to all. It would appear that John Wesley left the evangelisation of the Welsh-speaking areas to the Welsh leaders, while he preached to the English speakers mainly in the towns.

In 1763 he preached in Carmarthen on the Castle Green 'to a large and attentive audience' and the stone on which he was reported to have stood was later built into the wall of the Wesleyan Chapel in Chapel Street. On 11th August, 1769, John Wesley preached at Peter Williams' Tabernacle in Water Street, for he wrote in his Journal that 'the rain continuing, Mr. Peter Williams offered me his preaching house.' A few years later in 1774 he recorded that he heard a good sermon at St. Peter's Church and that later he preached in the Market Place to 'the largest congregation I ever saw in Wales.'

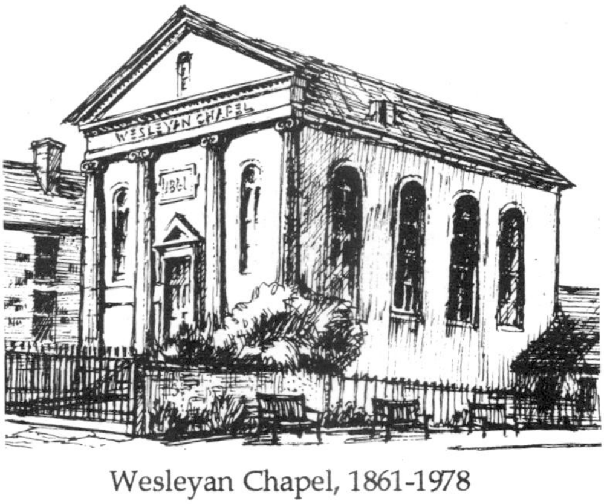

Wesleyan Chapel, 1861-1978

In 1775 the Wesleyans met for worship in a store house in what is now John Street and in 1779 Wesley preached in a room known as *Wesley's Room* in Red Lion Yard. On December

9th, 1804 the first chapel was opened in Chapel Place, later Street, and in the following year Carmarthen was made the head of a new Carmarthen Circuit, having previously been in the Haverfordwest Circuit. In 1821 the chapel was enlarged, but it would seem that the cellar belonged to a local brewery, for the following verse, found in some old papers, was written by one of the congregation:

There are spirits above,
There are spirits below,
There are spirits of love,
There are spirits of woe,
The spirits above are spirits divine,
The spirits below are spirits of wine.

In 1861 the Wesleyan Chapel was rebuilt in classical style, the windows of the old building being incorporated in the Sunday-School room. The interior of the chapel was damaged by fire in 1941, which necessitated further rebuilding and alterations to the 1861 design.

Finally, in 1978 the chapel was demolished to make way for the modern shopping-centre and a completely new Wesley Methodist Church was built nearby. A stone with the words *Wesleyan Chapel 1821* is incorporated at the entrance to the new building.

As far as Welsh Wesleyanism was concerned, a Welsh Society was set up in 1808 and a Carmarthen Welsh Circuit in the following year. But because the Welsh service was elbowed out of the main times of Sunday services, the Welsh Society built a chapel for itself in 1824, after worshipping in the open air for some time. During the later nineteenth century however, expansion ceased, congregations declined and the chapel, called Ebenezer, was abandoned about 1920. The building can still be seen near John Street car-park and adjacent to its old grave-yard on the corner of John Street and Barn Road. Now used for commercial premises, the chapel was for some years occupied by the Myrddin College.

An artist's impression of
Ebenezer Welsh Wesleyan Chapel
before 1920

Prominent in the history of Carmarthen Wesleyanism was the Hughes family, stemming from Hugh Hughes (1778-1855). His son was Dr. John Hughes, an interesting personality in the life of the town, who held almost every public or municipal position in the administration of the Borough and whose stern sense of duty earned him the title of 'Bismarck'. He

English Wesleyan Chapel, 1865

English Congregational Church, 1864

was, however, a tender-hearted person, with a deep love for Methodism and his country, and he was father of the eminent Wesleyan preacher Hugh Price Hughes, who was born at 10 King Street in 1847. Most of Hugh Price Hughes' work was done in London where the West London Mission, now located at Kingsway Hall, stands today as his monument. A powerful orator, he exerted a great influence on the public life of the metropolis and his redemptive work became known throughout the country. He died in 1902, the story of his career being told by his daughter in *The Life of Hugh Price Hughes.*

HEOL UNDEB CHAPEL
(Union Street Chapel)

Union Street Welsh Independent Chapel is an off-shoot of Lammas Street Independent Chapel, being built in 1846 and opened on 27th April, 1847. Its location reflects the town's expansion to the west in the mid nineteenth century.

PARC-Y-FELFED (VELVET) CHAPEL

Parc-y-felfed Unitarian Chapel, Mansel Street, was built in 1849 by Dr. David Lloyd, minister of the small Unitarian congregation at Carmarthen. (Unitarians rejected the doctrine of the Trinity in favour of the Uniperson of God). Dr. Lloyd was also the Principal of the Presbyterian College from 1835-1863, as were most of the subsequent ministers of Parc-y-felfed chapel. (Until 1835 when the Rev. David Peter, pastor of Lammas Street Chapel, retired as the Principal of the Presbyterian College, the latter had always been closely linked with Lammas Street Independent Chapel). Dr. Lloyd took an important part in improving educational facilities in Carmarthen and in providing a public hospital, The Infirmary, and the Cemetery.

ZION CHAPEL

Zion Presbyterian Church of Wales, (the Calvinistic Methodist Connexion), was built in Mansel Street in 1850 by English-speaking Calvinistic Methodists. These originally worshipped at Heol Dŵr Chapel in Water Street and included Mr. George Stephens, governor of Carmarthen gaol, who had been sent down from London to deal with the Rebecca Riots, together with some of the Militia then stationed at Carmarthen Barracks. In 1951 Zion Chapel was extensively renovated.

ENGLISH CONGREGATIONAL CHURCH

The foundation stone of Lammas Street English Congregational Church was laid by Mr. H. O. Wills of Bristol on 3rd July, 1861; it was opened on 21st May, 1862. The building was designed by Poulton and Woodman, Reading and built by Douglas and Sons, Llanelli.

Bethania Chapel

Heol Undeb

Zion Chapel

Parc-y-felfed Chapel

Priordy Chapel

English Baptist Church

ENGLISH BAPTIST CHURCH

Supported by Penuel and Tabernacle Welsh Baptists, Lammas Street English Baptist Church was built for English-speaking workers who had come to Carmarthen with the development of the railway and commerce. The church was opened on 21st June, 1870. Designed in Greek classical style by Carmarthen architect George Morgan of 24, King Street, the building features an attractive portico supported on four Corinthian columns and is listed as being of special architectural interest.

PRIORDY CHAPEL

Priordy Welsh Congregational Chapel, Priory Street was built in 1875 and opened on 28th May, 1876, the foundation stone being laid by Mrs. John Jones Jenkins. In 1971 the centenary of the meeting of the original congregation 'somewhere in Tanerdy' was celebrated.

BETHANIA CHAPEL

Bethania Welsh Calvinistic Methodist Chapel, Priory Street, is an off-shoot of Heol Dŵr Chapel and was built by the Welsh Calvinistic Methodists and opened on 9th September, 1902.

CHURCHES OF THE NINETEENTH CENTURY:

ST. DAVID'S CHURCH
(Eglwys Dewi Sant)

The response of the Established Church to the religious revival, as marked by the growth of Nonconformity and the building of chapels, was the foundation of St. David's Church in 1835 on Picton Terrace, at the west end of town. The proposal to build an additional church to that of St. Peter's was made in 1823, and the foundation stone of what was to be called St. Paul's Church was laid on the site of the present Christ Church on November 28th, 1824, the design by John Nash. However, difficulties arose over the ownership of the site and the foundation stone was taken up again. Eventually, a new site was obtained on Picton Terrace and the foundation stone of St. David's Church was laid by Bishop Jenkinson on 27th May, 1835. The church was opened on 19th January, 1837 and consecrated by Bishop Thirlwall on 3rd February, 1841. The architect was R. K. Penson. A new St. David's Parish was also formed out of St. Peter's Parish. By an order of the Queen in Council dated November 10th, 1843, the Parish of St. Peter was divided into three districts: St. Peter's, St. David's and Llanllwch. Subsequently, in 1857, these were constituted separate parishes.

There are two unusual features about St. David's Church. The first is the large battlemented tower which appears to be separate from the

St. David's Church

Penson's original design for St. David's Church

main body of the church. This is because the original building was constructed north to south with the main entrance through the tower. However the church was found to be too small and in the 1850's the Incumbent, the Revd. David Archard Williams, arranged the building of the present clerestoried nave with aisles and porch running west to east, and therefore at right angles to the older building. Further modifications were made in the 1880's when the old north-south nave was converted into the present chancel as a memorial to the Ven. Archdeacon D. Archard Williams.

The second feature is the very large west window, which is one of the largest in any parish church in Wales, and which is complimented by the modern stained-glass of the east window.

CHRIST CHURCH

Christ Church, Lammas Street, is the English Church of St. David's Parish which was built during the incumbency of the Revd. D. Archard Williams to provide services for the English speakers in his parish. The foundation stone was laid by Dr. Protheroe of Llandeilo on 2nd September, 1867, and the church was consecrated and opened by Bishop Connop Thirlwall on 21st September, 1869. One of the leading supporters of the new church was Col. Scott who had been sent down to deal with the Rebecca Riots and who became the first Chief Constable of Carmarthenshire. Some years ago the unusual pitched slated roof of the tower, having become troublesome, was removed and a more usual battlemented parapet was substituted.

ST. MARY'S CATHOLIC CHURCH

St. Mary's Roman Catholic Church, Union Street, was built to a

Christ Church

St. Mary's Catholic Church

Gothic design by Mr. Charles Hansom of Clifton and erected between April 1851 and August 1852 at the expense of Miss Katherine Frances Richardson, daughter of General Richardson and sister of Lady Straubensee.

The first priests-in-charge had established a mass-centre in 1851, catering in those days mainly for the needs of Irish immigrants, as the indigenous Roman Catholics were few in number. There were several changes of Rector in the early years, all of whom travelled widely to a scattered congregation.

In 1889 the Passionist Order[4] accepted the charge of the Carmarthen mission and their priests were to remain as Rectors of St. Mary's for 97 years. The Passionist Order was a body devoted to mission work and to establishing their faith in areas that were thought to be 'difficult'. In 1986, when they withdrew from St. Mary's, their place was taken by priests appointed by the Bishop of Menevia.

The work of the Church was assisted by the Religious Sisters who, driven from Brittany by persecution, arrived in 1903. Initially supporting themselves by private tuition, they soon opened a small school and after several moves finally settled in St. Winifred's Convent in Picton Place. The first Sisters, who belonged to the Order of the Daughters of the Holy Ghost, provided the head-teachers and teachers of St. Mary's school for many years until, in 1969, they withdrew from Carmarthen and their place was taken by an Order of Sisters of the Cross and Passion.

To the right of the steps leading to the church entrance is a medieval holy water stoup standing on a modern shaft. The shaft is inscribed 'Holy water stoup from St. Barbara's Chapel, Carmarthen, about the year 1300. Given by E. Spurrell, Esq. Erected by W. Davies, Sculptor.' The exact location of St. Barbara's Chapel, a small chantry chapel, is unknown but it is thought to have stood somewhere near the junction of Monument Hill and Job's Well Road.

ST. JOHN'S CHURCH
(Eglwys Sant Ioan)

St. John's Church, Priory Street, dedicated to St. John the Evangelist, is the Welsh Church of St. Peter's Parish. The foundation stone was laid on 25th June, 1889 by Bishop Alfred. G. Edwards of St. Asaph who had been vicar of St. Peter's Church at the time of his elevation to that See and who was chiefly responsible for organising the project and plans of the new Welsh church. Prior to the building of St. John's, the Welsh congregation had held services in Priory Street National School which was originally called St. Peter's 'School-Church' because it was built for two purposes: as a place of worship for the Welsh-speaking parishioners and as a day-school for the parish.

The ceremony for the laying of the foundation stone of St. John's Church was attended by the Mayor and corporation, the Principal, tutors and students of Trinity College, children of Priory Street school, many robed clergy, St. Peter's choir and the Fire Brigade. The service was conducted chiefly in Welsh.

Underneath the foundation stone was placed a bottle containing copies of the Journal and the Welshman for June 1889, St. Peter's magazine for June and coins of the current year.

The plans for St. John's Church were drawn up by Messrs. Middleton, Prothero and Phillott, architects of Cheltenham and Newport. The contract price was £2,300, Mr. Thomas Collins of Tewkesbury being the builder.

The architects were instructed to build a church to accommodate about 300 people but the site, which cost £75, was limited and so the plan was kept simple in design and detail. The style throughout was late perpendicular, the plan consisting of a clerestoried nave and chancel of the same height with a turret for two bells over the chancel arch, the north chancel serving as an organ chamber.

St. John's Church was consecrated and opened on Tuesday, June 15th, 1890 by the Bishop of St. Davids. Bishop Edwards of St. Asaph preached the sermon, the service being entirely in Welsh.

St. John's Church

Although St. John's was the last of the Anglican churches to be built in town, its dedication recalls the nearby Priory of St. John the Evangelist, founded in 1125. The Priory had itself absorbed the earlier Celtic Welsh church established there well before the Norman conquest.

ALL SAINTS, LIME GROVE

This small church was originally the Gaol Chapel, having stood within its walls on Castle Hill. It was removed, stone-by-stone, during the demolition of the Gaol and rebuilt as a chapel for the High School, behind their classrooms in Lime Grove Mansion. It was dedicated to St. Mary on June 8th, 1939. With the closing of the High School the Chapel passed into the care of St. David's Parish and was renamed All Saints. It re-opened for worship on October 21st, 1966, but is now no longer in use and has become derelict.

THE QUAKERS' MEETING HOUSE
(Now demolished)

The Society of Friends of Truth, usually called Quakers, was founded by George Fox in the mid seventeenth century. Quakers held that Christ's teaching was paramount and that man could experience the sense of the Divine and the direct working of Christ in the soul - the Inner Light - so making ordained ministers and consecrated buildings irrelevant. They worshipped without a set form of service and without any appointed minister, believing that God would use and inspire any worshipper as minister. The name 'Quaker' is thought to come from the spiritual trembling sometimes experienced at their religious meetings. They valued the moral qualities of simplicity, purity and truthfulness but their refusal to take oaths or pay tithes and their defiance of civil and spiritual authorities led to persecution under both the Puritan Commonwealth and the Royalist restoration.

When George Fox himself and his Welsh convert, John ap John, visited Carmarthen in 1657 they were given a very rough reception by the populace and were forced to ride quickly out of town. Apparently the County town would have none of the unconventional ways of the early Quakers!

However, by 1700, there was a Society of Friends meeting at Llanllwch, for in that year they had to vacate their Meeting House there because they were unable to pay the rent. At what date they first met in Carmarthen, or where they met, is not known but in 1725 the yearly meeting of the Friends in Wales was held at Carmarthen 'in a large warehouse at the Key'. In 1746 a Meeting House was built in Lammas Street, thanks to the efforts of Thomas Morgan 'Quaker and Malster'.This Meeting House was located in Quakers' Yard, the site of which is now reached through a narrow alleyway alongside the Midland Bank in Lammas Street. Reports of 1778 and 1787 show that 'large meetings' were held there, but towards the end of the eighteenth century numbers appear to have decreased, for in 1793 John Grubb speaks of the 'neat, pretty Meeting house', yet he found 'none of our Society in the town.' In 1807 there was only one surviving trustee and new trustees were added.

It is not known when the Quakers ceased to hold regular meetings but in 1820 the Meeting House was let to the Wesleyans while their own Chapel was being enlarged. In 1831 the house was sold to become a school conducted by Edward Donnard Evans, whose son Alcwyn, the Carmarthen antiquary, continued it until 1887. Between 1834 and 1849 the Meeting house was also used temporarily by the Unitarians, until they had built Parc-y-felfed Chapel in Mansel Street.

Until recently the site of the Quakers' Meeting House was identified by a stone tablet in a wall in Quakers Yard adjacent to a house known as The Retreat. The inscription read: *This wall and Pine End is the property of the People called Quakers, 1777.* This stone tablet has now been placed in the Museum.

The old burial ground also lies in the vicinity of Quakers' Yard where, in the past, human bones have been disturbed in building operations.

1 See *Some Carmarthen Personalities: Teachers and Preachers - Stephen Hughes.*

2 *Ibid - Revd. David Peter.* Also see *Education - The Welsh Academy.*

3 *Ibid - Revd. Peter Williams.*

4 Alan Randall, *The Passionists at Carmarthen, 1889-1986,* 1986.

Nott Square today

Nott Square in 1939

- 13 -

THE EIGHTEENTH AND NINETEENTH CENTURIES:

TOWN DEVELOPMENT

In the early part of the eighteenth century certain improvements in town amenities were made by the Corporation, such as the purchase of a fire engine in 1712, the construction of a conduit on the Common at Waundew to supply the town with water, also in 1712, and the repair of 'the little Kay leading from the ducking-stool to the old Water-gate, long since fallen into decay' in 1722. (This little Kay [Quay] was probably sited on the Wynveth Stream which was navigable at high tide as far as Dark Gate.) In 1723 £100 was laid out towards casting the bells of St. Peter's church, while in 1724 the bridge and town gaol were repaired out of the town rents. The Mayor's chapel in St. Peter's church was repaired in 1732 and in 1740 the Corporation agreed that the well and bathing-house, called Job's Well, should be repaired for the benefit of the public.

It was from the middle of the eighteenth century, however, that an increasing interest was taken in re-developing the town centre and in making improvements. In 1765 the Tudor Guildhall was in a very ruinous state and voluntary subscriptions were solicited towards erecting a new hall, while the Mayor ordered that '£500 be raised as expeditiously as possible by and out of the estates of the borough.' In 1766 the old Guildhall was demolished and the Mayor's Courts were removed to the Bumper Coffee Rooms until a more suitable building should be available. The meat shambles (butchers' stalls), which were around the Guildhall, were removed to nearby Clos Mawr, while other goods were removed to the medieval market Cross in Upper Market Street (now Nott Square).[1]

The Borough Order Book records that a temporary Hall was erected in November 1766 but then came a long delay before the present Guildhall was finally completed in 1777. It would appear that the reason for such delay was the Corporation's lack of finances, despite voluntary subscriptions and the mortgaging of borough property. In the Order or Minute Book the names Guild Hall, Shire Hall and Town Hall are all used at various times to describe the present Guildhall.

The Spilman Street Gate, near St. Peter's Church, was removed in 1768, reflecting the increasing amount of traffic. The narrow arched gateway was an impediment to wheeled vehicles, such as stage coaches, and to traffic to and from the recently established iron and tin works.

The stones were used to erect a 'conveniency' for the Free School.

In 1770, Quay Street, the busy thoroughfare from the Quay to Guildhall Square, was paved and lowered; in 1771 a new chapel (Heol Dwr) was built in Water Street, indicating housing development in this area, and in 1777 the bridge was widened by six feet. To enable townspeople to enjoy the Towy valley scenery, The Parade was constructed by public subscription in 1782 and subsequently in 1800 planted with trees.

In the town centre (now Nott Square) the medieval market cross was taken down in 1783 and a new covered market, built upon twelve pillars, was put in its place. This market was demolished in 1846 when a new market-hall was built on the present market site. Nott's monument was erected in the square in 1851.

St. Peter's Parish Church was given a new roof and ceiling in 1785 by the architect John Nash, while in the same year the first Baptist Chapel, Penuel, was built in Priory Street. In 1789 a new County Gaol was commenced by John Nash on the castle site, sweeping away the castle prison and the last remains of the castle interior. When the County Gaol was completed in 1792 the Prisoners' Gate (i.e. the East Gate with the town gaol above) between King Street and Nott Square was removed. At the same time the White Gate, at the other end of King Street by Conduit

The Old Market Place (Nott Square) showing conduit and stocks
Built in 1783 on the site of the Market Cross and demolished in 1846

Lane, was taken down.

On September 3rd, 1792 the first meeting of the Carmarthen Commissioners of Paving and Lighting was held; the result was that in the following year, 1793, King Street was paved with stone flags, followed by Dark Gate in 1797 and Spilman Street and Lammas Street in 1802. Iron water-pipes were laid down, on trial, in King Street in 1793 and then two years later in Lammas Street.

A major step was taken in 1796 when the medieval Wynveth Gate (Dark Gate) and the nearby Cock Mill were removed and the Wynveth Stream was covered over to form a wagon road, now Blue Street, to the Quay. This was to enable traffic to go directly from the Quay to a new market which was in the process of being sited in the Backway (the present Red Street), thus avoiding the congestion of Quay Street, Guildhall Square and Dark Gate. This new market was opened in 1800 chiefly for the sale of meat, poultry and cheese.

Meanwhile, in 1797, the original Queen Elizabeth Grammar School (on the site of the present Infirmary forecourt) in Priory Street had been replaced by a new school building.

With regard to lighting the town, in 1800 eighteen oil lamps were provided and four years later fifty more were ordered.

In 1802 Heol Awst (Lammas Street) Independent chapel was rebuilt and enlarged, the first meeting-house or chapel having been built as early as 1726. The Borough Order Book records on 14th January, 1803, that the Corporation subscribed £400 towards building a new Town Gaol. (The old one over the Prisoners' Gate had been removed in 1792.)

In 1804 an important new road, Castle Hill, was constructed from the bridge to Spilman Street, allowing through traffic to by-pass the town centre. In the same year the Quay was extended downstream to the Pot-house and in 1808-09 the Quay was built up to the bridge.

The first English Wesleyan chapel was opened on December 9th, 1804, in Chapel Street, indicating housing development in this area, just outside the medieval town wall. In the same year iron water-pipes, already laid in King Street and Lammas Street 'on trial', were laid down in other town streets replacing earlier wood and lead piping.

In 1805 a Poor-house, later converted into the Work-house in 1821, was built at the foot of Penlan Hill. Also in 1805 the Council voted £60

> 'to be expended in making a good road from the Dark Gate to the Quay.'

This was to improve the earlier wagon road covering the Wynveth Stream and so making what is now Blue Street. In the same year the Council ordered that

> 'the Mayor employ a Superintendent with a yearly salary of £5 5s. and also twelve men at a salary of £1 1s. each yearly to take care of, and work, the fire engines and that the Mayor pay them, in cases of fire, sums as he may deem proper.'

Castle Hill, constructed in 1804

It would appear that fire precautions were very necessary, for in 1811 three hundred barrels of gunpowder, enough to wipe out the town centre, were moved out of the castle area and a new magazine was ordered to be built. This was completed in 1813 near Pen Llwyn y Witch (later Penllwyn Park) and is now the site of the Barracks. It is marked Armoury Depot on John Wood's map of 1834.

In 1808 Mr. John Baile, silver-smith, was paid £133 'being the expenses in procuring a new clock for the Borough.' It was placed in front of the Guild Hall.

The new Borough or Town Gaol, as distinct from the County Gaol on Castle Hill, was completed in 1810 on the 'Old Bowling Green', later the John Street/Cambrian Place area. A record of 1816, probably referring to the Borough gaol, states:

> 'Two strong doors be immediately provided, together with wrought iron bars for the windows, at the expense of the Corporation, for the Lock-up House.'

The year 1812 saw the building of Tabernacle Baptist Chapel in Tabernacle Row, later called Waterloo Terrace, pointing to housing development in this area to the north of Carmarthen.

An important innovation occurred in 1822 when the gas works were built and the town was first lit with gas on September 25th. There were eighty public lamps and several shops were lit with gas. In celebration of the event, the Mayor and inhabitants walked in procession through the streets.

In 1824 a stretch of marshland called the *Wide Ocean,* where now are Red Street, John Street and the Market, was drained, so allowing more land for town development. The Welsh Wesleyan Chapel was built here in 1824 and though no longer used as a chapel, the building can still be seen at the entrance to John Street car-park.

The foundation stone of the first Picton's Monument was laid in 1825 at the top of Picton Terrace, an indication of the town's expansion to the west beyond Lammas Street. The Regency-period and early Victorian housing of Picton Terrace represents the prosperous middle-class housing which was then developing outside the town centre. So too does the mid-Victorian housing along The Parade and Esplanade.

In May 1835 the foundation stone of St. David's Church, Picton Terrace, was laid and the church opened in 1837, showing the growth of population in this area. In 1857 the Parishes of St. David and Llanllwch were formed out of the original St. Peter's Parish.

Development in Union Street and Mansel Street resulted in the building of Heol Undeb Chapel in 1846, Parc-y-felfed Chapel in 1849, Zion Chapel in 1850 and St. Mary's Roman Catholic Church in 1851. The west end of Lammas Street saw the foundation of the English Congregational Church in 1861 and Christ Church in 1867, while at the east end of the street the English Baptist Chapel was opened in 1870. By the end of the century Priordy Chapel, 1875, and St. John's Church, 1889, had been built in Priory Street.

Meanwhile another development in the public building programme had been taking place.

THE 1846 MARKET

In order to put an end to the centuries-old custom of goods being sold in various parts of the town, a completely new market was built in 1846 on Parc-y-felfed (velvet) fields, its central feature being a picturesque clock-tower. (This clock-tower, the only remaining relic of the 1846 market, has been restored and preserved as a feature in the new large market opened in 1981 on the same original market site.)

The 1846 market was opened on Saturday, 1st August, when for the first time in hundreds of years provisions ceased to be sold in Guildhall Square and Upper Market Street (Nott Square). A record states:

The Market Clock Tower

The Market Gates (demolished in 1939)

'the streets were comparatively deserted and everything outside the market walls wore a most quiet appearance.'

But inside the market-hall a variety of goods was now on sale under one roof. (Nott's Monument was erected in 1851 on the site of the covered, twelve-pillared, market demolished in 1846.)

Following the opening of the market, a cattle mart and new slaughter-house were built, just across St. Catherine Street in Pentrefelin fields, an indication of the importance of farming to Carmarthen's economy. However, the new mart did not stop the horse fairs, such as John Brown's fair, being held in Dark Gate, Lammas Street and Priory Street, a practice continuing into the early part of the twentieth century.

SCHOOLS [2]

In the field of education too, new buildings were being erected which added another dimension to the townscape. In 1848 the South Wales Training College (Trinity College) was opened, the first teachers' training college in Wales. In the following year the National and Practising School (the Model) was opened in St. Catherine Street, where the College students received their practical training. At first the Model School was limited to boys but in 1851 the girls' school was opened, to be followed in 1857 by the infants' school. Meanwhile, a new Lancasterian school for boys and girls was built in 1850 at Pentrepoth (the forerunner of the 1896 Pentrepoeth school) and this was followed in 1860 by the infants' school. The 1860's also saw the opening of St. Mary's Catholic School in Mill Street, Bridge Street and Towyside National Schools and Priory Street (St. Peter's) National School, the latter being built in 1869. Quay Street School was built in 1883 and a new Johnstown School in 1894, an indication of expansion in this area. To the north of the town, in Wellfield Road, an area also undergoing development at this time, the Diocesan High School for Girls was founded in 1879, while a new Queen Elizabeth Boys' Grammar School was built in 1884. The Carmarthen County Girls' School was built on an adjacent site in 1899.

To cope with the increasing social and welfare needs of the community, the second half of the nineteenth century saw the building of a number of social institutions such as the Assembly Rooms, the Infirmary and the Joint Counties Lunatic Asylum (now St. David's Hospital). Land was also allocated for Carmarthen cemetery and park.

THE ASSEMBLY ROOMS

The Assembly Rooms or Public Rooms, which played a large part in the social and cultural life of the town, were built by public subscription and opened in King Street on 21st November, 1854. The Lyric cinema was subsequently built on part of the site. The Assembly Rooms comprised a large hall, seating 600 persons, licensed for stage plays, operas and musical concerts, together with other rooms for lectures and a billiard room. Part of the building was occupied by the Carmarthen Literary and Scientific Institution which provided a lending library, reading room, supplied with newspapers and periodicals, and a games room for chess and draughts. A combination of instruction and amusement was the keynote.

The main part of the Assembly Rooms was converted into a cinema for silent films in 1918 and called the Lyric.[3]

THE CARMARTHENSHIRE INFIRMARY

'Founded 1847. Built 1858. Supported by voluntary contributions.'

The above inscription is lettered on the front of the Infirmary in Priory Street. However, it was first resolved to found the Carmarthenshire Infirmary at a meeting held on 24th October, 1846, during the mayoralty of Mr. Thomas Charles Morris. Subsequently, various committee meetings were held and public subscriptions and contributions requested. At a meeting of subscribers in early July 1847 it was resolved that the Borough Gaol in Cambrian Place, which the Town Council placed at the disposal of the subscribers, rent free for as long as they should require it, be fitted up as a temporary infirmary, with £200 allowed for alterations.

It was originally intended that the Barracks on Picton Terrace should be fitted out for the admission of infirmary patients, since there were plans for building new barracks near Pontgarreg, Johnstown, but the scheme had to be abandoned because the proposed new barracks were never built.

The election of officers for the new Infirmary took place at a meeting of subscribers in mid July, 1847, when a president (Lord Dynevor), vice-presidents, trustees and a house committee were elected. Recommendations for alterations to the Borough Gaol were passed and it was resolved that the first intake of patients should number twelve. This number rapidly increased, for the House Committee's third annual report of 1850 stated:

> 'This institution continues to increase in efficiency and usefulness as evidenced by the large number of patients who have been admitted to participate of its benefits during the past year . . . . . it has provided treatment for both in-door and out-door patients. Last year (1849) in-door patients numbered 78; out-door numbered 542; total = 620 patients.'

The Infirmary fund received money from all sections of the public - from annual subscriptions, donations and church and chapel collections. By the spring of 1857 the building committee was able to ask for tenders for a new Infirmary. The tender of £3,260 from William Lewis, contractor, was accepted. The foundation stone was laid by Bishop Connop Thirlwall on 14th May, 1857 on the site formerly occupied by the old

The Infirmary, 1861

Joint Counties Asylum, 1874

grammar school.

On the 1st July, 1858, the Infirmary was opened. It was

> 'a handsome and commodious building erected to contain between 30 and 40 in-patients and was well deserving the support and interest of a humane and benevolent public.'

The Infirmary continued on a voluntary basis until 1948 when the National Health Service was born and the state took over the control of all such hospital services.

WEST WALES GENERAL HOSPITAL, GLANGWILI

Today the Infirmary is part of the West Wales General Hospital, a prestigious and highly sophisticated complex built on an extensive site at Glangwili. At the end of the 1939-45 war Glangwili Hospital was little more than a collection of Nissen huts which had been constructed to provide hospital accommodation for the American Army, in anticipation of casualties following the invasion of Europe. In the event, the large number of casualties never materialised and the huts were quickly surrounded with barbed wire and used as a prisoner-of-war camp until hostilities ceased. In the years since, the huts have been gradually replaced with the present buildings and the hospital has been transformed into an ultra-modern general hospital with many specialist departments.

ST. DAVID'S HOSPITAL

St. David's Hospital was opened in November 1865 as the Joint Counties Lunatic Asylum for Carmarthenshire, Cardiganshire and Pembrokeshire. The original building cost £24,950. Occupying an eminent position in about 46 acres, the hospital was built by Mr. Pollard of Taunton to hold about 600 patients, officers and attendants. In 1895 it was enlarged by the addition of a new female hospital, a special hospital for infectious diseases, a new chapel seating 500 and various workshops and farm buildings. All the stone was quarried and the work done by the staff and patients of the hospital, to the design of Mr. Ernest Collier. In 1895 there were 286 male and 271 female patients.

Ward blocks and ancillary buildings have been added since the nineteenth century and the hospital now treats many out-patients as well as residents. Today there is an increasing emphasis on the rehabilitation of patients and their resettlement within the community and the outcome of this approach to the care of the mentally ill has been a reduction in the number of resident patients, together with increased provision for local community care and services.

THE CEMETERY

In July 1850 there was a recommendation to close St. Peter's churchyard for burials and to find another burial ground. The Borough Council allocated ten acres as a cemetery in 1853, reflecting the increasing need for burial facilities to cope with the expanding population. In April 1855 the Carmarthen Burial Board requested tenders for building two chapels, one Anglican and one Nonconformist, boundary walls and entrance gates at their new cemetery. In 1856 the cemetery was consecrated by Bishop Connop Thirlwall, and by a singular coincidence the first person to be buried there was James Brown, the parish clerk, in May 1856.

St. Peter's churchyard was closed for burials in 1856.

THE PARK

The twelve acre site was purchased by the Borough Council in 1899 and opened on Easter Monday 1900. It features a neat Victorian bandstand, a cycle track, rugby pitch and grandstand. More recent Gorsedd Stones mark the site of the National Eisteddfod Proclamation ceremony in 1973.

By the end of the nineteenth century town development had produced many features of the present townscape, presenting a very different picture from that of Carmarthen at the beginning of the eighteenth century.

Carmarthen Park Bandstand

CARMARTHENSHIRE ANTIQUARIAN SOCIETY
AND COUNTY MUSEUM

Although these do not belong strictly to the nineteenth century, their founders belonged to that century in spirit and character.

The Carmarthenshire Antiquarian Society and Field Club was founded in April 1905 to promote the study, collection and conservation of the County's history and archaeology. The Society's first officials were Mr. G. G. Treharne, M.A., President, a Carmarthenshire man who had practised as a solicitor in London; the Rev. M. H. Jones, Secretary; and Mr. Walter Spurrell, Treasurer.

Each week the Society published a column of notes, articles and reports of researches relating to the County's history in a newspaper called the *Welshman.* Twice a year these contributions were collected together and re-issued as a volume of *Transactions.* The *Transactions* proved extremely popular being a mine of information on all aspects of Carmarthenshire life: families, houses, industry, antiquities and archaeological finds. They continued until 1939, to be followed in 1941 by a new series called *The Carmarthenshire Antiquary.* This *Antiquary* still flourishes today as the annual Journal of the present Carmarthenshire Antiquarian Society.

The Honorary Secretary of the Society from 1906 until his death in 1939 was the indefatigable George Eyre Evans (1857-1939); in fact, in many ways he was the Society, being the editor and a prodigious contributor to the *Transactions* and the organiser of the Society's Field Days.[4]

The Carmarthen Museum was founded in 1908 by the Carmarthenshire Antiquarian Society whose initial collection is the basis of material in the present County Museum. George Eyre Evans made a great contribution to the founding of the Museum for he not only donated several hundred fascinating items himself, he also maintained the Accession Register, catalogued the collection, purchased, persuaded or cajoled people to donate interesting objects, acted as secretary and public relations officer and gave lectures to encourage a general interest in antiquities. Although he must be regarded as the creator of the museum, he was helped in his work by others, chief of whom was Ernest Vale Collier, an enthusiastic member of the Antiquarian Society and its Director from 1920 to 1932, who made many valuable contributions to the growing collection.[5]

The first museum was established at the rear of Spurrell's printing works at 37 King Street but then moved to a larger room on the premises of Messrs. Brigstocke at 54 King Street.

The *Transactions* record the donation of innumerable antiquities, not only from Carmarthenshire and Wales, but from places as far away as Tibet, Siam and Egypt. The Museum owes its collection of Egyptian artefacts to Ernest Harold Jones (1877-1911), son of William Jones, Principal of the Carmarthen School of Art. Harold, an old boy of 'The Gram', assisted in many Egyptian excavations in the Valley of the Kings, working as an archaeological illustrator. The Museum's Egyptian collection includes some of his original water-

E. Harold Jones

colours, drawings and photographs. Persistent ill-health resulted in his early death in 1911 and he was buried at Luxor in Egypt. His obituary, written by George Eyre Evans, included the line:

Towy's Quay has given a son to Luxor's Sand
and both in him are joined.

The Museum's collection was enhanced in 1919 by the gift of gold antiquities, including a Roman gold chain and pendant, found near the Roman gold mines at Dolaucothi. They were the gift of Lady Hills-Johnes in memory of her husband, Sir James Hills-Johnes, V.C. Other gold objects found at Dolaucothi are now in the British Museum.

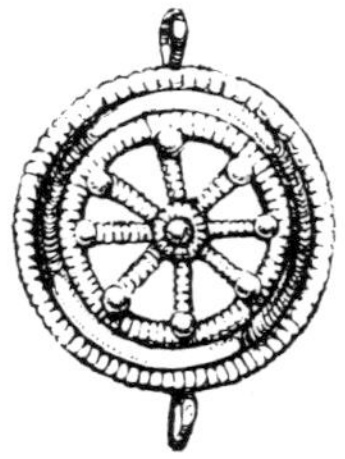

The Dolaucothi Gold Pendant

In 1920 the Antiquarian Society, together with the Museum, moved to 5 Quay Street, a house generously placed at its disposal by its President, Sir Owen Philipps, M.P., subsequently Lord Kylsant. The Society's library, stocked with many volumes and manuscripts donated over the years, and its reading room were also established here. In 1923 the Museum was affiliated with the National Museum of Wales. Visitors as well as gifts were increasing and by 1931 the Society was able to purchase its premises in Quay Street. Soon the problem was one of accommodation and in 1935 No.4 Quay Street was purchased. In 1937 the Museum had 3,500 visitors.

With 1939 came the death of George Eyre Evans and the bleak years of war. In 1940 the Museum was handed over to the Carmarthenshire County Council who became responsible for maintaining its exhibits and library. After the end of the Second World War, lack of funds prevented any development work taking place. The year 1975, however, saw the Museum's removal from Quay Street to the Bishop's Palace, Abergwili, under the auspices of Dyfed County Council. Subsequent years have seen the opening of new galleries and display areas, the housing of exhibitions, and many new acquisitions. The Museum's collections have been largely built up over the years through public bequests, loans and donations. In May 1989 the *Friends of Carmarthen Museum* was founded with the object of promoting the Museum's work and encouraging contact with schools and the public in general.

THE BISHOP'S PALACE

Before housing the County Museum, the Bishop's Palace, Abergwili, had been the residence of the bishops of St. Davids since the Reformation, since when it had undergone several restorations. Before that it was the site of a collegiate church founded by Bishop Beck or Bek in the late thirteenth century.

During the episcopate of Bishop Richard Davies (1561-81) the Palace

The Bishop's Palace

became a centre for clerics, scholars and men of literature. The Bishop invited William Salesbury, a notable Welsh scholar, to stay at Abergwili while they co-operated in translating the New Testament and the Book of Common Prayer into Welsh. After two years' work, in 1567, the translations were produced. The Welsh New Testament was largely the work of William Salesbury, while the Welsh Prayer Book was largely the work of Richard Davies.

The two books were printed in London 'at the costs and charges of Humphrey Toy'. In 1567 Salesbury stayed at Toy's residence in St. Paul's Churchyard in order to supervise the printing. Humphrey Toy was a prominent London bookseller, member of the Stationers' Company and nephew of the Carmarthen Humphrey Toy. The latter was a wealthy cloth merchant, property owner, mayor of the town in 1557 and public benefactor. It is uncertain which of the Toys actually paid the costs of printing, but it was probably the nephew in London.

The work done at Abergwili paved the way for William Morgan's translation of the Bible into Welsh in 1588.

1 See *Civic Dignity - The Guildhall.*

2 See *Education.*

3 See *18th and 19th Centuries - Social Conditions: Cinemas and Theatres.*

4 See *Some Carmarthen Personalities - Local Historians.*

5 *Ibid.*

- 14 -

THE EIGHTEENTH AND NINETEENTH CENTURIES:

SOCIAL CONDITIONS

Throughout the eighteenth century Carmarthen was still the most populous town in Wales but, by the middle of the nineteenth century, she was outstripped in size and population by her rapidly expanding industrial neighbours, Llanelli and Swansea. In 1801 Carmarthen's population was 5,500; in 1851 just over 10,000, and it remained at this figure for the rest of the century.

Carmarthen lay too far to the west of the South Wales coalfield to experience the industrialization of her neighbours. Her industrial enterprises were mainly service industries for the surrounding agricultural region. Carmarthen's rôle was that of a County town and an administrative, agricultural and commercial centre.

A valuable glimpse of Carmarthen and its neighbourhood in 1788 is given in a letter written by a young lady from Bath. She wrote:

> 'It is impossible for me to convey any idea of the beauty of the country . . . the rich scenery and the fertility of the soil . . . the abundance of fine fruit, such as apples and pares in every field and hedge, also full of nutts. Our coachman with his whip, as we rode under the branches of the trees, used to bring down such a load of apples and pares; and the footman would get off his horse and fill his pockets.
>
> 'I was surprised to hear many of the poor children speaking such good English. I often conversed with them . . . They have no provincial accent, therefore I was never more gratified to hear them talk.
>
> 'I was much pleased with a custom I observed the inhabitants had of every Saturday night going with flowers and plants, and strewing the graves of every relative with flowers.'

Her impressions, however, were not all complimentary and she had decided views on the old custom of carrying babies in shawls.

> 'The women look very sallow and unhealthy, and swaddle their children up in a kind of blanket fastened about them that they may have their hands at liberty to work. It makes the children poor ricketty things, and they can seldom walk alone until they are two or three years old.
>
> 'The working men are also poor looking creatures; they employ themselves in fishing, carrying their boats on their backs until they get to the water. As we rode out we often saw the women taking snuff, which they are dyed with, and seem quite indolent.'

The reference to the standard of English spoken by Carmarthen people in those days is not an isolated opinion. Iolo Morganwg, in his tour through the town in 1796, echoed the common opinion that the people were the 'politest in Wales' and said:

> 'The inhabitants speak very good English. The common people speak much better English than what we hear from those of the same rank in any town in England, London not excepted. The reason is that the English was not introduced into Wales till about the time of Elizabeth, when the language was nearly, if not quite, at its most pure degree of improvement . . .'

According to other tourist information, the local farmers living in the rich soil of the Towy valley enjoyed a higher degree of material comfort than those in the northern hilly regions of the country. Both farmers and their wives attended market on horseback and it was considered an undoubted sign of poverty to walk on foot to market. Some tourists expressed admiration at the easy way in which the people, even old ladies, rode their horses or ponies.

The dress of the womenfolk of the better-off farmer was described as a blue or brown jacket, a petticoat and a black beaver hat. The jacket was edged with binding of different colours. The women wore a short cap rounded at the ears and tied under the chin and over their shoulders a square piece of white flannel with a coloured binding.

However, the majority of the rural population consisted of poorer small farmers and agricultural labourers whose standard of living was extremely low; for while prices and rents rose substantially during the last decade of the eighteenth century, earnings and wages remained at starvation level - a situation which came about partly as a result of the war with Napoleonic France. Work on farms was long and arduous and many labourers were forced to supplement their starvation wages with parish relief. They were poorly housed and poorly dressed, sometimes going without shoes and stockings. Many quitted the land to seek work in town but they only swelled the number of unemployed and destitute who already thronged the streets of Carmarthen.

THE RIVERSIDE PEOPLE

Carmarthen's population in 1801 stood at 5,500 and of these about one third obtained their livelihood from the Towy, many living in the narrow crowded streets and alleys running down to the river. These were the coracle men, a close-knit community who lived in small dwellings on the Quay, in Towyside, Dan-y-banc, Kidwelly Fach, Bridge Street, Mill Street, Jolly Tar Lane and Little Bridge Street. Much of this area has now been swept away and is marked only by the name of Coracle Way. The coracle men snatched a precarious, seasonal living, but nevertheless had a reputation for longevity as well as one for hard drinking and fighting. At the beginning of the nineteenth century there were about four hundred coracles on the Towy; now only twelve pairs are allowed.

Other neighbours of the coracle men were riverside labourers, known locally as 'hobblers', and two colonies of Irishmen and Cornishmen. The Irish potato famine of the 1840's drove hoards of starving peasants into

Coraclemen about 1850-60

Wales and a small colony of Irish settled in the lane called Dan-y-banc (under the bank), and in Kidwelly Fach (Little Kidwelly). Along Dan-y-banc they lived in one-roomed cottages, now demolished, on one side of the lane and kept their mules in the recesses once in evidence on the opposite side. They used their mules for their trade of crockery dealing over a wide area. Below them, in Towyside, was a colony of Cornishmen who came to Carmarthen to work in the old Cystanog lead mine. The main entrance to this district was down the steps still leading to Dan-y-banc from Castle Hill.

THE LABOURING CLASSES

Poverty was rife not only among the riverside people but also among the labouring classes, often referred to in contemporary reports as 'the lower orders', who formed a large part of Carmarthen's population. They lived in the back streets behind the town's main commercial areas of Guildhall Square, Upper Market Street (Nott Square), King Street, Spilman Street and Lammas Street. Also the iron and tin-plate works near the old Priory employed a substantial number of men and women who lived in Priory Street and its environs, while tanneries, iron foundries, woollen mills and paper mills employed others in the area of St. Catherine Street and Water Street. The poverty of the working classes was largely due to the effects of the long-drawn-out Napoleonic war which resulted in high prices and a steep fall in the value of wages. Added to which, food was scarce resulting from a shortage of grain, which further increased the cost of food and reduced many workers to starvation level. Malnutrition then took its toll in the short life-expectancy of the poor. (With the exception of the coracle men, for whom salmon was the salvation!)

Living conditions too were grim - tiny, damp, insanitary dwellings, with four or five families to a cottage and very little furniture or bedding. It was no wonder that many sought solace in drink, available in the numerous pubs and gin-houses in every street of the town. Drunken brawls, family rows and unruly behaviour were a common feature of life throughout the nineteenth century. Such distress led to a general unrest which manifested itself from time to time in sporadic outbreaks of rioting, such as the *Cheese Riots* of September 1818. On 25th September a 'tumultuous assemblage' gathered on the Quayside to prevent the shipment of a cargo of cheese. They boarded the sailing-vessel and carried the cheese back to a warehouse. (Considering the poverty and hunger of the crowd, it is remarkable that the cheese was replaced in the warehouse and not stolen. It speaks volumes for the innate honesty of the Carmarthen mob!) Two days later another attempt was made to ship the cheese, but the infuriated crowd ransacked the vessel and again replaced the cheese in the warehouse from which it had come. To cope with the rioters the first Carmarthen troop of Yeomanry, the 'Derllys' troop of Yeomanry and the Carmarthen Militia were ordered out, and the cheese was shipped out without any more trouble on the 30th September. The rioting was the result of 'certain persons monopolizing cheese and butter for exportation'. Subsequently, 'considerable gratification was felt that some of the merchants had made up their minds to

The Quay with Bridge Street behind, 1937

dispose of their products locally in the future!'

Poverty, hardship and poor housing were to continue for many more years to come and indeed in the 1830's to increase, for by that time Carmarthen's population had almost doubled from about 5,000 at the beginning of the century to around 10,000 in 1831. It was to remain at this figure for the next 100 years or more. The 1840's, often called the 'Hungry Forties', were particularly severe on the poor of the town when the price of food rose to disastrous heights. The winter months were especially hard - and there were some very severe winters in the 1830's and 40's - when hundreds of poor families were reduced to destitution resulting in sickness and death. The mortality rate was high and life-expectancy was short.

In 1843 the Rebecca Riots[1] struck the town and the mob attacked the Workhouse - symptoms of the deep, underlying economic conditions and social unrest.

THE WORKHOUSE and other PROVISIONS FOR THE POOR

During the Middle Ages the poor and sick had been cared for by the Priory and the Friary until these were dissolved in Henry VIII's reign. Under the Elizabethan Poor Law of the late sixteenth century each parish was expected to look after its own poor, the cash to provide relief coming from a special Poor Rate paid by the inhabitants of the parish. In addition, there were many individual benefactors and a large number of charitable bequests to the poor and deserving of the town can be found in records going back to the early seventeenth century. In the eighteenth century it became more common for relief to be given to the poor inside the parish Poorhouse, although 'out-door relief' was still distributed.

St. Peter's Church Vestry Books dating from 1751 indicate that there was a Poorhouse at the Priory, or what was left of it, from about 1758 when £15 was paid out of the Poor Rate to rent the Priory 'for a workhouse for the use of the poor of this parish'.[2] It is not known how long this Priory Poorhouse continued in existence. A street plan of the town, drawn in 1786 by Thomas Lewis, marks a 'Poor House' in what was then called Water Street, but is now St. Catherine Street, and near to Morley Street. The Priory Poorhouse is not marked as such. The following entries in the Vestry Books may refer to the Poorhouse in Water Street or to the Priory Poorhouse:

April, 1786: Ordered that if James Rice does not teach the children to spell, read and write at the poorhouse, he be turned out of the poorhouse.

Aug. 1786: Leave given to William Williams to keep a school at the poorhouse.

Jan. 1791: Ordered that all the paupers who refuse to wear their badges be turned out of the poorhouse and that all such paupers who are able, that don't attend church, or some place of worship, shall have only water gruel for dinner every Sunday.

Aug. 29, 1793: Parish meeting at the Poorhouse to examine the accounts of the

Poor:- ordered that no shoes but wooden shoes be bought henceforward for the Poor of this parish. Ordered that if any pauper goes out of the Poorhouse without leave of Mr. Lewis (Master) or his wife, he shall be deprived of the next meal of meat.

Dec. 3, 1793: Parish meeting ordered that Mr. Lewis of the Poorhouse buy 70 yds. of flannel to make shirts for the paupers.

Dec. 2, 1794: At a meeting held in the Poorhouse, the following orders were made:- To John Davies a shirt; to Margaret Evans a pair of new leather shoes, her foot being so bad as not to be able to wear wooden clogs; to Thomas Evans a pair of wooden clogs and a pair of stockings; to Elias Price a pair of breeches; to Richard Basset a nightcap and shirt; to Mary Darby a shift and a pair of clogs and a shirt for her child.

Nov. 30, 1796: Parish meeting ordered that Lewis Lewis be removed from being Master of the Poorhouse and David Lewis be appointed to succeed.

May 5, 1797: David Lewis, Master, to receive the sum of 2s. 6d. weekly for maintaining each person now in the Poorhouse, being 32 in number till Michaelmas next.

Jan 12, 1798: Poorhouse Regulations to be read out every Monday morning by the Master: a bell would be rung a quarter-hour before breakfast, dinner and supper, provided in a communal room, to enable everyone to appear 'with hands and face washed clean and hair combed in a decent manner'. Paupers were not to go out of the Poorhouse without permission of the Master, they were to attend a public place of worship twice on a Sunday and they were to assist in any necessary work about or belonging to the House, without any gratuity, but if they were employed in any other work for which the Master received a profit, half the profit so earned was to be paid to the pauper earning it, 'as an encouragement to industry'.

From an entry in the Vestry Books, dated December 26th 1800, it would appear that a plan for a new Poorhouse and Workhouse was approved of. The Parish meeting ordered that a petition be presented to the Corporation of Carmarthen for the grant of a lease of a field at Wayndew (Waundew) for the purpose of erecting the said Poorhouse and Workhouse. However, nothing seems to have developed from these plans at the time.

In October 1801 entries show that the Water Street Poorhouse, which was rented from Richard Mansel Philipps, was to be repaired and major extensions undertaken and a 21 year lease taken out at an increased rent. But in February 1802 it was ordered that the building work be suspended and the lease not taken out. Subsequently, on September 27th 1803, it was ordered that the premises be returned to the landlord.

By October 4th 1803 the Ivy Bush was occupied as a temporary Poorhouse (It was in 1803 that the Ivy Bush Inn, situated in King Street, moved to Spilman Street and so this would account for the vacated premises in King Street being used as a temporary Poorhouse). Mr. Nott, proprietor of the Ivy Bush, was paid £20 rent by the Overseers of the poor.

Between 1805 and 1806 a new purpose-built Poorhouse was erected at the foot of Penlan hill for 'the reception, employment and maintenance of the poor of the parish'.

The Poorhouse became known as the Workhouse when on November 23rd 1821 an order was made to convert the Poorhouse into a Workhouse. In September 1822 the *Journal* records that the Rev. David Archard Williams, assistant master at the Grammar School, was appointed 'evening lecturer at the Workhouse of the Parish of St. Peter'; and in November of the same year the office of Assistant Overseer of the Poor of the Parish of St. Peter was advertised in the *Journal*.

At the same time as In-door relief was provided, there was also Out-door relief distributed to the poor and sick. Thus an entry in the *Journal* for February 1821 states: 'The Carmarthen Society for visiting and relieving the Poor met at St. Peter's Vestry. It was reported that coal, barley meal, bread, meat, blankets, wool and flannel had been distributed.'

The subscribers to this charity were also told that: 'every exertion has been made to enforce cleanliness in the persons and dwellings of the poor and to urge a regular and reverent attendance in whatever place of public worship they profess to belong to.'

The *Journal* contains many references to such distributions of food and clothing by the better-off townspeople.

The Poor Rate continued to be levied on the inhabitants, but with the increasing numbers of poor people during periods of unemployment and low wages, the old parish system was breaking down and unable to cope. The ever-increasing Poor Rate was unpopular with the people who had to pay it.

In an attempt to remedy the situation the *Poor Law Amendment Act* was passed in 1834. Out-door relief was no longer provided for the able-bodied poor; relief was now only obtainable in Workhouses. In order to make larger and more efficient units, parishes were grouped into Unions with one Union Workhouse between them.

Conditions in Union Workhouses were made as harsh and unattractive as possible in order to deter people from seeking admission. Husbands, wives and children were separated from each other, overcrowding was commonplace and the food hardly adequate. It was said that the rations given to the prisoners in Carmarthen Borough Gaol and the County Gaol were superior in both quantity and quality to those given to the inmates of the Carmarthen Union Workhouse. Many people preferred to live with their families on the verge of starvation and in abject poverty rather than give up their small cottages and enter the workhouse. All able-bodied men were set a daily quota of one-and-a-half tons of stone to be broken up for use in making the new Turnpike roads. It was no wonder that the Union Workhouses were hated and feared.

The new system ignored the causes of poverty and unemployment and assumed that the poor were responsible for their own poverty.

The *Carmarthen Journal* give continuous reports of the fortnightly meetings of the Board of Guardians which supervised the management of the Workhouse and received the Master's reports.

John Wood's map of 1834 shows a 'Poor House' at the bottom of Penlan Hill and in 1837, according to *Kelly's Directory*, 'a Workhouse building of stone, was built for 140 inmates.' In 1839 a Union Workhouse school was established.

During the Rebecca Riots of 1843 the Union Workhouse was attacked and stormed, although the inmates themselves resisted the rioters. The building was taken over and probably would have been set alight but for the arrival of the Dragoons.[3]

Throughout the 'Hungry Forties' and until the last decade of the century the Union Workhouse, for all its faults and prison-like regime, provided the basic necessities of life for many who would otherwise have starved. The Board of Guardians, representing the different parishes which made up the Union, did their best for the inmates, given the difficult economic circumstances. The Guardians attended to their food, clothing and medical needs and provided a rudimentary education for the children. In 1846 there were 58 children being taught in the workhouse school.

A few treats were provided from time to time, especially on Christmas Day when there was always plenty of roast beef and plum-pudding. A *Journal* report on Christmas Day 1858 rather pathetically states:

> 'It is a pleasant sight to witness the joyous and happy faces of these poor helpless people . . . old and young, the aged cripple and the little orphan . . . all alike seemed well satisfied and thankful for the repast and equally grateful to their worthy master and matron, Mr. and Mrs. Adams.'

In November 1873 the Board of Guardians suggested that the mistress take the children out for walks once or twice a week, as 'they scarcely know the difference between a cow and a camel or a horse and a pig.'

The Workhouse gateway

The year 1894 saw the last meeting of the Board of Guardians under that name, for new legislation in the form of the Local Government Act of 1894, introduced District Councils, urban and rural, which were made responsible for local government administration. At this time there were 99 inmates in the Workhouse and Out-door relief was given to over 1000 paupers. In 1906 a fire destroyed much of the original Workhouse and only the gateway, although altered, remains.

OUT-DOOR RELIEF

The Poor Law Amendment Act of 1834 had aimed to abolish Out-door relief but this it failed to do and throughout the nineteenth century food, clothing and fuel were distributed to the poor, sick and elderly. The Carmarthen Relief of the Poor Committee made regular distributions as did the Churches and Chapels. In January 1871 at the annual distribution of bread by the clergy and churchwardens of St. Peter's Church, 527 poor persons each received a sixpenny loaf. In addition 105 loaves were sent to the sick poor. 'It was painful to notice the wretchedness and poverty of most of those in attendance and some of whom came so early that they actually remained in the church three hours for the sake of getting a loaf.'

SOUP KITCHENS

Soup kitchens were also run for many years distributing bread and soup from January until March. In this way many poor families were helped through the winter until the fishing season began. On the usual charge of 1 penny, each poor person received 1 loaf and 1 quart of soup. The soup kitchens were usually under the control of the Mayor with a local committee and funds were requested from the public. From 1864 the *David Morris Charity* was a great help in this respect. David Morris, M.P., who died in 1864, left £2000 to the poor of the town; the bequest was invested and the proceeds arising from it used to furnish the soup kitchens. The *C. W. Jones Charity* was another source of benefit, given as a distribution of coal, which continues to the present day.

REPORT on the SANITARY CONDITIONS of THE BOROUGH, 1873

A most interesting report, dated March 1873, was that prepared for the Local Sanitary Authority by the Medical Officer of Health, Dr. John Hughes. The Report covers population, occupations, habitations, drainage, water supply, rainfall, food prices and rates of wages in the early 1870's.

According to the Census return of 1871 the population was 10,499 and the number of inhabited houses was 1,992. Dr. Hughes comments that the population of Carmarthen does not increase rapidly, the reason being

> 'the absence of any manufactories or other agencies which would give employment to all the native born young people and their necessary migration to other and especially the manufacturing districts.'

Moreover, this exodus of the young and strong left behind a larger proportion than usual of the aged and very young where the incidence of sickness and mortality was greater. This, together with the fact that many young men succumbed to diseases in the manufacturing towns and then returned sick and dying to Carmarthen, would account for the borough's high mortality rate.

Regarding occupations, Dr. Hughes states:

> 'The only manufactory of any importance is the Tinplate Manufactory of Messrs. Thomas, Lester & Co. which gives employment to about 190 men and about 100 women and children, supporting in all nearly 800 persons who are dependent upon that firm.'

Roughly 40 families were engaged in salmon and sewin fishing in the Towy while about 150 persons were employed in woollen factories and weaving sheds. Two foundries, two breweries and eight printing presses employed about 60 in each industry. Hat-making, formerly an important trade in the town, was in a very languishing condition. The number of hotels, inns and public houses amounted to 107, while the remaining population, consisting of persons in professions and trades, including a large number of small shopkeepers and artisans, was such 'as is usually found in an agricultural town.'

In 1872 only 550 houses were connected to the sewers and only 715 had water from the public waterworks laid on. There were between 60 and 70 pumps and wells but since some were situated among cesspools the water was unfit for consumption. There were 15 public conduits in different parts of the town.

Dr. Hughes also refers to an earlier report of 1849 (the year in which a cholera epidemic struck Carmarthen) in which it was stated that the mortality rate of Carmarthen was much higher than might be expected from the salubrious position of the town, that the parts in which epidemic sickness prevailed were the most deficient in drainage and were close, ill ventilated and ill supplied with water, and that the whole town was remarkably ill provided with privies and therefore in a very filthy state,

> 'rendered worse by the presence of foul open ditches in the suburb, by a want of proper dustbins, and of proper paving in the courts.'

The 1849 report recommended that a constant supply of soft filtered water should be laid on to every house in the town and a complete system of main and house drainage provided. Nevertheless, in 1873 there were two large areas of the town still undrained: the St. Catherine Street - Water Street area with its crowded houses, situated on a cold, wet bed of deep clay saturated with the contents of its cesspools, and the Priory Street - Richmond Terrace - Wellfield Road area. Here the new houses were too far from the existing sewers to be connected.

There were five 'common lodging-houses' licenced for 73 persons - two in Water Street and one each in Quay Street, Goose Street and on

Woods Row in 1973

The Quay.

In dealing with food prices, the report states that in 1872 the cost of flour per sack was 44s. 1d., beef was 7d. per lb., mutton 7d. and butter 1s. 1d. per lb. Potatoes were about 5s. 11d. per cwt., while Welsh cheese was at £1 6s. 1d. per cwt. Coal was at a famine price of 22s. per ton.

The wages at the Tinplate Works averaged: for puddlers 30s., roller-men 32s. 6d., hammer-men 35s., refinery-men 30s., tinhouse-men 30s. and labourers from 15 to 18s. a week. In the Iron Foundries the average rate was 25s. a week, while Weavers' wages were about 20s. a week. Masons earned from 24 to 27s., carpenters 21 to 24s., plumbers about 30s., painters 24s., printers about 22s., and labourers about 18s. per week.

One of the most disturbing features of the report was the amount of pauperism in Carmarthen. Dr. Hughes states:

> 'The number of poor relieved in the Workhouse is a little diminished, but the out-door list is simply enormous. The number relieved in the half-year ending Lady-day, 1872, was 103 in-door and 1,222 out-door, making a total of 1,325. This number represents 12.86 per cent of the population, the average pauperism of England and Wales being only 4.3 of the population. That is, this district has about three times as many paupers in proportion to the population as the whole of England and Wales has . . . . During the last 23 years the amount of pauperism in Carmarthen has about doubled. This excessive amount is partly caused by the number of people who get on the rate on account of the sickness, or death, of some member of the family, too frequently that of the breadwinner.'

Dr. Hughes concluded that the requirements necessary to put the town in a healthier condition seemed to be the construction and ventilation of proper sewers for those parts of the town without them, the proper connection of every house with the sewers, the abolition of the numerous cesspools, the provision of a sufficient number of water-closets, the more frequent removal of all refuse matter from house premises and a constant supply of good water laid on to every house.

Subsequent reports by Dr. Hughes show that these recommendations were not immediately carried out and that throughout the 1880's only about half the houses in town were connected to piped water which came from two reservoirs at Cwmoernant. The water was not filtered and was often contaminated. In the poorer districts of town very few houses were connected to the mains and many shared taps and standpipes. Some obtained water from wells and springs which were liable to contamination from numerous old cesspits. It was not until the mid 1890's that the problem of providing an adequate water supply was solved with the building of a new reservoir at Rock and Fountain near Cynwyl Elfed.

The sewerage system too was completely inadequate for the needs of the town: Dan-y-banc with 38 houses and 128 residents had only 2 water-closets and 5 privies, while Duke Yard had 5 houses and 16 residents all sharing the same privy!

The death rate in the 1880's was higher than the average death rate for England and Wales; the causes of death were chiefly tuberculosis, pneumonia, bronchitis and pleurisy, all caused by the cold, damp and poor living conditions. There were also periodic epidemics of measles, whooping cough and scarlet fever, which took a heavy toll among children. Fortunately, the earlier epidemics of cholera (1849 and 1866) and typhoid fever were now over and most children were vaccinated against small-pox, which had been the scourge of the eighteenth century.

CULTURE AND ENTERTAINMENT

Although there was much poverty in Carmarthen during the nineteenth century, there was also a good deal of prosperity for some more fortunate sections of the community. Being a county town, an administrative, judicial and commercial centre, a busy port and an agricultural market town, Carmarthen was the home of prosperous professional and business classes. The prosperity of its commercial centre co-existed with the poverty of its back streets. In 1840 Carmarthen was described as 'one of the most wealthy and polite towns in Wales.' A wide range of cultural activities and entertainment was available for many inhabitants.

THE ASSEMBLY ROOMS

The Assembly Rooms, which played a large part in the social and cultural life of the town, were opened in King Street on 21st November, 1854. Part of the site later became that of the Lyric cinema. The Assembly Rooms, sometimes called the Public Rooms, comprised a large hall seating 600 persons and fully licensed for stage plays, a commodious suite of rooms and a billiard room. Part of the Assembly building was occupied by the Carmarthen Literary and Scientific Institution which provided a lending library, a reading room and a room for conversation, chess and draughts. Both the Carmarthen Musical Society and the Choral Society held regular concerts in the Rooms, often before packed audiences, while visiting opera and

The Assembly Rooms, 1858

drama companies were also a regular feature. The *Journal* contains many notices such as that in January, 1855:

> 'A grand vocal concert, under Distinguished Patronage, by the celebrated Drury Lane English Opera Company.'

In March 1870 Mr. Manley's Opera Company included in their week's programme:

> 'La Somnambula', 'The Barber of Seville', 'The Bohemian Girl', 'Il Travatore', 'Faust' and 'The Daughter of the Regiment'. Doors were opened at 7.30 p.m. to commence at 8 and 'carriages may be ordered at 11.'

Mr. D'Oyle Carte's Opera Company gave performances of Gilbert and Sullivan in the 1880's and 1890's while Mr. Vance's Concert Party rendered compositions 'that can be sung in any drawing room'.

The Assembly Rooms were also used for some of the grand balls which were a feature of Victorian times, such as the Carmarthenshire Assize Ball held in July 1855 at which

> 'the company was of the highest character and the arrangements as to the music and supper were excellent . . . The affair was more like a drawing-room dance than a set ball.'

Fashionable clothes for these fine occasions could be purchased from establishments such as that of D. & W. Davies, Guildhall Square, who advertised their 'Paris and London' fashions in the *Journal*.

An annual event held at the Assembly Rooms was St. Peter's *Christmas Tree*, a fund-raising bazaar, with numerous stalls and other attractions, first held in 1868. Carmarthen Dramatic Society also gave performances there during the 1890's.

THE CARMARTHEN AMATEUR OPERATIC SOCIETY

This society, which was founded in 1891 and which is still presenting annual operatic productions, staged many of its early performances such as *Patience*, *The Mikado* and *Merrie England*, in the Assembly Rooms. After the First World War St. David's Memorial Hall became the venue for many of the Society's successful shows, to be followed later by productions in St. Peter's Civic Hall.

LATER HISTORY OF THE ASSEMBLY ROOMS

The main part of the Assembly Rooms was converted into a cinema and concert hall in March 1918 and its name was changed to the *Lyric*. At this time films were 'silent' and the *Lyric* management guaranteed that they were free from any form of vulgarity. The chief film for opening week was *Rasputin*.

'Talking' films came to Carmarthen in 1930 when in March of that year the *Lyric* put on the 'talkie' *Sonny Boy* featuring Al Jolson. In the following year considerable refurbishment was carried out before the *Lyric* reopened on April 4th, 1931. Five years later, the proprietor, Mr. W. E. Morgan, practically rebuilt the cinema, making the new *Lyric*

King Street with the
Lyric Buildings behind

Theatre comparable with any in the country. Built to the design of architect William S. Wort of Cardiff, the *Lyric* offered luxurious accommodation for 1,000 persons in elegant surroundings with modern accoustics. The opening programme on April 6th, 1936, featured Richard Tauber in *Heart's Desire.* The cinema flourished until the advent of television led to its gradual decline and eventual closure. However, in recent years the *Lyric* has undergone a major restoration, thanks to the dedicated work of the Carmarthen Youth Opera and to financial assistance from local authorities and it has now reopened as a theatre, cinema and concert hall.

The other well-known cinema in town, the *Capitol,* was built in 1930 on the site of the old Tannery in John Street. Costing £10,000, the cinema provided seating accommodation for 800 people and opened in August 1930 with a showing of *The Desert Song.* It has now been converted into bingo and snooker halls.

Before the 1914-18 war there were two cinemas showing silent films: one in Old Station Road called the *Rink,* because the building was originally a roller-skating rink, and the other in Blue Street known as *Vint's Electric Palace* owned by Mr. Leon Vint. The *Palace,* designed by Ernest Collier, opened on April 1st, 1912 and provided seats for 600 people with 'modern' electrical heating, ventilation and plumbing. As well as being a cinema, Vint's *Palace* was also a theatre for the staging of plays and variety performances. In February 1914, however, the *Palace* closed and then reopened one week later as the *Empire Theatre,* putting on a wide range of variety acts and 'pictures'. The *Empire Theatre,* which had its own orchestra, remained open until the 1930's when it became the Oscar Chess garage.

18th AND 19th CENTURY THEATRES

Various theatres are recorded in the town in the eighteenth and nineteenth centuries but their precise locations are difficult to determine.

They varied in the quality of performances and audiences and in the degree of comfort they offered. Some performances ended in near riotous behaviour - whistling, shouting, jumping and fighting - with the police being called in to restore order.

Two theatres are recorded in the town in the late 18th century, one of which was situated in Little Water Street. This theatre must have been a substantial building as it had a pit, gallery and boxes and was well patronised by local townspeople and the gentry. The *Journal* of 1817-40 carried many notices of plays and entertainments at this theatre. The proprietor in 1813 was one 'Henry Dunn, Comedian'. In 1819 Nathaniel Awbery was the occupier.

The other theatre was in King Street and attracted the best actors of the day, including Edmund Kean and John Kemble. John Nash acted as an amateur in this theatre in 1786. Lord Nelson and Lady Hamilton were in the audience at one performance when they stayed at Carmarthen in 1802.

The original building in King Street was replaced by a new theatre which opened on 7th September, 1830. Twenty years later a Journal report of 1850 states:

> 'Mr Barton the manager has set up a respectable and excellent company of actors and actresses . . . . Mr. Barton has paid attention to the comfort of the theatre. The place is well-aired and well-lighted . . . . On Friday, under the patronage of Chief Magistrate Valentine Davis, the house was literally crammed . . . On Wednesday under the patronage of Col. Love the house was filled and overflowing.'

But this theatre could not have lasted long for in 1855 the *Journal* reported that

> 'the Carmarthen theatre was reopened after a considerable lapse of time. The Company now performing at this place of amusement under the management of Mr. Chadwick is able and talented.'

Later in the century there was the *Star Theatre* run by Mr. John Noakes whose performances were carried out

> 'with a very fair regard to decorum as well as decency.'

There was also *Jennings Theatre* in the Market Place,

> 'conducted in a most respectable manner . . . the entertainment including plays ranging from high tragedy to low comedy, all being most creditably performed.'

A record of 1820 tells of a lease being granted for the building of a theatre in Blue Street, but whether this was the same theatre or cinema which stood in Blue Street in the early part of this present century (i.e. Vint's Palace, followed by the Empire Theatre) is not known.

THE LITERARY AND SCIENTIFIC INSTITUTION

Carmarthen Literary and Scientific Institution was founded in November 1840 when it was first called the Carmarthen Mechanics' Institute. Its purpose was to improve the standard of education for mechanics, i.e. tradesmen, by providing lectures and evening classes in return for a membership fee. It was started by a group of young townsmen, among whom were William and George Spurrell, George Bagnall, T. Mostyn Davies, Dr. David Lloyd (Principal of the Presbyterian College) and Dr. John Hughes. The Institute was first located in Hall Street and soon afterwards in Guildhall Square. In 1846 its name was changed to The Literary and Scientific Institution and by 1852 its members numbered 130, the secretary being the antiquary Alcwyn Evans. Lectures were given on a variety of topics including literature, public health, local history and scientific subjects, whilst evening classes were held in French, German and mathematics. The Institution moved to the Assembly Rooms, King Street, when these were opened in November 1854. A lending library, a reading room supplied with newspapers and periodicals and a room for conversation, chess and draughts were provided. There was also a small collection of local curiosities forming the nucleus of a museum. With the outbreak of war in 1939 the Institution eventually ceased to function.

Bull Lane
(drawing by Ernest Collier)
The building on the right was at one time the Empire Theatre

Another society called the *Lammas Street Library and Reading Institution* flourished in the mid nineteenth century and was also the venue for lectures.

"WINTER EVENING ENTERTAINMENTS"

These were held weekly at the Guildhall or in the Assembly Rooms and took the form of talks, poetry and prose readings, musical recitals and songs, all given by local talent and often in aid of various charities. One such 'Entertainment' was given by the Venerable Archdeacon Archard Williams, in December 1867, when he gave an amusing account of the last Court of Admiralty held on the Towy (i.e. until its revival in 1971). His talk went as follows:

> "Some forty years ago the Mayor and body Corporate, relying on the promise of a fine day, risked their precious persons in a boat on the river and shaped their course towards the bar. Everything went on as merry as a marriage bell until they approached the seaward limit of the Mayor's jurisdiction as Conservator of the river, when suddenly the wind chopped round to the south-west and sent in what the sailors call a heavy lop of a sea over the bar. The Conservator of the Towy did not hesitate to take charge of the helm and steer the boat . . . Whilst it glided gently on the bosom of the placid river, the seamanship of the Chief Magistrate of Carmarthen was loudly extolled; but when the wind freshened and the white crested billows came tumbling over the bar, and the boat with its interesting freight of civic dignitaries began to perform certain ascents and descents and rollings about, the worshipful 'Palinurus' proved sadly unequal to the emergency, for instead of keeping the head of the boat to the wild waves, he acted on the Sheriff's advice, and ported his helm so as to bring it between the watery furrows broadside on to the running sea; and it would in a few minutes have been inevitably swamped, had not one of the sailors on board sprung to the helm and brought the boat back to its proper position - thus averting the catastrophe which would otherwise have consigned the Conservator and his companions to a watery grave. The situation had become extremely critical; the jubilant strains of 'Rule Britannia', in which the whole party had been vociferously indulging, ceased, and gave place to some subdued aspirations to that tutelary guardian of the British main that - if she really ruled the waves - she would be pleased to rule them 'straight', as their upheavings and irregular motions had rendered the boat party extremely uncomfortable. A perceptible change had come over the countenances as well as the spirits of the Mayor and his fellow voyagers. The faces which a few minutes before were rosy and rubicund and radiant with smiles and animation had assumed a pallid hue and woeful expression; quite as much the result of uneasy physical sensations, as of a consciousness of the danger they were in. Many of the municipals, the Conservator of the Towy included, and not excepting the learned Recorder of those days, might be seen hanging over the boat's side, gazing intently on the vasty deep and trying to discover some of the 'gems of purest ray serene' which we are told 'the dark unfathomed caves of ocean bear'; while others were interestingly occupied in studying the habits of the finny tribe feeding in their native element. Thanks to the skill of the sailors, and a flood tide, the gallant craft, after numerous tossings and buffetings, reached home safely with its interesting freight of frightened Civic Dignitaries - plentifully saturated with spray, and quite ready to repair to the 'Six Bells' to partake of the usual annual dinner . This was the last visit of the Mayor of Carmarthen, accompanied by his officials, to the seaward limit of his jurisdiction, to inspect under serious difficulties the state of the river, and to contest with Neptune the sovereignty of the surging estuary of the Towy."

THE SOCIAL SCENE

The Boar's Head in Lammas Street and the Ivy Bush, originally in King Street but in 1803 moved to Spilman Street, were well-known coaching inns and favourite meeting places for the socially élite. They both had Assembly Rooms which were used for military balls, hunt balls, musical concerts and glittering social gatherings. The *Carmarthen Journal* has many references to such occasions, describing the select company present usually with the names of the local gentry and well-to-do townspeople in descending order of importance. In the mid nineteenth century the popular dances were the *polka, waltz* and *quadrille,* the fashionable *polka* seemingly the favourite. Times had changed since the 1780's when at a ball given by Sir Cornwallis Maude, father-in-law of John Vaughan of Golden Grove, the dances were the *minuet, cotillion* and *'the hop'.*

The ability to dance, and so take part in the social whirl of the winter season, was regarded as a necessary accomplishment for the more affluent classes and so children were taught the intricacies of the different steps. A *Journal* report of 1850 states:

> 'Miss Saunders Juvenile Assembly. - Miss Saunders gave her annual assembly at the Boar's Head, which was fully and fashionably attended. The programme exhibited polkas, waltzes, mazurkas, quadrilles and several fancy dances which were danced by the pupils with extraordinary proficiency and elicited repeated plaudits from the assembled company. Miss Saunders deserves infinite credit for the pains she takes in instructing the little ones . . . The dancing was kept up by the company until a late hour, when they departed highly pleased with the treat provided for them.'

In January 1855 Mrs. Loder advertised her Academy for Dancing and Deportment with due deference:

> 'Mrs Loder has the honour to inform the Nobility, gentry and inhabitants of Carmarthen and its vicinity that her Academy for Dancing, Deportment and Calisthenic Exercises will re-open at her Residence in Spilman Street.'

As the century progressed, the gap between the social classes was gradually narrowing and the first Tradesmen's Ball was held at the Boar's Head in the season of 1856-1857.

BOAT-RACING AND STEEPLE-CHASING

There were annual boat races on the Towy for large and small rowing boats and coracles which attracted many entries, for there were valuable cash prizes to be won. The town's inhabitants turned out in full force to watch the events. Many other celebrations, such as royal weddings and accessions to the throne, were marked by races on the river and other sports in which all sections of the community took part.

Steeple-chasing too, held at Alltycnap, attracted much interest, the races of 1830 being 'superior to anything witnessed here for many years.' (As early as 1801 the Corporation subscribed £25 towards purchasing a Plate for the races.) A steeple-chase was a horse race over jumps or rough country, which today would be called a point-to-point; it was so named as it was formerly a race having a church steeple or tower in view and all intervening obstacles had to be cleared in racing towards this finishing post. Race week was marked by two balls, one held at the Ivy Bush and the other at the Boar's Head and both were 'numerously and respectably attended.' About four or five days were devoted to the annual steeple-chases and the accompanying balls and hunts.

A CHRISTMAS EVE CUSTOM

In December 1849 a *Journal* report on Christmas Eve activities in Carmarthen stated:

> 'According to immemorial custom the town streets were thronged with crowds of idle, disorderly boys and adults who amused themselves and annoyed others by throwing squibs, crackers and other fireworks at each other and at the peaceful passers-by, much to their discomfort...A large blazing tar-barrel was drawn through the streets at a rapid pace and there was firing of pistols.'

This 'immemorial custom' continued to be practised for another twenty years but faced mounting criticism. Thus in 1864 it was stated:

> 'On Saturday evening (Christmas Eve), as is customary in this town, the foolish display of torches, squibs, rockets, etc. took place. The number who took part in the proceedings fell very far short of former years, and very fortunately too, or the business of the town would have been seriously interfered with.'

The custom was stopped on Christmas Eve, 1870, by order of the Mayor.

ROYAL WEDDING CELEBRATIONS, 1863

To mark the marriage of Edward, Prince of Wales, to Alexandra of Denmark on 10th March, 1863, the Mayor's Committee resolved that 'tea and cake' should be provided for the school-children and for the paupers of Carmarthen Union and that the 'male paupers receive an additional half-ounce of tobacco, and the female paupers 1d. worth of snuff.' It was also resolved that 'one third of the amount collected be distributed amongst the aged and deserving poor of the town, in food and other necessaries.'

In addition, the following programme was arranged:

> 'The day will be ushered in with ringing of bells, firing of cannon etc. The volunteers, friendly societies, and clubs of all denominations, and the public in general will meet in Guild-hall Square, at 11 o'clock. At 12 o'clock the volunteers will fire a royal salute, and form procession through the principal streets of the town, headed by their bands. At 2 o'clock the rustic sports will commence. There will be climbing the greasy pole in Nott-square, Guild-hall square and Lammas-street for legs of mutton and other prizes. There will be foot racing in Lammas-street, King-street and Spilman-street, and hurdle racing in the upper part of Lammas-street. Fireworks will be given away gratis . . . A ball at the Assembly Rooms will wind up the festivities of the day and at 12 p.m. a large bonfire will be seen blazing from the top of Penlan.'

Top: Red Street today
Bottom: The same scene before redevelopment;
the building on the right, adjacent to Merlin Lane,
housed the Borough Council Offices

Clearly the people of Carmarthen knew how to enjoy themselves in spite of the harsh economic and social conditions which governed the lives of so many of the town's inhabitants in the nineteenth century.

CARMARTHEN ATHLETIC SPORTS CLUB

Programmes show that from 1877 the Carmarthen Athletic Sports Club held annual sports and bicycle races on Whit Mondays at the Mansel Athletic ground which was in a field near Picton's Monument. (The public Park with its cycle track was not opened until Easter 1900.) Sporting events included flat running races, hurdles, high pole jumps, walking, cycling, sack races, tug-of-war and pony trotting races. Cycle races also took place around town on 'high wheelers' or penny-farthings, starting in John Street, going down St. Catherine Street, round Picton Monument, down Lammas Street and finishing in front of the Guildhall. Competitors came from as far afield as Bristol and Cardiff, attracted no doubt by the generous monetary prizes, such as £3 for the 100 yards foot race and 20 guineas for the one-mile flat. However, in races exclusive to workhouse children, prizes had to be taken in books.

A VICTORIAN FUNERAL PROCESSION

In September 1870 one of the last of the old-fashioned funeral processions took place, following the death of one of the wealthiest women in the county, namely Mrs. Catherine Bridget Florentia Davies of Lime Grove, Carmarthen. All invited to the funeral were invested with rich silk hat-bands and scarves, and all the tenants wore long black cloaks and silk hat-bands. The hearse and mourning coach, heavily plumed, were drawn by four black horses appropriately caparisoned for the solemn occasion, all having a most imposing appearance. The procession left Lime Grove at eight in the morning, and the cortège took five hours to cover the twenty miles to Llangadog, at a pace that permitted the foot mourners to accompany the coaches. Two mutes (hired mourners) headed the funeral procession.

MASONIC AND FRATERNAL SOCIETIES

The history of the Masonic and Fraternal Societies in Carmarthen appears to start with a Lodge which had been working in the town prior to 1717 when a Provincial Grand Lodge was formed in South Wales. However, the first known Masonic Lodge in Carmarthen, indeed in the whole of Wales, was warranted in 1724 as No. 34 to meet at the Bay Nag's Head and Star in Dark Gate. In 1733 the Lodge removed to the Bunch of Grapes and was renumbered No. 30. The earliest Lodges were generally known by numbers and the names of the taverns at which they met.

Lodge No. 30 appears to have lapsed after some years and a new warrant was granted in 1753 to Lodge No. 240 which was named the Lodge of Perfect Friendship in 1767. Its name was subsequently changed to Temple Lodge and in 1777 it was erased from the roll. Its meeting places had included the Three Crowns in Upper Market Street (Nott Square), the Red Lion in Guildhall Square and the Shakespeare in Market Street (Hall Street). From 1777, for the next 34 years, there was no Freemasons' Lodge in Carmarthen.

In 1811 two Lodges were warranted, clearly in rivalry to each other. They were the St. David's Lodge of Perfect Friendship which met at the King's Arms under the Grand Lodge of *Moderns* and the Union Lodge which met at the Old Ivy Bush under the Grand Lodge of *Ancients.* The St. David's Lodge lasted until 1822 while the Union Lodge is last heard of in 1829. The two rival Grand Lodges had amalgamated in 1813 and it is possible these two local lodges had also joined forces at some time before 1829, as documents exist referring to 'The Ancient and Modern Lodge' in Carmarthen.

The last chapter in this saga of formation and closure commenced in 1841 when St. Peter's Lodge was formed at the Ivy Bush in Spilman Street, to continue without interruption until today. Originally numbered 699 this was later changed to 476. The first Master of St. Peter's Lodge in 1841 was Samuel Tardrew, a chemist, whose shop was at 59 King Street and who was Mayor in 1846. The Master in 1845 was F. Bolingbroke Ribbans who was headmaster of Powell's School on the Parade and who was well connected in Masonic circles having been associated with the earliest Masonic Girls' School in London. The Lodge was held at the Ivy Bush and then at Napier House nearby until 1899 when the first Masonic Hall was built in Spilman Street. The present hall was built on the same site in 1911. Other Lodges now meeting in the building (with dates of formation) include: Merlin R.A. (1855), Mansel Mark (1870), Kensington I.M. (1913), Maridunum R.C. (1923), Caerfyrddin (1927) and Coracle R.A.M. (1931).

The Loyal Order of Moose was constituted in Carmarthen as the Carmarthen Lodge No. 74 in 1928 and, after meeting in various rooms, finally purchased the redundant Towyside Mission Church in Old Station Road in 1957 as a Lodge headquarters. The Royal and Ancient Order of Buffaloes are also represented in the town.

Newspaper reports and records of civic processions and funerals show that in the nineteenth century Carmarthen was also host to societies of Ivorites and Oddfellows, both of which have now ceased to function in the town.

1 See *Political Strife - Rebecca Riots.*

2 See *The Priory - Priory Poorhouse.*

3 See *Political Strife - Rebecca Riots.*

Woods Row, 1937

- 15 -

EDUCATION

CARMARTHEN: AN EARLY SEAT OF LEARNING

Carmarthen has long enjoyed the tradition of being an early seat of learning, owing to the presence and influence of the royal castle, St. Peter's Church, the Priory and the Friary. It is probable that St. Peter's Church, being the original parish church of Carmarthen, maintained a school in the Middle Ages, as did most of the larger parish churches in Wales, but there is no direct evidence for such a school to date. By the time of the dissolution of the monasteries in the sixteenth century, the medieval schools associated with monasteries, cathedrals and parish churches, which had provided virtually the only avenues of education for many centuries, were in sad decay. The need for the establishment of schools for the education of both clergy and laity was becoming increasingly recognised and the result was the foundation of the Tudor grammar schools which were such an outstanding feature of this period. Some grammar schools were endowed from monastic and church property, others were founded by successful merchants, landed gentry, ecclesiastics and patrons of learning; an indication of the tremendous interest being taken in education and the awareness of its value for the Tudor civil service and the professions. However, although these efforts did much for the education of the upper and middle classes, the education of the lower classes was almost entirely neglected and remained so until the nineteenth century, with only a few free places being offered at the grammar schools to poor scholars.

THOMAS LLOYD'S SCHOOL, 1543-47

The first authentic record of a grammar school in Carmarthen occurs in 1543 in Henry VIII's reign. Since Carmarthen was the most populous town in Wales in the sixteenth century, it is hardly surprising that an endowed grammar school should have been founded here. Although it lasted for only four years, it was one of only three such schools founded in Wales during Henry's reign, the other two being Christ College, Brecon (1541) and King Henry VIII's Grammar School, Abergavenny (1543).

The founder of the first Carmarthen Grammar school was Thomas Lloyd, about whose early life little is known.[1] He may have been a native of Carmarthen, or its environs, in view of his desire to establish a school in the town. It is known that he was educated at Oxford

University and admitted to the degree of Bachelor of Civil Law in 1524. Later he became Precentor of St. David's Cathedral (i.e. head of the Cathedral Chapter) and holder of several lucrative benefices in the diocese. Thomas Lloyd had cherished plans for founding a grammar school in Carmarthen for several years before they finally came to fruition. As early as January 1536, Henry VIII licensed him to found a school in 'New Karmarden' to be known as 'Thomas Lloyd his skole'. However, nothing appears to have been done in the matter at this time, possibly because Lloyd became engaged in a quarrel with Bishop Barlow of St. Davids and also in a law suit concerning his claim to certain lands in Pembrokeshire.

In 1538 the Franciscan Friary at Carmarthen was dissolved and all its goods and contents surrendered to the King. The dissolution gave the incentive to Thomas Lloyd to petition for a school again. In 1539 the mayor and aldermen of Carmarthen sent a petition to Thomas Cromwell, who had been responsible for sending the royal commissioners round the monasteries, urging him to persuade the King to grant the Friary and its adjoining land 'so that they may have a Grammer scoole at the coste and charge of Mayster Thomas Lloyd, chauntier of Sainte David.' The petition stated that the Friary had fallen into ruin and decay, there was no lead upon any part of it and it was a pity that such a building should not be put to some convenient use for the common good. They offered Henry VIII £40 for the property and Thomas Cromwell £20 for using his influence with the King!

Eventually, after a long delay, in February 1543, the King issued new Letters Patent for the school which was to be known as 'The King's Scole of Carmarden of Thomas Lloyd's fundacion'. Lloyd was granted, at an annual rental of three shillings and four pence, the house of the Friars with its gardens and closes and its adjoining properties. The profits accruing were to be used for the maintenance of the school. He was also given a new licence to make over to the Canons of St. Davids lands in Dewsland, Pembrokeshire, to the value of £20 a year, to sustain the school.

A master and an usher (assistant master) were appointed and the school was not restricted to boys and youths within the town only, but also catered for those 'of the country theretoe adjoining'.

Unfortunately, the school did not last long after Lloyd's death in 1547. In his will he left the site of the Friary, together with his other property in Dewsland, Pembrokeshire, for the maintenance of the school, but his executors betrayed their trust and the Friary properties were appropriated by William and John Parry (or ap Harry), thus causing the school to be closed. The Pembrokeshire property was appropriated by John Davies (or David) of Trefin. The mayor, aldermen and inhabitants of Carmarthen brought a Bill of Complaint against the three offenders shortly after Lloyd's death, with the object of reviving the school, but the lawsuit was not heard for several years until early in Elizabeth I's reign. Then John Parry denied ever having entered the Friary premises at all, while his brother, William, claimed that he had legally taken a lease of the premises. His claim was successful and his family remained in possession of the Friary until the early seventeenth century. In 1632 the property was sold to Lord Vaughan of Golden Grove and became part of the Golden Grove Estate. Thus ended Carmarthen's first grammar school after only four years. Nevertheless, its influence must not be underestimated, for it was probably one of the factors which brought the Queen Elizabeth Grammar School into existence nearly thirty years later.

THE QUEEN ELIZABETH GRAMMAR SCHOOL, 1576-1978

One of the oldest and most celebrated grammar schools in Wales, the Queen Elizabeth Grammar School was founded by Letters Patent dated 7th July, 1576, and continued in existence for just over four centuries until its closure in July, 1978. The school Charter was granted by the Queen in response to a petition by Walter Devereux, Earl of Essex, Richard Davies, Bishop of St. Davids, Sir James Croft(e), Controller of the Queen's Household, Griffin Rees and Walter Vaughan, Aldermen of Carmarthen and Robert Toy(e), a Councillor of the town. The Charter stated that the school was to be called 'the free grammar school of Queen Elizabeth . . . . for the education, instruction and teaching of boys and young men in grammar and other lesser studies.'

The founders were all local men of influence who took an interest in the welfare of Carmarthen. The principal founder, Walter Devereux, first Earl of Essex, was born at Carmarthen castle about 1540 and buried in St. Peter's Church in November 1576, shortly after the foundation of the grammar school. He was the grandson of Walter Devereux, Lord Ferrers, who was made Chamberlain and Chief Justice of South Wales in 1525 and was Mayor of Carmarthen on several occasions.[2]

The Bishop of St. Davids, Richard Davies, was also keen to found a grammar school, for he was well aware of the widespread illiteracy in the diocese, the scarcity of able preachers and the need for education to further the cause of religious enlightenment and the spread of Protestantism.

Of the other founders, Sir James Croft (or Crofte) had connections in Carmarthen in that his sister, Lady Joyce Gamage, née Croft, married Griffith Leyshon, High Sheriff, who lived in the Priory after its dissolution. In his will of June 1555 Griffith Leyshon bequeathed the Priory, described as his 'mansion house', to his wife who subsequently left it in 1588 to 'James Croft, the third son of my brother, Sir James Croft.'

The two aldermen, Griffin Rees (Griffith Rhys/Rice) and Walter

Vaughan, were both members of distinguished county families - the Rices of Newton (Dynevor) and the Vaughans of Golden Grove.

The last founder to be named, Robert Toy(e), was a councillor who became mayor in 1582. He was a member of a notable and prosperous merchant family living in St. Mary Street, his father Humphrey being mayor in 1557 and also interested in education, for in his will he left money towards a free school.

The Charter also named twenty 'guardians and governors of the school', consisting of the mayor, aldermen and councillors. Many of these first governors were former mayors or subsequent mayors and many were merchants and ship-owners. There was to be one master and an under-master, called an usher, their appointments and salaries being vested in the governors.

The Charter, unfortunately, gives no information on the number of scholars admitted, or at what age, but the fact that there were two masters indicates a school of reasonable size. Nor does the Charter make specific provision for the admission of poor children although the school was called *free.*

A CLASSICAL CURRICULUM

The Charter stated that the school was 'for the education, instruction and teaching of boys and young men in grammar and other lesser studies.' This indicates that the Carmarthen Grammar School followed the classical curriculum common to all Tudor grammar schools. Latin grammar was the foundation of learning, with a certain amount of Greek, followed by the study of classical literature. Lessons consisted chiefly of learning the texts by heart, continuous oral repetition and the composition of Latin prose and verse. Classics were necessary for entry into the Universities (only Oxford and Cambridge at this time) and into the learned professions.

Since the Carmarthen School was also licensed by the Bishop to give theological training to students, leading to their ordination into the Church, theology formed an important part of the curriculum. This remained so until 1827 when St. David's College, Lampeter, was opened specifically for theological training.

Unfortunately, no definite evidence has yet been discovered about the early history of the Grammar School between 1576 and 1619. Indeed, there is even some doubt as to whether it actually came into existence after its foundation by Charter in 1576, and even if it did so, it may not have enjoyed a continuous existence. Speed's map of Carmarthen of 1610 does not show the school. However, there are two pieces of evidence which could indicate the existence of the school. The first is that a number of eulogies, composed in Latin, appear in the funeral service for Walter Devereux, the chief founder. According to Martin Evans:[3] 'These eulogies had much in common both in content and treatment, and were probably composed as exercises by the scholars of the Grammar School for this special occasion. Since the School Charter was granted on July 8th, 1576, and the funeral took place on 26th November 1576, it appears that the school did open and exist in these early months.'

The second piece of evidence is that of the will of Edward Myddleton (Middleton), dated 1587, one of the first governors of the school, who left an annual sum of money 'to the free schoole of Carmarthen if it goe forward and be maintained.' This suggests that the school may have been in existence at this time but there was some doubt as to whether it could be maintained. Its location is unknown.

THE SEVENTEENTH CENTURY

From 1619 more definite official evidence emerges about the building of the school. At this time there was a good deal of correspondence concerning money collected in Carmarthenshire, originally for sending soldiers to Ireland, but subsequently re-allocated, in part, to the building of a free school in Carmarthen. From 1619 to 1622 there was some delay in getting the money to be used for building the school. Eventually, according to the Minutes of the Common Council, the school house was built in 1622 with 'money levied in Carmarthenshire towards furnishing a hundred soldiers for Ireland, partly in expenses for the soldiers and the remainder in payments for the free school in Carmarthen.'

The next reference also occurs in the Minutes of the Common Council dated 18th September 1633, when certain monies 'received towards the building of the free school' were ordered to be paid to Mr. Morgan Owen towards its maintenance. The Rev. Morgan Owen, M.A., who was born at Myddfai, was Headmaster from about 1622-1633 and so far as is known to date, the first recorded Headmaster. In 1640 he was consecrated Bishop of Llandaff. In his will, proved on 12th December 1645, Bishop Morgan Owen states: 'I give twenty pounds annuity to the school at Carmarthen or to maintain apprentices to the Common Council of that town to be paid out of the Rectory of St. Ishmael's for ever.' (Presumably this endowment was to be used to maintain apprentices if the school should cease to exist.)

None of these references to the Grammar School mentions its location but subsequent references show that the school stood on what is now the forecourt of the Priory Street Infirmary and that it was a low single-storey building of limestone.

A picture of the Grammar School in the mid seventeenth century is provided by some letters written in 1673-74 by the Rev. Nicholas Roberts, Headmaster at that time. The letters, dealing with the preceding thirty years, were in response to a questionnaire sent by a Christopher Wase of Oxford University to the Grammar Schools of the period. This correspondence was discovered in the Bodleian Library, Oxford, by Mr. Benjamin Howell, M.A., Headmaster 1955-72, whose findings were published in *The Carmarthenshire Historian*, 1966. The most informative letter, dated April 1st 1674, states: 'The fabric was built at public charge about the beginning of the late rebellion.' (The Civil War began in 1642 so this date does *not* correspond with that of the building in 1622). The letter also states that the school had been endowed by Morgan Owen 'with £20 per annum charged upon the Impropriation of St. Ishmael's' and 'the Schoolmaster is to be approved of by the Mayor and Common Council consisting of 22'. In another letter to Wase, the Rev. Nicholas Roberts states that Morgan Owen gave a house 'in Priory Street Ward to be ye schole house (and so it is) with an acre of land thereto adjoyning.' (This land could be the school-yard shown on Bucks' print of 1748.)

According to Roberts' letter of April 1st 1674, there had been eleven Headmasters, most being in Holy Orders, since the endowment of Morgan Owen, though he states that 'many eminent persons taught here long before'. The reason for such a large number of headmasters in the comparatively short space of about thirty years, lies in the fact that many, being clergymen, usually left to take up appointments in the Church. Of the headmasters listed, perhaps the best known is William Jones, a vicar of St. Peter's Church and later Archdeacon of Carmarthen. He was a generous benefactor of the School, for in his will dated May 2nd 1676, he gave 'ye house and lands Next to ye Free Schoole to ye Mastr of ye said Free Schoole for Ever.' This house was occupied by successive Headmasters until the grammar school was amalgamated with Sir Thomas Powell's School in 1857. William Jones is buried in St. Peter's Church.

Finally, the Rev. Nicholas Roberts states that the School had a large library before the Civil War (1642-48) but afterwards not one book was left. However, he had procured a considerable number from several gentlemen in order to refurnish it, together with a small sum of money. (Headmaster Roberts was himself a considerable scholar, interested in Welsh antiquities, who corresponded with Edward Lhuyd, Keeper of the Ashmolean Museum, Oxford. His letters to both Lhuyd and Wace are preserved in the Bodleian Library.)

In August 1684 the Duke of Beaufort, as Lord President of the Council in Wales, visited Carmarthen in the course of his Progress through the Principality. He was accompanied by Thomas Dineley who recorded and illustrated places of interest in his Diary, now known as *The Beaufort Progress*. Since only hasty notes could be taken, Dineley was not always accurate in his facts and descriptions, but his pen-sketches at Carmarthen of the 'ffree schoole', the bridge and the quay, and St. Peter's church are most intriguing. His Diary records: 'At the Entrance into Carmarthen from Golden Grove you have on the left hand the ffree schoole belonging to the Town, built of white hard stone . . . It is endow'd with thirty pounds a year, carrying in the ffront towards the street, the Armes of the Corporacon cut in stone, after the same manner as I have exhibited it, from the Common Seal . . .' (The School stood in Priory Street on the site of the present forecourt of the Infirmary.)

Thomas Dineley's drawing of the School Building in 1684

Beneath the Corporation Arms was a Latin inscription to the effect that the School was 'renewed' during the mayoralty of John Scurlock. Dineley gives the date as 1662 but the stone, now preserved in the Old Maridunians' Chapel in St. Peter's Church, is inscribed *MDCLXVI* (1666). Dineley also records that there was an inscription in Greek over the school door which was at the back of the building. Spurrell states that two fragments of a stone tablet bearing two lines of a Greek inscription were found when the old school building was demolished in 1857. Subsequently, after Spurrell's death, two more inscribed stones were found in the garden wall of Picton House, near the Infirmary, the one being the stone with the Latin inscription mentioned above and the other being the lower part of the Greek inscription recorded by Dineley in his diary. This stone had a border in relief and appeared to be complete in itself and not part of the original two Greek lines discovered in 1857. Mr. E. S. Allen, Headmaster at the time of the discovery of these two later stones, had them removed to the Grammar School, where the stone discovered earlier was also housed. Translation of the Greek inscription, however, always proved a problem since the Greek was inaccurate, but it was generally rendered as:

To build a house without foundations is labour in vain,
To learn without grammar is as empty as the winds.
From the birth of Christ 1668.

Unfortunately, the Greek inscribed stones were lost in a disastrous fire at the school in 1969, but the Latin inscribed stone is preserved in St. Peter's Church. Another casualty of the fire was a stone crowned head, reputed to be that of Elizabeth I, which was found in the foundations of the original grammar school when it was demolished.

In 1686 the administration of the free Grammar School became the reponsibility of the Common Council when the latter became responsible for the appointment and payment of the Masters. John Maddocks was appointed 'Schoolmaster' in 1686.

THE EIGHTEENTH CENTURY

During most of the eighteenth century the Grammar School

continued to provide an education based on Classics and Theology. All of its headmasters, without exception, were in Holy Orders. It still maintained its close connection with the Established Church since it was the chief centre in the diocese licensed for theological training, hence its name *Free Licensed Grammar School.* The term *free* could be something of a misnomer, however, since there is little evidence to show that the Grammar School provided for the sons of the poor labouring classes; its pupils were chiefly the sons of clergymen, prosperous tradesmen and local gentry who could afford to pay fees for the privilege of education. Nevertheless, in the year 1711, the first reference to poor children occurs in the Corporation or Borough Order Book, when the Headmaster, John Maddocks, was asked to give an account of the number of poor children taught by him and was informed that in the future he was to teach 'such a number of poor children as the Mayor and major part of the Common Council shall appoint yearly.'

The Mayor and Common Council were responsible for appointing the Headmaster and his usher (assistant master), paying their salaries and maintaining the Grammar school in good repair. The Corporation Order Books show that they took their duties seriously and that they were interested in the welfare of the school. An entry of 1733, when John Evans was appointed Headmaster, reveals that there were then about fifty scholars or more although the number of poor boys admitted free was no more than six.

In 1748 *The Free School* was marked on Samuel and Nathanial Buck's print of Carmarthen. The view is taken from the river and shows the school-house in Priory Street as a single-storey building with a back door and an enclosed yard.

With the appointment of the Rev. William Higgs-Barker as Headmaster in 1767, an appointment which lasted for the next thirty years, the school entered upon a period of expansion in numbers and of a wide reputation for instruction in Classics and Divinity. In addition the curriculum was being expanded and instruction was also given in English, Writing, Arithmetic, Drawing, Dancing and Philosophy. The

The School Building in 1748, rear view (detail from Samuel and Nathaniel Buck's engraving of the town)

The School Building, 1797-1857

school also took boarders at £15. 15s. per annum, with 'parlour boarders' at £21 per annum. (The latter probably lived with the Headmaster and received better meals and accommodation).

In 1797 in order to accommodate increased numbers, the Common Council decided that the old school-house in Priory Street should be demolished and a new school-house built on the same site. It was a long, low building with its front door directly onto the street, its back door onto a playground. It could accommodate one hundred boys with desks and benches on raised wooden platforms on both sides. The master's seat and usher's seat were opposite the front door. The school-house had two fireplaces, one at each end, and 'was like a college chapel and very comfortable'.

Rev. William Higgs-Barker
Headmaster, 1767-1797

THE NINETEENTH CENTURY

The close link between the Grammar School and the Established Church continued beyond the middle of the nineteenth century. From 1867, however, none of the Headmasters was in Holy Orders. Some indication of the subjects studied in the 1820's is given in a *Journal* advertisement of January 1822. The Rev. T. Hancock was then Headmaster with the Rev. David Archard Williams as his assistant. In addition to Classics there were the following subjects at different terms per quarter: Mathematics, English Grammar, Use of globes, Elocution, Composition, Geography, Writing and Arithmetics. Also available were French, Drawing and Dancing, which were regarded as social accomplishments. The school catered for boarders as well as day scholars: 'Each young gentleman to provide himself with a tablespoon and six towels.'

With the opening of St. David's Theological College at Lampeter in 1827, the Grammar School suffered a decline in numbers owing to the removal to Lampeter of senior scholars seeking ordination. After 1834 the School ceased to be recognised as an institution from which young men were admitted to Holy Orders and numbers dropped accordingly.

In 1847 the Report of the Commissioners of Inquiry into the state of Education in Wales revealed that the Grammar School was conducted by a master and two assistants, the subjects taught being Latin, Geography, Mathematics and History. The standards were reported to be very modest. The school-room was 'a good-sized room; pews on the sides, desks and a stove in the middle.' There were six free places for foundation scholars.

At this time the Grammar School was experiencing competition from Sir Thomas Powell's Charity School which had been founded under Thomas Powell's will of 1729. (See below.) In 1857 the two schools were amalgamated under the name of *The Endowed Schools* and the Grammar School moved from Priory Street to Sir Thomas Powell's School which was located on the Priory Field to the east of The Esplanade. This building, completed in November 1846, still exists and is known as *The Old Grammar School.* The school-house in Priory Street was demolished in May 1857 and the foundation stone of the Carmarthenshire Infirmary was laid to the rear of the site.

With amalgamation came an increase in numbers so that the *Journal* could report in August 1858 that the Endowed Schools had 51 pupils on the register as against 27 at the corresponding period of the previous year. Under the Headmaster, Mr. Benifold, pupils were prepared for the University examinations of Oxford, Cambridge and Durham.

The Grammar School remained on the Priory Field until January 1884 when a new school was built on a new site between Richmond Terrace and Wellfield Road. This site, the gift of the Charity Commissioners, was known as the Prisoners' Field, having been left in trust many years previously for the benefit of debtors in Carmarthen gaol. (This charitable bequest goes back to the seventeenth century: 'The Lady Elizabeth Morgan of Inniswen [Ynyswen] gave by her will Augt ye 30th 1674 fifty pound to purchase Lands, ye rent to be distributed among ye prisoners of this county Borough of Carmarthen for ever.')

In December 1885 the Headmaster, Mr. H. S. Holme, advertised in the *Journal:* 'Excellent classroom accommodation for 150 boys at the new school. The course of instruction is such as will thoroughly prepare boys for the Matriculation, Civil Service, Oxford Local, Cambridge Local, Preliminary Professional, Prelim. Medical, Prelim. Pharmaceutical and Prelim. Law examinations.'

From a photograph taken in 1888 it would appear that there were then about sixty pupils in the school.

In September 1894 the Grammar School was established as an Intermediate School under the Welsh Intermediate Education Act, whereby the County Council gave grants for a few entrance scholarships covering free tuition. Scholarships were open to boys who had been in a public elementary school for not less than three years. The Intermediate School prepared pupils for the Universities of England and Wales, and so for the first time an educational ladder was set up between elementary school and university.

At this period in the Grammar School's history the Headmaster was Mr. E. S. Allen, (1892-1929), with a staff of two assistant masters plus part-time teachers for drawing, music and short-hand. According to a

The Headmaster's house and dormitories

Journal report of December 1894, there were then only about 33-36 boys in the school, the annual fees of £5. 5 shillings being hardly sufficient to cover salaries! But following on the Welsh Intermediate Education Act the school experienced a steady development and in 1899 a new Headmaster's house and a boarders' wing were erected.

THE TWENTIETH CENTURY

From a school photograph of 1904-05 it would appear that the number of pupils in school was just over 100. Thereafter numbers continued to rise as did the achievements and reputation of 'The Gram', as it became affectionately known. After the First World War the school experienced a further period of expansion; a new wing was added in 1931 and by 1934 there were 335 on the register. When in 1958 the Girls' Grammar School, which had been built on an adjacent site, moved to Johnstown, the Boys' Grammar School occupied all the buildings on the Wellfield Road site. Sadly the oldest portion of the school was severely damaged by fire in 1969 and considerable rebuilding work had to be undertaken.

To mark the 400th anniversary of the founding of the school by Royal Charter, a formal visit was made in October 1976, by Her Royal Highness the Duchess of Gloucester, representing the Queen. The Duchess was welcomed to the school by the Headmaster, Mr. D. J. Evans; this ceremony was followed by a service at St. Peter's Church. However, the 400th anniversary celebrations were tinged with sadness, in view of the impending closure of the school under the scheme for reorganising secondary education.

In September 1978 a new pattern of secondary education in Carmarthen was introduced. The Boys' and Girls' Grammar Schools ceased to exist as such and three new mixed comprehensive schools, ages 11-18, came into being. For a few years the boys already in the Grammar school remained on the Wellfield Road site, as an annexe to the new Queen Elizabeth Maridunum Comprehensive School in Johnstown, sharing the Wellfield site with the Welsh medium school, Ysgol Gyfun Bro Myrddin (District of Merlin Comprehensive School). Eventually the latter took over the entire site.

The last issue of the Grammar School magazine, the *Maridunian*, which had appeared regularly since 1888, was produced at Midsummer 1978, when it was recorded that there were 524 boys on the roll and 33 members of the staff under the last Headmaster, Mr. D. J. Evans. There was a large sixth form of 110 boys and a wide curriculum. Since the first recorded Headmaster, Morgan Owen (c.1622-33), there had been thirty-nine headmasters, the great majority of whom had been clergymen of the Established Church.

Throughout the centuries the Queen Elizabeth Grammar School always maintained its traditional link with St. Peter's Church, the Founders' Day service and the Christmas Carol service becoming annual events held in the church. The church's south porch, dating from the

The Richmond Terrace buildings
The oldest building in the foreground was burnt down in 1969.
Inset: The school crest and motto *Nid da lle gellir gwell*
(It is not your best if you can do better)

14th century, was converted into a Chapel of Rest by the Old Maridunians' Association in memory of former pupils who gave their lives in the two world wars and subsequent conflicts.

Many scholars who received their early education at 'The Gram' have won distinction in various spheres, including the church, universities, civil service, medicine, law, the arts, commerce and sport. For generations of pupils the school offered opportunities and opened avenues for advancement by representing all that was best in the tradition of Welsh grammar school education.

SIR THOMAS POWELL'S SCHOOL, 1729-1857

Sir Thomas Powell's School was amalgamated with the Grammar School under a Court of Chancery scheme in 1857. At this time Sir Thomas Powell's School, a progressive educational establishment in the town, was located on the Priory field to the east of the Esplanade, and it was to this building that the Grammar School pupils moved when the old school building in Priory Street was demolished. The two amalgamated schools were known initially as 'The Endowed Schools'. Powell's school building, completed in November 1846, still exists, being now divided into four private houses still known as 'The Old Grammar School'.

Sir Thomas Powell (1664-1720) of Broadway, Laugharne and of Coldbrook, Monmouth, was created a baronet in 1698 and served as M.P. for Monmouthshire from 1705-08 and for Carmarthenshire from 1710-15. According to the inscription on his monument in Laugharne Church, he was the son of Sir John Powell of Llanwrda who was one of the judges who acquitted the seven bishops of seditious libel in the famous trial of 1688, just before James II was deposed.

Sir Thomas Powell's School
(*now* The Old Grammar School)

Sir Thomas Powell's Charity School came into existence as a result of his will, proved in 1729, leaving certain premises to be used for charitable purposes. It would appear from later evidence that the premises consisted of three houses in Lower Market Street (now Hall Street) and that the rentals from these houses were used for the purpose of paying a master to give instruction to poor boys. Although there is no clear information on the school's history in its early years, such as when it actually came into existence, some information is supplied in a letter written by the Rev. David Peter, Master of the Charity School, to the

Cambrian Society, prior to the Carmarthen Eisteddfod of 1819. The letter, dated 13th May, 1818, states:

> 'Many years back a Gentleman in this town (Sir Thomas Powell, Bart.) left three houses in trust for the education of six boys in reading, writing and the mathematics. On the demise of the twelve trustees appointed by the said gentleman, the Common Council Men of the County Borough of Carmarthen became trustees and guardians of the said Charity, and in them alone is invested the power of choosing the Master, and superintending the Charity. In the year 1792 Mr. Peter was chosen by the Common Council Men of Carmarthen to be Master of the said Charity School. From 1792 to 1813 the aggregate rent of the three houses left for the education of the six boys amounted to no more than £22 per annum; but on the expiration of the leases, in 1813, the aggregate rent of the three houses was advanced to £70 per annum. In consequence of this advance of salary the number of scholars was doubled, and ever since Mr. Peter has on that Charity from 12 to 15 boys, nominated and recommended by the Common Council Men.'

(The master was allowed to take an unlimited number of paying scholars.)

The Rev. David Peter (1765-1837) was also the minister of Lammas Street Chapel and, in addition, in 1795 he was appointed Tutor of the Welsh Presbyterian Academy. He held these three posts until 1835 and in consequence of this both the Charity School and the Academy classes were housed in the Lammas Street Chapel buildings. By 1846, according to the Report of the Commissioners of Inquiry into Education, Sir Thomas Powell's School was located in 'a detached building on the slope under the Parade', but the school-room was very small and inconvenient. A new and more substantial building had been built by subscription and was ready for occupation in November of 1846, being sited on the Priory field to the east of the Esplanade. The Master was Mr. F. B. Ribbans, assisted by his son. There were 15 foundationers (free-place scholars) and 34 pay-scholars. Subjects studied were Latin, Greek, Geography, History and Mathematics. It is recorded that Mr. Ribbans, who was appointed in March 1844, put new life into the school and he is described by a contemporary as 'a scholar, short of stature, choleric and lived for a while on the Parade'.

The new building was dedicated in April 1847. It was to this building (now known as the Old Grammar School) that the Queen Elizabeth Grammar School was moved in 1857 on amalgamation with Thomas Powell's School.

MEYRICK'S CHARITY SCHOOL AND LIBRARY

Edmund Meyrick (1636-1713), a native of Merioneth and a kinsman of the Vaughans of Golden Grove, was chaplain to Richard Vaughan, second Earl of Carbery. He held a number of church livings at the same time, including St. Peter's, Carmarthen, (Vicar 1672-89) and he also became a Canon and Treasurer of St. David's Cathedral. A generous benefactor to Jesus College, Oxford, he bequeathed much property for the foundation of scholarships and exhibitions there for the benefit of Welsh students. He died at Carmarthen in 1713 and was buried in St. Peter's vestry, which he had restored at his own expense. There is a memorial tablet to him in the chancel.

In one of the *Tables of Pious Benefactors to the Town of Carmarthen*, dated 1715, which can be found in St. Peter's Church, it is recorded that 'Edmund Meyrick, M.A., gave a convenient house and garden for ye use of a charity school and lending library for ever.'

According to the *Schools Inquiry Commission 1869, Vol XX* (based on the Charity Commissioners' Report for 1834), it was in 1708 that the Rev. Edmund Meyrick gave premises in Priory Street for a library, library-keeper and schoolmaster for instructing poor children. There is some confusion, however, as to what eventually happened to Meyrick's school. According to one report, it fell down in 1727 when the boys were in school, fortunately without loss of life. On the other hand, in *The Story of Carmarthenshire* A. G. Prys-Jones states that Meyrick appointed a local man, Evan Griffiths, as its Master and that he intended to endow the school. Owing to some dispute, however, he changed his will and instructed that the Master should remove to Bala and set up the school there. Later this became the Bala Grammar School.

ASHBRIDGE'S SCHOOL, 1869-1887

This school, also known as the 'Carmarthen Collegiate School', existed from 1869 to 1887 and was a continuation of 'The Carmarthen School' at 7 and 8 Spilman Street. This latter school was taken over by John Hales Ashbridge who soon found it necessary to move to larger premises at 4, St. Mary Street. To its principal, Mr. Ashbridge, many Carmarthen men owed their secondary education. About 170 boys attended the school and in the words of George Eyre Evans, himself a pupil, 'Mr. Ashbridge was in many ways abreast of the educational methods of his day, never letting a pupil pass from a subject until he was assured the boy had mastered it.'

PARC-Y-VELVET ACADEMY

In 1849 a school was opened in connection with Parc-y-Velvet (Felfed) Unitarian Chapel, Mansel Street. The school or academy was carried on with varying fortunes during the second half of the nineteenth century. In 1894 under the name of Old College and Parc-y-Velvet Schools, it advertised its numerous successes in various examinations, including London matriculation, preliminary medical, law and chemists' exams, mathematics, physics and theoretical mechanics, and in examinations for theological colleges.

BLUE STREET ACADEMY

In the latter part of the nineteenth century this Academy prepared candidates for London matriculation and entry to theological (Baptist) colleges.

THE WELSH ACADEMY or PRESBYTERIAN COLLEGE, c.1704-1963

Until its closure in 1963 the Presbyterian College, located on The Parade, was the oldest surviving centre of higher education in Wales and one of the first Theological Colleges in Britain. Its origin can be traced to the private school or 'academy' conducted by the Revd. Samuel Jones, M.A., who was one of the Puritan clergymen ejected from their livings after the passing of the Act of Uniformity in 1662. In spite of persecution he maintained a school at his home, Brynllywarch, in his old parish of Llangynwyd, Glamorgan. A former Fellow and Tutor of Jesus College, Oxford, Samuel Jones was a cultivated and tolerant man, held in high esteem by both Nonconformists and Anglicans. By 1689, when the Toleration Act was passed, his Academy was a well known establishment for preparing students for the ministry and for other professional careers.

With the passing of the Toleration Act relieving Protestant Dissenters of persecution, the Presbyterians and Independents co-operated together to establish the London Presbyterian Fund Board in 1690. One of its purposes was to train students for the Nonconformist ministry. Since Oxford and Cambridge, the only Universities at this time, were not open to Nonconformists, the Presbyterian Fund Board sent students on scholarships to the dissenting academies, such as that conducted by the Rev. Samuel Jones at Brynllywarch. This was the first and most famous academy in Wales and was known as *The Welsh Academy.* Although the academies could not confer degrees, the best provided a standard of education which compared favourably with that of the old universities.

When Samuel Jones died in 1697, the Welsh Academy continued under other tutors at Brynllywarch until 1699. It then moved to Abergavenny but in about 1704 came to Carmarthen. Its first tutor was William Evans, a zealous dissenter who was working hard to establish Independent congregations in the area. Until his death in 1718 he conducted the Academy in premises in Priory Street, 'where five or six persons are instructed under him for preachers for the Dissenters.' He was also Minister to a small congregation of Independents meeting in Priory Street.

William Evans was succeeded as tutor and minister by the Revd. Thomas Perrot who moved with his congregation to premises in Lammas

Street. In 1726 a new Meeting House was built - Heol Awst or Lammas Street Chapel. Here Perrot conducted a private grammar school in connection with the Academy, both being open to Anglicans as well as Nonconformists. However, numbers became too large to be properly supervised, the Academy's reputation suffered a decline and on Perrot's death in 1733 the Academy's students were transferred to a school at Llwynllwyd, near Hay, by the Presbyterian Fund Board. It was because this Board was the main support of the Academy that the name *Presbyterian* was applied to the Academy, or College as it was subsequently called. It had no association with the later Presbyterian Church of Wales (the Calvinistic Methodist Connexion).

In 1741 the Academy was transferred to Haverfordwest, only to come back again to Carmarthen in 1743. Samuel Thomas was now Independent minister of Lammas Street Chapel and he became Junior Tutor and then, in 1759, Senior Tutor of the Academy. He was succeeded in 1764 by Dr. Jenkin Jenkins but gradually during the ensuing fifteen years there was a decline in standards and in 1779 the Academy was removed from Lammas Street to Rhydygors House, Johnstown, where the students, twenty-three of whom were supported by the Presbyterian Fund, had to reside under strict regulations. The move, however, failed to have the desired effect and in 1784 the Academy's 'present low reputation' was noted, with the comment, 'great abilities and great Character for Wisdom and Goodness are necessary to retrieve it.'

In 1785 the few remaining students were moved to Swansea but ten years later, in 1795, the Academy returned to Carmarthen for the third time. The Revd. David Peter, minister of Heol Awst Chapel, was appointed Senior Tutor or Principal (there were only two tutors at this time, senior and junior) and he remained in this post for the next forty years until his retirement in 1835. College classes were held in the Chapel premises as were those of the grammar school which David Peter also conducted. In a letter, dated 1818, he wrote: 'There is at Carmarthen a Presbyterian College, under the superintendence of the Rev. D. Peter and his Colleague, the Rev. D. Jones, where twelve young men are educated for the Christian ministry. This College is supported by Legacies and annual Collections and its affairs managed by the Presbyterian Board in London .... Mr. Peter has also a Grammar School, where between forty and fifty boys are instructed in the languages, Arts and Sciences ...'

The close association between Lammas Street Chapel and the Academy continued until David Peter's retirement in 1835. He was succeeded by Dr. David Lloyd, a classical scholar and a Unitarian minister, who had his own small Unitarian congregation. He built Parc-y-Felfed (Parc-y-Velvet) Chapel in 1849. From Dr. Lloyd's appointment in 1835, with very few exceptions, all the Principals of the

The Presbyterian College, The Parade (closed in 1963)

Academy were Unitarians and pastors of Parc-y-Felfed Chapel.

In 1840 the Academy was moved from Lammas Street to rented premises on The Parade and in 1842 became affiliated by Royal Warrant to the University of London. Thus it was the first institution in Wales to offer training for a University degree. It was about this time that the Welsh Academy became known as the Presbyterian College. In 1847 a third tutor was appointed and in 1860 the Presbyterian Fund Board purchased the Parade premises which were considerably enlarged in 1894.

With the opening of the Welsh University Colleges, however, the Carmarthen Presbyterian College became purely theological in 1896 and was recognised as an affiliated theological college of the University of Wales. Subsequently it presented graduates for the higher Welsh University degrees in Theology.

In 1959 the Independent tutors and students withdrew from the college, amalgamating with Brecon Memorial College to form a Congregational College at Swansea. The reduced number of students, together with economic and financial considerations, finally compelled the Presbyterian Board to close the College, still located on The Parade, in 1963. It was then merged with the School of Theology at University College, Cardiff.

So ended the close association between the Presbyterian College, formerly the Welsh Academy, and Carmarthen - an association that lasted for over 250 years. During that time the College made a significant contribution to the educational and religious life not only of the town but also of the County and the Principality. Being open to students of all denominations, the College offered a training in liberal theology and education fostering a critical spirit of free enquiry. It not only trained students for the various Nonconformist ministries but, prior to the opening of St. David's Theological College at Lampeter in 1827, many Anglican students received their training at the Academy. Its importance for higher education in the days before the establishment of the Welsh University Colleges and before Oxford and Cambridge Universities were open to Nonconformists, cannot be over-estimated.

At the same time the Academy was the seat of unorthodox doctrines and especially during the later part of the eighteenth century it was 'the fountain-head of Unitarianism in Wales.'

During its long history a great many preachers, teachers, writers and public men were trained at the College, including Thomas Charles of Bala; Griffith Jones of Llanddowror; Rev. Watkin Williams (Watcyn Wyn); Rev. David Davies, Castellhywel, who translated *Gray's Elegy* into Welsh; Rev. David Peter; Sir John Russell, eminent chemist and soil scientist and a former President of the British Association for the Advancement of Science; Rev. Elfed Lewis of Blaen-y-coed, Cynwyl Elfed, poet, hymnologist and a former Archdruid; and David Williams, eighteenth century radical reformer, whose writings on political, religious and moral issues were praised by Frederick II of Prussia, Voltaire and Rousseau. His defence of the American colonists in his *Letters on Political Liberty* so influenced the French revolutionaries that he was invited to France and made an honorary citizen of the Republic. He was the founder of the *Royal Literary Fund* to help struggling writers in their studies.

Tŷ Coffa Elfed
(Elfed's Memorial House), Cynwyl Elfed
The restored birthplace of
Rev. Elfed Lewis, a student at the college

TRINITY COLLEGE

Founded as the South Wales and Monmouthshire Training College, Trinity College was the first teacher training college to be established in Wales. The foundation stone was laid by Connop Thirlwall, Bishop of St. Davids, on July 16th 1847 and the building was formally opened on October 24th 1848. The College came into being largely through the influence of Bishop Thirlwall with the strong support of the Welsh

Education Committee of the National Society, an Anglican organisation founded in 1811 *for Promoting the Education of the Poor in the Principles of the Established Church.*

The Welsh Education Committee of the National Society was set up in 1846 to promote the spread of primary education in Wales and to administer funds raised for this purpose. Recognising an urgent need for trained teachers, the Committee (of which Bishop Thirlwall was a member) resolved to build a training college at Carmarthen and in December 1846 an architect, Henry Clutton, was directed to prepare plans. In May 1847 a tender to build the college for £5,853, submitted by contractor W. P. James, was accepted. The same contractor was also engaged to build a National and Practising School, known as the Model School, at a cost of £2,425, where the college students were to receive their practical training. The proposal to erect a 'model' school for boys, girls and infants was originally discussed by the St. Davids Diocesan Church Union Society Committee, meeting at Abergwili on August 14th, 1846, and it was probably this proposal which drew the attention of the National Society's Welsh Committee to Carmarthen and influenced its decision to locate the South Wales Training College here. The final outlay for the College, including the site of 10 acres, amounted to £9,000 which was met by the Welsh Education Fund from donations, by the National Society and by a grant from the Privy Council's Education Committee. The S.P.C.K. also gave £1,000.

According to a *Journal* report, the day on which the foundation stone was laid, July 16th 1847, was kept as a public holiday; shops were closed

The Training College in 1864

and a procession over a mile long proceeded from the Guildhall to the College. Headed by a Marshall and brass band, the procession included the Mayor and Corporation, police officers, the architect and clerk of works, the Ancient Order of Druids in full dress, the Order of Oddfellows and over 500 children of St. David's Sunday School. Many magistrates, clergymen and county gentlemen were also in the procession, followed by the Lord Bishop of the Diocese in his carriage.

The formal opening of the College on October 24th, 1848, was marked by a service in St. Peter's Church attended by the Mayor and other dignitaries and was followed by a 'cold collation' (light refreshments) at the College when many speeches were given.

The first Principal was Canon William Reed, former Principal of St. John's College, York, while the Vice-Principal was chosen as being 'able to speak, read and write the Welsh language.' For the first seven years the college was managed by the Welsh Education Committee meeting in London but then a local College Council was formed by Bishop Thirlwall. The cost of maintenance was borne by the National Society, Welsh public subscriptions and students' fees.

Accommodation was provided for 60 Anglican male students but there were 28 when it opened, increasing to 49 a year later. The building consisted of a chapel, school-room, library, dining-room, a house for the Principal and rooms for the Vice-Principal and assistant masters. In 1903 twenty day-students were admitted and 'as such students were admitted subject to a conscience clause, it became possible to extend the benefits of the college to Nonconformists.'

In 1931 a new Chapel was dedicated and it was then that the college was designated 'Trinity College'. Women students were admitted for the first time in 1957, with a corresponding expansion in teaching and administrative staff.

The College Chapel

Trinity College is now the only Church Voluntary College in Wales. Over recent years it has expanded greatly and as an Associated Institution of the University of Wales it now offers students a range of degree courses in addition to teacher training. Being a bilingual college, most courses may be pursued in either English or Welsh; the number of students able to teach through the medium of Welsh has increased progressively. Recently a Centre for Theology and Education has been established whilst the College is also committed to developing a post-graduate degree programme.

Situated on the edge of Carmarthen in a rural environment, the college campus covers a large area with buildings which are a mixture of the original Victorian architecture, modern teaching blocks and residential hostels. New student residences, furnished to the highest standards, have been completed recently. College buildings include a fine chapel, concert hall, theatre, providing facilities for music and drama performances, a new library, well-equipped computer unit and indoor swimming pool with sports facilities. The college farm and gardens are used for teaching purposes. An innovation in 1983 was the establishment of the East Dyfed Health Authority's School of Nursing on the campus site.

Another innovation was the opening in 1989 of The Halliwell Centre comprising conference rooms, a theatre and dining suites to serve both the local community and the College and to provide facilities for commercial and industrial organisations.

THE DIOCESAN HIGH SCHOOL FOR GIRLS 1879-1964

The High School was founded in 1879 by the St. David's Diocesan Board of Education for 'female secondary education in the Diocese' and was the first secondary school for girls in the town. It started in three adjoining houses in Wellfield Road (Nos. 20-22), its first principal being Mrs. Prince. In 1883 there were thirty-two boarders and sixteen day girls. In 1937 the school moved to Lime Grove House, with The Grange added in 1942.

The High School was primarily for boarding pupils but there were always day students and, at times, junior boys. At its peak there were over one hundred pupils, but the numbers declined and financial considerations caused it to close in 1964.

The school Chapel was originally the chapel of the County Gaol but when the latter was demolished, the chapel was removed, stone by stone, and rebuilt in Lime Grove. It was dedicated to St. Mary on June 8th, 1939. With the closing of the High School, the chapel passed into the care of St. David's parish and was renamed All Saints. It was reopened for public worship on October 21st, 1966, but has now closed.[4]

THE GRAMMAR SCHOOL FOR GIRLS, 1895-1978

The Girls' Grammar School was founded as the Carmarthen County Girls' School in September 1895, and was also known as the Girls' Intermediate School. It started with 35 pupils and was originally situated at No. 10 Quay Street, which had previously housed a private school - the Girls' Collegiate School - run by Mrs. W. Marles Thomas. The first Headmistress of the County Girls' School was Miss B. A. Holme, M.A., who held the post for 31 years. In 1899 the school moved to new

The Girls' Grammar School, Richmond Terrace

premises adjoining the Boys' Grammar School between Richmond Terrace and Wellfield Road.

In 1958 'The Girls' Gram' as it was affectionately known, moved again, this time to Llansteffan Road, Johnstown. The new buildings were formally opened by H.M. Queen Elizabeth the Queen Mother in May 1959, and the name of Queen Elizabeth II Grammar School for Girls was formally bestowed.

However, with the new pattern of comprehensive education introduced in Carmarthen in September 1978, the Girls' Grammar School ceased to exist as such, becoming a mixed comprehensive known as the Queen Elizabeth Cambria School.

During the years of its existence, the Girls' Grammar School enjoyed the dedicated services of four distinguished headmistresses: Miss B. A. Holme, Miss E. A. Davies, Miss M. M. Anthony (Mrs. Ben Howell) and Miss M. M. Wooloff who continued as headmistress of the Cambria School until her retirement in 1983.

CARMARTHEN SCHOOL OF ART

The Carmarthen School of Art, believed to be the first establishment of its kind in Wales, was founded in 1854 in Parade Road. It was housed 'in a dingy, barn-like building', originally the National School for Boys, at what are now Nos. 7, 8 and 9. By 1887 it had established branches in Llanelli, Haverfordwest and Tenby. The original premises in Parade Road were proving inadequate to meet the growing number of students and so in January 1891 a tender of £1,165 10s. was accepted for building a new school in Church Lane, opposite St. Peter's Church. The architect

The School of Art

was George Morgan of 24 King Street and the builder was Thomas Morris of Water Street. A public subscription list was drawn up and various events organised to raise funds; the biggest effort was one called 'Ye Fancye Fair' held in the Market Place in July 1891, raising £480. The new Art School, built in a distinctive red brick typical of late Victorian architecture, was opened with due ceremony on September 22nd, 1892. Accommodation for 70 students was provided (the majority at that time being part-time) and the Principal was Mr. William Jones, a native of the town, who is still remembered for his local etchings. He was also the father of Ernest Harold Jones, artist, archaeologist and Egyptologist.

In the early 1950's Carmarthenshire County Council took over control of the Art School in Church Lane and in 1958 moved the school to Ucheldir, a large house in College Road. The Church Lane premises, which were too small for the larger number of students, were left empty. In 1969, however, a further increase in student numbers resulted in the Church Lane building being once more occupied in conjunction with the main school. In September 1971 the Carmarthen School of Art combined with that of Llanelli to form the Dyfed College of Art, to provide full-time vocational courses for art students as well as non-vocational courses in pottery, painting and photography.

A new modern college was built in Job's Well Road in 1979, resulting in the final closure of the old Art School in Church Lane. In September 1985, under a reorganisation scheme, the new Art College became part of the Carmarthenshire College of Technology and Art which also embraces the Technical and Agricultural College at Pibwrlwyd and colleges at Llanelli and Ammanford.

For several years there have been plans to re-develop the Church Lane buildings into an art gallery and visual exhibition centre.

CARMARTHEN TECHNICAL AND AGRICULTURAL COLLEGE, PIBWRLWYD

In 1970 Carmarthen Technical and Agricultural College was formed by the union of Pibwrlwyd Rural Technical College and Golden Grove Farm Institute, Llandeilo. Pibwrlwyd Rural Technical College was founded by the Carmarthenshire Education Committee as Pibwrlwyd Farm Institute and opened in January 1927 with the object of giving both theoretical and practical training in agriculture, horticulture, poultry-keeping, dairy husbandry and rural domestic science to young men and women who chose a career connected with the land. The Institute was equipped with facilities for the purpose, having a 200 acre farm and a dairy and domestic science room.

In 1952 the Pibwrlwyd Farm Institute became the first residential Rural Technical College in Wales, responsible for all aspects of agricultural education in the county, while Golden Grove Mansion, once part of the Vaughan and later Cawdor estates, became Golden Grove (or Gelli Aur) Farm Institue. The subsequent growth of Pibwrlwyd's technical and commercial departments necessitated large-scale building extensions, the completion of which coincided with the merger of the two establishments in 1970.

As the Carmarthen Technical and Agricultural College, attracting students from West Wales and even further afield, the College provided courses in agriculture, dairying, engineering, business studies, home-economics and catering. It also ran its home farm.

In September 1985, under a reorganisation scheme, the Carmarthen Technical and Agricultural College became part of the Carmarthenshire College of Technology and Art, which is based on campuses at Carmarthen, Llanelli, Ammanford and Gelli Aur, Llandeilo.

19th CENTURY PRIVATE ADVENTURE SCHOOLS

In early nineteenth century Carmarthen there were numerous, small private establishments, sometimes known as *private adventure schools*, providing various standards of education in return for fees. These ranged from select establishments for young ladies and gentlemen, commercial academies for business and trade (reflecting the growing numbers of middle-class professionals and tradesmen), right down to the *dame schools*, usually run by elderly women who needed the few 'school pence' charged to make ends meet.

JOHN WHITE'S SCHOOL

One of the earliest schools was established by Mr. John White who also founded a well-known family printing business together with his wife Hannah. Born in 1762 at Knowstone, Devon, John White was appointed Headmaster of The Great House School, Chard, in Somerset in 1787. He came to Carmarthen at the close of 1803 and on March 31st 1804 he went to live in 44, Priory Street. A cultured and educated man, he became a noted school-master in the town. Mr. John White's School,

A NEW CIPHERING BOOK;

OR

THE TEACHER'S EASE,

AND

THE SCHOLAR'S HELP:

CONTAINING

A GREAT VARIETY OF INSTRUCTIVE AND AMUSING SUMS AND QUESTIONS,

IN THE SIMPLE AND COMPOUND PARTS OF

The Four first Rules of Arithmetic,

AND THE

RULE OF REDUCTION.

TO WHICH IS ADDED, THE MOST

Complete Set of Arithmetical Tables extant;

THE WHOLE IS ADAPTED

To Ladies and Gentlemen's Schools,

AND

PRIVATE FAMILIES.

By J. WHITE. Schoolmaster.

THE SECOND EDITION.

CARMARTHEN:

PRINTED AND SOLD BY THE AUTHOR: SOLD ALSO, BY LACKINGTON, ALLEN AND CO LONDON; HOBDAY AND CO. BIRMINGHAM; JENKINS, SWANSEA; PRIDHAM, NEWCASTLE, &c.

1809.

Priory Street, gave instruction in English grammar, useful and ornamental penmanship, arithmetic, fractions, decimals, extraction of roots, logarithms, geometry, trigonometry, land surveying, navigation, the use of globes and other sciences. The strictest attention was also paid to the 'morals and improvement of the pupils committed to his care.'

Subsequently he moved to King Street, where he kept a school called *The Writing, Commercial and Mathematical School,* which gave instruction in the same subjects as previously mentioned. Strict rules on behaviour, dress, cleanliness, tidiness and discipline were laid down and had to be observed. (see page 258)

In 1796, before his arrival in Carmarthen, John White produced *A New Ciphering Book or The Teacher's Ease and The Scholar's Help,* containing a great variety of instructive and amusing sums and questions, together with a complete set of Arithmetical Tables. It was for use in Ladies' and Gentlemen's Schools and private families. In 1809 he produced the second edition which was printed at Carmarthen. Advertisements for his school, showing the subjects taught, together with the financial terms, were printed by 'J. White and Sons, at the

Commercial Printing Office, Carmarthen.' According to one advertisement: 'the rapid progress pupils make under his care, is a convincing proof of the attention paid to their learning, many of whom have far exceeded the expectations of their parents.'

John White died on Sunday, 2nd August, 1818 and was buried in St. Peter's churchyard. His wife Hannah continued the printing business until her death in 1860.[5]

PARADE HOUSE SCHOOL

Another early school was Miss West's Seminary for Young Ladies, established in 1810 at Parade House. It was also known as *Miss West's French and English Boarding School for Ladies.* Subjects taught were reading, writing, grammar, arithmetic, geography, history, French, drawing, music and dancing - a wide range. Fees varied from 15 shillings to £1. 11s. 6d per quarter, while Board was 'liberally provided' at £21 per annum. If tea was taken twice a day then the charge was £2. 2 shillings per annum. Each boarder was to bring six towels and one spoon!

Parade House boarding school changed hands in 1816 when Mrs. Charles Brown 'a lady of great respectability and adequate qualifications such as might be expected from the daughter and grand-daughter of clergymen' took over. Mrs. Brown assured parents and guardians 'that every possible attention on her part shall be devoted to the comfort, improvement and morals of the ladies entrusted to her care.' However, the school closed quite suddenly in 1818 when Mrs. Brown's husband, Captain Charles Brown, left town.[6]

Later in the same year, 1818, Miss Rees opened her *Ladies' Seminary* in Spilman Street, followed by Miss Lander and Mrs. Kenge's *Ladies' Boarding and Day School,* also in Spilman Street.

By 1825 there were the following schools available: R. Owen's School, Dark Gate; Mrs. Williams' and Miss Jardine's School, Spring Gardens; James Puddicombe's Mathematical and Commercial Academy, Spilman Street; the Tabernacle Grammar School, later called the Tabernacle Classical, Mathematical and Commercial Academy; David Thomas' Commercial and Mathematical School, Bridge Street; and M. W. John's Academy, King Street (later Lammas Street). At John's Academy one could become accomplished in 'Elocution, Rhetoric, Logic, Versification and Theme Writing' for 15s. per quarter; 'the mathematics in all its various branches' for 21s., while European and 'the Oriental languages' each cost £2. 2s. per quarter. For 21s. the 'young gentleman' could acquire 'the Latin, Greek and Hebrew languages', whilst there was 'on reasonable terms accommodation for two respectable parlour boarders.'

Other schools recorded were: The Rev. David Lewis Jones' School, Guildhall Square, 1828-30; Miss Margaret Price's Ladies' Boarding School, Priory Street in 1830, later moved to Spilman Street; Mrs. Charlotte Smith's English and French Establishment for Young Ladies at Carmarthen House in Spilman Street 1828, later located at Furnace Lodge in 1835. Mrs. Smith took up to ten young ladies 'to educate with her own daughters'. Miss Woozencroft's Boarding School for Ladies in Spilman Street was established before 1830; Martin's Drawing School, The Parade, c.1830+; J. P. Brodribb's School or Carmarthen Commercial Academy, finally located in Lammas Street after several moves, 1828+; Mrs. Lewis Williams' School, Temple Gardens, succeeded in 1830 by Mrs. Davies; and Mr. Torckler's Clarendon House Academy, 8 Church Street, 'a select and genteel academy' for young gentlemen boarders, 1834+. Fees were 20-25 guineas per annum for which the young gentlemen were given a sound classical and commercial education 'exempt as much as possible from all coercion or corporal discipline.' James Brown's Commercial and Mathematical School, King Street, 1828+ combined business with education. Any person who wished to go in for the 'tallow-chandlery business' could be supplied with a 'large iron boiler, mould and other articles at a fair valuation', and strict attention was given to 'the morals and improvement of the pupils.' Spelling and reading were available at 7s. per quarter; writing, arithmetic, geography and English grammar at 10s. 6d. per quarter; vulgar and decimal fractions, extraction of roots and duodecimals at 12 shillings per quarter. The syllabus also included logarithms, geometry, trigonometry, merchants accounts, navigation, land surveying and mapping estates, all taught 'on reasonable terms.'

Other subjects covered by some of the schools were Lunar and Sidereal Observations (moon and stars), gauging and navigation, and use of globes.

Last, but not least, was the *Ladies' School* conducted in the 1840's by Mrs. Philip Fowke of Picton House, Picton Terrace. According to an advertisement in the *Journal* Mrs. Fowke 'begs to say she devotes her entire and undivided energies to the promotion of the health, domestic comfort and mental culture of those committed to her care. She instructs in Music and Singing herself; Drawing and Dancing are taught by a highly talented lady, her assistant, and French by a Parisienne resident in the establishment.'

PUBLIC ELEMENTARY EDUCATION

Although the Welsh educational movement of the eighteenth century began in Carmarthenshire, under the inspired leadership of Griffith Jones of Llanddowror, founder of the Welsh Circulating Schools, it was not until the early years of the nineteenth century that the first steps were taken towards establishing some form of public elementary education. Indeed it was not until the 1870 Education Act that a state system of elementary education was introduced by Gladstone's Liberal government. Only very gradually during the nineteenth century did the desire for government intervention in educational matters, as also in other matters, gain ground.

For the mass of the population in both England and Wales the fee-paying Public schools (a misnomer) and Grammar schools were completely out of reach, although the latter provided some free places for poor children - an avenue for intellectual and social advancement. The only schools that were available for providing some form of basic elementary education - reading, writing and arithmetic - were Voluntary schools run by religious groups and by private individuals. The best organised of the Voluntary schools were those run by the Established Church and by the Nonconformists. The Anglicans organised their schools through the *National Society (The National Society for promoting the Education of the Poor in the Principles of the Established Church)* founded in 1811 by Andrew Bell. The Nonconformists worked through the *British and Foreign Schools Society* established in 1814 under the influence of Joseph Lancaster, a Quaker, who had earlier formed the Royal Lancasterian Society and who ran his own schools at Borough Road in London.

Both the National Society and the British and Foreign Schools Society provided funds for the building of schools from income completely dependent on voluntary sources. However, in 1833 the Whig government made the first grant of £20,000 to the Anglican and Nonconformist School Societies to help them provide more school buildings. The government did not provide any schools itself - it merely made cash available to these voluntary societies. The National Society inherited, to some extent, the experience, prestige and resources of the *Society for Promoting Christian Knowledge* (the S.P.C.K. founded in 1698) which had been active in Carmarthenshire. Consequently more 'National' (i.e. Church) Schools were founded in the county than 'British' Schools. Nevertheless, it was a British Lancasterian school that was the first to be established in Carmarthen town itself.

Both Andrew Bell and Joseph Lancaster followed the 'monitorial' system of tuition in their schools. Older pupils called monitors taught small classes of younger children and were responsible for their behaviour and cleanliness as well as their instruction, thus economising on teaching staff and finances. Religious education was an important basis for all teaching in the schools, but in the British schools the Bible was taught 'without note or comment', thus giving non-sectarian instruction in the Scriptures.

THE LANCASTERIAN SCHOOL FOR BOYS, 1813

The Lancasterian school came into being as the result of a public meeting convened on the 16th February, 1813 by the Mayor, Mr. David Morris. The meeting was addressed by the Rev. David Peter, Principal of the Presbyterian College, the Rev. William Higgs Barker, vicar of St. Peter's and Dr. Morgan. Public subscriptions were raised from all denominations and the school was opened on January 25th, 1814 for 50 boys. It was held 'in a room lent by the Corporation over the old slaughter house,' in Cambrian Place. (Subsequently this became the site of the Malt House and is now roughly the site of the Day Centre in John Street.) In 1815 the Carmarthen Corporation gave the sum of ten guineas towards the support of the 'Royal Lancasterian School'.

A *Journal* report of March 1821 stated that there were about 200 boys receiving regular instruction in the school and making rapid progress. 'Much benefit to the town is anticipated.' In May 1823 it was reported that there were then about 161 boys in the school and their orderly conduct and improvement gave great satisfaction. The children were taught to read and revere the Bible but without attachment to any particular denomination. The 1846 Report of the Commissioners of Inquiry into the State of Education stressed the need for a new school-room and for a girls' school.

THE NATIONAL SCHOOL FOR GIRLS, 1820

This school was established by voluntary subscriptions aided by a grant from the National Society. The school-room was built in 1820 at the bottom of Parade Road beneath the Parade. The Corporation Order Book records in December 1819:

> 'ordered that a piece of land near a well walled in under the west end of the Parade 95ft. in length x 90ft. in breadth, be granted by lease by this Corporation to the Rt. Rev. The Lord Bishop of St. Davids for 99 years at a yearly rent of 2 shillings and 6d., for the building of a school for female children.'

In February 1820 a *Journal* report stated:

> 'Carmarthen National Female School: The Committee having the management of this establishment inform the Subscribers to the Fund for building a school-room that a piece of ground contiguous to the Parade has been liberally granted by the Corporation of Carmarthen for that purpose; and that the intended building will be commenced as soon as an adequate portion of the sum already subscribed shall have been paid into the hands of the Treasurer. The Committee cannot apply to the National Society for their grant of £50 until they can show that a sum equal to the estimated expense of carrying the above-mentioned object into effect has been actually deposited in the Fund.'

This report was followed by another in May 1820:

> 'The building of a commodious School-room has been commenced and must be completed in the course of four months. The spot on which

> the building is now in progress is near the west end of the Parade. It was granted by the Corporation for the purpose.'

There is no report of the actual opening of the school but it must have been open in October 1820 because at this date the Journal states: 'there is some prospect of the Carmarthen Sunday School for Boys being shortly made into a permanent national school, like the Girls' school, under the auspices of the National Society.' Also in October a special sermon was preached at St. Peter's Church and a collection made for the joint benefit of the National Female School and the Sunday School for Boys. (Spurrell states that a Sunday School was established at Carmarthen in 1787, the first in South Wales.)

In March 1821 the *Journal* reported that the children at the National Female School numbered about 120 and were making most satisfactory progress. Moreover

> 'it would be gratifying to the supporters of the Charity to know that for every guinea subscribed by them in the future they would be entitled to send 3 instead of 2 girls to the school - a regulation which will considerably augment the number of scholars.'

At the first public examination of the school held before the Bishop in November 1821, when 105 children were present, the Bishop expressed to the school mistress, Miss Wright, his satisfaction at the efficiency of the National system and his thanks to the Ladies' Committee for visiting the school and watching over its interests. On New Year's Day, 1822, about 100 girls were given one shilling each by Mrs. Morris, wife of the Mayor.

In December 1823, at the annual public examination, there were 108 girls present out of 130 on the register: those in the third or junior class being on average 7 years of age; those in the second class 9 years and those in the first class 11 years of age. Rewards of books were distributed to each deserving child, while Miss Wright was given a gratuity for the progress, order and management of the school. (Records of the 1830's show that the school mistress was then Mary Harris while in 1844 Ann Adams had the post.)

The National School for Girls also served as a Sunday School and so it is sometimes referred to as the Girls' National Day and Sunday School. This was the name given in the 1846 Report of the Commissioners of Inquiry into the state of Education.

THE NATIONAL SCHOOL FOR BOYS, 1822

This was also known as the Boys' National Day and Sunday School since it originated from the Carmarthen Sunday School. (i.e. St. Peter's Sunday School - since there was only one church in Carmarthen at this time.) It was opened in November 1822 and was located near the bottom of Parade Road, not far from the Girls' National School. In 1854 it became the site of the first School of Art and is now the site of numbers 7, 8 and

9 Parade Road.

At the school's first annual examination, held in November 1823, before the Bishop of St. Davids and the Committee of supporters, it was stated that there were 110 boys then present, but 149 altogether on the school register. Average daily attendance was 100 and a greater number on the Sabbath, since several boys had weekly employment which kept them away from the Day School but they attended the Sunday School. Tribute was paid to the school's progress during the year under the master, Mr. Nathaniel Leigh. Reports of 1835 and 1844 show that the master was then Mr. Cornelius Bland.

THE 1847 REPORTS OF THE COMMISSION OF INQUIRY INTO THE STATE OF EDUCATION IN WALES

As the result of a *Commission of Inquiry into the State of Education in Welsh Schools*, 1846, a detailed survey of the provision for education in Carmarthen was published in 1847. This survey is sometimes referred to as the *Blue Book Reports*. In addition to listing the schools then in existence in the town, including the Sunday Schools, the reports also contain comments on the Schools and evidence given to the Commissioners by certain residents familiar with the prevailing educational conditions.

Before giving the list of schools, some of the general comments made will be of interest. Mr. William Morris, assistant Commissioner, who visited several Carmarthen schools in November 1846, stated:

> 'The prevailing language of this town among the poor is still Welsh. I was particularly struck at the time of my visit with the great deficiency of public institutions for female education, the only school of the kind being the Girls' National school, with an average attendance of 75 in a female population of 5,260!
>
> 'The two grammar schools, i.e. Queen Elizabeth and Sir Thomas Powell's schools (between them educating 21 free-place boys) stand in an isolated and anomalous position. The foundationers are nominated by the Corporation from a class (i.e. working class) in proportion to whose numbers the accommodation of two such schools (21 free places) is as nothing.'

Mr. Morris suggests that

> 'the foundationers, instead of being arbitrarily appointed, be elected into the grammar schools by open examination from the primary schools. In this manner provision could be made for continuing the education of specially deserving pupils and for bringing the poor within the scope of influences . . . . enabling and encouraging them to prolong the period of education.'

The Rev. David Archard Williams, Perpetual Curate of St. David's stated:

> 'In the case of day-schools the mass of the population is commonly too poor to keep their children long enough at them, even if they wished it. The great number of little day-schools existing in the town are chiefly resorted to as infant-schools; convenience of locality, the low rate of charge, often a wish to serve the person keeping the school, make these schools frequented; there is no other public instruction provided than the National and Lancasterian schools, and the free foundations at Powell's and Queen Elizabeth's grammar schools, which are available for only 21 boys; for girls, excepting the National school, there is no such instruction whatever; the girls are put out to service at a very early age . . . The Sunday-schools have been the great supplement of our educational machinery.'

Mr. James Mortimer, Superintendent of the Calvinistic Methodist Sunday school said:

> 'The poor are rather careless about sending their children to the Sunday-school; this, however, proceeds in some degree from their being unable to provide proper clothes for them. The majority of the day-schools are very badly managed. A great majority of the poor cannot afford to pay towards the education of their children; our congregation subscribes chiefly to the Lancasterian school. Greater facilities of day-school education are much wanted here; the Lancasterian school is not so well attended as we could wish; the poor express a desire to educate their children, but show little practical earnestness in sending them to school.'

Mr. Edward Warren, Superintendent of the English Wesleyan Sunday school said:

> 'The poor in general show no active desire for education, nor do they appreciate the advantages of it . . . There is no gratuitous education for the poor of the town, except the National and Lancasterian schools and the free foundations for 21 boys at the grammar and Powell's schools. The present day-school accommodation is by no means adequate to supply the wants of the town. The numerous small day-schools which exist are frequented chiefly by the children of the little tradesmen and superior mechanics, who object to the notion of a charity-school; persons above the poorer class rarely apply to have their children admitted to the Lancasterian school, but we have more applications than we can accommodate . . . . The mass of the poor are Dissenters . . . . I should say that the majority of the adult labouring population in this town cannot read either in Welsh or English . . . a considerable proportion of them have attended, but few are still attending, Sunday-schools. One of the first and cheapest benefits which could be conferred on the poor of this town would be to give them increased facilities for day-school instruction; there is no deficiency of Sunday-school accommodation; but the provision for day-schools is most inadequate.'

The Rev. David Lloyd, Classical and Mathematical Tutor of the Presbyterian College, stated:

> 'Most of the children in the town from 8 to 10 years old can read

either English or Welsh. This has been learnt in the Sunday-schools, which the children of the poor almost universally attend. The education of females is decidedly at a lower point than that of the males; there are more who cannot read than among the men. Very few of them can write, Such of them as can read, learn this in the Sunday-schools where writing is, I believe, never taught.'

The 1847 Report lists the following schools and some of the comments made about each school are given:

QUEEN ELIZABETH FREE GRAMMAR SCHOOL: 'The school-room is a good sized room; pews on the sides, desks and a stove in the middle. The school is conducted by the master and two assistants.' The subjects taught were Latin, Geography, Mathematics and History but it would appear that the standards were very modest. (In 1846 the Grammar School stood on the forecourt of the present Infirmary in Priory Street.)

POWELL'S SCHOOL (i.e. Sir Thomas Powell's School): 'Conducted by a Mr Ribbans, assisted by his son, who is in Orders. There are in this school at the present 15 foundationers and 34 pay-scholars. Subjects studied are Latin, Greek, Geography, History and Mathematics. The boys acquitted themselves well in answering questions set by the visiting assistant commissioner. The day-books of the school appear to be kept with great regularity and neatness . . . . The present school-room is very small and inconvenient being a detached building on the slope under the Parade, near the Girls' National school. A new one has been built by subscription upon a site granted upon lease by Jesus College, Oxford, not far from the present building. The new room is a large and substantial edifice . . . No religious instruction is given in the school, but it is opened and closed with prayer and the Scriptures are read without comment.' (The 'new' building referred to is now the 'Old Grammar School' near the Esplanade.)

BOYS' NATIONAL DAY AND SUNDAY SCHOOL: (This stood at the bottom of Parade Road): 'Established 1822. Number of children on books = 73. Monitorial method used; number of monitors = 6. School-room and copy-books untidy; the boys extremely noisy and unmanageable. Two boys barefooted and many very ragged, but a few boys answered well. The master had a good faculty of teaching and the faults could be removed with a little judicious visiting . . . School was maintained by voluntary subscriptions. Subscribers could each recommend one child for every 5 shillings annually subscribed. Those scholars who learn writing pay a halfpenny per week, the rest pay nothing. More than $^4/_5$ are children of Dissenters. Attendance at church is supposed to be enforced . . . but the excuse of "having no fit clothes to go to church in" is generally received. Not more than 40 children out of 73 on the books attend church on Sundays . . . The poor dislike the idea of a charity-school. Parents will take their children away from gratuitous schools during prosperous times of the year and pay 2 pence or 3 pence per week for them at inferior schools. They bring them back again when wages are low or they are out of work or the markets rise. Probably religious objections as well as love of independence have something to do with their conduct.'

GIRLS' NATIONAL DAY AND SUNDAY SCHOOL (This also stood at the bottom of Parade Road, beneath the Parade.): 'Number of children on books = 103. Monitorial method used, number of monitors = 7.

School-room spacious, airy, scrupulously clean and neat. The course comprises religious instruction, reading, writing, the multiplication table and sewing. The children's reading is confined to the Scriptures. Some ladies come and read to the girls from an instructive or entertaining book while they are sewing in the afternoon. Such a practice puts within the reach of poor children an acquaintance with books which no one of them will perhaps ever be rich enough to purchase . . . On Sundays, besides the week-day scholars, 50 were said to belong to the Sunday-school exclusively . . . There had existed at one time a strong prejudice against teaching the girls even so much as writing.'

LANCASTERIAN SCHOOL FOR BOYS: 'Established 1813 (British and Foreign School Society.) Number of children on books = 145. Monitorial method; number of monitors = 10. Held in a room lent by the Corporation over the old slaughter house (Cambrian Place) . . . . The present room in the summer is both offensive and unhealthy . . . A better room would add both to the efficiency and respectability of the school. The Lancasterian School is mainly supported by Dissenters, although there are some persons who subscribe both to it and to the National school . . . . We want a Lancasterian school for girls and increased funds to support that for the boys, but more especially for the purpose of supplying a new room . . . . . Almost all the funds for managing the school are absorbed in paying the master.' It was also reported that reading books were few and had to be passed along the rows of desks!

UNION WORKHOUSE SCHOOL (Penlan Hill): 'Established 1839. Number of children on books = 58. Monitorial method; number of monitors = 6.'

TIN WORKS SCHOOL: 'Established 1844. Number on books = 55. A room in the master's house which was far too small to contain the number present of 40, although generally attended by 50. Master seemed well qualified to discharge his duties. Writing good and some answered questions readily on what they had been reading . . . 1d. per week from the men employed in the tin-works.'

PRIVATE SCHOOLS

The 1847 Report also lists a number of private schools which were frequently run by untrained teachers who had had previous occupations and who depended for their meagre income on the few 'school pence' which they charged their pupils. The latter tended to be 'the children of the little tradesmen and superior mechanics, who objected to the notion of a charity school.' The 1847 Report refers to these schools as Day schools in order to distinguish them from the Sunday schools which were also featured in the Report and which were doing great work to supplement what facilities were available. Also listed are a few Dame schools, run by elderly women who needed the few school pence to make ends meet.

DAY SCHOOLS

Mr. David Aaron's School, Little Water Street: Established 1832. Number on books = 32

Cambrian Place Day School: Established 1846. Number on books = 19.

Castle Green Day School: Established 1816. Number on books = 8. 'Very dirty . . . . the master being the very picture of poverty and wretchedness.'

Catherine Street Day School: Established 1843. Number = 19.

Chapel Street Day School: Established 1840. Number = 21.

Chapel Street Reading School: Established 1838. Number = 40.

Church Lane Day School: Established 1831. Number = 24. 'Crammed with children sitting on old boxes, six or seven on the bed . . . . in a room where the 60-odd year old mistress lived day and night.'

Mr. T.R. Davies Academy, Priory Street: Established 1846. Number = 12.

Guildhall Square Day School: Established 1845. Number = 7. 'In a wretched garret in a house in Guildhall Square. The master was an old man of 78. Previous occupation a farmer. Seven children present - two, the old man's grandchildren, were taught gratis, and 1s.3d. per week from the others + 2s. per week relief from the parish.'

Mr. Watts' Lammas Street Commercial School: Estd. 1823. Number = 70. 'Teacher keeps a victualling and a lodging house . . . . small cramped room completely filled with children. There were no lessons, maps or prints of any kind . . . copy books were ill written and dirty except for two of them . . . He had a good control over the children.'

Parade Row Day School: Established 1846. Number = 17. 'where the dame also lives. Began school when ill-health disabled her as a washerwoman. . . . Incapable of keeping the infants quiet.'

Pentre Poth Day School: Established 1818. Number = 40. 'Schoolroom tolerably good. There are no lessons, prints nor maps of any kind. Master appears to be very efficient according to his means sparing no pains to teach his scholars. Scholars' progress appeared to be satisfactory; they read well, wrote fairly well and were very quick in the arithmetical tables. Upon the whole this was not a bad school.'

(This small private school should not be confused with the later Pentepoeth school.)

Mr. Prees' School, The Quay: Estd. 1843. Number = 16. Teacher's previous occupation = Mariner. 'School held in master's dwelling room. Few scholars present were very disorderly; while he is engaged in teaching some individually, the rest are idling and playing.'

Quay Street Day School: Estd. 1846. Number = 34. 'Previous occupation = Lady's maid. Most scholars under 5 years of age. Children very disorderly.'

Mrs. Anne Reynold's School, near the bridge: Estd. 1842. Number = 24. 'School in room where mistress, aged 75 and her husband live. Previous occupation = housekeeper and dressmaker.'

Smith's Day School, Catherine Street: Estd. 1811. Number = 9. Master's age = 84; previous occupation = Glover. 'School conducted by grand-daughter aged 14 as master was unwell upstairs . . . Labourers' children and very poor. A few only understood English . . . Read well and answered well. Master receiving parochial relief.'

Wood's Row Sewing and Reading School: Estd. 1840. Number = 35. Previous occupation = milliner. 'School-room filled with respectable girls and a few boys . . . . governess an amiable woman, governing her pupils by gentle means. Some read with ease and answered the questions put to them readily. Elder girls worked samplers which appeared very good. Course of instruction limited; only small books, no prints, maps nor cards. Both teacher and taught appeared extremely happy together.'

SUNDAY SCHOOLS
(listed in the 1847 Report)

'The Sunday-schools have been a great supplement of our educational machinery', said the Rev. David Archard Williams in giving evidence to the Commission of Inquiry. It was in the Sunday schools that many of the children of the poor learned to read either in Welsh or English through the medium of the Scriptures.

The Report listed the following Sunday schools:

Boys' National Day and Sunday School: 'In the Sunday School the master manages all, as on a week-day.'

Girls' National Day and Sunday School: 'Besides the week-day scholars, 50 were said to belong to the Sunday school exclusively.'

St. David's Church Sunday School: 'held in the Church and had a large attendance. The Bible, Chatechism and a small collection of hymns and prayers were used. Prizes of Bibles and Prayer Books were given for superior merit. A syllabus of lessons was dawn up for each Sunday of the month together with a list of Rules for the Sunday-school . . . . In Jan. 1847 there were above 500 children with no other opportunity of receiving instruction . . . 50 teachers devote their gratuitous services in this benevolent and Christian cause.' *In June 1851, a report in the Carmarthen Journal showed that St. David's Church Sunday school had over 700 pupils, both adults and juveniles, with 70 teachers.*

Penuel Sunday School, Priory Street: 'conducted in Chapel. There were a number of male and female classes reading the Old and New Testament in both English and Welsh. Questions were subsequently asked about the texts.'

Cwmaurnant Sunday School: 'Junior and adult classes were held in two rooms and even on the stairs of a dwelling house; a new school-room was being built. There was not nearly enough of light to enable those of an advanced age to see distinctly.'

Lammas Street Sunday School: 'held in the Chapel. Few in this school who are not able to read the Scriptures in Welsh or English . . . . 100 of the scholars attend a Day school . . . . systematic and efficient instruction.' This Sunday school had been in existence from about 1821.

Tanerdybach School: A branch of Lammas Street Independent Sunday school. Held in a public-house near Cwmaurnant School but also held in other houses in rotation . . . There were two classes reading the Welsh Testament and one class reading the English Testament, collectively, both sexes together. They complained that they wanted a proper school-room.'

Bethel School: 'Two male Testament classes, one female Testament class and three elementary classes taught individually.'

Water Street School: Held in the Chapel which was a large, well-lighted and spacious building. There were adult and junior classes. 'The males, both adults and boys, occupied one side of the chapel and the gallery immediately over them and the females the other side.' Water Street Chapel Sunday school had been in existence since the early 1820's.

English Wesleyan School, Chapel Street: 'This school is held in the morning and afternoon in a large room attached to the chapel. The boys are taught on one side and the girls on the other, by very efficient teachers. The scholars are made to understand what they read.'

Ebenezer (Welsh Wesleyan) School: held in the chapel. There were male and female Bible and testament classes and elementary classes. 'Most of the teachers question the scholars on what they read . . . The school at present is not in a flourishing state.'

Wood's Row Phonotypic School: 'held in a small underground room, hired by voluntary contributions of the pupils for the purpose. The Superintendent was a member of an institution established to promote the simplification of written and printed characters. Adult and junior reading classes . . . . some of the younger portion of the school read very correctly and with ease. They answered common Scriptural questions.'

SCHOOLS ESTABLISHED AFTER THE 1846 SURVEY

THE NATIONAL AND PRACTISING SCHOOL or THE MODEL SCHOOL (St. Catherine Street)

A proposal to erect a 'model' school for boys, girls and infants was originally discussed by the Church Union Society Committee of St. Davids Diocese, under Bishop Thirlwall, on August 14th, 1846. In December 1846 the Welsh Education Committee of the National Society resolved to build a training college for teachers at Carmarthen and in May 1847 the contractor for the college, W. P. James, was also engaged to build a National and Practising school, known as the Model School, at a cost of £2,425, where the college students could receive their practical training as teachers. A *Journal* report of October 1st, 1847 states: 'the foundation stone of the Model School will ere long be laid'.

In October 1848, at the formal opening of the Training College, it was stated in one of the speeches that 'the Model Schools were fast approaching completion.' The *Carmarthen Journal* of February 9th, 1849 recorded that 'a meeting of the friends of popular education was held at the Model Schools to arrange for the early opening of the Schools which have just been completed.' However, it was also stated that the Infants School had not yet been built because of lack of funds. The original intention was to cater for a total of 450 pupils, boys, girls and infants. A shortage of money also delayed the opening of the main school, for a *Journal* report of 18th May, 1849, stated that a meeting of the town's inhabitants had been held for the purpose of adopting measures for the speedy opening of the Model Schools. From a review of the situation given at the meeting by the Rev. D. Archard Williams, it would appear that the cost of the building was to be met partly by grants from the National Society, the Welsh Education Committee and the Government and partly by local private subscriptions. The latter, however, had not reached the amount originally promised and in addition, money was needed for necessary furniture, fittings and apparatus for the school. Accordingly the reverend gentleman then appealed to the meeting for public subscriptions to enable the school to be opened without delay. He also informed the meeting that the monitorial system of teaching (whereby the older children were put to teach the younger ones) would not be pursued in the Model Schools; instead students from the training college would attend the school everyday to instruct the children. Furthermore, there would be fourteen pupil-teachers, eight boys and six girls, selected from the most proficient pupils and distinguished for their superior merit, who would be entitled to receive an annual stipend from the government as Queen's scholars and who would also be apprenticed to the master and mistress of the school. The boys, at the conclusion of their apprenticeship, would be entitled to compete for the Queen's Exhibitions at the Training College.

Regarding the rate of payment, the Rev. D. A. Williams stated that in order to include even the very poorest class, the rate of admission should commence at 1d. per week for the lowest class, gradually increasing, but the precise amount of gradation had not been settled. The time of attendance would be from nine to twelve in the morning and from two to five in the afternoon and all payments would have to be made in advance.

The Model School

It would appear that the original plans for a Boys' school, a Girls' school and an Infants' school were too ambitious financially and could only be carried out as circumstances permitted. Accordingly, the Boys' school was the first to be opened.

THE MODEL SCHOOL FOR BOYS, 1849

The school was opened for boys on August 6th, 1849. A *Journal* report of Friday, August 10th stated:

> 'The opening of the Boys' School took place on Monday last, and such was the desire displayed by parents to obtain admission for their children, that the master was obliged to defer receiving a great many until the next week, by which time the necessary classification and arrangement will have taken place. The Boys' School is calculated to accommodate about 200 and already nearly 100 have been admitted and next week a great many more will be received so that it is fully expected in a few weeks the school will be filled . . . The Master, Mr. Davies, appears to be an exceedingly active and intellectual young man and he has received the highest testimonials.'

A week later, on August 17th, the *Journal* reported that at a meeting of the Committee of the Model Schools arrangements had been made for an early canvas of the town for subscriptions.

'There is still a deficiency in the building fund; we hope this will be paid off and a large surplus realised so as to provide the necessary furniture and apparatus for the school.'

On September 28th the *Journal* stated:

'We are glad to learn that the Model School is progressing very satisfactorily and considering the short period the pupils have been under instruction the progress they have made is certainly surprising. Mr. Tearle the organising master of the National Society has been engaged in organising the school which no doubt in a very short time, if the progress at present is continued, will become a Model School not only in name but in reality . . . There are now three pupil teachers in the school. The students from the Trinity College daily attend the school and thus obtain practical knowledge of the proper management of a school. The master, Mr. Davies, in addition to his other qualifications, has a pleasing method of communicating knowledge. The Lord Bishop of St. Davids visited the school and expressed his approbation and surprise at the progress made in so short a time.'

Apparently the cost of the building was still not entirely defrayed and again an appeal was made for subscribers.

In January 1850, at the first public examination of the school in Scripture, Geography, English grammar and vocal Music, the pupils had made surprising progress.

MODEL SCHOOL FOR GIRLS, 1851

A meeting was held on March 1st, 1850, to devise measures for the speedy opening of the Girls' school. Apparently £160 was still due on the building account and an annual subscription would be necessary to enable the school to be opened forthwith. It was decided to divide the town into five districts and to canvass for annual subscriptions.

The school was opened on Monday, 12th May, 1851; a *Journal* report of May 9th stating that the Committee of the Girls' Model School agreed

'that the School be opened for the reception of girls at 9 o'clock on Monday morning next (i.e. 12th May) and that the school be divided into two divisions. Girls in the first division should pay 3 pence per week and they should be taught reading, cyphering, the elements of English grammar and geography, writing in copy books, sewing, knitting and marking. In the second division the girls should pay 2 pence per week and be taught reading, writing on slates and number arithmetic, general instruction and sewing. All books for reading and writing, slates, pencils and all other school materials should be provided by the Committee without any extra charge. No children under six years of age should be admitted.'

Apparently good progress was made, for in December of that year, the Bishop congratulated the teachers on the excellent performance of the children.

At the annual examination of both schools in December 1856, the girls were examined in scripture, mental arithmetic, geography, grammar and reading, while the boys were examined in scripture, arithmetic, geography, grammar, reading, English history, music, drawing and penmanship. The Bishop expressed his satisfaction at the results and his belief in the high position of the two schools in regard to training and instruction.

MODEL SCHOOL FOR INFANTS, 1857

The Infants' School, which had been part of the original plan, was not completed until November 1857.

After Forster's Education Act was passed in 1870, establishing a state system of elementary education, the Model continued as a Voluntary National school. (A Church school aided by the National Society.) It remained in St. Catherine Street for over 100 years until the need for new buildings and the movement of population away from the area prompted the building of a new school in College Road. Thus it was that in 1987 the old school was finally closed and the pupils moved to a brand-new Model School in close proximity to Trinity College.

THE LANCASTERIAN SCHOOL FOR BOYS, 1850 and FOR GIRLS, 1851 at PENTREPOTH

To replace the Lancasterian school-room, opened in January 1814, and 'lent by the Corporation over the old slaughter-house', in Cambrian Place, a new Lancasterian school was built in 1850. It was built at 'Pentrepoth' on a piece of land between Little Water Street and what was Orchard Street.

The money was raised by a Committee of the Lancasterian School by means of donations and subscriptions. The school was of two storeys, the ground floor being one large school-room for the boys while the upper storey, for the girls, was reached by means of steps incorporated in a 'tower'. Adjoining the school was the Master's House with two ground floor rooms and three bedrooms.

THE LANCASTERIAN BOYS' SCHOOL, 1850

The Boys' School was opened on 25 November, 1850. The first permanent Master was Mr. George Revell who had been trained at the Borough Road Teacher Training School, London, which was started by Joseph Lancaster. The Master was helped by pupil-teachers who came earlier and left later in the day, so that they could be instructed by the Master before passing on their knowledge to the pupils. The average number of boy pupils was 148. They paid 1 penny per week for spelling and reading and 2 pennies for anything more. School hours were from 9

The Lancasterian Schools at Pentrepoth
and the Headmaster's house, 1850-1896

until 12 in the morning and from 2 until 5 in the afternoon, with school on a Saturday morning. Attendances varied according to the season of the year, for many pupils had to help on the land especially in the spring and at harvest time. Others, especially girls, were kept at home to look after younger members of the family (often very large) while their parents went out to work.

THE LANCASTERIAN GIRLS' SCHOOL, 1851

On January 20th 1851 the Girls' school was opened in the upper storey of the Boys' school under the care of Miss Gillespie from the Glasgow Training College.

In July 1851, at the Annual Meeting of Subscribers to the Lancasterian Schools, it was reported that the average weekly attendance for the boys was 145 and for girls 164. 'Additional evidence of the willingness of the less educated classes to profit by the advantages held out to them.' The Committee asked for a continuance of support by subscriptions, which were given by all denominations.

In October 1858 the *Journal* reported:

> 'The Boys' School now stands in the very first rank of elementary schools, while the Girls' School is now one of the most efficient girls' schools in the district in every respect.'

PENTREPOTH INFANTS' SCHOOL, 1860

In July 1860 a new school for infants was opened on the site, with Miss Samson as Mistress in charge. Children between the ages of 3 and 7 were accepted. By 1865 there were 135 on the roll but in 1882 the numbers had to be limited to 132.

Pentrepoth Infants' School was re-built in 1892-93.

PENTREPOTH BOARD SCHOOL, 1871

After the 1870 Education Act, the Lancasterian schools were transferred, in 1871, to the Carmarthen School Board which was allowed to levy a local rate for financial support. (Schools supported by locally elected School Boards were often called 'Board' schools.)

In 1884 Kelly's Directory states:

> 'Board School, Pentrepoth for 210 boys, 214 girls and 132 infants.'

In 1894 Pentrepoth Board School was enlarged for 310 boys and 260 girls.

THE 1896 PENTREPOETH SCHOOL

In 1896-97 a new red-brick, solid, late Victorian school was built by Carmarthen architects, George Morgan and Son. This was the school which was so well-known to generations of children and was often called 'The Lancy' from its Lancasterian origin.

Pentrepoeth School (demolished 1990)

Top: Little Water Street Entrance *Bottom:* Orchard Street Entrance

In 1902 the Balfour Education Act abolished School Boards and made County Councils and County Borough Councils responsible for schools through their own Education Committees. Pentrepoth now came under Carmarthen Borough Education Committee.

As a result of the 1944 Education Act the functions of the Carmarthen Borough Education Authority were transferred to the Carmarthenshire County Council and it was about this time that the name and spelling of the school became *Pentrepoeth.*

In 1951 the Girls' School and the Boys' School were united and called the Pentrepoeth Junior School.

An innovation was made in 1955 when a Welsh language class for 21 children was established in the school, which subsequently grew into the first Welsh primary school in the town. Called Ysgol y Dderwen, the school moved in 1967 from Pentrepoeth to the site of the former Grange School.

For several years the threat of closure overhung Pentrepoeth school on the grounds of cramped, outmoded conditions. Closure finally came to pass in 1988, when a newly-built school was waiting in Richmond Park to accommodate the pupils of Pentrepoeth, together with those of Priory Street School. Both the Infant and Primary schools were demolished (despite some public protestation) early in 1990.

The new amalgamated Richmond Park Primary School was opened in September 1988, and as it is built on part of the site of Roman Carmarthen, the design of the building incorporates Roman features to reflect its historical past.

ST. PETER'S 'SCHOOL-CHURCH', 1869 (PRIORY STREET NATIONAL SCHOOL)

Although this Voluntary National (i.e. Church) School was not founded until 1869, its ancestors were the National School for Girls established in 1820 and the National School for Boys established in 1822 at the bottom of Parade Road.

In January 1851, the Girls' National School became an Infants' School, while in 1854 the Boys' National School became Carmarthen's first Art School. It is possible that the pupils then went to either the Lancasterian or Model Schools. However, by 1869 St. Peter's parish needed a new school and this was built in Priory Street. The foundation stone was laid on 29th June (St. Peter's Day) 1869 by Mrs. William Morris and the building was opened on the same date one year later in 1870. (A sealed bottle, containing a printed record of the event, gold and silver coins and local periodical publications, was placed in a hollow in the foundation-stone).

The school was originally called *St. Peter's School-Church* because it was built for two purposes: as a Day-school for the parish and as a place

Priory Street School

of worship for the Welsh-speaking parishioners of St. Peter's. (St. John's Welsh church was not opened until 1890). It was a neat and spacious building with a beautiful stained glass window at the east end, giving it an ecclesiastical appearance. A master and mistress were appointed to take charge of the Day-school which was to be under government inspection.

The new building was also urgently needed for Sunday-school purposes, since the 300 scholars and teachers of St. Peter's Sunday-school were then meeting weekly in very cramped conditions in the Grammar School, sited on the Priory Field.

St. Peter's School-Church was the last of the *Voluntary schools* to be founded before a new era in elementary education began.

In 1988 Priory Street School amalgamated with Pentrepoeth in a new school at Richmond Park.

ESTABLISHMENT OF A STATE SYSTEM OF ELEMENTARY EDUCATION

FORSTER'S EDUCATION ACT, 1870

W. E. Forster was head of the Education Department in Gladstone's Liberal government. His Act marked the beginning of a new era in education - the provision of a state system of elementary education. For the first time the state took responsibility for the education of the nation's children. Under the Act the existing Voluntary schools i.e. church schools aided by the National Society and undenominational schools aided by the British and Foreign Schools Society, were allowed to continue, with increased grants from the government. In areas where there was no voluntary school or where the existing schools could not provide enough places, a locally elected School Board was to be set up, empowered to organise *Board Schools* for children aged five to twelve. In addition to government grants, the new Board Schools were to receive extra finance from a special local rate to be collected by the Board. (The Voluntary schools received no money from local rates). Each School Board could decide whether religious education was to be given in its schools; if so, it should be undenominational and restricted to Bible study only. Attendance was not yet made compulsory or free but School Boards could pay the fees for poor children, either in the Board schools or in the Voluntary schools.

Although the 1870 Act came in for criticism from all sides, it 'filled up the gaps' in the existing voluntary system as new Board Schools came into being all over the country.

CARMARTHEN SCHOOL BOARD, 1871

In January 1871 a School Board of seven members was formed for Carmarthen. At its February meeting the Board expressed doubts as to whether some of the schools existing in the Borough would qualify for government grants. Before any grant was made to a school the Education Department had to be satisfied that the school was conducted as a public elementary school within the terms of the Elementary Education Act, including the provision of premises which were healthy, well lighted, drained, ventilated and properly furnished with sufficient space for each child. It was stated at the Board meeting that Llanllwch National School was held in a room 39 ft. long by 15 ft. wide and only 9 ft. high; Johnstown British School was held in a chapel belonging to the Independents (probably Salem Chapel); Priory Street National School was held in a church, although it was generally held that the premises were originally built primarily as a school; while in both Towy Side National Church School and in the Ragged School at Kidwelly Fach religious services were also held.

Nevertheless, the reports of School Inspectors, who visited some of the schools, were very encouraging. Johnstown British School was

> 'in excellent order and thoroughly well conducted in every respect . . . much credit was due to the tact and industry of the Mistress, Miss Bevan.'

In March 1871 Priory Street National School was visited by a School Inspector who reported:

> 'This comparatively new school has made a good beginning . . . The building, desks, apparatus and furniture seem exceedingly well adapted for educational purposes . . . The managers have provided a very liberal staff of paid teachers.'

Of Towy Side National School (associated with St. Peter's Church, like Priory Street National) the H.M.I. report stated:

> 'This is a block of buildings which has been converted into a school-room. It is situated in a low part of the town where the population are mostly very poor. It has been very fairly furnished with suitable teaching apparatus . . . it is necessary, however, that a proper wall should be built to prevent the children falling into the river which runs close by . . . The building is of a good length; it is rather narrow but the great objection is the height . . . this defect should be remedied at once and proper means of ventilation adopted . . . The managers have decided that this school should be for younger children only and the older children

should be encouraged to attend one of the other elementary schools in the town.'

The School Board meeting of March 1871 reported that pupil accommodation in the Borough was as follows: Model National Practising Schools 559; Lancasterian Schools 412; Priory Street National 282; Roman Catholic School 72 (then in Mill Street); Ragged School 73; Towy Side School 59; Johnstown British School 89; Llanllwch National School 73.

There was also Bridge Street National School having accommodation for 162 pupils. This was a building in Bridge Street that was being converted into a school by the Ven. Archdeacon Archard Williams, vicar of St. David's parish. The school had not yet come under inspection. It was located in Bridge Street where the road forked into Little Bridge Street (now demolished for Coracle Way).

In December 1871 the Lancasterian school for boys and girls at Pentrepoth was transferred to the Carmarthen School Board which was allowed to levy a local rate. Johnstown British School was also transferred to the School Board.

1881 saw attendance at elementary school being made compulsory for children aged between five and ten. This increased the need for more school accommodation.

In 1883 the Carmarthen School Board was responsible for building Quay Street Board School. (This was really in Little Bridge Street, at the Quay Street end). The construction of Coracle Way caused the school to be closed and partly demolished; it is now used as Council offices and can be seen alongside the new road.

Little Bridge Street
(showing the end of
Bridge Street National School
with school bell)
Engraving by William Jones

KELLY'S DIRECTORY OF 1884 lists the following schools:

Board School, Johnstown (mixed) for 117 children; average attendance, 84.

Board School, Quay Street (mixed) for 100 children.

Board School, Pentrepoth, for 210 boys, 214 girls and 132 infants. Average attendance 210 boys, 133 girls and 136 infants.

National and Practising School (Model), Catherine Street (mixed and infants). (No numbers given).

National School, Bridge Street (mixed) for 164 children; average attendance 74.

St. Peter's National, Priory Street, for 200 boys and 120 girls. Average attendance 180 boys and 100 girls.

National Towy Side (mixed). Tutors at present from Training College. (No numbers given).

St. Mary's Catholic, Mill Street (mixed) for 60 children. Average attendance 48.

Ragged School, Kidwelly Fach (Dan-y-banc). (No numbers given).

FREE ELEMENTARY EDUCATION

In 1891 elementary education became free and in Carmarthen the last decade of the century saw a spate of school building.

1892-93: The School Board was responsible for the rebuilding of Pentrepoth Infants' School.

1894: School Board was responsible for rebuilding Johnstown School. H.M.I. report of May 1894: 'It is to be hoped that the new building will soon be got ready as it is very much needed.'

1894-95: School Board was responsible for extending and rebuilding accommodation at Quay Street School.

1894: Board School at Pentrepoth was enlarged for 310 boys and 260 girls. There were also 160 infants in the Infants' School.

1896-97: The familiar red-brick Pentrepoeth School for Boys and Girls was built between Little Water Street and Orchard Street, closely adjoining the site of the former Lancasterian School. (The new school was still called The Lancy).

1902: The Balfour Education Act abolished the School Boards and made County Councils and County Borough Councils responsible for running both Voluntary and Board schools through their own education committees.

Only at the beginning of the twentieth century could it be said that there was <u>free</u> elementary education for <u>all</u> children.

STEPS TOWARDS FREE SECONDARY EDUCATION FOR ALL

The next step was to make secondary education available for all, with the ultimate goal of free secondary education for every child.

1906: All Secondary schools receiving government grants had to reserve 25% of their places for children from elementary schools awarded scholarships on the special entrance examinations.

1918: H. A. L. Fisher's Education Act raised the school-leaving age to 14 years. More scholarships were made available to secondary schools and State scholarships were introduced to enable secondary school pupils to go on to University.

1926: The Hadow Report marked the break between primary and secondary education at 11 years and recognised the principle that everyone was entitled to some secondary education.

1944: The R.A. Butler Education Act made secondary education available to all, free and without restriction. The school-leaving age was raised to fifteen (taking effect in 1947). There were to be three types of secondary schools - grammar, technical and secondary modern.

The **1950's** were marked by debates on the relative merits of grammar schools and comprehensive schools as the idea of comprehensive secondary education gradually gained ground. The 1960's and 1970's saw more determined moves towards comprehensive education as more and more grammar schools became comprehensive.

In 1976 the Queen Elizabeth Boys' Grammar School celebrated the 400th anniversary of the founding of the school by Royal Charter in 1576. Shortly afterwards, in September 1978, the new pattern of secondary education in Carmarthen was introduced and three mixed comprehensive schools came into being - Queen Elizabeth Maridunum, Queen Elizabeth Cambria and Ysgol Bro Myrddin.

YSGOL Y DDERWEN

Carmarthen's first Welsh primary school, Ysgol y Dderwen, grew out of a Welsh-language class for 21 children established in Pentrepoeth School in January 1955. For eleven years this embryonic Welsh school had no name but in May 1966 *Ysgol y Dderwen* (Oak Tree School) was adopted. In February 1967 the school left Pentrepoeth to take over the old Grange school site in Heol Spurrell. At first conditions were very spartan but the school flourished and in September 1985 a new, modern class-room complex was opened.[7]

1 Glanmor Williams, *Thomas Lloyd his Skole: Carmarthen's First Tudor Grammar School* in *The Carmarthenshire Antiquary, Vol X, 1974.*

2 See *Some Carmarthen Personalities*

3 Martin Evans, *An Early History of Queen Elizabeth Grammar School 1576-1800.*

4 A history of the Diocesan High School has been compiled by the last Headmistress, Miss M. E. Hodges.

5 See *Trade and Industry - Family Businesses;* also *Printing Pioneers.*

6 Alan Randall, *The Education of Young Ladies of Distinction* in *The Carmarthenshire Historian, Vol. XVI, 1979.*

7 Peter Hughes Griffiths and Rhys Gwyn Jones, *O'r Fesen Derwen y Dyf (From an Acorn an Oak will Grow).*

TO BE OBSERVED IN

Mr. White's School,

CARMARTHEN.

1. THAT every Pupil come into the School silent, clean, and decent; walk to his place immediately, and proceed to his duty in the School.

2. That every Pupil is to be silent during the time he is in the School, and not to speak to any but to the Master.

3. If any Pupil talks, or idles his time, during School-hours, he is to be fined not less than one mark, nor more than a penny (ten marks is one halfpenny); the like fines are to extend to those who neglect their duty or learning which they are requested to perform.

4. If any Pupil talks, or indolently neglects his duty, in or out of School, and refuses to pay his fines for such talking or neglect, or disobeys the Master, he or she, so offending, will be expelled the School.

5. All the fines are to be kept in the Master's desk, which will be doubled by the Master every vacation, and the amount thereof distributed as prizes to the Pupils, according to merit, at the time the School breaks up.

6. No new books, paper, slates, or any other School articles will be admitted, but such as are purchased at the School.

Strict rules imposed at Mr. John White's *Writing, Commercial and Mathematical School* in King Street in the early 19th century.

- 16 -

CIVIC DIGNITY

THE MAYORALTY

The office of Mayor cannot be traced back with certainty to any definite historical date, for the earliest holders of the office which might compare, in some respects, with that of the Mayoralty, were called Reeves or Bailiffs. However, these were appointed officials and not elected representatives. In the *Cartulary of the Priory,* a collection of documents relating to land-grants to the Priory, the Latin word *prepositus* is used for reeve; *prepositus regis* (King's reeve) is sometimes used in connection with New Carmarthen, whilst *prepositus prioris* (Prior's reeve) is sometimes used in connection with Old Carmarthen.

The earliest recorded reeves appear in the late thirteenth century. Among the reeves of New Carmarthen were Meylor Matthew (c.1277-80), Nicholas Le Kyng (c.1277-80), Simon Bideford (c.1280), Meylor (Meilyr) Vachan or Vychan (c.1280-1301), Robert Jafes or Japhes (1284-1300), Thomas Bulpen (c.1288) and Henry Kastel (c.1287-1307). In the fourteenth century some reeves of New Carmarthen included John Young (1305-6 and 1308-9), John Wynter (1312-13), Thomas Louring (1314-15), Thomas Wynter (1327-28), Bernard Saundre (1340-41 and 1349-50), John Andrew Coubrigge (1351-2, 1354-5, 1357-8 and 1360-61), Thomas Japhes (1352-54 and 1358-59) and John Laurence (1356-57 and 1359-60).

Some reeves of Old Carmarthen (the Prior's reeves) are recorded in the *Cartulary* as Llewellyn Cruth (Crowdder? c.1268), Adam Felach (c.1281), David le Grosker (the Grocer? 1340), Adam le Skynner (1350), John Streynen (1356), John Hopkyn (tourker or tucker, 1358), David Gilbert (1359), John le Scriveyn (the Scribe, 1360), John Iorwerth (Sept. 1361), Henry Traharne (Nov. 1361), Walter Lloyd (1364 and 1368), Robert Ricard (1366), and John Hugon Raulyn (1371).

The actual term *maior* (mayor) as distinct from *prepositus* (reeve) is first recorded in the *Cartulary* in three documents relating to land transactions. In two documents dated December 1368 and August 1369 (Nos. 94 and 96 in the copy of the Cartulary kept at the Carmarthen Record Office), John Andrew Coubrigge (Cowbridge) is named as a witness and is referred to as *maiore nove ville de Kermerdyn* (mayor of the new town of Carmarthen). In another document (Carm. Cart. No. 84) John Andrew Spilman is referred to as *maiore eiusdem ville* (mayor of the said town). Unfortunately, this document, which is an Indenture between Prior William Symons and Robert de Penres, Lord of Llanstephan, whereby the Prior is granted 2 acres of meadow and 7 acres of marshland, to which John Andrew Spilman is one of the witnesses, is not dated (except that it is sealed on the Lord's Day following St. Michael and All Angels, the latter being on September 29th.). However, since William Symons is also named as Prior in the document dated August 1369 when John Andrew Coubrigge is recorded as Mayor, this gives some indication as to the date of John Andrew Spilman's mayoralty. The latter has been tentatively fixed soon after Sept. 29th, 1369, although there can be no certainty.

The Cartulary documents do not follow a chronological sequence; thus the Indenture, in which John Andrew Spilman is recorded as mayor, is preceeded by a document dated 1369 (regnal year Edward III quadragesimo tercio) and followed by a charter dated Nov. 13th, 1361 (regnal year Edward III tricesimo quinto).

There has been some speculation that John Andrew Coubrigge (Cowbridge) and John Andrew Spilman might be the same person owing to the similarity of names and owing to the fact that both are referred to as 'mayor' and the dates of their mayoralty are very close. However, it would seem that this could not be the case since both their names appear together as separate witnesses in the same document, dated 1359, in the Cartulary (Carm. Cart. No. 89). Moreover, the Spilman family had held land at Rhydygors from about 1280, whilst John Andrew Coubrigge is recorded as importing and trading in wine in the 1350s and also holding land at Canon Hill (Capel Evan) in 1358 and 1360.

Apart from the above references to 'mayor' in the Cartulary, there is an earlier reference to John Laurence being 'mayor' in a letter dated 20th April, 1356. The letter was to the people of Barnstaple, Devon, requesting that Carmarthen burgesses should not be arrested whilst trading in their town. John Laurence was mayor again in 1382 when he was nominated to take impoverished Talley Abbey into the King's hands.

Carmarthen's early mayors were Mayors-Escheator, i.e. they had the duty of dealing with escheats - land and property lapsing to the Crown through lack of heirs or through forfeiture because of treason and felonies. They were officials who collected incomes from escheated estates on behalf of the Crown.

The concept of an *elected mayor* was recognised by a Charter of Richard II, dated 1386, when the burgesses of New Carmarthen were allowed to freely elect a Mayor every year (on the Monday after the feast of St. Michael, which was on September 29th) .

A list of mayors, with sources, is given in Appendix I.

THE PORTREEVE

The Portreeve was the chief officer of a town or borough usually dependent upon a port for trading purposes. The position might be identified as equivalent to that of Mayor. There are two early references to a Portreeve at Carmarthen, both appearing in Petitions to the Crown. The first, dating either to the reign of Henry III (1216-1272) or Edward I (1272-1307), is a request from the burgesses of Carmarthen that: 'the Portreeve (who collects the King's monies there) be charged in the Exchequer for the amounts of his receipts so that those who have paid their rents and dues to him be not charged for them again in case of his default.' They also petitioned that: 'the Portreeve henceforth be elected after this manner, to wit, the burgesses to choose four suitable burgesses and present the same to the Constable of Carmarthen, who, in the name of the King, shall choose one of them.'

In the second petition dating to Edward III's reign (1327-1377) probably before 1330, the burgesses complained that in a certain case of trespass within their town the Justiciar of South Wales wrongly enforced them to plead before him when they had the right to plead before their own Portreeve in their Guildhall. The burgesses received a reply in their favour.[1]

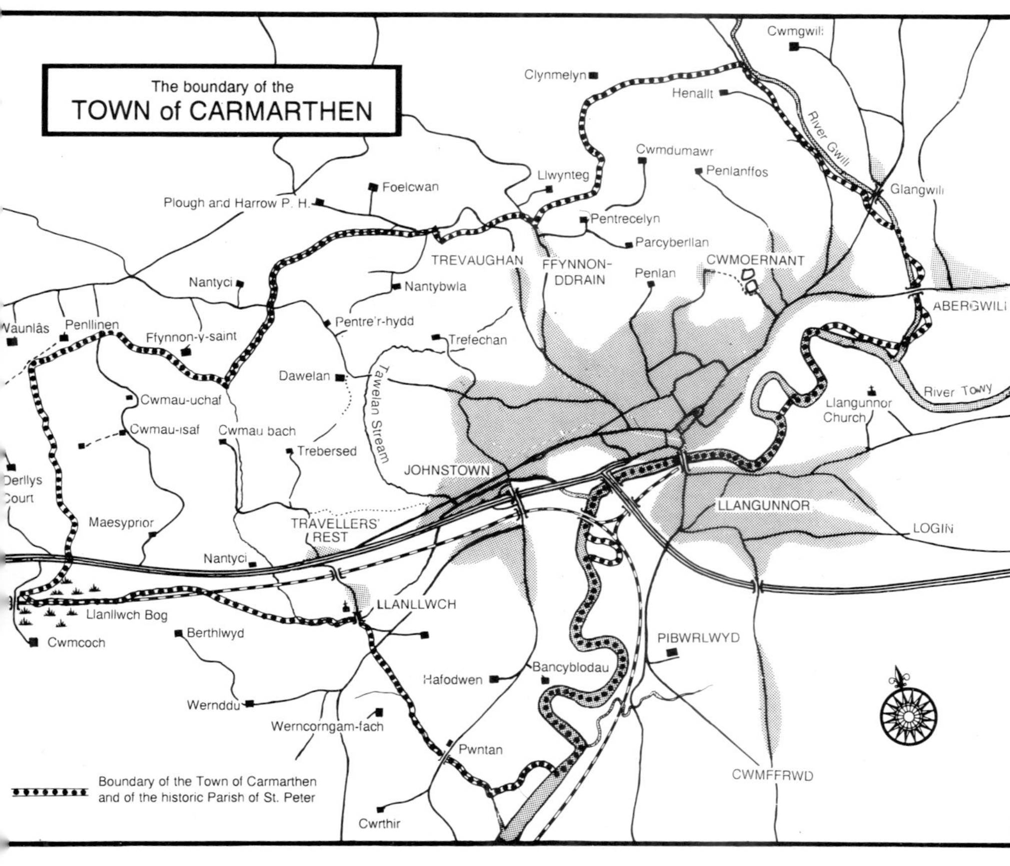

ADMIRAL OF THE PORT

The Mayor also has the title of Admiral of the Port of Carmarthen, granted by the Charter of Henry VIII in 1546. The Charter gave the Mayor authority over the river and its banks from Carmarthen bridge to the bar of the Towy.

This Charter recalls the years when the Towy was a thriving artery connecting Carmarthen and its hinterland with the sea, bringing trade and prosperity to the town. However, the silting up of the river and, to some extent, the coming of the railway, gradually reduced its maritime trade which finally came to an end in 1938 when the last cargo boat left the Quay.

It was customary in the days when Carmarthen was an important port for the Mayor and Corporation to voyage down to the bar of the Towy on 'Admiral's Court Day', when it was the Mayor's duty to hold a Court of Admiralty for the purpose of preventing obstructions and nuisances in the river. During the nineteenth century the custom lapsed, the last Court of Admiralty being held on the Towy about 1828, but the custom was revived again in 1971 and is now an annual event.

THE CIVIC REGALIA

THE STATE SWORD

By the Charter of 1546 Henry VIII granted to the Mayor the privilege of having a sword carried before him by a sword-bearer, Carmarthen being the only town in Wales allowed such a privilege at the time. The charter stated that there should be

> 'a sword-bearer of the said mayor, who shall freely and lawfully carry the Sword before the said Mayor, in manner as is accustomed to be done in our City of London.'

The sword is reversed to form a cross when carried into church, as is the custom on Mayor's Sunday. It is also customary for the sword to be carried unsheathed in time of war and in its scabbard in peace-time. The sword was the gift of Richard Birt, presumably a relative of Robert Birt, Mayor in 1564. The blade is inscribed with the name of Andrea Ferrera, a famous sword-maker of Toledo, Spain.

THE SILVER MACES

The two present silver maces were the gift of Lord Cawdor, Mayor in 1808-09. But there must have been earlier maces, which have since disappeared, since in the town Charter of 1546 Henry VIII ordered that there should be

> 'two sergeants-at-mace, who shall have and carry maces with our arms engraved thereon.'

Also the following extract from a manuscript dated 1563 states:

> 'Carmarthen . . . . which is a greatly privileged town, the Mayor having the King's sword before him, and two bailiffs before him, and

two sergeants bearing the two maces of gold and silver, in two liveries every year, at the expense of the mayor and the bailiffs, and every high feast each man who has been mayor is in a gown of red scarlet, with a tippet of black velvet, and in a similar manner each of their wives. And it is incumbent upon each mayor to paint the door of his house red without and blue within, to show that he is a royal mayor'

The Medallion on the Mayor's chain of office

The Maces are also referred to as early as 1540, six years before Henry VIII's Charter[2]:

On Tuesday, in Easter week, 30th March, Thomas Awbre, of the town of Old Carmarthen and Deputy Steward of it came to the Mayor of New Carmarthen then being within the liberties of Old Carmarthen, demanding of him why he suffered the maces to be carried before him in Old Carmarthen being out of the liberties of New Carmarthen, whereof he was Mayor . . . . To whom the Mayor answered that he would carry his maces there, spite of his 'tethe'. Whereupon the Deputy Steward laid handle on the maces, being in the servant's hand, intending to reason the matter, and as he did so the mayor, with divers other persons his adherents, haled Thomas Awbre, being a man of 80 years of age, or thereabouts, and threw him to the ground, caused the common bell to be rung, and thence out of his own office caused him to be led to the gaol of New Carmarthen.

In 1800 the Sergeants-at-Mace were provided with 'a decent cocked hat each, trimmed with silver lace' which they were ordered to wear at every public meeting of the Corporation. The Sword-bearer was also provided with 'an elegant velvet hat'.

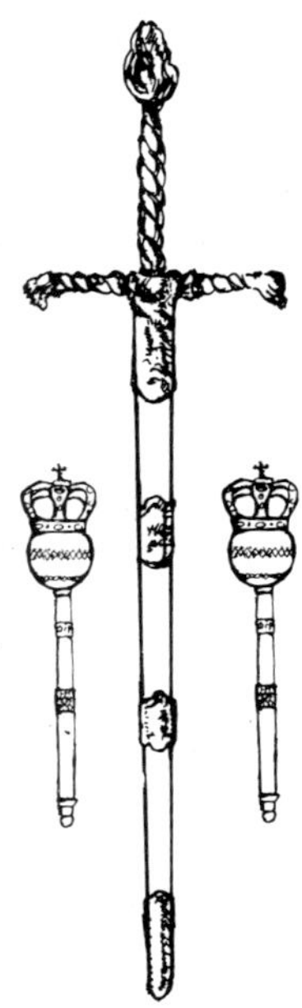

The State Sword and Maces

THE SILVER OAR

An interesting item of regalia is the Silver Oar, 1ft. 6in. long, a symbol of the mayor's office as Admiral of the Port of Carmarthen. The original silver oar disappeared from the Corporation regalia about 1648 during the Civil War; the present replica was presented in 1954 from an over-subscribed public fund, raised to provide a chain of office for the Mayoress and sponsored by the local Rotary Club.

THE BELLMAN'S STAFF AND BELL

The Staff dates from the reign of George III (1760-1820) and was used, together with the Bell, by the Town Crier.

THE MAYOR'S CHAIN

The Mayor's Chain of office is dated 1892 and consists of an enamel medallion, depicting the town's Coat-of-Arms, suspended on a gold chain linked with shields carrying some of the names of past holders of the office. It was purchased from a fund subscribed to by members of the Council.

CARMARTHEN'S COAT-OF-ARMS

The Coat-of-Arms was granted to the Borough by the College of Heralds in 1936, based on the original sixteenth century Seal of the Borough. The motto *Rhyddid, Hedd a Llwyddiant* means Freedom, Peace and Prosperity. Until 1936 the Coat-of-Arms used by the Council

Carmarthen Town Coat of Arms
Granted by the College of Heralds 9th April, 1936

The design is officially described:
Gules, a Castle tiple towers between two ostrich feathers erect in fesse Argent on each of the outer towers a Cornish Chough proper respecting the centre tower and in base a lion passant regardent Or. And for the Crest on a wreath of colours a fisherman carrying a Coracle proper.

The Welsh motto means: Freedom, peace and prosperity

was not registered with the College of Heralds. As will be seen from the illustrations, the central portion of the crest is based on the original Seal, the coracle man is a comparatively modern addition. An interesting detail concerns the position of the two birds, traditionally regarded as the ravens of Sir Rhys ap Thomas of Dynevor, now officially described as Cornish choughs. On the state Sword and Mayor's Chain they face outwards and on the Maces and Coat-of-Arms they face inwards.

Crests used before the present official design was adopted

THE CIVIC OFFICE HOLDERS

By tradition, the sword-bearer and the two accompanying sergeants-at-mace, dressed in their long official cloaks and three-cornered hats, accompany the mayor at all civic services and other ceremonial occasions.

The town crier, whose duties in the past were more extensive than those of today, was at one time called upon to announce royal proclamations such as royal weddings and deaths and to advertise local events such as carnivals and fairs as well as announcing lost property. All announcements would commence with the cry 'Oyez! Oyez!' and end with the traditional 'God save the King' (or Queen). At one time the town crier's uniform consisted of a dark blue frock-coat with red collar and cuffs and a dark blue 'shako' peaked cap but it is now similar to that of the sword bearer.

THE GUILDHALL AND ITS HISTORY

The only known medieval reference to a 'guildhall' appears in a petition to Edward III (1327-77) and thought to date before 1330, in which the town's burgesses claimed the right to plead before their own Portreeve in their Guildhall. There must have been trade guilds in medieval Carmarthen but there is no documentary evidence of them until the sixteenth century. There is a record of a 'Shirehall' in 1540 when Thomas Awbre, deputy steward of Old Carmarthen, objected to the mayor of New Carmarthen having the mayor's maces carried before him in Old Carmarthen, which was outside his jurisdiction. After a scuffle, Thomas Awbre was put in the gaol of New Carmarthen; whereupon Richard Devereux, son of Walter Devereux, steward of Old Carmarthen, requested the mayor of New Carmarthen to release his prisoner, but the mayor refused. Devereux then went in person 'with 4 or 5 servants and the mayor raised a cry so that 300 persons whom he had laid in bushment and hid in the *Shirehall* came out with bills (halberds), glaives (swords) and clubs. They followed him (Devereux) to the Market Place.'[2] It is not known when this 'Shirehall' was built.

In 1569 a *gwyld* (guild) hall is recorded in the Borough Order Book while in 1576 it was ordered that all wool bought and sold within the town was to be brought to the Guildhall to be weighed 'at the common beam and by the common balances and weights there appointed by the Mayor', at the charge of one penny per stone to the seller. On January 4th, 1579, the Mayor and Common Council 'assembled themselves in the Guyld-hall' and agreed that all the highways throughout the town should be paved. In 1580 Robert Toy paid a rent 'for the shop under the Shire Hall' and so too did the 'Buchers for the Arches under the Shire Hall.' References to orders and decrees being made at the 'Guildhall' appear in the Borough Order Book in 1581, 1582 and 1585.

There has been some confusion caused by William Spurrell's statements in *Carmarthen and its Neighbourhood 1879* that 'the Hall was built by Robert Toy, as tradition goes' and that 'the tower (housing the hall bell) was built in the Mayoralty of Robert Toy in 1582.' The sources on which he based his statements are not known; the Borough Order Book makes no reference to the above, so far as is known.

John Speed's map of 1610 shows a building which could be the Guildhall but it is not named. During the later 17th century the Borough Order Book contains certain references, such as a lease being granted on 1st Nov., 1655, 'of a house lying and being over against the east end of the Towne Hall, the wall of the Rood Church on the south side and the streete called St. Marie's Streete on the north side'. In 1675 'one little chamber under the Shire Hall, now in the occupation of Wm. Rees, mercer' is referred to, while references are also made to 'the oven (bakery?) of Dawkin Gove, alderman in the Great Close (Clos Mawr), over against the Shire Hall' and 'a high way to go from the Great Close, over against the Shire Hall with horses and carts to the Gorse.'

The Seal of the Borough
as drawn by Thomas Dineley in 1684

A record of 7th March,

1711, states that the Guild Hall Tower was to be 'rough cast forthwith'. (The names Guild Hall, Shire Hall and Town Hall appear to be interchangeable.)

The Borough Order Book (i.e. Minute Book) records on Sept. 30th, 1765, that the Guild Hall was 'out of repair in a very ruinous state and condition' and that voluntary subscriptions were begun towards erecting a new hall 'in a substantial and proper form'. The Mayor also ordered that '£500 be raised as expeditiously as possible by and out of the estates of the borough' (i.e. Corporation property to the value of £500 was to be mortgaged).

On May 26th, 1766, the Order Book records again that a voluntary subscription had already been begun by the Corporation, inhabitants and gentlemen of the County towards erecting a new hall. It was ordered that the old hall 'be razed and pulled down and a new hall erected in a substantial and proper form instead and in the same street with all the expedition possible.' It was also ordered that 'until such Hall be completed the Mayor's and Sheriffs' Courts be held at the new Bumper Coffee Rooms until a Booth shall be erected or a more proper place can be thought of and provided.' Furthermore, it was ordered that 'until a more convenient market place shall be thought of and procured, the present Shambles and Butchers' stalls that now are round and adjoining to the present outside walls of the Guild Hall be removed and that, instead of the same, proper shambles and stalls shall be erected and fixed within Clos Mawr.' On the same date, May 26th, 1766, it was also ordered that 'until a more convenient place can be thought of and provided, the market place for oatmeal and such other perishable commodities shall be at or under the Cross in Upper Market Street or some convenient market place adjoining.'

The Borough Order Book records on Nov. 7th, 1766, the payment of several bills in connection with 'the erection of a Temporary Hall'. A few months later, on March 16th, 1767, it was ordered that the Hall Bell be fixed in some convenient place at the new market in order to inform the public of market opening times and also to sound an alarm in case of fire. (According to Spurrell this hall bell was dated 1671 and was sold in 1846 when the market hall in Nott Square was demolished.)

Nothing more is heard of the new hall for over two-and-a-half years until on Nov. 27th, 1769, the Borough Order Book records the following information: 'It now appearing necessary that Mr. Thomas Evans, then Surveyor, having laid the foundation and prepared the pillars and free-stonework should be fully empowered to erect a proper and substantial emplacement, or other sufficient necessary work to surround the said foundation in a substantial manner, in order that the said pillars and stonework which are prepared and ready to be placed and fixed upon the said foundation may be sufficiently secured and the Building carried on as early as possible the next Spring. Therefore it is ordered that Thomas Evans without delay proceed to erect . . . such emplacement or other sufficient necessary work to surround the said foundation. . . . and to complete the same with all possible speed.'

However, nothing more is recorded of the hall's progress until four years later when on Dec. 23rd, 1773, the Borough Order Book confusingly states: 'It is ordered that the present Temporary Town Hall be pulled down and another erected in its stead within the new Hall.' After a lapse of three more years the Book records on Sept. 30th, 1776, 'William Williams, Postmaster, be paid 20 guineas for accommodating the Common Council with a Room for their Assembly for twelve years last past.'

On Oct. 6th, 1777, the Order Book states: 'It is ordered that the meeting of the Common Council be held at the Dwelling house of David Edwards in Quay Street in the stead of the house of William Williams where the same hath hithertofore been held.'

No reference is made to the new hall nor are any further references made in the succeeding Minutes of the Council. However, the Order Book always begins each meeting with the heading 'The Borough of Carmarthen at the Guild Hall of the said Borough' and this applies even in the period 1766-1777 when the old hall was pulled down and the new one was in the process of being built.

It would appear that the reason for the delay in completing the new Guildhall was the Corporation's lack of finances. In spite of voluntary

The Guildhall

subscriptions and the mortgaging of Corporation property, £700 was still required to complete the Hall in 1774.[3]

The situation was saved when John Adams of Peterwell, Cardigan, made a gift of £4,000 to the Corporation. Significantly, he was elected M.P. for the Borough in the same year, 1774. However, the money was not intended specifically for the construction of the Guildhall, although a part of it, £887. 6s. was thus spent. The greater portion was used in discharging the debts of the Borough which had been incurred in obtaining the new Borough Charter of 1764.

Some hand-written notes made by John Vaughan (on a copy of the *Charter for Carmarthen* printed in 1765) give the following information:

1768 The building of the Hall stopped owing to a dispute arising between the Trustees.

1770 On May 23rd. they began upon the building of the Hall

1774 The High Sessions first held in the new Hall 30th March, and not yet finished.

1777 The inside of the Hall, and the Market-house finished.

According to Spurrell 'the first stone of the new Shire Hall' was laid on April 10th, 1767, by Vaughan Horton, Mayor. Spurrell's next reference is May 23rd, 1770, when 'building the Hall begun', and then in 1777, with no month given, Spurrell states 'Hall and Market-house finished'. Since no further evidence is available, it must be assumed that the Guildhall was completed in this year.

Two curved flights of steps leading up to the Courtroom in the front of the building were constructed in 1811 but were removed in 1862. The present building contains the Crown Court, the Magistrates' Court and jury rooms and is now administered by the County Council.

The Guildhall in 1861

Inset in a wall on the Hall Street side of the building is a bronze plaque commemorating the birth-place of Brinley Richards, composer of *God Bless the Prince of Wales.*

END OF A TRADITION

By a decision of the Lord Chancellor, Carmarthen lost its separate Commission of the Peace and Quarter Sessions on 1st October, 1951, the town being thus deprived of its Recorder, Clerk of the Peace and Quarter Sessions. The Recorder and Clerk followed the Sword of State for the last time in a ceremonial procession to the civic service (Mayor's Sunday) at Penuel Baptist Chapel on 17th June, 1951, the last Quarter sessions being held on 10th September, 1951. By this implementation of the Justice of the Peace Act there passed away another of Carmarthen's old institutions, for the town had had its own Commission of the Peace and Court since the 1546 Charter of Henry VIII. The Charter of William IV (1830-1837), renewing the grant of Quarter Sessions to the Borough, still hangs in the Mayor's Parlour.

With the implementation in 1972 of the Crown Courts Act of 1970, the new Crown Court at Carmarthen took over the work of the County (as opposed to the town) Quarter Sessions and most of that of the Assizes, apart from the more serious cases which go to Swansea and Cardiff.

CARMARTHEN TOWN COUNCIL

With the reorganisation of Local Government following the 1972 Act, Carmarthen lost its Borough status and many of the Borough Council's former powers and responsibilities were handed over to the newly formed District Council. The Mayor now has the title of Town Mayor and the Mayor's Parlour and the Town Council Offices are located in St. Peter's Civic Hall, formerly St. Peter's Church House, Nott Square. In the Mayor's Parlour are displayed all the civic regalia previously mentioned, the charters of James I, 1604, William IV, 1836, and the College of Heralds, 1936, together with many other interesting items collected over the years. The remains of the Old Oak are displayed in the Civic Hall's foyer. The Town Council has eighteen members who annually elect a Mayor, Deputy Mayor and Sheriff. The latter office, originally granted in 1604, is comparatively rare since there are now only fourteen city and town sheriffs (as opposed to county sheriffs) in England and Wales; Carmarthen and Haverfordwest are the only two in Wales.

CARMARTHEN DISTRICT COUNCIL

Carmarthen District Council is now responsible for many of the duties formerly exercised by the Borough Council together with those exercised by the former Rural District Council. The Council Chamber and offices are located in a much-extended property at 3 Spilman Street, formerly the residence of Mrs. M. M. A. Reid of the Kylsant family which then became the home of the County Club and was subsequently purchased by the Rural District Council. The latter was absorbed into Carmarthen District Council under the 1972 Local Government Act.

County Hall and the bridge

COUNTY HALL and DYFED COUNTY COUNCIL

With the amalgamation of the three Counties of Carmarthen, Cardigan and Pembroke, Carmarthenshire County Hall became the administrative headquarters of Dyfed County Council. Built on the site of the County Gaol, which itself was built on the site of the castle, County Hall was started in 1938 but remained unfinished until the end of the Second World War. The eye-catching chateau-style building, designed by Percy Thomas, now dominates the river skyline as did the gaol and castle before it. Dyfed County Council Chamber, the Chairman's room, committee rooms and some of the major departments are housed in the building, but the large expansion in local government has meant that the original idea of housing all departments under one roof has now given way to a succession of offices scattered around the town. Tentative plans have been put forward for a new building outside the town to accommodate all departments.

It is fascinating to recall that the name Dyfed is supposed to have been derived from the Demetae, the Celtic tribe living in this area of south-west Wales when the Romans arrived over nineteen hundred years ago, and that Moridunum Demetarum, now Carmarthen, was their tribal 'capital'.

1 *Ancient Petitions* No. 14713 and No. 15527 (P.R.O.) in *Transactions Carms. Antiquarian Society,* Vols. 17 and 18.

2 *Letters and Papers Henry VIII,* Vol. XV, No. 427 in *Transactions Carms. Antiquarian Society,* Vol. 18, Part 45.

3 M. C. S. Evans, *Expenses incurred by the Borough of Carmarthen, 1764-1775, in relation to the obtaining of a new Charter* in *Carmarthen Antiquary,* IV, 1962.

Jackson's Lane

- 17 -

TRADE AND INDUSTRY

CORACLE FISHING

> To fish or cross streams they use boats made of willow, not oblong nor pointed at either end, but almost circular or rather in the form of a triangle, covered without but not within with raw hides. When a salmon thrown into one of these boats strikes it fiercely with its tail, it often oversets it and endangers both vessel and boatman. In a clumsy manner, in going to or coming from a river, the fishermen carry these boats on their shoulders.
>
> *Giraldus Cambrensis, A.D.1188*

Coracle fishing for salmon and sewin (sea-trout) has been known for centuries on Welsh rivers but it has declined so rapidly in recent years that today coracle fishing is limited to three West Wales rivers - the Tywi, Teifi and Tâf (St. Clears).[1] There is a surprising lack of evidence for coracle fishing on the Tywi (Towy) until the eighteenth century, although in a sketch of the Quay, drawn by Thomas Dineley in his Diary of 1684, there appears to be a man fishing from a coracle. Both the 1740 and 1748 Bucks' prints of the town show coracles on the river from which men are fishing by rod and line.

Further evidence for coracle fishing appears in a poem, *Llangunnor Hill*, dating from 1794:

Upon the glittering stream below,
Those fishermen of courage bold,
In numerous pairs, pursue their trade
In coracles themselves have made;
Form'd of slight twigs with flannel cas'd
O'er which three coats of tar are plac'd
And, as a porter bears his pack,
Each mounts his vessel on his back,
When first his usual work's begun,
And when his fishing toil is done.

In 1796 Sir Christopher Sykes, while visiting Carmarthen, saw 'many fishermen returning with their coracles upon their backs.'

An entry in the Llanegwad Vestry Book on 7th September, 1798 states: 'that John Harry, overseer, do purchase flannel and other things necessary to make a coracle for John Lot.'

However, there are much earlier references to coracle fishing, although not on the river Towy. One such reference appears in the *Gododdin* poem of Aneirin, which can be dated to the seventh century; it has one line which reads 'ef lledi bysc yng corwc' (he would kill a fish in his coracle). The medieval Welsh laws give the value of a coracle as eight pence (corwc wyth keinhawc kyfreith).

The first clear description of a river coracle, reproduced at the head of this chapter, is that which appears in the writings of Giraldus Cambrensis, who made a journey through Wales in 1188. Unfortunately, Giraldus does not indicate where in Wales he encountered the coracles although he describes the river Teifi and its environs in some detail.

There are also several references to craft, similar in construction to the coracle, by Roman writers such as Julius Caesar and Pliny the Elder. In his *Civil Wars*, Bk. I, 54, Caesar states that he ordered his men to build ships for crossing a river (in Spain) of the kind that his experience in Britain in previous years (55 and 54 BC) had taught him to make. 'The keels and the first ribs were made of light timber; the remaining body of the ships was made with woven osiers (willows) and covered with hides.' Unlike the Welsh river coracles, Caesar's boats had keels and were long enough to hold several men; they were conveyed on wagons coupled together, one in front of the other.

Writing about 100 years after Caesar's account, Pliny the Elder in his *Natural History*, Bk. IV, XVI, states that the historian Timaeus (probably the Sicilian historian who flourished c.262 BC) reported that the Britons crossed to an island named Mictis (probably St. Michael's Mount off Cornwall because of the reference to tin being found there) in boats made of osiers covered with stitched hides. Pliny further states in *Natural History*, Bk. VII, LVI, 'Even now in the British ocean vessels are made of wicker (i.e. osiers) with hide stitched around.' However, Pliny's descriptions would seem to refer to sea-going vessels and to be similar to the curraghs of Ireland rather than to the Welsh river-fishing coracles.

It is interesting to note that in the above classical references the Latin word *corium* is used for *hide* and it has been suggested by Sir Ifor Williams (Canu Aneirin, 1938) that the word *coracle* is derived from the Latin *corium.*

Vessels mentioned in the *Mabinogion* would appear to be sea-going, keeled boats of the curragh type, designed for crossing between Ireland and Wales.

CONSTRUCTION AND USE OF THE TOWY CORACLE

The construction of the coracle is a family tradition handed down from generation to generation. The materials consist of nothing more than strong calico or canvas stretched and sewn over a framework of interwoven ribs of sawn ash laths, the material then being well-coated with pitch or tar. Before the use of calico it was usual to use prepared Welsh flannel covered with three coats of tar. Much older versions were covered with animal hides. When coracles were hide-covered, they must have been a considerable weight, presumably giving rise to the old Welsh proverb: *Llwyth gwr ei gwrwgl* (a man's load is his coracle), i.e. do not overload the willing horse. Today a coracle seldom weighs as much as 30lbs and some are now made of fibreglass.

The coracle is carried on the fisherman's back with a heavy leather strap, fixed to the seat, passing over the fisherman's shoulders. Once the coracle is in the water the fisherman sits with his feet in the broad end and with one arm controls the single oak or ash paddle, performing a figure-of-eight motion in the water. The fish are caught in the net which sweeps the river suspended between two coracles, each man holding an end of the net in his free hand. When a fish is enmeshed the coracles are quickly drawn together by pulling in the net and the fish is killed by a blow from a *cnocer,* which is a wooden club about 15 inches long normally fixed by a strap to the end of the seat. Fishing usually takes place at night on the tide, either coming in or going out, below the town bridge. The fishermen, after floating gently from one convenient set of launching steps to another, walk back to their starting point with their coracles on their backs, repeating the process until the tide has gone out.

Coracle fishing has tended to remain a family tradition but increasingly strict fishery laws have now limited the coracles to twelve pairs, with licences only available to descendants of the present holders. Whereas fishermen at one time had no other occupation, they now tend to have other jobs and fish only in their spare time. In the 1860's there were about 400 coracle-men on the Towy.

The coracle is incorporated in the town's coat-of-arms.

THE PORT OF CARMARTHEN

Long before the existence of other South Wales ports such as Cardiff and Swansea, ships were sailing up the Towy to Carmarthen with a variety of goods. The importance of the river to the trade of the town is evident from the frequent references to it in many old records.

In fact the origin of the port can be traced right back to Roman times when a military fort was established in about AD 75, to be followed by the Roman town of Moridunum (meaning Sea-fort). Since Moridunum became the civitas capital of the Demetae - the tribe inhabiting south-west Wales - it probably became a busy port with vessels bringing in an exciting variety of goods from the Mediterranean and the continent, including a wide range of pottery, wine, oil and Roman jewellery. When the Normans arrived a thousand years later and built their castle and new town, ships sailed up the Towy bringing supplies of men, armaments, food and wine, initially for the castle garrison and for the other castles in the district. Commercial expansion followed and Carmarthen carried on a flourishing trade with other ports, especially Bristol and others in the west country, such as Barnstaple and Bideford.

In the Middle Ages, owing to the lack of roads, the river was the main highway of transport. The site of the Medieval quay was at Island Wharf (now demolished), where the Wynveth Stream, just before running into the Towy, divided into two branches on either side of a tract of land. At high tide this area of land became an island and was probably surrounded by timber wharfs and quays.

The Wynveth Stream, later covered over in 1796 by what is now Blue Street, was also navigable at high tide, when small boats could discharge their cargoes nearly as far as the Wynveth Gate (i.e. Dark Gate) for the Wynveth was also lined with wharfs.

In the mid sixteenth century there is evidence that the main quay was rebuilt in stone and that subsequently attention was paid to keeping it in good repair. John Speed's map of 1610 shows the quay below Quay Street but not extending as far as the bridge. The present stone quay was built up to the bridge in 1808-09.

To return to the Middle Ages: in 1244 the bailiffs of Bristol were ordered to put 40 tuns of wine, 200 quarters of wheat and 200 pigs on board one or two good ships and convey half to Carmarthen castle and half to Cardigan castle.

In 1284 the bailiffs of Bristol were ordered to supply 20 tuns of wine to the castle at Carmarthen; wine was an important trade commodity at this time with large quantities being brought from Gascony (France), and

Portugal to supply the castle garrison. Between 1302 and 1324 forty-four vessels brought cargoes of wine, and by 1335 this number had risen to fifty-two. Some of the ships in the thirteenth and fourteenth centuries had names such as *Le Nicholas de Kermerdyn, Le Julien de Kermerdyn, Le Syapnnol de Haverford* and *Seynt Marie Cogge de Pembrock.* John Andrew Coubrigge, an early mayor of the town, imported wine, selling two tuns to the castle in 1353-54, and shipping a further two tuns in the cog *St. Mary* in 1359-60.

Exports were mainly wool, woolfells (skins with the fleece still on) and hides. Much raw wool was exported to Flanders, the main textile producing region.

THE 'CUSTOM' TAX AND THE 'STAPLE'

It had long been the custom for a tax to be levied on all exported wool and in order to make the collection easier it was decreed that all wool had to be exported through selected towns, known as *Staple* towns. (The Staple was originally a depot where traders voluntarily deposited their wares). In 1326 Carmarthen was selected as a staple town for the export of wool, hides and woolfells. There were three such staples for Wales, the others being Cardiff and Shrewsbury, and eight for England. The objects of the staple were to make it easier for the King's officials to calculate and collect the tax, called *the custom,* levied on exports, which was a very valuable source of revenue, and also to help trade by giving purchasers a guarantee of fair dealing under royal supervision, since the quality of the goods was strictly scrutinised. Each Staple had a 'Mayor' appointed by the King.

In 1326 the mayor and bailiffs of Carmarthen were ordered to publish and observe the *Ordinances* made by the King concerning the staple and also the bailiffs were ordered to choose two of the richest burgesses to go to London and give full particulars regarding the staple of wool, hides and woolfells so that a mayor might be elected for the local staple of Carmarthen.[2] In 1327 Edward III commanded that all merchants coming to the King's staples were to remain there forty days before leaving with their goods (an attempt to check fraud) and in 1332 the officials of Carmarthen were instructed to choose faithful and honest men to receive the King's customs (taxes) and to be keepers of the weigh-beams of wool.

Finally, in 1353, Edward III issued the famous *Ordinance of the Staple* which regulated all previous measures in a systematic and orderly way. Carmarthen now became the only staple town in Wales and was authorised to sell wool, hides, wool-fells and tin to foreigners. Accordingly, in 1354 Carmarthen's exports jumped from 119 sacks of wool and 148 dikers of hides (a diker was a set of 10 hides) to 734 sacks of wool, 11 lasts (a last was 12 dozen hides) and 8 dikers of hides and 296 woolfells. The amount of duty increased from £43 to £252. In 1358 exports rose to 825 sacks of wool and 12 lasts, 7 dikers of hides and 60 woolfells yielding a revenue of £284. From this peak year the figures dropped to barely 36 sacks in 1389, reflecting, to some extent, the effects of the Hundred Years' War with France. At this time, too, the town's ships were often commandeered by the King to transport 'armed men and archers' to the continent.

However, another reason for the decline in the exports of raw wool in the late fourteenth century was that a large proportion of the wool produced in Wales was being absorbed by the growing cloth-manufacturing industry. During the fifteenth century the cloth trade became very flourishing, cloth being taken from Carmarthen to Bristol and then exported to Europe. It was also taken by cloth merchants to the numerous fairs and markets, including the great annual cloth fair of St. Bartholomew's in London. The woollen cloth industry was encouraged by levying a high duty on exports of raw wool but a low duty on exports of finished cloth.

During the sixteenth century Carmarthen's importance as a centre of the cloth trade and its manufacture was reflected in the existence of Trade Guilds. In April 1574 the Fraternity of Weavers was incorporated while in May of the same year a Guild for the Tuckers, Clothworkers, Fullers and Shearmen was likewise incorporated. Unfortunately, the restrictive practice of the Guilds, in trying to prevent the development of the craft industry in country cottages and farmsteads outside the town, was partly responsible for the decline of the cloth trade, so that by 1600 the export of cloth had virtually ceased.

In the early sixteenth century records show evidence of certain trade relations with Portugal: the King of Portugal himself thanked Carmarthen Priory for the manner in which his merchants had been entertained there.

From the middle of the sixteenth century Carmarthen was recognised as the most convenient and most suitable place for both coastal and foreign trade. When John Leland visited Wales between 1536 and 1539 he stated in his *Itinerary* that Carmarthen was rapidly supplanting Kidwelly as a port, owing to the silting up of the latter's harbour, although the Towy itself was experiencing some difficulty with the same problem. Leland noted that there was a sand bar at its mouth and that the river was full of sand banks so that larger ships lay at anchor off Green Castle while small balingers were used to ferry cargo to and from the quay at Carmarthen.

In 1546 Henry VIII granted a Charter to the Borough which included, among other privileges, the right of the Mayor to be Admiral of the Port from Carmarthen bridge to the bar of the river. He had the power and authority to do all the things appertaining to the office of Admiral.

The Quayside in 1939
From the left: Quay Street School, Jolly Tar Lane, The Jolly Tar Inn, Justices Lane, Rank's flour warehouse

At this time Carmarthen's export trade, in particular, increased considerably. The inland port was sufficiently distant from the sea to be almost immune from pirates and smugglers who were particularly active along the coast of West Wales. French and Breton seamen were the worst offenders but many Carmarthenshire men, too, were guilty of piracy or of aiding and abetting. Successful attempts by the Tudors to suppress piracy were of great benefit to trade as were their reforms in customs administration which brought Wales into line with England. A Customs House was established at Carmarthen where customs officials were instructed to record both coastal and foreign trade in their *Port Books.* Although not all of these *Port Books* have survived, those that have done so supply interesting information on trade in the latter half of the sixteenth century.[3] An extremely valuable analysis of these books has been made by Michael C. S. Evans[4] who shows that whereas 'trade during the later Middle Ages had been mainly an inward one in the hands of alien merchants, the sixteenth century saw the transfer of this trade to Carmarthen men and its shipping. But the character of this trade remained the same. . . . The Port Books, despite their inadequacies, clearly show that the town was the commercial and maritime centre of the shire in the latter half of the sixteenth century.' Carmarthen's merchants had a virtual monopoly over certain trade routes, especially the Carmarthen-Bristol trade. It was the coastal trade with Bristol, and to a lesser degree with Barnstaple and Bideford (all entrepôt ports), which was the mainstay of the town's commerce. Trade with Ireland and Scotland was infrequent, while foreign trade was chiefly with France. Imports included salt, barley, household goods such as pewter-ware, bedsteads and coffers, oil, wine and luxury silks and velvets. Exports were mainly cloth to Bristol and coal to France, La Rochelle being the chief centre. However, imports of wine and salt decreased later in the century, as did exports of cloth. A scarcity of corn in the last decades led to a heavy import of barley malt from ports on the River Severn. The *Port Books* reveal the names of at least 63 Carmarthen merchants, but the majority were traders on a small scale, commissioning only a few shipments each. Of the 28 vessels registered at Carmarthen with names such as *Le Trinitie, Le Nightingale* and *The Wheele of Fortune,* none was very large or of heavy tonnage, for the silting up of the Towy was a real and growing problem.

In 1592 the merchants of the town complained to the Court of Admiralty that four of their ships laden with silks, velvets, wine and oil to the value of £10,000 had been despoiled by pirates, while on their way to Carmarthen from Bristol.

In the early seventeenth century an extract taken from James I's *Geography Book* states that Carmarthen 'beforetimes was a convenient haven for ships arriving, but now is sore pestered with sands and shelfes. Notwithstanding some small vessels ascend up the river unto the Bridge of the Towne.'

With the rise of the landed gentry in this century, the cargoes discharged at Carmarthen reflected the tastes of the newly wealthy. Some of these cargoes included soap, pewter, vinegar, sugar, fruit of all kinds, ginger, marmalade, bedsteads, brass goods, playing cards, pins, buttons, chests, trunks, earthenware, wines and other liquors.

In spite of the difficulties of navigation, the river's importance in the town's history is seen in many records. One tells the story of a party of Welsh men and women emigrating to America. Hailing from Montgomery, they were due to board the *Maria,* of Bristol, at Carmarthen in 1795, but arrived to find that the ship was too big to come up the river. Because the press gang was aboard another boat in the river they could not risk the voyage from the town so decided to walk to Bristol, leaving their womenfolk and goods at Llansteffan to follow later. The story of their trials and their ultimate reunion is told in a letter reproduced in the *Carmarthenshire Antiquarian Society Transactions, Vol. VIII.* In those days the town often had raids by the press gang in search of able-bodied men for naval service.

In the early part of the eighteenth century Carmarthen possessed 57 vessels of a total tonnage of 2,293, compared with Cardiff's 22 vessels of

789 tons. A directory of 1794 gives a list of some of the vessels belonging to the port of Carmarthen as follows:

At 'Pickle-Herring Wharf' (London): *Race Horse, John, Sally, Neptune, Industry, Welcome, Lovely Cruiser, Union, Elizabeth.*

At 'The Back' (Bristol): *Lark, Speedwell, Providence, Constant Trader, Ceres, Polly and Betsy, Emlyn, John and Mary, Mayflower.*

Dr. Pococke, an English traveller in Wales in 1751, wrote of Carmarthen: 'There is a good key to which ships of 150 tons can come up, as they have eleven feet of water. They have a great trade in butter to London, and of wheat, barley and beans to all parts, mostly coastwise; and they are famous for pickled salmon.'

In addition to pickled salmon there was also a good trade in pickled herrings. It was the custom to sell pickled herrings direct from the ships when they berthed at Carmarthen. Up to near the end of the nineteenth century local inhabitants could buy these herrings in any quantity, from a couple to a salted barrel-full.

Some records of the port's activities are also given in Samuel Lewis' *Topographical Dictionary of Wales, Vol. 1,* which gives the following information for the year ending 5th January, 1830: The exports were chiefly timber, bark, marble, slate, bricks, lead ore, manufactured goods, butter and eggs. Shipments for this year were 136,857 bushels of oats, 1,470 barley, 760 wheat, and 740 of malt. The average quantity of butter shipped was 22,000 casks (80lbs. each) and the average value of the year's egg exports is given as over £6,000.

In 1831 thirteen foreign vessels of 1,503 tons, and 420 coasting vessels of 16,850 tons entered the port, the amount of duty paid being £3,000. The registered number of vessels belonging to the port was 51, and the number of men employed was 152. Labour at this time was considered cheaper in Carmarthen than in any other part of Wales. A great deal of trade at this period was done with Bristol, but it was not an uncommon sight to see sailing ships in the river from Devon, London, Ireland, Scotland and from as far away as America.

In consequence of Henry VIII's Charter of 1546, by which the Mayor was made Admiral of the Port, it was the duty of the 'Court of Admiralty' to prevent any nuisances or obstructions in the river. On 'Admiral's Court Day' it was the custom for a barge, carrying the Mayor and Corporation, to set out on a voyage to the Bar of the river bearing the silver oar, the sign of the Mayor's jurisdiction over the Towy. Up to 1835 the Court was still sworn in 'for the sake of custom.' This was stated in the *Report of the Commissioners on Municipal Corporations in England and Wales, 1835,* which also stated that 'no attempt has been made to remove or prevent obstructions in the river for many years past.' These obstructions, it was said, had taken place to such an extent that vessels which formerly came up to the Quay had to discharge their

Carmarthen Bridge in 1748
(detail from Samuel and Nathaniel Buck's engraving of the town)

The Bridge, 1874

cargoes at considerable expense two miles down the river. (After a lapse of well over a century the old custom of Admiral's Court Day was revived in 1971.)

Obviously the silting of the Towy was still a problem and some larger vessels were forced to discharge their cargoes below Green Castle from where they were transported to the Quay in smaller boats (just as Leland had noticed in the 1530's). Alternatively some vessels waited for high tides to take them up but this could be inconvenient and expensive. Throughout the nineteenth century there was much talk, but little action, on how to tackle the problem and in the end virtually nothing was done.[5]

The first steam-ship, as opposed to sail, between Bristol and Carmarthen came into service in November 1830. The paddle-steamer *Frolic*, capable of carrying freight and passengers, the latter with the comfort of cabins and dining-room facilities, arrived in the Towy but since the steamer could not get up as far as the Quay, 'an immense concourse of the inhabitants went some miles down the river in a fleet of boats to greet her arrival.'[6] Unfortunately, this first paddle-steamer foundered only four months later off the Glamorganshire coast, with heavy loss of life. Losses at sea were nothing new and many ships were wrecked, especially on the treacherous sandbanks of Carmarthen bay.

The 1840's saw the heyday of the port with both sail and steam ships. In March 1849 the paddle-steamer *Phoenix* of the Bristol Steam Navigation Company made a record-breaking voyage from Bristol to the Towy in just 8 hours and 20 minutes (and in the teeth of a heavy head-wind). It was the practice for larger vessels to anchor at Black Pool, below Green Castle, where passengers and goods were off-loaded.

Although the opening of the South Wales Railway in 1852 reduced Carmarthen's dependence on the river, paddle-steamers continued to serve the town and sailing ships still brought cargoes to the Quay, but according to *Journal* reports, there was a general feeling of gloom for the future prospects of the port. This was due to a combination of adverse circumstances, including the continuous silting up of the Towy. Dredging work was undertaken but not enough to remove the sandbanks; ships had to wait for high tide to negotiate the river.

Kelly's Directory of 1884, under the heading 'Water Conveyance', states: 'To Bristol, *Cambria*, and *Neath Abbey* steamers to and fro once a week; John Lloyd, the Quay, agent.' and 'To Liverpool, *Ibis* and *Lady Kate* steamers, once a fortnight; John Lloyd, the Quay, agent.' Liverpool was one of the ports from which hopeful emigrants sailed for the New World.

The Customs House was situated on Island Wharf, while the Stamp Office was at No. 22 Quay Street.

Photographs of the early 1900's show that river traffic was still busy, with sailing ships and steamers bringing cargoes of grain, flour, seed, timber, slates and building materials to the Quayside yards and warehouses. In 1904 the Western Counties Agricultural Society warehouse was completed. Built to a new French design, it was one of the first reinforced concrete structures in the country. (It was demolished in 1979.) One of the best known steamers was the S.S. *Merthyr* which regularly carried cargoes, mainly flour, between Bristol and Carmarthen. The 1914-18 war caused an interruption in the trade and although it resumed in the 1920's, the tonnage carried fell away in the 1930's and the last coaster to leave the Quay departed in 1940.

Shipping in the Port of Carmarthen

		number during year (f=foreign)		*total tonnage*
1920	...	-	...	-
1921	...	2	...	127
1922	...	20	...	1211
1923	...	22	...	1337
1924	...	20	...	1523
1925	...	1f	...	170
1925	...	17	...	1226
1926	...	1f	...	163
1926	...	16	...	987
1927	...	3f	...	406
1927	...	24	...	1858
1928	...	1f	...	146
1928	...	35	...	2480
1929	...	18	...	1380
1930	...	22	...	1517
1931	...	22	...	1239
1932	...	13	...	911
1933	...	12	...	961
1934	...	10	...	466
1935	...	7	...	355
1936	...	6	...	233
1937	...	8	...	411
1938	...	5	...	439

SHIP-BUILDING

Before the introduction of iron and steam, ship-building was an important feature of Carmarthen's trade activities. The stocks were situated along the Pothouse Bank to the west of Island Wharf.

Lower Quay Street in 1937

Ships of two to three-hundred tons were turned out of the yards, such as the brig *Mary Anne* launched in 1805, the *Priscilla* in 1806, the *Albion* of 220 tons in 1813 and the brig *Hero* of 220 tons in 1814. The schooner *Margaret* of 140 tons was launched at the Pothouse in 1834, the brig *Naiad* in 1838 which was employed on the Baltic timber trade, while in 1841 the barque *Princess Royal* of 330 tons took to the water. Several smaller boats such as the *Carmarthen Packet* and *Bristol Packet* also came off the stocks during these years. In 1865 the last boat to be launched from the Pothouse was the small pleasure steamer *Lily* which was to ply between Carmarthen and Ferryside. (However, a small yacht, built for the Mayor, was launched at the Quay in 1869.)

THE TRADE GUILDS

There must have been Craft Guilds in medieval Carmarthen but it is not until the sixteenth century that there is any record of them and even then little is known apart from the dates of their charters and their annual payments to the Corporation. There were guilds of tanners, glovers, weavers, tailors, shoemakers, saddlers, hatters, tuckers (cloth finishers) and hambermen or hammermen i.e. goldsmiths, silversmiths, ironsmiths, cutlers, pewterers, plummers and tinkers.

The tanners, shoemakers and hammermen were granted their Charter in 1569, the weavers, tuckers and clothmakers in 1574 and the glovers about 1575. Masters and wardens were chosen to supervise the guilds and to see that the rules for their trade were carried out.

Mention of a Guildhall appears in 1576 when there were complaints about the diversity of weights used for wool and the Council, in an effort to prevent the sale of wool in secret places and to stabilise the trade, ordered that no wool was to be weighed 'save only at the common beam and by the common balance and weight thereof appointed by the Mayor and remaining within the Guildhall.'

It was not until 1651, however, that the last of the guilds, the 'Hatters and Feltmakers,' were incorporated, paying the 'some of Twenty shillinges of good and lawful money of England.' This Guild marks the existence of the beaver and felt hat industry at Carmarthen which possibly started in the early 1630's. Such hats were then becoming very fashionable. In 1633 Lewis Lloyd, a hatter, petitioned to be a burgess of the town and the Council, 'finding our town destitute of such a tradesman, hath agreed to admit Lewis Lloyd to be one of the burgesses of the town and to execute his trade.'

WATER MILLS

In addition to the craft industries, some of the medieval corn mills, such as the Cock Mill near Dark Gate and the Priory Mills, continued to function during the sixteenth and seventeenth centuries. The Cock Mill was demolished in 1796 while the Priory Mills continued into the nineteenth century.

IRON AND TIN WORKS

Carmarthen's old and vanished industrial activity centred on the north bank of the Towy, just to the east of the site of the Priory. What remains today of the iron and tinplate works can give only some small indication of their former importance and extent. From the middle of the eighteenth century to the beginning of the twentieth they played an important part in the industrial and economic life of the town, employing a substantial number of men and women.

Almost all the iron works of the county owe their origin to Robert Morgan, who owned concerns at Carmarthen, Kidwelly, Cwmdwyfran and Llandyfan about the middle of the eighteenth century. He already owned works at Kidwelly when he came to Carmarthen in 1748 and rented his land from Lady Trevor. Some years later Robert Morgan owned a furnace, forge, rolling-mills and tin mills. The early iron works were sited in woodland areas because the latter were rich in timber, charcoal being considered the best fuel for producing the highest grade pig-iron. The timber used for smelting was oak and elm, containing 23% and 19% respectively of charcoal. (At the same time the bark of the oak was considered ideal for tanning purposes and a big trade arose in exporting this commodity from Carmarthen). The Gwili running into the Towy also provided an excellent water-supply, while the iron-ore was brought to Carmarthen up the Towy. The latter was the chief means of transport to the early iron works, though the old stone bridge limited the passage of the bigger vessels. From here on it was customary to float the cargoes up to the works on rafts and small boats, where they were unloaded at the small jetty.

A contemporary picture of Carmarthen Ironworks, 1790

In 1750 about one hundred and fifty tons of bar iron were being produced and in 1788 four hundred tons. The tin mills produced tin plate which achieved an international reputation, the products bearing the mark of *M.C.* (Morgan Carmarthen). In 1808 a stock book of the tin works showed that the total value of stock was over £8,000.

Between 1777 and 1800 Robert Morgan's son, John, managed the business. To facilitate his business John established the Carmarthen *Furnace Bank* in 1792 and issued his own coins and tokens which were payable in London, Bristol and Carmarthen, the bank being subsequently taken over by David Morris. In 1800 John Morgan leased the tin works to his nephew, John Morgan junior, who eventually entered into partnership with William Morris, Thomas Morris and William Morgan, under the name of *John Morgan and Company.*

When John Morgan died in 1820 the property was devised to W. O. Brigstocke, Thomas Morris of Carmarthen, and Samuel Harford of Bristol, on trust with certain interests to the widow. The firm was then carried on under the name of *Morris, Morgan and Co.* In 1822 a seven-year lease was granted to Robert Smith, who, having been joined by John Reynolds of Bristol, traded as *Reynolds and Smith.*

The works were very active in about 1823, the labour employed being engaged in smelting, milling the plates and tinning. There were increasing orders for tinplates for export. In June 1823, however, there was a destructive fire at the Tin works. In 1826 Reynolds and Smith moved to Aberavon with their Carmarthen employees despite protests that this industry, so important to Carmarthen, might die out. Concern was also expressed that 'the M.C. brand-mark which has brought these works into such repute is used by Smith at Aberavon . . . Carmarthen as a trading and manufacturing town will sink into insignificance.'

The decline of many early iron works, located in inland wooded areas, in the nineteenth century, was the result of adopting coal for smelting purposes instead of charcoal. This necessitated the migration of many iron works to the South Wales coalfield. However, in 1831, the Carmarthen iron and tinplate works were restarted by Henry Ridout Downman, Hugh Downman, Thomas Gratrex and Nicholas Price, but according to an indenture of 1836, the Hon. H. M. Yelverton and his wife became the owners of the iron furnaces, rolling mills and tin houses in that year. The many changes had not yet finished, for in 1844 the works were reopened by Wayne and Dunn, following another disastrous fire and in 1865 they were rented to *Thomas Lester and Co.* Lester worked them with great success, his two sons coming into control in 1894.

Up to the end of the nineteenth century the industry seemed to flourish, with five mills in full production and a substantial number of local workmen and women employed. Nevertheless, in 1900 the tin works closed down, following a wage dispute which culminated in a strike. Carmarthen tin works could no longer compete with the large imports of American and continental steel and iron-bars at a cheap rate. The closure was a severe economic blow to the eastern side of the town, where most of the workers lived. The works were dismantled in 1902, so ending a great tradition of iron and tinplate manufacture extending over a period of 150 years.

FURNACE HOUSE

Furnace House in 1969

Furnace House in St. Peter's Street was the home of the Morgan family of ironmasters. Probably built by Robert Morgan about 1760, the house provided a good example of a well-proportioned Georgian town dwelling. The façade and forecourt have been preserved and restored although the rear of the property has been rebuilt as the modern County Library. The preserved features include a raised porch with Corinthian columns, a forecourt enclosed with walls at each end decorated with pineapple finials and iron entrance gates and railings, the latter being cast at Robert Morgan's works. Above the gateway is a lantern supported on iron pillars with the words M. BUSTEED FECIT 1761 (M. Busteed made it) cut into one them.

The story is told of Sir Thomas Picton dining at Furnace House on 25th May 1815, before leaving for Waterloo, and on taking leave of Mr. Morgan, saying: 'Now for a peerage, or a glorious grave.'

LEAD WORKS

Carmarthen's lead works were located on the site of the old Priory and were owned by John Campbell of Stackpole, Pembrokeshire. They were probably started just after 1760 and appear to have flourished until about 1800 when they were closed down. Most of the lead ore came from Campbell's mine at Rhandirmwyn. The smelting houses can be seen on Thomas Lewis's map of 1786 standing in the south-eastern part of the Priory enclosure. In their disused state the lead works came into the possession of Earl Cawdor, who dismantled them and removed them to Llanelli in 1812. The remains of the Carmarthen works were demolished in the mid nineteenth century when the railway line was laid through the area.

The nearest lead mine to Carmarthen is the Cystanog mine, Llangunnor, which having been previously abandoned, was reopened in 1852 by the Vale of Towy Silver and Lead Mining Company, when the lead was reported rich in silver. The mine was again in operation from 1865 to 1881 with the Bryn Towy and Nant Mining Company working it for barytes (native sulphate of barium). Another abortive attempt to work the mine was commenced in 1951 with the same objective but the mine is now unprofitable to work.

IRON FOUNDRIES

There were three iron foundries, one in Priory Street and two in Blue Street, the latter (shown on John Wood's map of 1834) sited upon the Wynveth Stream which had been covered over in 1796. Two foundries, those of Thomas Jones and Sons, Priory Foundry, and William Isaac and Son, Blue Street, gave employment to about sixty men and boys in 1871 and were still active in the town until early this century. Examples of their work in the shape of manhole covers, railings and grids are still in evidence about Carmarthen. In the 1840's Thomas Bright kept a large iron foundry and coalyard in Blue Street.

OTHER INDUSTRIAL ENTERPRISES

Other industrial enterprises in the town in the nineteenth century were tanneries and woollen mills still dependent upon the medieval mill stream (the Wynveth). One tannery stood on the corner of John Street and St. Catherine Street; a little further upstream stood St. Catherine's Woollen Mill (near the site of the present Mart); while two woollen mills were sited in Glannant Road. One of these was shown as a paper mill on John Wood's map of 1834.

There are several references to paper mills in Carmarthen, the earliest being mentioned in 1799 when the baptism of Rachel, daughter of Samuel Davies, Paper Mill, is recorded in Heol Awst Chapel Register. Later a mill is recorded as being in the occupation of David Charles 'one of Wales' sweetest singers' and the author of the famous hymns *O fryniau Caersalem* and *Rhagluniaeth fawr y nef.* In February 1821 the mill was destroyed by fire, but apparently it managed to survive and was carried on by David Charles' son until the middle of the century. David Charles and his son were also rope and twine makers who owned a rope factory and lived in King Street.[7] Rope-making was carried on in town where four rope-walks are recorded in the nineteenth century. A rope-walk was a stretch of ground or building where ropes were laid out and spun or twisted.

There were also two brickworks in the town, one near Old Station Road and the other near the Gas Works. The Gas Works, now demolished, dated from 1869 and replaced an earlier building of about 1822, the year when Carmarthen was first lit with gas. (Carmarthen was one of the first towns in the country to be lit in such a manner). On September 25th 1822 the Mayor and inhabitants walked in procession through the streets to mark the event. There were eighty public lamps and several shops were lit with gas.

In the early decades of the nineteenth century Carmarthen was a centre for stage-coach and mail-coach routes.[8] Consequently, trades associated with horses and stabling flourished, employing leather workers, harness makers, shoe smiths and coach builders.

RAILWAYS

The South Wales Railway reached Carmarthen in September 1852, although by this time it had been taken over by the Great Western Railway (G.W.R.). Its station was about one mile outside Carmarthen at Myrtle Hill, Pensarn, later called Carmarthen Junction.

The first train to travel the single line track from Swansea to Carmarthen on September 6th 1852, however, carried no passengers but only materials for the line. Nevertheless, 'crowds watched as it pulled its train of wagons at a terrific speed of 15 m.p.h.'

The official opening took place on Friday, September 17th, when three trains left Swansea complete with dignitaries and a military band which played at each of the stations along the line. Carmarthen was now no longer dependent for trade and transport on the river, as it had been for centuries, or on the more recent stage-coaches. It soon became an important railway junction with tracks radiating out in all directions.

In 1857 the Carmarthen and Cardigan Company cut the first sod near Myrtle Hill Junction for a line to Cardigan but it was not until March 1860 that the first mile of this track together with the new Town Station were opened. The Town Station (now called the Old Station) was sited in the area known as Kidwelly fach, below the Parade. The Carmarthen and Cardigan Company never reached further than Llandyssul, however, having spent over £$^1/_2$ million on engineering works with liabilities of £1 million. A Receiver was appointed in November 1864, although the company managed to survive until July 1888 when it was bought by the G.W.R.

Both the South Wales and the Carmarthen and Cardigan Railways were built on the Broad Gauge and not converted to Narrow Gauge (i.e. the present standard 4ft. 8$^1/_2$in.) until 1872. The present station was opened in 1902. If one considers the three stations (Myrtle Hill, old Town and present Carmarthen station) then it can be said that the following companies sent passenger trains to Carmarthen at some time in their history: South Wales; Carmarthen and Cardigan; Llanelli Company 1865-1871 - via the Towy valley from Llandeilo [this railway from Carmarthen to Llandeilo and Llandovery was opened on June 1st 1865]; Manchester and Milford 1866-1872 which ran from Pencader to Strata Florida, with a later branch to Aberystwyth from Strata Florida; Pembroke and Tenby 1868-1872 using the loop they built from the bridge to the Carmarthen and Cardigan line; L.N.W.R.; G.W.R. and L.M.S.

RAILWAY BRIDGES

The iron bridge near the old town station (L.M.S.) was commenced in March 1858 to carry the line from Myrtle Hill Junction to the Station and thence on to Llandeilo and central Wales. Passenger traffic ceased in 1965 and freight traffic in 1973, but occasional trains continued to cross to

The view from Mount Pleasant, 1865

Gwili Vale, 1874

supply the coal yard on the town side until May 1983. The iron bridge was demolished in January 1984.

The other bridge built to carry the tracks over the Towy in the direction of Pembrokeshire was constructed to open so as to allow the river traffic to reach the Quay. From its inception it was referred to as the *White Bridge.* In 1911 this bridge was replaced by a stronger bridge supported on fourteen steel cylinders sunk to a depth of over 100ft. It took nearly three years to construct the new bridge which has a single opening span of the rolling bascule type - a design that is relatively uncommon in bridge building. In recent years the opening mechanism has become unworkable, so effectively preventing the raising of the lifting span. This, together with the building of Pont Lesneven to carry the by-pass road, prevents anything except smaller boats from reaching the Quay.

PRINTING PIONEERS

Carmarthen was the home of the earliest Welsh printers, becoming the chief centre of the Welsh book trade in the late eighteenth century. The first printing press in the Principality was set up at Adpar, near Newcastle-Emlyn in 1718 by Isaac Carter, a press he brought to Carmarthen in 1725. Before this, most of the Welsh printing had been done in London or Shrewsbury. In 1721, four years after Carter's start at Adpar, Nicholas Thomas started printing in Carmarthen, followed in 1725 by Isaac Carter and in 1730 by John Breden. These three printing presses at Carmarthen were the first three in Wales.

There followed a succession of master printers, the most famous in the eighteenth century being John Ross. It is said of him that he printed and circulated nearly as many books in the eighteenth century as all the rest of the printers in Wales put together.

What John Ross was in his time, so became William Spurrell, the founder of the firm whose classical output in the Victorian era is well known to antiquarian book lovers and Welsh scholars. What is little known is that William Spurrell designed the standard type-case which was used by all printers at one time.

The following information about these local craftsmen gives the dates of their known printing existence in the town, the locality of their plant and one or two of their best-known publications (where this information is available).

Isaac Carter: (1725-1733). *Maddeuant i'r Edifairiol; Gwaith a Gwobr.* Carter was buried in St. Peter's churchyard.

Nicholas Thomas: (1721-1741). *Pedwar Ugain o Argoelion o Dyfiant a Phalliant mewn Duwioldeb.* (This was the first book printed in Carmarthen - 1721); *Cyffes Ffydd . . . Henuriaid a Brodyr amryw Gynnulleidfaoedd . . .* (Although the date of this is given as 1721 also, its appearance indicates that it followed Pedwar Ugain . . .); *Llun Agrippa* - 1723. Thomas died in 1741 and was buried in St.Peter's churchyard.

John Breden: (1730). Only one book has come to light from this printer: *Ychydig Ymholiadeu Ynghylch Credu a'r Petheu sydd iw Credu Gan Ewyllyssiwr Da i bob Enaid Dyn.*

Samuel Lewis, King Street: (1743-1749). *Aleluja* of Williams, Pantycelyn; *Leaves from the Tree of Life.*

Evan Powell, Priory Street: (1752-1765). *Canwyll y Cymru* by Vicar Prichard. Evan had a brother David, and under their names appeared *Pantheologia.*

Rhys Thomas, Lammas Street: (1760-1764). *Golwg y Ffyddloniaid ar Degwch a Gogoniant Iesu Grist.*

John Ross, Lammas Street: (1763-1807). Born in 1727, Ross printed hundreds of books in English and Welsh, including three editions of *Beibl Peter Williams.* He was first in partnership with Rhys Thomas (1763) and printed for some time in conjunction with John Daniel, though both seem to have had their separate plants. They printed together certain numbers of *Cylchgrawn Cymraeg.* In conjunction with others he published fifteen fortnightly numbers of a Welsh magazine called *Trysorfa Gwybodaeth, neu Eurgrawn Cymraeg.* Ross is said to have been a Scotsman who learned to read and write the Welsh language and became a prominent figure in the life of the town. He was a deacon of Lammas Street Chapel and a Sheriff of the Borough. He printed copies of the 1764 Charter. His daughter, Ann Scott, carried on his business for some years after his death. She married Walter Scott who kept a nursery behind Scott Terrace in Water Street. A Civic Society plaque is placed on Heol Awst Chapel Schoolroom.

John Daniel, King Street and Lower Market Street (Hall Street): (1784-1823). He served his apprenticeship with Ross and was the most skilled of all the early Welsh printers. He produced a Welsh Bible and he was the first to print music notes (staff notation) for in 1797 he printed *Cyfaill mewn Llogell* . . . He was also the printer of *Richard's English-Welsh Dictionary.* In conjunction with others he promoted and published the *Carmarthen Journal* which, soon afterwards, was printed by David Rees of Carmarthen. Daniel was born in the town, of which he was made a free burgess. He was buried, with his wife, in Llangunnor churchyard.

John Evans, Priory Street and Lower Market Street - next door to John Daniel in Lower Market Street: (1795-1830). He printed four editions of the New Testament and six of the Bible of Peter Williams. In 1806 he printed the only two numbers issued of *Trysorfa Effangylaidd.* He also bought the printing and publishing rights of *Seren Gomer* and printed the first numbers of *Y Brud a Sylwydd.* He was also the proprietor and publisher of the *Carmarthen Journal* for many years and was a deacon of Lammas Street Chapel and a Sheriff of the Borough. His three sons David, John and William were also master printers.

David Evans, Spilman Street: (1820-1823). Son of John Evans. *Carmarthen Journal, Testament Newydd. . .*

John Evans, Red Lion Court (Red Lion Yard) and Lammas Street: (1823-1840). Another of the sons of the already-mentioned John Evans.

William Evans: (1830-1847). Succeeded to his father's business. Printed the *Carmarthen Journal, Seren Gomer,* and last six-monthly numbers of *Cylchgrawn y gymdeithas er Taenu Gwybodaeth Fuddiol.*

Zecharias Bevan Morris, Lower Market Street: (1817). Proprietor of the office he called 'The Gomerian Printing House.'

Jonathan Harries, King Street and Dark Gate: (1807-1832). Peter Williams' Bible and Welsh Concordance, *Mynegair Ysgrythurol.*

John Powell Davies, King Street and Spilman Street: Most of his work as a jobbing printer was turned out about 1828 to 1833. He printed copies of the 1764 Charter.

Rev. Joshua Watkins: (1809-1811). He was a Baptist minister at Penuel Chapel from 1796 to 1841, who printed mostly religious matter. He traded at the beginning as 'White and Watkins' in King Street, and then as 'Watkins and Lloyd' in Priory Street. He came to Carmarthen in 1793 to help his friend Morgan John Rhys produce his *Cylchgrawn Cymraeg.* He does not appear to have been a practical printer in the beginning, his first partnership with the well-known White printers in King Street, in 1809, lasting less than a year. In the same year (1809) we find him trading as 'Watkins and Lloyd' in Priory Street as printers, booksellers, bookbinders, etc., and becoming sole proprietor in 1810. This business was eventually bought by Evan Jones and carried on by him until his death in 1832, his son-in-law, Daniel Jones, subsequently taking it over. At this time the office was considered a very attractive one because it possessed a wooden press. Daniel Jones died in 1902 at the home of his son-in-law, Harry Williams, Parcydrissy. The business was continued into the present century by J. R. Lewis of 104 Priory Street, who was well known for his music printing, and the business was continued by his nephew Mervyn Lewis until it closed in 1961. The iron Columbian press used by them can be seen in the museum. (Daniel Jones was the father of Maurice Jones a well known headmaster of the Pentrepoeth School in the early years of the twentieth century, and also of Professor D. E. Jones of

Aberystwyth, who worked with the great German physicist Hertz in developing the early electro-magnetic transmissions that were the forerunners of radio, radar and television.)

Daniel Harries: (1832-1836). Succeeded Jonathan Harries.

John Lewis Brigstocke, Lammas Street: Left John Evans and became publisher of the *Welshman* (first issue 1832); new edition of Peter Williams' Bible. Lived in Bridge Street. Buried in Carmarthen cemetery in 1865.

Hannah White, King Street: (1809-1860). Wife of John White, a highly respected school-master in the town who had been Headmaster of Chard School in Somerset. Until her husband's death in 1818, Hannah traded on her own, employing several men in printing. From 1818-1860 she traded as 'H. White and Sons,' printers, booksellers, stationers etc. Two of their sons, George White White and Isaac White White, were later partners in the printing business with their mother at Carmarthen. Another son, Henry White White, was a master printer at Merthyr and in 1850 was High Constable of Merthyr. George's son was Henry Brunel White, solicitor, town clerk and mayor four times, whose son, Howard, was also town clerk. Both were Freemen of the Borough. (See *Family Businesses* later in this chapter.)

Hannah White *

William Spurrell: For this famous printer and local historian, see *Some Carmarthen Personalities.*

Josiah Thomas Jones, Blue Street: Started Welsh weekly called *Y Gwron Cymreig* in 1852, which he moved to Aberdare in 1856.

William Morgan Evans, Hall Street: Established *Seren Cymru* (1851) and started the *Carmarthen Weekly Reporter* (1860) and the *Carmarthen Express* (1873). Printed *Mathetes' Dictionary* and many other books.

William Thomas, 3 Bridge Street (Gwilym Mai): (1849-1872). Bard, author and jobbing printer.

The following printers are also found in the mid nineteenth century:

John Philipps, Conduit Lane, King Street (1841);

David Williams, King Street (1842);

Charles Watling Wisbey, Picton Terrace and **Joseph Spawforth,** Union Street (1843);

Isaac Edwardes (1844);

Benjamin Jones, Guildhall Square (1844);

Joseph Higginbottom, Guildhall Square (1845);
Alice Williams (1845);
John Powell Davies (1848);
Mary Jones, Priory Street (1849);
John Thomas, Priory Street (1849);
William James Morgan, Chapel Street and Howell Davies, Waterloo Terrace (1861);
S. Jones, Priory Street (1863);
Edward Joseph, 2 Mansel Street (corner of Morley Street 1866-1868); Printed *Carmarthen Weekly Reporter* for a time and sold it to William Lawrence.
John Evans, Caxton Office, 13 Queen Street (1867-1883); Printed the *Carmarthen Times* at 2 St. Mary Street (1875) before moving to Queen Street.
The Lawrence Family[9] were connected with the book-binding and printing trades from the late eighteenth century to the present one. The first of the family to settle in the town, as a book-binder in the 1780's, was Thomas John Lawrence who lived in Red Lion Yard and who was buried at St. Peter's Church in 1824. His eldest son, John, continued the book-binding business as did John's youngest son, Richard, who died in 1870. John's third son, William Lawrence (1833-1889) was a printer who gained experience in London, Swansea and Cardiff. In 1873 he purchased the plant and copyright of the *Carmarthen Weekly Reporter* from the proprietor Edward Joseph. He succeeded in establishing a flourishing jobbing printing and newspaper business on Joseph's premises at 2 Mansel Street before moving to new offices at 3 Blue Street in 1875. After his death in 1889, his wife Mary and his son, William Loveden Lawrence, carried on the printing business together with the publication of the *Carmarthen Weekly Reporter*, until the latter was forced to close in 1921. After Mary's death in 1928, the general printing business was continued by William who modernised the plant. He was the first Carmarthen printer to install the Linotype composing machine. From 1935-38 William was chairman of the Carmarthenshire branch of the South Wales Master Printers' Federation. A bachelor, he died in May 1940, so ending the family's long association with the printing and book-binding trades. He was survived by two unmarried sisters who lived at 3 Blue Street, the last of whom died in 1963.

NEWSPAPERS

The first edition of the *Carmarthen Journal* was published on March 3rd, 1810 by John Daniel of Market Street, following a meeting of gentlemen of the county who had gathered in a local hotel to discuss such a possibility. The paper was to carry national and local news, political views, advertisements for trade and property as well as market and sale reports. Its full title was *Carmarthen Journal and South Wales Weekly Advertiser.* Subsequently North Wales was added to the title and by 1850 it was *Carmarthen Journal and Weekly Advertiser for the Principality.* For the first few years it had to struggle against the *Cambrian,* a rival paper from Swansea which had commenced some five years previously. There were several changes of ownership and editorial in the following years but politically the *Journal* faithfully continued as a supporter of the Tory faction in the county. Until the present century the *Journal* regularly carried reports of national as well as local events and was an important source of national news for the district. It has been the *Journal's* proud boast that it has appeared weekly without a break from 1810 until the present day.

In 1820 a Reading Room containing London and Provincial news publications was attached to the *Journal* office in Spilman Street and open to subscribers. Daily, weekly and Sunday papers were available. Maps were also hung in the Reading Room. In 1822 the *Journal* Reading Room was removed to the premises of John Evans, proprietor and publisher of the *Journal,* in Lower Market Street.

The *Welshman* appeared in January 1832 as a local rival paper supporting the reform and liberal groupings in the county and it continued to provide the strongest opposition to the *Journal* for most of its life. In 1944, however, the *Welshman* ceased publication and its title was acquired by its older rival. For the next forty years just fifty copies of the *Welshman* were produced each week by the *Journal* but finally in 1984 production could no longer be continued and the *Welshman* is now incorporated in the Journal.

During the nineteenth century several other weekly newspapers were started in the town. The *Carmarthen Weekly Reporter* was printed for a time by Edward Joseph of Mansel Street (1866-68) who then sold it to W. H. Lawrence and Son at 3 Blue Street. It was discontinued in 1923. The *Carmarthen Times and Joint Counties Weekly Gazette,* printed by John Evans at 2 St. Mary Street, lasted for some time in 1875. The *Carmarthen Miscellany,* a monthly periodical printed by the Welshman Publishing Company at 103 Lammas Street, flourished for a short time in 1892, edited by journalist Arthur Mee. The *Celtic News,* printed by D. L. Evans at 108 Lammas Street in 1923, was altered to the *Cymric Times* in 1927 and its copyright left the town in 1936.

A new weekly newspaper, the *Carmarthen Times,* was published in 1962 reviving a title from a former publication of 1875. In 1989 the weekly paper became a free publication under the title *Carmarthen and District Times and Citizen.* Subsequently it was acquired by the *Journal* and is published as the *Carmarthen Citizen.*

EARLY BANKS

The first record of a bank in the town is that of *David Parry's Bank*, established sometime before 1791. At this date it was taken over by David Morris, a Carmarthen merchant, who was then established somewhere in Dark Gate. David Morris' family originated in the parish of Llansteffan. Morris also took over The *Carmarthen Furnace Bank* founded in 1792 by John Morgan, the owner of the tinworks. Later on, after the failure of *The Carmarthen Bank*, conducted by Walters, Jones and Company, Morris assumed the name of *The Carmarthen Bank*. The bank thrived and a descendant, William Morris, moved to Coomb near Llangain in the 1860's, building a large mansion there which is now Coomb Cheshire Home. In 1834 there were three banks in the town: *Morris' Bank*, Spilman Street; *Biddulph Brothers and Company's Bank*, Quay Street; and *Wilkins, Wilkins, Jones and Company's Bank*, King Street. Soon afterwards the joint stock banks began their extensions and the *National Provincial Bank of England* opened a branch in the town in November 1864. It was at 59 King Street, the former shop and residence of Samuel Tardrew, chemist, druggist, seedsman and wine merchant. In 1871 *Morris' Bank* was taken over by the *National Provincial Bank* which in recent years has become the *National Westminster Bank*.

FAMILY BUSINESSES

The early years of the nineteenth century saw the founding of several well-known family businesses.[10]

David Brigstocke, whose family had been long established in west Wales, carried on a successful business at 61 King Street as a painter, decorator, glazier and paper-hanger. His contracts included painting and decorating the Guildhall in 1805 and painting 'The King's Arms' to be placed inside St. Peter's Church in 1820. He was the father of John Lewis Brigstocke, printer, Charles Brigstocke, wine-merchant of St. Peter's Street and Thomas Brigstocke, an accomplished artist.[11] David Brigstocke died in 1854 and was buried in St. Peter's.

Charles Brigstocke, his son and wine-merchant, was followed in the wine business by his son, Thomas Edward Brigstocke, J.P., who had his premises at 54 King Street. It was here in 1908 that the newly-founded Museum was given a room in which to display its initial collection. Thomas Brigstocke, faithful member and churchwarden of St. Peter's, produced a booklet on its history in 1924 entitled *Notes for Visitors*. The family wine business was continued under Mr. Frederick T. Brigstocke until it finally closed in the middle of this century.

Another son of Charles was James Brigstocke who established a pharmacy in 1869 at 25 King Street which was subsequently acquired by *D. King Morgan* at the beginning of this century and continued by his sons who are still giving service to the people of Carmarthen.

The Coffee Pot
preserved as a reminder of the grocery shop, specialising in coffee, kept by Miss Puddicombe and then by her nephew, Ald. J. O. Morgans, Mayor 1935-37 and Honorary Freeman 1953.

The Malt House in John Street (now demolished)

George and James Bagnall were the sons of John Bagnall, a prosperous draper, who owned a fashionable draper's shop at 2 Guildhall Square (now part of Littlewoods). George (1805-1900) took over the business and when he retired, to live in King Street, the shop continued under the name of D. and W. Davies. Later this became *The Emporium.* George became a Borough councillor in 1835 and a Justice of the Peace. His life spanned the nineteenth century and among his reminiscences, he recalled seeing King George IV, the former Prince Regent, being driven through Carmarthen in the royal coach at break-neck speed. The year was 1821 and sixteen year-old George ran after the carriage as far as Priory Street but was unable to keep up further. George kept weather diaries for fifty years from the 1840's.

James, the younger brother, set up his own business in corn, flour and butter, with premises next to the Old Oak in Priory Street. He was a J.P., a governor of the Priory Street Infirmary and lived in Castle Hill House on the corner of Castle Hill and Spilman Street.

Samuel Tardrew ran a very successful business in 1807 as a chemist, druggist, seedsman and wine-merchant, his premises being at 59 King Street. He took an active interest in local affairs; in 1841 he was the Founding Master of St. Peter's Lodge of Freemasons, Mayor in 1846 and subsequently a governor of Priory Street Infirmary. In about 1850 he retired to Starling Park, his shop and premises being occupied by his former apprentice, and later partner, John Smith. Samuel Tardrew died in 1864 and in November 1864 the National Provincial bank of England opened a branch in his former home at 59 King Street. It is now the National Westminster Bank.

A well-known family business was that founded by *John and Hannah White.* John White, born in 1762 at Knowstone, Devon, was appointed Headmaster of The Great House School, Chard, Somerset in 1787. He came to Carmarthen at the close of 1803 and became a noted school-master, keeping a school first in Priory Street and then in King Street.[12]

In addition to keeping the school, John and Hannah White also established a printing business and sold books. They opened a circulating library and a reading-room in King Street in 1815. John died on 2nd August 1818. He and Hannah had a family of seven sons and one daughter; the latter died in infancy.

In 1809 Hannah traded as a printer in partnership with the Rev. Joshua Watkins, a Baptist Minister at Penuel Chapel. However, the 'White and Watkins' partnership in King Street lasted for less than one year. Subsequently, until the death of her husband in 1818, Hannah traded on her own at 50 King Street, employing six or seven men in printing and binding. From 1818 until 1860, when Hannah died, the business was known as 'H. White and Sons,' printers, book-sellers and

A selection of engraved labels used to mark books by White and Sons
(reproduced actual size)

stationers, incorporating a reading-room and library. (Her husband's school-room was taken over by the Rev. John Evans).

Two sons joined her in the partnership, namely George White White, fourth son and Isaac White White, fifth son. On 26th November 1840 George married Betsey Thompson of Doric Place, Woodbridge, Suffolk. Betsey, a well-educated, genteel young lady, had come to Carmarthen in 1834, at the age of twenty five, to teach at Miss Woozencroft's School, a ladies' boarding school in Spilman Street. She was the daughter of George Thompson, County Surveyor for Suffolk, and sister of Francis Thompson, architect to Robert Stevenson for the North Midland Railway and later, architect for the Grand Trunk Railway of Canada. On their marriage in 1840 Betsey and George set up home in King Street. They had five children.

Meanwhile Hannah White, a woman of great character and determination, remained in the family business until she died in 1860 and was buried in St. David's churchyard. Sons George and Isaac continued the business until 1861 when they retired, the business being sold by auction. Isaac died in 1866.

George White White, a Justice of the Peace and church warden, who died in 1888, is commemorated by a stained glass window in St. Peter's Church, erected by two of his children, Henry Brunel White and Georgiana M. E. White. Henry Brunel White, a solicitor, became Town Clerk and Clerk to the Justices and he was also Mayor of Carmarthen four times in 1894, '95, '96 and 1897. He commissioned the architect, George Morgan, to build The Grange in Lime Grove to be his private residence.

Henry's eldest son, Howard Belmont White, M.C., also became Town Clerk and Clerk to the Justices. He retained the latter office until his death in 1955. Both father and son were made Freemen of the Borough.

From the early nineteenth century the *Timmins* family carried on business as timber merchants and owned a substantial amount of property in town, including a large piece of land in King Street which was where the Ivy Bush Inn had stood before it moved to Spilman Street in 1803. Previously in the eighteenth century it was the site of the Scurlock family house in which Sir Richard Steele died in 1729. When the Timmins family sold their property, the Assembly Rooms were built on the site in 1854. The present Lyric cinema and neighbouring properties now stand on the site.

Aaron Timmins, son of Joseph, the founder, had a house and timber yard here and also traded as a grocer, draper and general warehouse man. He became Mayor in 1827 and 1833. Aaron's sons, Joseph and Charles, carried on the business as timber merchants, grocers, tea dealers, linen drapers and general warehousemen until the property was sold in 1854. A third son, John, had a timber business at Bridge Wharf and lived at Mount Hill. His son, Dr. Timmins, became physician at the Infirmary in Priory Street.

A long-running family business was that of *David Jones and Sons,* painters and decorators of 15 King Street. Established in 1845, the business continued in the same family until 1970, the longest established business on the same premises in King Street. David Jones had two sons, Arnaud and Robert. Arnaud and his family lived over the shop, whilst Robert and his family lived in Waterloo Terrace. One of Arnaud's sons became Professor Percy Mansell Jones (1889-1968) who was born at No.15.

Another interesting and unusual family business was carried on in King Street by the *Jeffreys* family from the middle of the nineteenth century until the 1940's. They were carvers, gilders and taxidermists. Their skills in taxidermy were highly regarded and much sought after by museums, county families and antiquarians.

Among the many cabinet-makers were David Morley (1760-1831) whose portrait, painted in 1824 by Hugh Hughes, hangs in the museum and his son, also *David* (1792-1837), a councillor in 1835. They occupied extensive premises between Lammas Street and St. Catherine Street and gave their name to Morley Street. Other cabinet makers were Thomas Humphreys, Henry and Daniel Ayres in King St., Isaac and John Davies from the 1820's to about 1870, Evan Vaughan and son and Henry Jones and son in Lammas Street.

Nineteenth century Carmarthen was also well supplied with drapery and millinery establishments. In the early part of the century there was John Bagnall's shop at 2 Guildhall Square, continued by D. and W. Davies and later by William R. Edwards, (Mayor 1886), who called it *The Emporium.* This was subsequently taken over by Henry Thomas who had previously kept a drapery and millinery business at The Golden Anchor on the corner of King Street and Queen Street. In the 1920's this became the well-known *Anchor Café* and high-class cake and chocolate shop. The Emporium in Guildhall Square was not the first of this name.

There was an earlier Emporium at Nos. 1, 2 and 3 King Street which in about 1883 became known as *Cloth Hall.* This family business was a thriving drapery establishment which expanded further into King Street and Queen Street setting up millinery and ladies' fashion departments. The same family business is still continued today at No. 1 King Street.

The Emporium, 2 Guildhall Square, run by Henry Thomas and Sons from the early 1900's until 1947, was a most impressive Victorian building in classical style. A large, elegant drapery store housing several departments, including gentlemen's and ladies' outfitting, millinery, soft furnishing and haberdashery, it provided quality goods with personal service in a leisured, well-mannered ambience. In 1954 the Emporium, with its distinctive façade of five arches supported by six classical columns, was pulled down and replaced by a modern retail store.

OLD ESTABLISHED.

The Emporium

Commerce House in Guildhall Square, now Barclays Bank, was another flourishing drapery and millinery business, run by John Lewis from the early 1860's to the 1890's. Originally apprenticed to Mr. Puddicombe, who had a linen and woollen drapery here from 1851, John Lewis succeeded to the business in 1862 and built it up into a prosperous concern. He became Mayor, a J.P. and a governor of the Grammar School. He died in 1895 and a few years later the site was sold to Barclays Bank.

An early motor business was run by D. E. Jones (Bradbury Jones) who kept *The Leader Cycle and Motor Works* in King Street, with workshops in Woods Row. He sold bicycles called 'Bradburys' which became extremely popular at the time. Cycling was taken up enthusiastically by all sections of the public, a cycling club was formed and a cycling track was laid down in the park which was opened in 1900.

A well-known family of printers, stationers and book-sellers was that of David Jones, whose four sons were all gifted musically, the family forming a group known as 'Jones' Quadrille Band'.

Two highly-esteemed family businesses, founded towards the close of the nineteenth century, were those of *Crown Stores,* high-class grocery, confectionery and restaurant, founded by George James in King Street (originally in Little Water Street), and *The Old Curiosity Shop* founded by David Williams in King Street, dealing in antique furniture, new and second-hand books, leather goods, silver, jewellery and greeting cards.

The business of churn making was represented in the town by the works of *John Morgan, Cooper,* in Blue Street. This business was founded in 1842 by the father of John Morgan and continued until the 1940's by his son Stephen. They kept a stall on the market where churns of all descriptions, pails, buckets, casks and all sorts of dairy utensils for butter, milk, cheese and cream were displayed. Samples of their work are on display in the County Museum.

To complete the picture of a bustling, prosperous town there were also iron-mongers (e.g. Colby Evans in Dark Gate), boot and shoe makers, tea dealers, saddlers, upholsterers, silver smiths, ladies' and gentlemen's tailors and watch and clock makers, among many others.

John Morgan's Churns

At the end of the nineteenth century Carmarthen had come a long way from the original small settlement of traders and artisans which grew up outside the gates of the Norman castle in the twelfth century.

1 J. Geraint Jenkins, *Nets and Coracles,* 1974.
2 *Transactions Carms. Antiquarian Society,* Vol. 18, part 45 and Sir John E. Lloyd, *A History of Carmarthenshire,* Vol. 1, 1935.
3 E. A. Lewis, *Welsh Port Books,* 1550-1603.
4 M. C. S. Evans, *Carmarthen and the Welsh Port Books* in *The Carmarthen Antiquary, 1960.*
5 Terrence James, *Shipping in the River Towy: problems of navigation* in *The Carmarthenshire Antiquary, Vol. XXII, 1986.*
6 Pat Molloy, *Four Cheers for Carmarthen,* 1981.
7 See *Some Carmarthen Personalities - David Charles.*
8 See *Inns And Taverns - Coaching Inns.*
9 Richard E. Huws, *The Lawrence Family of Carmarthen and their contribution to the Book Trade, 1796-1940* in *The Journal of the Welsh Bibliographical Society.*
10 For information on some *Family Businesses* we are indebted to detailed research by Mrs. Edna Dale-Jones.
11 See *Some Carmarthen Personalities - Thomas Brigstocke.*
12 See *Education - Private Adventure Schools.*
* The drawing of Hannah White is taken from a contemporary portrait, by the Welsh artist Hugh Hughes, painted sometime after 1818. The portrait now belongs to one of her descendants, The Rt. Hon. Sir David Croom-Johnson.

Quay Street

Quay Street Bank

- 18 -

FOLK-LORE AND CUSTOMS

THE OLD OAK AND MERLIN

Until it was removed in 1978, the Old Oak was Carmarthen's most famous landmark, standing at the junction of Priory Street and Old Oak Lane. For many years it had been nothing more than a withered stump buttressed and encased in concrete and surrounded by iron railings. Since it was thought to constitute a traffic hazard, the relic was removed to St. Peter's Civic Hall where it is now preserved in a glass case.

Very little is known about the history of the Old Oak, which is also referred to as Priory Oak and Merlin's Oak. According to A. Stepney-Gulston[1] there was a hand-written memorandum on the back of an old play-bill of the Theatre Royal, Covent Garden, stating: 'Old Oak in Priory Street was planted by an Ancestor of President Adams, of America, May 29th 1659.' This memorandum was written in the nineteenth century; the play-bill, part of which is now in the Carmarthen County Record Office, was once owned by Stepney-Gulston who thought that the Oak may have been planted to commemorate the return to power of King Charles II after the death of Oliver Cromwell. Charles was proclaimed at Carmarthen on 19th May 1659, a year before he landed at Dover and finally entered London on May 29th, 1660.

According to Spurrell[2] 'the old oak-tree is said to have sprung from an acorn planted there by one Adams, master of Queen Elizabeth's Grammar School, in this town, and an ancestor of one of the American presidents of that name.' However, no reference can be found in the school records to any master of the Grammar School by the name of Adams.

On Thomas Lewis' *Street Plan of Carmarthen* of 1786 the tree is simply, but clearly, marked as 'Oak'. It is recorded by Spurrell that the oak-tree was killed by a 'dose of poison introduced through an auger-hole into its centre.' Tradition has it that this deed was done in the early nineteenth century by a nearby tradesman who disapproved of the practice of people congregating under its spreading branches at all hours of the day and night. It is clear that the tree was dead in 1856 for in that year Alex Aitken wrote a poem about the oak, including the lines:

> No mark of life adorns me now,
> But rugged antlers crown my brow.[3]

By the turn of the century the decayed trunk was 'walled up with cement and ribbed with iron bands.' This description was given by D. Parry Jones[4] in recalling his boy-hood memories of the Oak. He

The Old Oak in 1939

continues 'a brown, dry mummy, it has survived in its coffin for over half a century. I never knew it in its glory. On a plaque may be read the following prophecy of Merlin:

When Priory's Oak shall tumble down,
Then will fall Carmarthen town.'

This prophecy, supposedly made by the famous sage and magician, Merlin, was well-circulated about the town and neighbourhood and was taken very seriously. Another version of the same theme was:

When Merlin's Tree shall tumble down,
Then shall fall Carmarthen town.

There were other prophecies attributed to Merlin regarding the destruction of the town which was to be overwhelmed by water. Thus Spurrell states: '1727 Aug 12th. great consternation caused on the fair day by a big man, with long hair, ragged clothes, and eyes shining like two stars, crying, 'Mae tref Caerfyrddin i suddo o'r golwg am ddau o'r gloch heddyw.' (The town of Carmarthen will sink today at two o'clock). Spurrell continues: 'It had been noised about the country that Carmarthen would sink some time, and that Merlin had said,

Y Gaer fawr, ti gei oer fore,
Daiar a'th lwnc, daw dwr i'th le.
(Carmarthen, thou shalt have a cold morning,
Earth shall swallow thee, water take thy place.)

MERLIN'S PROPHECIES

These local prophecies attributed to Merlin were just a small part of the widespread medieval legend of Merlin which had a tremendous influence for many centuries over the minds of people, not just in Wales and England, but throughout Europe. It was Geoffrey of Monmouth who first published in Latin in 1135 *The Prophecies of Merlin (Prophetiae Merlini).* He then incorporated them in his *History of the Kings of Britain (Historia Regum Britanniae)* in about 1136, a publication which enjoyed wide acclaim and made a tremendous impact on European literature. (It is thought that Geoffrey was descended from a Breton family who had come over with the Norman Conquest and settled in Monmouth. Geoffrey seems to have lived in Oxford from 1129 to 1151 during which time he wrote his *History,* the *Prophecies of Merlin* and the *Life of Merlin.* He became Bishop of St. Asaph in 1152 and probably died in 1155.)

Merlin's prophecies, all rather obscure, dealt with the Saxon invasions of Britain and predicted the coming of a British (Welsh) champion and deliverer who would eventually defeat the Saxons. During the Middle Ages such prophecies became very popular and over the centuries many other sayings of a prophetic nature, written by others, were attributed to Merlin.

In Wales in particular Merlin's prophecies were taken very seriously and copies were sold in fairs and markets so that nearly every household possessed a copy. During the nineteenth century several publications containing his so-called prophecies were printed in Carmarthen and enjoyed a widespread sale.

However, some of these prophecies, especially those of a more local nature and significance, although attributed to Merlin, are now thought to be the work of the Rev. David Williams, (Dafydd o'r Nant), Vicar of Penllin, near Cowbridge, c.1460-1490.[5]

It is interesting to note, also, that none of the prophecies about the destruction of Carmarthen or about the Old Oak, which are now attributed to Merlin, were part of the original *Prophetiae Merlini* of 1135. The Old Oak prophecy probably dates only from the 19th century.

The legend that Merlin or Myrddin was born in Carmarthen (Caerfyrddin), that he gave his name to the town and that he lived in a cave on Merlin's hill and is buried there, must now be investigated.

THE LEGEND OF MERLIN

Who, then, was this Merlin described as sage, seer, prophet, wizard and magician, whose name is linked with that of King Arthur and who features in the literature of Europe from medieval times?

The legend of Merlin, a strand of the Arthurian legend, was the chief Celtic contribution to European literature in the Middle Ages. As previously mentioned, it was Geoffrey of Monmouth who first popularised the Arthurian legend in his *History of the Kings of Britain* c.1136 which has been described as 'the most influential book ever to have come out of Wales.' Written in Latin, Geoffrey's book was intended to be read as a history book but much of the material is pseudo-historical, coloured with Geoffrey's vivid imagination. He gives a glorified account of the ancient British race and especially of the Welsh and Breton connection. About one fifth of the book is devoted to the post-Roman period and the legendary Arthur. The *History* was later translated into French which gave the Arthurian legend, and hence the Merlin legend, an even wider appeal and attracted more literary contributions.

Geoffrey was the first to link Merlin and Carmarthen in literature and the first to use the name *Merlinus* which he Latinised from the Welsh Merddin or Myrddin. In his *History* Geoffrey relates how the boy Merlinus was found in a town, which was afterwards called Kaermerdin, by messengers of Vortigern, King of the Britons. Vortigern, fleeing from the Saxons, had been advised by his magicians to build a strong tower in which to seek refuge. However, whatever was built one day the earth swallowed up the next. Vortigern's magicians then advised him to find a boy without a father, kill him and sprinkle the mortar and stones with his blood. The foundations would then hold firm. The King's messengers 'came to a town which was afterwards called Kaermerdin and there they saw some lads playing by the town gate . . . A sudden quarrel broke out between two of the lads, whose names were Merlin and Dinabutius. As they argued, Dinabutius said to Merlin: "Why do you try to compete with me, fat-head? How can we two be equal in skill? I myself am of royal blood on both sides of my family. As for you, nobody knows who you are, for you never had a father!" The messengers examined Merlin closely . . . They were told that no one knew who his father was, but that his mother was the daughter of a king of Demetia and that she lived in the same town, in St. Peter's Church, along with some nuns.'

Merlin and his mother were sent to King Vortigern, when Merlin amazed the King by proving to him that his magicians had lied. He told the King that there was a pool under the earth which was preventing the tower from standing. Accordingly, the pool was found and Merlin then predicted that at the bottom of the pool would be found two hollow stones in which two dragons were sleeping. The King ordered the pool to be drained and there emerged two dragons, one red and one white. They began to fight each other and Merlin explained that the red dragon represented the British people, while the white dragon represented the Saxons. At first the British people would be overrun by the Saxons but in the end they would prevail when the Boar of Cornwall (King Arthur) drove out the Saxons.

Geoffrey then attributes to Merlin a long series of obscure prophecies, the *Prophetiae Merlini.* As we have seen, these had been published separately in 1135 before his *History of the Kings of Britain* incorporated them. The prophecies became a medieval 'best-seller' and because their chief characteristic was obscurity, they called forth a torrent of literary commentary, criticism and interpretation.

Geoffrey's story of Vortigern and the discovery of Merlin was not a product of his fertile imagination but was taken from the *Historia Brittonum* compiled about 800 A.D. by the Welsh priest Nennius, who called the fatherless boy Ambrosius and set the place of his discovery in Glamorgan. However, Geoffrey changed the name of the boy from Ambrosius to Merlinus and the place of his discovery from Glamorgan to Carmarthen. (At first Geoffrey called the boy Merlinus Ambrosius and then dropped the Ambrosius, simply calling him Merlinus, for the greater part of his narrative.)

Nennius' characters were not wholly imaginary but had their origin in the post-Roman era of the 5th century and, by the time of Nennius, they had assumed legendary form.

The question now to be asked is why did Geoffrey change the name of Ambrosius to Merlinus and why did he associate him with Carmarthen rather than Glamorgan? The answer is provided in scholarly detail by Professor A. O. H. Jarman in his absorbing book *The Legend of Merlin.*[6] Professor Jarman writes:

> 'There was in Welsh verse and saga in the twelfth century a fully-developed legend of Merlin, or Myrddin, of which Geoffrey had heard in general terms, but the content of which he only knew very vaguely and incompletely. What he did know seems to have amounted to this: that in the distant past, but later than the Roman period, there was a prophet or seer named Myrddin who was associated with Carmarthen or Caerfyrddin, and after whom that town was named. He knew, too, that there existed certain political prophecies in Welsh of which Myrddin was reputed to be the author, and some references in the *Prophetiae Merlini,* such as the linking together of Cynan and Cadwaladr as national deliverers whose coming was expected by the Welsh, suggest that he knew something of what the prophecies contained. And that was all.'

The Vortigern story, the association with Arthur and most of the prophecies in the *Prophetiae Merlini* were 'all extraneous themes which Geoffrey deliberately brought into association with the traditional seer of south-west Wales.' During the Middle Ages a vast crop of legends grew up around Merlin until he became a famous character in European literature and far removed from the original Myrddin of the Welsh legend.

Who, then, was this original Myrddin? According to Professor Jarman, the Welsh legend was a version of the primitive theme of the Wild Man of the Woods - a theme which was widely used in both Medieval art and literature. It was early in Celtic literature, however, that it first appeared, there being Scottish, Irish and Welsh versions of the same theme - that of a madman, an outcast from society, who, having lost his reason in the strain and stress of battle, fled to the woods where he lived like an animal, but nevertheless possessed prophetic powers.

The Welsh version has come down through the centuries not in the form of a prose saga, although originally it must have been transmitted orally, but embedded in several poems such as the *Afallennau* (Apple-trees), the *Hoianau* (Greetings), the *Cyfoesi Myrddin a Gwenddydd ei Chwaer* (Conversation of Myrddin and his sister Gwenddydd) and the *Ymddiddan Myrddin a Thaliesin* (The dialogue of Myrddin and Taliesin). These poems are preserved in several medieval manuscripts such as *The Black Book of Carmarthen* (late 12th - early 13th century) and *The Red Book of Hergest* (c. 1400). Myrddin is portrayed as a seer and madman living in Coed Celyddon (the Caledonian Forest) in southern Scotland towards the end of the sixth century. At that time this region was Welsh speaking. His madness is attributed to the Battle of Arfderydd, a genuine historical battle which probably took place in AD 573 near Carlisle and which was itself the subject of a full-length saga. However, although the setting for the Myrddin legend is sound historically, there are no grounds for believing that Myrddin himself was anything more than a purely legendary personage and no grounds for maintaining that he was a contemporary of Aneirin and Taliesin.

In the Scottish version of the legend the equivalent of Myrddin is Lailoken or Llallogan, who also lost his reason in a battle identified, on good authority, as that of Arfderydd. In the Irish version Suibne is driven mad at the battle of Moira, which actually took place in AD 637.

During the Dark Ages, possibly sometime between the seventh and ninth centuries, this theme of the Wild Man of the Woods, plus its accumulated saga, spread from the Welsh speaking kingdoms of southern Scotland to Wales, where it achieved widespread popularity thanks to the bards at the courts of the Welsh princes. But how did the central character come to be called Myrddin? And how was he connected with Caerfyrddin? Was Caerfyrddin named after Myrddin or was Myrddin named after Caerfyrddin?

The answers to these questions can be best understood by considering the origin of the name Myrddin. Professor Jarman states:

> 'Although in the Middle Ages Myrddin was accorded a place alongside of Taliesin, Aneirin and Llywarch as one of the founders of the Welsh poetic tradition, and numerous prophecies were attributed to him, his name does not occur in any of the genealogies of the "Men of the North" or in any other early northern source . . . . There are in fact no grounds for believing that any historical person of the name of Myrddin, whether king or poet, existed in the North in the sixth century. The name Myrddin is simply the second element of the place-name Caerfyrddin and is derived from the British "Moridunon", meaning "sea-fort". The Welsh form (Myrddin) was no doubt established by the end of the sixth century but its meaning was probably obscured by the phonetic development it had undergone.'

This phonetic development is further explained by Professor Jarman[7] where he states:

> 'During the fifth and sixth centuries the Brythonic language developed into Early Welsh by a regular process of phonetic change. The terminations -i and -on were dropped from *-mori* and *-dunon,* and these two forms became *Mer* and *ddin* respectively, thus giving the form Merddin. Myrddin is a variant of Merddin . . . Merddin or Myrddin, then, was a place-name. Why did it develop into Caer-fyrddin? The reason was that, whereas speakers of Brythonic understood the meaning of Moridunon, "sea-fort", being familiar with its constituent elements, speakers of Early Welsh in the sixth century would have found the new formation Merddin obscure . . . As there was a fort at Carmarthen it was natural that the common prefix *Caer* (fort) should be attached to the new name, thus giving *Caer-fyrddin.* (During this period Caer was commonly used in the names of places which had been Roman forts.) The next step in the development was the aquisition of a totally new meaning by the second element in the name, *-fyrddin;* this came to be understood as a personal name, that of the presumed founder of the *Caer* which perpetuated his memory.'

In this way Myrddin was created as a founder-figure out of a mere place-name. Thus Caerfyrddin was interpreted as the Fortress of Myrddin, whereas in fact 'caer' simply denoted the former Roman fort, while 'fyrddin' (myrddin) was derived from Moridunon.

Since nothing was known of the shadowy founder-figure, gradually over the years various attributes were attached to him and when the Scottish legend of the wild man, Llallogan, endowed with prophetic powers, and other northern folklore reached Wales, they too were gradually attached to the shadowy Myrddin and eventually the name of Llallogan was replaced by that of Myrddin. Nevertheless the northern setting was retained, as illustrated in the Welsh medieval poems embedding the Myrddin legend. Although these poems deal with the political state of Wales and contain many political prophecies, Myrddin is portrayed as a seer living in Coed Celyddon, i.e. the Caledonian Forest, at the end of the sixth century.

To return now to Geoffrey of Monmouth. When Geoffrey wrote his

History of the Kings of Britain incorporating the *Prophetiae Merlini (Merlin Prophecies)* in 1136, there was already this fully developed Myrddin legend in Welsh, but since Geoffrey was not of Welsh origin and not fully conversant with this legend, he confused two totally unconnected legends, giving the name of Merlinus to the wonder-child Ambrosius in the Vortigern story as told by Nennius in c.800 A.D. However, he knew that the Myrddin legend was connected in people's minds with the town of Caerfyrddin and so it was in Carmarthen, and not in Glamorgan, that his Merlinus was discovered. The changing of the names Ambrosius and the Welsh Myrddin to Merlinus is Geoffrey's entire responsibility. That Geoffrey eventually realised his early mistake is apparent in his *Vita Merlini (Life of Merlin)*, a poem which appeared between 1148-51, some twelve years after his *History of the Kings of Britain*, and which differs completely from the earlier work. In the *Vita Merlini* Merlinus or Merlin is presented as king of the Demetae who engages in war with the king of Scotland. After three of his brothers have fallen in battle Merlin's grief deranges his mind and he flees to live as a wild man in the Caledonian Forest. Much of the poem deals with Merlin's life in the wilds and he is portrayed as the Myrddin of the Welsh poems, remaining in the Caledonian Forest. Geoffrey realised his earlier mistake and his fusion of two distinct legends but instead of admitting to it, he merely stated that his *Life of Merlin* referred to a later period in Merlin's life.

Such then is the origin of Merlin - not a historical person but a name derived from the Welsh Caerfyrddin, which was itself derived from the ancient British place-name Moridunon (Roman Moridunum) meaning a sea-fort, with the later addition of 'caer' denoting a Roman fort, and to which has been attached the northern legend of the wild man possessing prophetic powers. A fusion of two distinct legends in the Middle Ages by Geoffrey of Monmouth associated Merlin, alias Myrddin, with the Arthurian cult and so profoundly influenced European literature to the present day. Carmarthen can take pride in the fact that the world-famous Merlin owes his name to that of Caerfyrddin.

OTHER ASSOCIATIONS OF MERLIN WITH CARMARTHEN

Geoffrey of Monmouth's *Historia* was such a best-seller in the Middle Ages that it had a profound effect on European literature, influencing poetry, drama and romantic fiction down the centuries. Merlin and Carmarthen are referred to in Edmund Spenser's *Faerie Queene*, 1590, and in Michael Drayton's poem *Polyolbion*, 1622. Both refer to Merlin's cave, Merlin's intention to build a wall of brass around Carmarthen and to Merlin's final imprisonment in his subterranean cave at the hands of a beautiful fairy maiden identified as the Lady of the Lake by Spenser. In Book III of the *Faerie Queene* Spenser writes:

To Maridunum, that is now by change
Of name Cayr Mardin call'd, they took their way;
There the wise Merlin whilom went, they say,
To make his wonne, low underneath the ground.
In a deep delve, far from the view of day .....

And if thou ever happen that same way
To travel, go to see that dreadful place;
It is an hideous hollow cave they say,
Under a rock that lies a little space
From the swift Barry tumbling down apace,
Amongst the woody hills of Dynevowre; .....

A little while,
Before that Merlin dy'd he did intend,
A brazen wall in compass to compile
About Cayrmarden, and did it commend
Unto his sprights to bring to perfect end;

In *Polyolbion* Michael Drayton says:

Now Merlin by his skill and magic's wound'rous might,
From Ireland hither brought the Stonendge in a night:
And for Caermarthen's sake would fain have brought to pass,
About it to have built a wall of solid brass,
And set his fiends to work upon the mighty frame, ...

According to Alan Randall[8] the reference to the wall of brass seems to be Spenser's personal contribution to the legend and may have been suggested to him by Giraldus Cambrensis' description of the town as being 'enclosed by walls of brick'. The location of the cave may also have been suggested to him by Giraldus' description of Dinefwr Castle as being 'built on the top of a high hill which overlooks the River Tywi'.

The association of Merlin with Carmarthen was also attested in a local poem entitled *Llangunnor Hill*, composed by an unknown author in about 1794:

There with delightful pleasure view
Carmarthen town, both old and new
The place where Merlin claim'd his birth,
That mighty prophet when on earth,
Who in Allt' Fyrddin form'd a cave,
Which serv'd him for his house and grave ....

Merlin's Hill, Abergwili, the site of an Iron Age hill-fort, probably became associated with Merlin sometime after *Spenser's Faerie Queene* of 1590 and had certainly become associated by 1767 when Sir Joseph Banks stated in his *Journal of a tour in Carmarthenshire* that Merlin's 'residence is said to have been a little hill, which still bears his name: it is

Gwili Weir and Furnace Pond, 1874

Towy Valley with Abergwili and Merlin's Hill (1st on left), 1853

situate about one mile from the town'.

In the early nineteenth century both Donovan and Malkin recorded the local belief that the hill was the location of Merlin's cave and chair, the latter being a rock, near the brow of the hill, upon which Merlin used to sit when uttering his prophecies. Even one hundred years later Ceredig Davies recorded in his *Folk-lore of West and Mid-Wales,* 1911, that many residents of Abergwili still believed that Merlin was imprisoned in his cave on the hill and that the clanking of his chains could be heard at twilight!

HENRY TUDOR - THE SON OF PROPHECY

Whatever we may think of Merlin, there is no doubt that his prophecies coloured the political thought of Wales for several centuries. When Geoffrey of Monmouth produced his *History of the Kings of Britain* in 1136 containing the Prophecies of Merlin there was already a very long tradition of prophetic poetry in Wales, dating back to Taliesin and the traditional Celtic Myrddin, predicting the coming of a national hero who, one day, would lead the Welsh to victory. Thus Merlin, with his prophecy that the Red Dragon would ultimately be victorious over the Saxon White dragon, became a national prophet, while the Red Dragon became a national emblem. The Welsh bardic tradition transferred these prophecies from generation to generation culminating in the enthusiastic and effective support given to Henry Tudor by the Welsh poets in his bid for the English crown. By the time Henry marched to Bosworth Field in August 1485, under his banner of the Red Dragon, his cause was well publicised throughout Wales giving him widespread support. His victory and accession to the throne fulfilled the hopes and dreams of past generations - the ancient prophecies had at last come true.

THE EISTEDDFOD

The first competitive eisteddfod of which there is a trustworthy record is the great festival held by the Lord Rhys in 1176 at Cardigan castle. The name eisteddfod may be loosely translated as 'session'.

The Carmarthen Eisteddfod of 1450 was an important development in the history of Welsh bardism.[9] Held under the patronage of Lord Gruffydd ap Nicholas of Dynevor, it was significant for its development of the rules of poetry given in the bardic schools. It was probably held in the precincts of the Priory. Here Dafydd ab Edmwnd won fame and a miniature silver chair for his codification of the traditionally strict metres of the formal alliterative ode, rules which have remained unbroken to this day, and for his many other contributions to Welsh poetic art. His bardic teacher was Maredudd ap Rhys, and he himself was an uncle of Tudur Aled. Both in their turn held the distinguished rank of *Pencerdd*

(Chief Bard).

Such meetings were common throughout Wales during medieval times. A notable one was that held in Caerwys in 1568. The Eisteddfod at Corwen in 1789, however, was the first on a national scale. This was organised by the London Welsh Society of the Gwyneddigion (Welsh exiles from Gwynedd). Others that followed were more regional than national.

It was the Gwyneddigion eisteddfod that reverted to the old custom of proclaiming the festival and its subjects a year and a day in advance, thus giving competitors time to prepare worthier odes and essays than could be expected from more impromptu efforts.

The next development came when the erudite, if romantic, Edward Williams, who was invariably known by his bardic name of Iolo Morganwg, introduced a ritual which he purported to be that of the druids and in 1792 he held the first Gorsedd meeting, or meeting of bards, on Primrose Hill in London. (Gorsedd = throne.) These imaginative inventions he combined with the Eisteddfod ceremonial and at Carmarthen in 1819 the Gorsedd became an integral part of the Eisteddfod. It is believed that part of this first Gorsedd ceremonial with the (now) traditional stone circle took place in the garden of the Ivy Bush Hotel in Spilman Street.

Another Eisteddfod was held in the town in 1823 when it is recorded that William Williams, son of a Carmarthen musician, won the silver harp.

The Llangollen Eisteddfod of 1858 was the next notable gathering and from this time it became customary to hold an annual ceremony on a national scale.

The Archdruid's Crown, Sceptre and Breastplate

In 1867 the National Eisteddfod was held in Carmarthen when it was housed in a large wooden pavilion erected on land in Priory Street which was later used for building St. John's Church and Priory Street School.

The next visit of the 'National' to Carmarthen took place in August 1911, by which time the event had taken on the form of the modern gathering with many cultural events accompanying the main competitions and occupying the best part of a week. The pavilion on this occasion was a substantial structure erected in the Park using the slope of the ground and the cycle track to form the tiered seating.

The last National Eisteddfod held in the

town, the *Bro Myrddin* (Region of Merlin) Eisteddfod, was proclaimed in June 1973 in the Gorsedd circle of stones erected for the purpose in the Park, where they remain today. This event was an elaborate ceremony with a procession of bards and civic dignitaries through the town culminating in the Proclamation Ceremony. A year later, the 1974 Eisteddfod Bro Myrddin was an outstanding success. The pavilion was erected on fields immediately below Castell Pigyn, Glangwili, and the competitions were held in the week of 5th-10th August, attracting large crowds.

THE WELSH HAT AND NATIONAL COSTUME

Carmarthen was a centre of the beaver and felt hat industry in the middle of the seventeenth century, the guild of hatters and felt-makers being incorporated in 1651. The origin of the Welsh hat and costume is a subject that has caused much speculation, but invaluable information is to be found in *Welsh Costume* by Ken Etheridge and in the Welsh Folk Museum's publication *Welsh Peasant Costume* by F. G. Payne.

It would appear that the Welsh 'national' costume is based on the peasant wear of the eighteenth century - the every-day, common dress of the peasants, farm servants and cottagers. However picturesque these costumes may appear today, they were made for hard wear and unremitting toil. The characteristics of the female costume were the open fronted gown (bedgown or betgwn), its skirt hitched back displaying the petticoat, the long apron protecting the petticoat front and the wide neckerchief or shawl. The materials used for the garments were chiefly local flannel, striped and checked. The tall, wide-brimmed, steeple-shaped beaver hat, however, did not arrive until the late eighteenth century and, when it did arrive, it looked very much like a revival of one of the seventeenth century styles. (A pamphlet published in Trefriw in 1778 refers to the hat as 'a recent and hideous fashion.') This so-called 'Welsh' hat, under which a mob-cap or bonnet was worn, was not a universal fashion but was prevalent in the larger towns such as Carmarthen. Beaver hats varied a good deal in form and shape; some were cone-shaped, others were shallower and squarer in shape. However their price was prohibitive to all but the fairly well-to-do. Therefore other hats of straw and felt were widely worn. The hooded cloak was also popular among country women.

During the eighteenth century the everyday working dress of the common people changed very little, owing to remoteness and lack of contact. But then garments of a similar kind and cut, although of different materials, were worn by English country-women too in the rural areas. However, the gentry and the well-to-do in Wales, as in England, followed the general fashions of the day in so far as they were able. Towards the end of the eighteenth century Wales was being opened up to English travellers by means of the stage-coach and from then onwards Wales was 'on the map'.

The nineteenth century saw a much closer relationship between England and Wales and English visitors were eager to observe any customs or modes of dress that were different. By this time England was enjoying the new fashionable materials pouring from the textile factories and mills of the Industrial Revolution, bringing rapid changes in fashion. These new materials and fashion changes eventually came into Wales, leading to the decline of the peasant costume, as they had done in England. But it was at this stage that the Romantics took over in Wales. In 1828 the romantic novelist T. J. Llewelyn Prichard published *The Adventures of Twm Shôn Catti* which was designed to attract English visitors to different parts of Wales. Welsh costumes were described as varying from county to county; thus for Carmarthenshire: 'the stout Carmarthenshire lass with her thick bedgown and petticoat of a flaring brickdust red.' However, a writer of 1826 says of Carmarthen that 'the women uniformly dress alike, viz., men's hats over their white caps, blue or black and red gowns with short sleeves with linen arm covers, dark blue stockings and cloth habits or cloaks of a dark colour.' On a market day he sees 'Welsh women coming into the town on horseback, dressed in men's black hats, habits, coats and cloaks, with saddle bags well loaded.' Much later in the century, in 1893, Marie Trevelyan in *Glimpses of Welsh Life and Character* states that Carmarthen girls are dressed in 'thick dresses resembling bedgowns and petticoats of red brick coloured flannel, sometimes with a pin-mark stripe of black or white.'

It was Lady Llanover (Mrs. Augusta Hall) of Gwent, however, who did more than anyone else to standardise and promote a Welsh national costume, at least for women. At the Gwent and Dyfed Eisteddfod of 1834 she gained a prize with her essay entitled 'The Advantages resulting from the Preservation of the Welsh Language and National Costumes of Wales.' She herself took to wearing Welsh flannels in stripes and checks and she also persuaded her friends to dress in this fashion at the

The Market, c. 1850-60

eisteddfodau and at other public occasions. According to F. G. Payne 'it was she who turned farm servants' working clothes into a conscious, or rather self-conscious, national costume.'

Furthermore, her water-colours of various costumes influenced the numerous prints which were produced to attract tourists to Wales from the 1840's onwards. These prints of country costumes were accepted as being national costumes, the implication being that Welsh people in general dressed in this manner in the mid nineteenth century. But F. G. Payne states: 'There is absolutely no evidence at all that Welsh women in general dressed in this way. There are vast numbers of portraits in existence showing the dress of nineteenth century Welshwomen . . . . It is surprising how few of the subjects of these portraits wear the so-called national costume . . . . Very few of them depicted the bedgown, petticoat and tall beaver hat.'

It would seem that from the mid nineteenth century, just when the 'national' costume was being so well publicised by the print designers, the flannel bedgown and petticoat were being dispensed with, even in the most rural areas, while the Victorian bonnet replaced the tall beaver hat. Most Welsh women, like their English counterparts, were keen to wear the new materials and fashions then available. However, the shawl and apron being so useful and adaptable, still continued to be worn, while the old country dress could still be seen on market days. Whether the scenes at Carmarthen market pictured in the engravings reproduced here are entirely genuine is debatable. It is possible that at that time some farm servants would have come to town in variations of the 'national' costume but the townswomen would have been dressed in the fashions of the day.

In the latter half of the nineteenth century, as part of the campaign to attract visitors, the print publishers were taken over by the picture post-card sellers and souvenir makers. It was they who were responsible for the 'phoney' photographs of Welsh women spinning, weaving, knitting and churning, implying that these were illustrations of contemporary Welsh life. For the studio photographs, in particular, the Welsh costume was altered and prettified, blouse and skirt replacing the old bedgown, lighter and brighter materials replacing the duller flannel, lace frills under the hat replacing the bonnet and shorter, fancy aprons. 'What was being done at the end of the century was to turn the so-called national costume into a fancy dress.'[10]

Thus what we see today is not the rough country dress of the eighteenth century but a much altered and prettier version, partly the creation of romantic fancy.

LOVE SPOONS

An old Welsh courting custom prevalent in Carmarthen and district

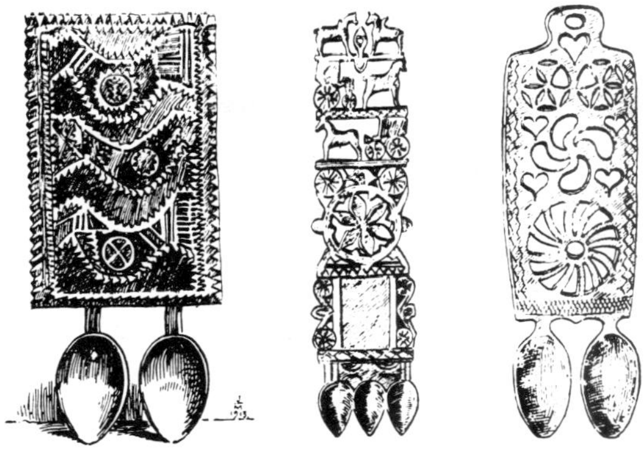

Love Spoons

in the eighteenth century was the giving of a carved wooden spoon by a young man to the lady of his love. In the early part of the century the spoons were merely copies of the metal spoons used by the wealthier people of this period, but in the course of time they became very elaborate specimens of the carver's art, and the more ornate they were, the more they were thought to express a lover's feelings. Sometimes the name of the lady was carved into the design. Traditional features included the heart, chain and ring. Even the most elaborate of spoons was traditionally carved from one piece of wood. The best type was carved in the early years of the nineteenth century but at the end of the Victorian era the custom of giving love spoons died out. The term 'spooning' may have originated with this custom.

THE BIDDING LETTER

A pleasant old Welsh custom practised in Carmarthen in the nineteenth century was the Bidding Letter, a general invitation to all the friends of the bride and bridegroom to meet them at the houses of their respective parents, or other houses appointed for the occasion. It was understood that every person who attended contributed some kind of gift.

In this fashion the young couple were given a big start in making their home. Whatever donation was given to the couple concerned, an equal amount was expected to be returned to the giver or a member of the giver's family, should a similar event take place in that circle.

In the early nineteenth century a Bidder *(Gwahoddwr)* went from house to house announcing the invitations (the Bidding) verbally, in prose or verse. At a later date he merely delivered the bidding letters. It was customary in some parts for the Bidder to have a bell attached to a ribbon and hung either around his neck or from a coat button.

Carmarthen, June 6th, 1836

As we intend to enter the Matrimonial State on Tuesday, the 28th day of June, we purpose to make a BIDDING on the occasion, the same day at the sign of the Fox and Terrier, situate in Water Street, when and where the favour of your good and agreeable company is respectfully solicited; and whatever donation you may be pleased to confer on us then will be thankfully received, warmly acknowledged, and cheerfully repaid whenever called for on a similar occasion,

By your most obedient Servants,
THOMAS THOMAS
MARY DAVIES.

The Young Man, his mother (Elizabeth Thomas, Bridge Street) his Brothers and Sisters (David, John, Mary and Margaret), and his Brother-in-law and Sister (Benjamin and Eleanor Jones), desire that all gifts of the above nature due to them be returned to the Young Man on the above day, and will be thankful for all additional favours granted.

The Young Woman, her Mother (Sarah Davies, Green Grove), together with her Brother and Sisters (Richard, Ann and Margaret), her Uncle and Aunt (Mr. Griffiths and Mrs. Griffiths), also her Aunt (Mrs. Thomas) desire that all gifts of the above nature due to them be returned to the Young Woman on the above day, and will be thankful for all additional favours conferred on her.

SPORT AND EARLY SPORTSMEN - "Crickett" in swan-skin jackets

An early reference to cricket in Carmarthenshire appears in a letter 'from Rd. Jones, Pantglas, 12 July 1783, to Jno. George Philipps, Cwmgwilly.' (Cwmgwili Manuscripts).

Dr. Philipps,

I have frequently heard you talk of crickett as a favour't game and that you would willingly make one of a sett (team) at any time. The following gentlemen are prepared upon to enter into my list and are willing to meet any sett which you can produce.

There is a very good place on the little common between me and Court Henry. We may fix the tent near and dine in it. Batts, balls etc. shall be provided by me. If you accept the challenge it should be soon as the ground and weather are favourable.

The dress, if you approve it, may be a swan-skin jacket with sleeves edged with coloured ribband which will not stand each person above 2s. 6d. or 3s. 6d. at the utmost and be of use afterwards.

If you should not be able to make up a sett we may meet and toss up for choice of partners, as I am sure there will be number sufficient to make up a double wickett.

Yours sincerely,
Rd. Jones.

THIRSTY FOOTBALLERS

If cricket was an early pastime of local sportsmen, there were devotees of other games in 1796. The following curious account could refer to an early game of football.

> This wrote by John Rosser of Treherion, Llanstephan parish, County of Carmarthen, South Wales, 18th July, 1796.
>
> 1st, played about 5 games and 1/2 of ball at Llanstephan, before hurting my foot, then I stept wrong upon plain ground with my right foot as it bent out a little in my ancle: then I plaid that game out, and one other game, and no more we were to plaing; and drank 6 quarts of ale on the plain between us, and gave share to many others. Drank the first quart after ending the 2nd game, and the 2nd quart after the 3 games, and so on the best of my knowledge .... but I sweat considerable, but I sweat so much many times, according to my knowledge in the summer by working, as I now by playing ball.

We now follow John for a brief period after his exertions, realising that whatever game he played was a very thirsty one!

> We then came down four to the publick house only wearing our coat and handkerchief, without catching cold.
>
> We 4 in the house drank between us 3 or 4 quarts of ale, and eat some food. Afterwards walked home, that was about 2 miles of way, and my foot began to swell since it first happened, and regularly then it swelling and some pains, and going warmer, and yet was sleeping every night. The 2nd day I went to Coomb action, and eat and drank some, also, according to my want, not to any excess. That night I felt my foot going worse. Afterwards, in 3 or 4 days, I applied to a woman, who had been with me just upon the like occasion 2 or 3 years preceding, but not by the same reason, that is by sweating and then I was made well. Then I took a sweting ale made of some herbs boiled in ale, but I am now convinced that the sweting was more by the abundance of cloathes upon the bed, than from strength of the sweting ale....

MANY MILES TO SCORE A GOAL

A game called *Knappan or Cnapan,* said to be the forerunner of modern Welsh rugby, was played in this locality up to the eighteenth century, its origin being lost in the distant past.

The game was played over a large area of countryside, with the 'pitch' stretching over many miles between two goals. The wooden ball, greased and held in the hand, was slightly larger than a cricket ball. The object of the game was to carry or pass the ball from one player to another as far as the goal line. Often horsemen were used as a forward 'front line'. Since the game was of a very rough nature, some of the participants were often injured or even killed.

There were regular contests between two districts which took place on festival days, as many as 2,000 players taking part. The game (or some form of it) was a regular fixture on Good Friday between Llandyssul and Llanwenog. It is said that Knappan (Cnapan) was a survival of an early form of war training.

1 *Transactions of Carmarthenshire Antiquarian Society,* Vol.4, p.56.

2 W. Spurrell, *Carmarthen and its Neighbourhood,* 1879.

3 Alex Aitken, *Poetical Pieces,* 1856: *Transactions of Carmarthenshire Antiquarian Society,* Vol.18, p.29.

4 D. Parry Jones, *Welsh Country Upbringing,* 1976.

5 Alan Randall, *Carmarthen and Merlin the Magician* in *The Carmarthenshire Historian,* 1980.

6 A. O. H. Jarman, *The Legend of Merlin,* 1970.

7 A. O. H. Jarman, *The Legend of Merlin and its associations with Carmarthen* in *The Carmarthenshire Antiquary,* Vol. XXII, 1986.

8 Alan Randall, *Carmarthen and Merlin the Magician* in *The Carmarthenshire Historian,* 1980.

9 National Eisteddfod Proclamation Booklet, 1973.

10 F. G. Payne, *Welsh Peasant Costume;* a Welsh Folk Museum publication.

- 19 -

THE PENAL CODE AND THE POLICE FORCE

Before John Nash built the new County Gaol (1789-92) on the castle site, the town had two squalid and dilapidated prisons, one in the remains of the Castle and the other over the East Gate, called Prisoners' Gate, between King Street and Nott Square. From the latter prison debtors were accustomed to lower down bags soliciting aid with the phrase 'Remember the poor debtors'. With the completion of the County Gaol in 1792 this gate and prison were removed.

When John Howard, the philanthropist and 'inspector' of prisons, paid one of his visits to the castle gaol in 1774 he found it in a shocking state, like most other prisons at this time. There was no water inside, the cells were very small with mud floors and 'the condemned dungeon was damp'. On another occasion in 1788 he found 'a number of idle and profane people playing at tennis. The gaoler lived far from the gaol and was paid no wages, existing on fees and tolls extracted from the prisoners and their friends.' It was following Howard's recommendations for improvements in 1788 that John Nash got his first job to build the new County Gaol, commenced in 1789.

The penal code was inhuman in its severity, public hangings and transportations for comparatively trivial offences being ordinary and frequent events. At the beginning of the nineteenth century crimes or felonies punishable by death were very numerous, including not only murder but also highway robbery, house-breaking, forgery, coining and horse and sheep stealing. Executions were public spectacles attracting crowds of people from miles around. It was not until the 1820's that Robert Peel, as Home Secretary, began to reform the penal system and abolished the death penalty for over a hundred crimes.

As far as Carmarthen was concerned, before 1818 public executions of convicts from the County took place at Pensarn, on the site where Babell Chapel now stands, while executions of those from the town took place on the Royal Oak Common in Johnstown.

In 1739 a man from Llandyfaelog was hanged at Pensarn for pilfering, a servant girl at Job's Well was hanged on the Royal Oak Common for killing her child, and two lads were executed for stealing cider from the Greyhound Inn, Bridge Street. In 1752 Griffith Philipps of Cwmgwili wrote to his son George in London:

> There are this day to be hang'd at Carmarthen two men for house

> breaking, which I suppose will draw all ye country peoples together, it being a very uncommon thing here to get 'em hang'd by pairs.

In 1767 a man was hanged at Pensarn for murdering his sweet-heart and in 1804 another was hanged there for horse stealing. A letter dated 1788 from Richard Jones, Carmarthen, to John George Philipps, M.P. stated:

> We had three persons condemned, two for horse stealing and one for stealing goods and breaking into a house in the day-time; this last was the hangman in the gaol, - a person not 20 years of age, who had been tried at our bar three times; not half an hour after he received sentence he hung himself in the gaol . . . .

However, juries were often reluctant to convict people for trivial offences when this entailed the death penalty and reprieves were frequent, except for persistent offenders.

After 1818 condemned men were hanged on a platform raised above the County Gaol wall facing Spilman Street. The last public execution was in 1829 when an estimated crowd of 10,000 packed the streets to see the event. It was on this occasion that a distressing circumstance took place. When the first attempt to hang the convicted killer proved abortive, he pleaded for his life on the grounds that he could not be

Entrance to the County Gaol, facing Spilman Street

punished twice for the same offence. His pleas were rejected and the crowds got their 'Roman holiday'.

However, it was to be the last, for there were no more executions at the County Gaol for nearly sixty years, until 1888, and then it was no longer a public spectacle.

Inspite of its reputation as a drunken town prone to street brawls and near-riotous behaviour, Carmarthen was never a town with a high crime rate - murder, theft and break-ins were negligible considering the poverty and poor housing conditions of many of its inhabitants. But there was imprisonment for debt, among many other offences, and prisoners had to work hard on the tread-wheel (supplying the gaol's water), at stone-breaking for roads, brick cleaning, cooking, sewing, clog-making, mending and cleaning.

A report of 1834 on the Borough Gaol and House of Correction, which had been completed in 1810 on the Cambrian Place site, stated that it was much inferior in accommodation and management to the County Goal. There were four rooms and a yard for debtors but no day-room. The average number of debtors in confinement was seven or eight but frequently there were twelve and once there had even been eighteen. The accommodation was quite insufficient.

There were eight cells for criminals, with a day-room and yard for male prisoners and the same for female prisoners, although the women's yard had been broken up by the gaoler for a garden. A surgeon and a chaplain were appointed by the town corporation.

EARLY GUARDIANS OF THE PEACE

Some of the earliest attempts to maintain law and order can be traced back to the *Watch and Ward* patrols of Edward I's reign (1272-1307), when at dusk a curfew (*couvre-feu* = cover the fire) was imposed, the streets emptied and the town gates closed. Such a practice was probably followed in medieval Carmarthen. In the seventeenth century there is a reference to *constables* in the Minute book of the Common Council, when there are entries concerning the playing of tennis and fives in St. Peter's churchyard, fighting and flinging stones. Children were 'to receive due correction in presence of one or more constables.'

Apparently the constables were in the employ of the Common Council for on 17th August, 1709 nine constables were sworn before William Gower, the Mayor - three each for St. Mary Street, Gell (i.e. Lammas) Street and Priory Street. In 1726 the chamberlain (treasurer) was ordered by the Common Council to pay 'John Tindall for painting thirteen staves for the constables of the County of the Borough of Carmarthen such sum as John Roberts, Mayor, and any three of the Common Council shall agree.'

In 1803 in consequence of press-gang riots in the town, it was ordered 'that the Chamberlain pay out of the rents in his hands such a sum of money as the magistrates of this borough shall direct to the constables employed in suppressing the riots for their loss of time and trouble.'

However, these 'constables' should not be regarded as 'policemen' in the present sense of the term for they were employed, more or less temporarily, by the Mayor and magistrates as and when their services were required and could just as easily be discharged. It was the Mayor and magistrates (the Mayor being the chief magistrate) who were responsible for keeping law and order in the Borough and who could call out the troops as a last resort. Besides 'constables' there were also night-watchmen but these were often elderly, illiterate, drunken men who could do little else but walk the streets and were not very effective at keeping the peace.

At the beginning of the nineteenth century Carmarthen had only one such watchman and he was called Wil y Lôn (Wil the Lane) commonly known as 'Wil Alone'.[1] Armed with his watch-pole, lantern and truncheon, he would report to the Mayor before setting out on his nightly rounds and lighting the oil lamps dotted around the town which was much smaller in those days. At the end of his watch he would extinguish the lamps and report back to the Mayor.

In 1804 a small lock-up, known as the Roundhouse, was erected in Cambrian Place and on the same site in February 1810 a Borough Gaol was completed, to which prisoners were taken.

In 1810 we hear of 'watchmen' being engaged to supervise the festivities celebrating the fiftieth anniversary of the coronation of George III. The following day they were discharged from their office.

In the year of Waterloo, 1815, watchmen were again appointed, the Mayor and magistrates being authorised 'to retain and employ any number of persons they may think proper for the purpose of watching the town.' The Mayor was also authorised 'to have any police officer from London to this town for the purpose of giving such instructions in respect to the manner of carrying on the matters aforesaid in the most efficient way.'

The first mention of a 'Chief Constable' occurs on 16th February, 1827, when the Council appointed James Evans, of Spilman Street, brightsmith and zinc worker, to be 'Chief Constable of this borough in the room of Charles Wilson, and that he be allowed a salary of £20 a year for discharging the office faithfully.' As in the case of the constables mentioned above, this term must not be confused with the present meaning of a Chief Constable.

In the following year his salary was increased to 10s. per week, and the Council ordered 'a pair of pistols, mole and case to be purchased for the Chief Constable of this county borough for the use of himself and his successors as Chief Constables.'

It is interesting to note that at the same meeting the Council appointed 'four watchmen' to be paid 10s. each per week - the same as the Chief Constable!

During the Parliamentary election riots of 1831[2] when the Carmarthen mob held sway, the Chief Constable and his four watchmen were powerless to preserve the peace of the town and seventy extra 'special' constables had to be pressed into service. These constables, drawn from the same 'lower orders' as the mob and virtually dragged in from the streets, illiterate and just as prone to drink as the rioters themselves, were unable to restore law and order. Eventually the Home Secretary sent to Carmarthen six policemen from the London Metropolitan Police Force - Sir Robert Peel's *Bobbies* - a police force founded only two years earlier in 1829. The London police came in for special attention from the mob who resented their presence and several were quite seriously injured. They were reinforced with a large number of local special constables and eventually some semblance of order was restored to the town, although there were recurring sporadic outbreaks of violence. One of the London policemen, John Lazenby, remained in Carmarthen and was appointed Chief Constable of the force, consisting of four constables, who were employed on a year-to-year basis. John Lazenby worked hard to mould the illiterate, often drunken men under his command into something resembling a peace-keeping force. But his days in Carmarthen were numbered!

THE BOROUGH POLICE FORCE, 1836

The Municipal Corporations Act of 1835 sought the reform of local government and Carmarthen held its first democratic (hopefully) Borough Council elections on 26th December, 1835. The Whig radicals (the *Blues*), backed by the mob, defeated the Tory *Reds* and set about making changes, including a new police force which was made compulsory under the Act. In January 1836 the Carmarthen Borough Police Force was created.

Unfortunately the new Borough Council was so tainted with past political rivalry that it dismissed Chief Constable Lazenby, who had put the Whig mob rioters in gaol in 1831, and replaced him by a Whig party voter with no qualifications and with no salary. New constables were also appointed but these were all drawn from the mob rioters of 1831. Thus Carmarthen's new police force still consisted of unruly elements.

In June 1836 the Watch Committee, headed by the Mayor, gave its new police force the London-styled uniform of blue tail-coats with silver buttons, white trousers and black leather top-hats. Unfortunately, the force was constantly changing because of dismissals for drunkenness; but then the policemen were no better or worse than the majority of the poorer townspeople for whom life was harsh, food and money scarce,

A Bobby or Peeler
A member of the Metropolitan Police Force founded by Sir Robert Peel

housing conditions appalling and life expectancy short. So many escaped the realities of life by drowning their sorrows in drink.

During the Rebecca Riots[3] the Borough's police force was reprimanded on several occasions for failing to deal firmly with the rioters, although when the Workhouse was stormed, on 19th June 1843, the police overpowered the mob and about one hundred arrests were made. No proceedings, however, were taken against the majority of the rioters who all pleaded that their lives and houses were at risk had they not joined the Rebecca march. Only five ring-leaders were committed for trial at the Assizes.

During the mid nineteenth century most of the cases dealt with by Carmarthen's police force appear to have been connected with drinking, since drunken brawls were a common occurrence. On many occasions the police themselves were violently assaulted and suffered injuries, for they were regarded at first as a force for the suppression of liberty rather than one for law and order.

In 1848 a new Chief Constable was appointed - Samuel Kentish - who brought discipline and stability to the Borough force, for he remained in control for the next twenty two years until his retirement in 1870.

"THE CARMARTHEN SHILLING" 1857

In 1857 the Borough police at last reached a strength of twelve - the twelve coppers - and so became known as *The Carmarthen Shilling.* Their uniform also changed - the helmet replacing the top-hat and the belted tunic the tail coat.

With the passage of time came gradual improvement in social and economic conditions and this, together with free elementary education for all and the growth of the temperance movement in the latter part of the nineteenth century, led to less drunken brawling in the town which had been such a feature earlier in the century.

But for all its political riots and heavy drinking, Carmarthen had never been a town with a high rate of crime. Considering the grinding poverty and squalid housing of many inhabitants, theft and break-ins were negligible. There were no executions for murder at the County Gaol for almost sixty years, between 1829 when the last public execution took place and 1888.

In addition to its main peace-keeping duties, the Borough Police

Force also maintained and manned the Fire engine, with the assistance of several auxiliary firemen, and this system continued until the 1939 war years when the National Fire Service took over. With the outbreak of war another change took place when *The Carmarthen Shilling*, consisting of Chief Constable, two Sergeants and nine Constables, was increased in number to sixteen.

Finally on 31st March, 1947, the Carmarthen Borough Police Force ceased to exist as a separate entity when it was taken over by the Carmarthenshire Constabulary. This too, was subsequently amalgamated with the Cardiganshire Constabulary, the joint body later becoming the Dyfed-Powys Police Force.

1 Pat Molloy, *A Shilling for Carmarthen*, 1980. (A history of the Borough Police Force).

2 See *Eighteenth and Nineteenth Centuries - Political Strife.*

3 See *Political Strife - The Rebecca Riots.*

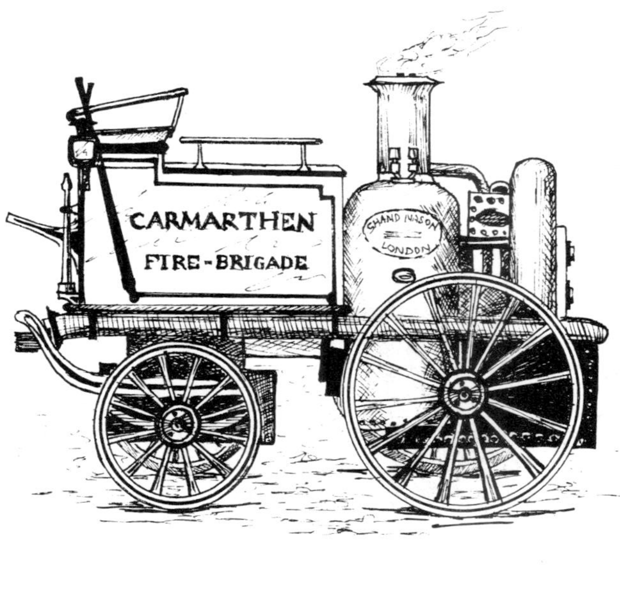

The Borough Fire Engine, 1896

A 'New Volunteer' horse-drawn, steam powered, fire engine by Shand Mason & Co.

Penllwyn Park

The Esplanade

- 20 -

SOME CARMARTHEN PERSONALITIES

THE DYNASTIES OF DYNEVOR AND DEVEREUX

SIR RHYS AP THOMAS (1449-1525)

Sir Rhys ap Thomas was the third son of Thomas ap Gruffydd and the grandson of Gruffydd ap Nicholas, founder of the House of Dynevor. Related to the earlier dynasty of Dinefwr, the House of Dynevor was based on the 15th century manor-house of Newton, Llandeilo. This was later rebuilt and enlarged and from 1782 was known as Dynevor Castle. It stood close to the ruins of the much older Dinefwr Castle.

Rhys ap Thomas was born in 1449 and lived for a time with his father at the court of the Duke of Burgundy. Here he received his early military training. On the death of his elder brothers, he succeeded to the wide estates of the family, to which was added the inheritance of his first wife, Eva, the heiress of Henry ap Gwilym of Cwrt Henry.

The most influential county magnate, Rhys ap Thomas was instrumental in putting Henry Tudor upon the throne of England and securing his accession as Henry VII. He was a courageous warrior, though cautious and cunning, ambitious, able and dominating. For some years before Henry Tudor landed at Dale, near Milford Haven, in August 1485 in a bid for the crown, Rhys ap Thomas had been secretly negotiating with him in exile in Brittany. However, the Carmarthenshire magnate did not immediately join Henry and his small army but waited until they had collected more support before meeting them near Welshpool. Under his banner of the Black Ravens, Rhys led some thousands of Carmarthenshire men up the Towy valley and through Breconshire to meet up with Henry Tudor and other Welsh contingents. From Welshpool they marched to Bosworth where they attacked Richard III's superior army on August 22nd, 1485. Richard was killed and his crown, which was picked up from a bush on the battlefield, was placed on the head of Henry Tudor. The honour of a knighthood was bestowed upon Rhys ap Thomas for the services he had rendered, as well as many rich rewards of estates in south-west Wales. He was also appointed Chamberlain (Treasurer) at Carmarthen castle.

Throughout Henry VII's reign Sir Rhys ap Thomas continued to serve the King, being present at the battle of Stoke in 1487 when the impostor, Lambert Simnel, was taken prisoner. In 1492 he accompanied the King to France on a military expedition with a force of Welshmen, whose exploits were highly extolled. He was present at the battle of Blackheath, 1497, where Lord Audley and his Cornish rebels were defeated. It is said that Sir Rhys, on his famous horse *Llwyd y Bagsau* took Lord Audley captive and presented him to the King. He was duly rewarded with the gift of Audley's estates. It was also Sir Rhys who besieged Perkin Warbeck, another impostor of Henry's reign, and took him prisoner.

After Henry VII's death in 1509 Sir Rhys continued to serve Henry VIII, being present at the battle of the Spurs in France in 1513 and at the Field of the Cloth of Gold in 1520. By this time he was seventy-one years old and by this time, too, he was the undisputed ruler of south-west Wales.

From 1495, when Sir Rhys became Chief Justice, he ruled this area with a power and authority that brooked no opposition; so much so that it enjoyed a long period of peace unknown to other parts of Wales which were torn by the armed feuds of local lords.

Sir Rhys ap Thomas' landed estates were so extensive that there was a popular saying of the time: 'The King owns the whole island except that part which belongs to Sir Rhys.' Among his estates were his seats at Abermarlais (Llansadwrn), Dynevor (Llandeilo), Derwydd (Llandybie) and Newcastle Emlyn Castle, which he made a place of residence. Carew Castle was also a place of residence and Sir Rhys' home for many years. Other castles which were in his hands for some time were Kidwelly, Laugharne, Carreg Cennen, Dryslwyn and Narberth. He was also Chamberlain of Carmarthen and Cardigan; Chamberlain and Steward of

The effigy of Rhys ap Thomas in St. Peter's Church

Haverfordwest; Constable and Steward of Brecon and Steward of Builth. He was Mayor of Carmarthen on three occasions. In 1505 he was created a Knight of the Garter and a Privy Councillor by Henry VII.

Nevertheless, inspite of all his power and wealth, Sir Rhys ap Thomas was quite unscrupulous in adding to his vast possessions. It was said of him that he repaid the loyalty of his friends by robbing them of their estates and that within twenty miles around the place where he lived 'there was not in the possession of the poor farmers any land which, if he fancied it, he did not obtain, either as a gratuity or by purchase, without consulting the owners.' He was omnipotent and untameable, living in an age when the strong and selfish survived in prosperity and when cruelty and torture were the normal procedures.

On the other side of the coin, however, Sir Rhys was a patron of the bards, his praises being sung by Tudur Aled, Lewis Glyn Cothi and Lewis Morgannwg. He was also the most outstanding Welsh personality of his age. Nevertheless, he was the last of the medieval landed magnates to exercise such power and authority, for under the Acts of Union of 1536 and 1542 new shires were created which became units of local government in both legal and administrative affairs.

Sir Rhys ap Thomas' last years were spent in Carew castle which he then left to enter the Franciscan Friary at Carmarthen. Here he died in 1525 at the age of seventy-six and was buried in the Friary Church. After the Dissolution the tomb of Sir Rhys and his second wife, Janet, was taken to St. Peter's Church and placed in the north-east corner of the chancel. In September 1865 it was dismantled prior to its restoration by Lord Dynevor, a lineal descendant. In April 1866 after much restoration it was placed under the arch between the chancel and the consistory court. In 1886 it was moved again, a few yards further west, to make room for the organ. Here it remains but records, by mistake, the name of his first wife, Eva.

The tomb of Sir Rhys ap Thomas
before restoration in 1866

In his will Sir Rhys left '£20 to the Freres of Kermerden; £6.13s.4d. to the Priory of Kermerden; a vestment price £2.13.4. to the Rode Church (i.e. St. Mary's); a vestment and a Chalice price £5 to St. Peter's Church; a vestment price £2 to St. Barbara's Chapell; a vestment price £2 to St. John's Chapell and the same to St. Katheryn's Chapell'.

SIR RHYS AP GRUFFYDD or SIR RICE GRIFFITH FITZURIEN (1508-1531)

The vast estates of Sir Rhys ap Thomas passed on his death, in 1525, to his seventeen year old grandson, Rhys ap Gruffydd, for Sir Rhys ap Thomas' son, Gruffydd, had predeceased him in 1521. The young Rhys liked to call himself 'Rice Griffith fitzUrien' because of his family's reputed descent from Urien Rheged, an early Celtic prince. The Ravens of Owain ap Urien Rheged also formed part of his family's coat-of-arms. However, since Rhys, or Rice, was too young to undertake the judicial and administrative responsibilities of his grandfather, the post of Chief Justice and Chamberlain of South Wales went to Walter Devereux, Lord Ferrers of Chartley. There was already enmity between the families of Dynevor and Devereux, the Dynevors having supported the Lancastrian cause, while the Devereux family had been Yorkist supporters. In March 1529 the young Sir Rhys complained to Cardinal Wolsey, his grandfather's old friend and chief minister to Henry VIII, that his tenants and servants were being badly treated by the officials of Lord Ferrers. He also requested that he be appointed Deputy to the Chief Justice. However, he received no reply and when in June 1529 Lord Ferrers came to Carmarthen to hold the Sessions, quarrels about lodgings broke out between the retainers and servants of the two rivals. One of Sir Rhys's men was arrested, whereupon Rhys, accompanied by armed followers, burst in upon Lord Ferrers in his castle apartment and a furious dispute ensued. Sir Rhys was placed in custody and sent to London. His wife, Lady Katherine Howard, daughter of the Duke of Norfolk, appealed to Cardinal Wolsey who 'for the love he bore old Sir Rhys ap Thomas' ordered the prisoner to be set at liberty.

Some weeks later the feud flared up again and one of Ferrers' officials was killed. Both Sir Rhys and the Chief Justice appeared before the Court of Star Chamber at which Wolsey presided. They received a stern warning and were ordered to cease their hostility.

With the fall of Cardinal Wolsey, no one was safe who was suspected of loyalty to him or of disapproval of Anne Boleyn's friendship with the King. It would appear that Sir Rhys was a devout Catholic, whose sympathies were with the Queen, Catherine of Aragon, and who was against any break with Rome. Moreover, Rhys' wife, Katherine Howard, is reported to have made some disparaging remarks about Anne Boleyn, although the two were cousins. Henry VIII, too, was probably envious of the great wealth of the Dynevors in west Wales and ready to seize any opportunity to diminish that power and influence.

It was against this background that Sir Rhys was arrested and kept prisoner in the Tower of London. In November 1531 he was tried on a charge of treason. The charge was that he had conspired, with two of his fellow countrymen, to raise a rebellion in Wales and, with the help of

The Seal of
Sir Rhys ap Thomas

King James of Scotland, to make himself Prince of Wales. Sir Rhys' claim to descent from Urien Rheged, together with the Ravens of Owain ap Urien Rheged on his coat-of-arms, only served to strengthen the charge of treason against him, for it was stated that the conspirators 'had often repeated that there was in Wales an ancient prophecy that King James with the Red Hand and the Ravens should conquer all England.' (The Red Hand probably referred to assistance from Ulster.)

Sir Rhys was found guilty and executed on 21st December, 1531. That the charge of high treason was a flimsy one is substantiated by a letter written to the Emperor Charles V by his ambassador, Chapuys, on the morning of Rhys' execution. This letter, which appears in the 'Calendar of Spanish State Papers', states that 'there is a rumour about town that, had it not been for the lady (i.e. Anne Boleyn), who hated him because he and his wife had spoken disparagingly of her, he would have been pardoned and escaped his miserable fate.' His estates passed to the Crown under the Act of Attainder which was passed soon after his death.

Later, in Elizabeth I's reign, some of the family lands in Carmarthenshire and Pembrokeshire were restored to Griffith Rice, son of Sir Rhys, including the manor of Dynevor (Newton, Llandeilo), and in the course of time more lands were regained.

THE DEVEREUX FAMILY

The man who was appointed Chief Justice of South Wales in 1525, on the death of Sir Rhys ap Thomas, was Walter Devereux, Lord Ferrers of Chartley. Taking a keen interest in local affairs, he was Mayor of Carmarthen in 1531, '32, '34 and '35. In 1550 he was created Viscount Hereford, the Devereux family coming from Herefordshire. Walter's son, Richard, also became Mayor in 1536 and was Member of Parliament for the County in 1545 and 1547. However, Richard died in 1547 before his father, leaving a son, Walter, who had been born in Carmarthen castle about 1540. This Walter Devereux was created first Earl of Essex in 1572 for his loyalty to the Crown. Later he was appointed Governor of

Walter Devereux Earl of Essex

Ulster and in 1576 Earl Marshal of Ireland.

It was in 1576 also that Walter Devereux, Earl of Essex, was the principal founder of the Queen Elizabeth Grammar School. Through his influence the Grammar School was founded by Letters Patent dated 7th July, 1576, and shortly afterwards he died in Ireland at the age of thirty-five. His body was brought back to Wales and he was buried in the chancel of St. Peter's Church on November 26th, 1576. The exact site of the grave is not known but Donovan in his *Excursions in South Wales* in 1804 noted that the sexton of St. Peter's Church, while preparing a fresh grave in the chancel, had observed the coffin and it was described as follows: 'The outer coffin was of oak but of singular construction. It was somewhat cymbiform (boat-shaped), pointed at both extremities, and strongly bound with iron. The inner shell was of lead, in which the body lay embalmed in a curious sort of spirituous liquor, that had retained its purity in an astonishing manner . . . . .'

Walter Devereux's son, Robert, second Earl of Essex, was the handsome dashing young courtier who won Elizabeth I's favour but whose ambition for power eventually led to his downfall. Having obtained the post of Lord-Lieutenant of Ireland, he was charged with the task of suppressing Tyrone's rebellion in 1599, but his wastage of men and money led to his recall and disgrace. Furthermore, his impetuosity caused him to plot with other hot-heads to compel the Queen to dismiss his rivals from her Council. He was executed for high treason in 1601.

The third Earl of Essex was the son of the above, also named Robert. A high-minded Puritan, he commanded the Parliamentary forces in the early years of the Civil War, but resigned his command in obedience to the Self-denying Ordinance of 1645. A year later he died, the earldom becoming extinct; the Devereux family then reverted to its older title of Viscount Hereford.

WELSH BARDS

LEWYS GLYN COTHI or LLYWELYN Y GLYN (c.1420-1489)

Nothing much is known about the early history of Lewys Glyn Cothi, one of the greatest Welsh poets of the fifteenth century. His bardic name suggests that he came from the Vale of Cothi and it is thought that he may have belonged to a family of some social standing. His close association with Carmarthen is seen in his eulogy on the Priory which he wrote for the Prior, Morgan ab Owain ab Einon (c.1450-1464). In it he gives us a picture of life in the Priory in the mid fifteenth century where he says that those under its pastoral charge numbered five hundred. He praises the singing of the choir which 'surpassed even that of the birds', the music of the organ 'sweet as the honey of bees' and he admires the gold and silver vessels, silken vestments and ornamented books. It is possible that he was in the Prior's service during his youth and received some education under him.

Lewys Glyn Cothi lived in the days of the Wars of the Roses and there is a tradition, not based on fact, that he fought for the Tudors; and in his poems we read of the battles of Mortimer's Cross (1461), at which he was probably present, Banbury (1468) and Bosworth Field (1485). However, his support of the Lancastrian cause did not prevent him from composing poetry for patrons who were Yorkists. A cultured and versatile poet, he wrote elegy and eulogy for his patrons, specialising in genealogy and heraldry. His wanderings as a bard led him far afield and in his writings we hear of his regard for patrons in Powys and Gwynedd and also his animosity for places where he was shabbily treated in his travels. The poems of Lewys Glyn Cothi have been published by Evan David Jones, an authority on the poet's works.

TUDUR ALED (c.1480-1526)

Tudur Aled was a native of Llansannan, Denbighshire, who received bardic training from his famous uncle, Dafydd ab Edmund. A cultured gentleman, Tudur Aled passed through the various grades of the bardic course and reached the rank of Pencerdd (Chief Bard). One of the 'Poets of the Gentry', he probably became the *bardd teulu* (household bard) to Sir Rhys ap Thomas, a generous patron of the bards, whose praises Tudur sang in several of his poems. A master of the poetic art, Tudur Aled's work includes poems in praise of Welsh noble families whose hospitality he enjoyed so much, elegies and love songs. It was in his poetry that the bardic tradition of the Middle Ages reached its climax. Tudur Aled retired to Carmarthen Friary where he assumed the Franciscan habit at the end of his life. He died in 1526 and was buried at the Friary.

His Carmarthenshire poems can be found in *Gwaith Tudur Aled* by Dr. T. Gwynn Jones.

TEACHERS AND PREACHERS

BISHOP ROBERT FERRAR

Among those who suffered for their Protestant beliefs in the reign of Mary Tudor was Dr. Robert Ferrar, Bishop of St. Davids. He was burnt at the stake in 1555, an event which was brought about by a very unfortunate set of circumstances.

Before the dissolution of the monasteries Robert Ferrar had been an Augustinian monk and Prior in his native Yorkshire. He then joined the reformers, found favour with Archbishop Cranmer and was appointed Bishop of St. Davids in 1548 in the reign of the Protestant Edward VI. Unfortunately, he quarrelled with a group of his canons led by the

Bishop Robert Ferrar

Cathedral chancellor and the precentor. Bishop Ferrar accused the canons of having 'made great spoil of the plate and ornaments of the Cathedral', of selling church livings and of general bribery. In reply, the canons virtually accused their bishop of not being sufficiently active and zealous in the pursuit of Protestant reforms. Thus, one of the charges brought against him was that when George Constantine, the reforming Archdeacon of Carmarthen and vicar of St. Peter's, had taken down the high altar in the chancel and replaced it by a communion table in the nave, Dr. Ferrar had ordered Constantine to put back the communion table in the chancel.

Other charges were brought against him, some hardly worthy of consideration, but he was arrested and was already in prison when Mary Tudor, an ardent Roman Catholic, came to the throne in 1553. In 1554 Dr. Ferrar was deposed from his bishopric for heresy and for having married, and he was given a preliminary trial in London before Stephen Gardiner, Bishop of Winchester. When he refused to recant, he was sent back to Carmarthen for a further trial.

Dr. Ferrar was then taken to St. Peter's Church by Griffith Leyshon the County Sheriff who, ironically, was now the owner of the dissolved Priory which was described as his 'mansion house'. Robert Ferrar was tried before Bishop Henry Morgan, his successor as Bishop of St. Davids, and by George Constantine. He was offered a pardon if he would renounce his errors and conform to the Roman Catholic faith but Ferrar challenged the authority of his judges and refused to reply to the charges of heresy. The court in St. Peter's was adjourned on several occasions to give Dr. Ferrar time to renounce Protestantism but he remained unrepentant and said that he would appeal to Cardinal Pole and the Queen. Finally, having failed to persuade him to recant, Bishop Morgan pronounced him 'a heretic excommunicate' and handed him over to the civil authorities.

On March 30th, 1555, the deposed Bishop Ferrar bravely met his death by burning at the stake 'in the market place where the cunditt standeth' and 'at the southside of the market cross'. Nott Square is now the site of the old market place and in 1902 a memorial tablet was placed within the railings of Nott's Monument, bearing the following inscription:

The noble army of Martyrs praise thee.
Near this spot suffered for the truth
Saturday, March 30th, 1555.
Dr. Robert Ferrar Bishop of St. David's.
We shall by God's grace light such a candle
in England, as shall never be put out.
Erected by a Protestant of this Town.

Another memorial tablet, dated 1843, is to be seen in the Consistory Court in St. Peter's Church. It is said that the stone, which supported the stake to which Bishop Ferrar was bound, now forms the apex of the spire of Abergwili Church. His martyrdom was lamentable and his fate a hard one in that having been imprisoned in Edward VI's reign for not being enough of a Protestant reformer, he was executed in Mary's reign for his refusal to renounce Protestantism.

RHYS PRICHARD (1579-1644) *Yr Hen Ficer - The Old Vicar*

Vicar Prichard is held in high esteem, not only as the author of *Canwyll y Cymru* (The Welsh People's Candle), but also as a great pulpit orator whose eloquence and zeal profoundly influenced the later growth of evangelical Nonconformity. However, he himself was a strong upholder of the Established Church and the monarchy, an orthodox conformist Protestant, leading a devout, disciplined life and working for the enlightenment of the poor and uneducated.

Born at Llandovery in 1579, it is believed that he received his early education either at the Queen Elizabeth Grammar School, Carmarthen, or Christ College, Brecon. After graduating from Oxford, he was ordained in Essex in 1602 but was soon appointed vicar of Llandingat and Llanfair-ar-y-bryn in his native town. Additionally in 1613 he was appointed rector of Llanedi (Carms.) and shortly afterwards he became Chaplain to Robert Devereux, third Earl of Essex. The plurality of his appointments increased when he became prebendary in the Collegiate Church of Brecon and then in 1626 Chancellor of St. Davids and a Cathedral canon.

Prichard's reforming zeal did not end with his sermons from the pulpit which attracted huge crowds. He also preached in the open air thus anticipating the Methodist revival of the eighteenth century. But his great concern was the ignorance, illiteracy and poverty of the majority of his fellow countrymen and the ill effect this had upon their standards of social behaviour and religious life. He tackled the problem by writing the mass of verses now known as *Canwyll y Cymru* (The Welsh People's Candle). These homely simple verses, which could be understood by all, were based upon the Bible, the Book of Common Prayer, Bishop Bayly's *The Practice of Piety* and other devotional publications. They also contained practical and moral guidance for all sorts and conditions of men, for young and old, for all classes of society and various kinds of occupations. Moreover, they could be sung to well-known folk-tunes and so easily remembered.

During Vicar Prichard's lifetime his verses were circulated in manuscript form exerting a widespread influence throughout the countryside. After his death they were collected, printed and published in various editions by Stephen Hughes who gave the title *Canwyll y Cymru* to the 1681 edition.

The complete English version of these poems by the Rev. William Evans, Vicar of Llawhaden, appeared in 1771 in which he wrote: 'Scarce anything else was to be heard in any House, Street or Field but those Godly songs and carols; they soon made an almost entire change in the morals and behaviour of the whole Country . . . .'

This English version was printed by John Ross of Carmarthen.

STEPHEN HUGHES (1622-1688)

Very little is known about the early years of the great Nonconformist leader, Stephen Hughes, except that he was born in Carmarthen about the year 1622. He is said to have been educated at the Queen Elizabeth Grammar School, his father and brother John being mayors of the town in 1650 and 1659 respectively.

During the Commonwealth period Stephen Hughes was appointed to the living of Merthyr (Carms.) in 1650 and then in 1655 to Meidrim. Like Vicar Prichard, he was deeply aware of the ignorance and illiteracy of the ordinary Welsh people and his great contribution to their enlightenment was his publication of books in Welsh for the poor and untutored. He recognised the value of Prichard's simple verses, both for religious instruction and for teaching the people to read and so, in 1659 he printed and published a selection of these verses, to be followed by another selection shortly afterwards.

With the restoration of Charles II, Stephen Hughes was ejected from Meidrim in 1661 and from hereon he turned his back on the Established Church and played an important part in the Puritan movement in Wales. During the period of bitter and prolonged persecution after his ejection, he retired to Swansea, but he continued to journey through the county of Carmarthen visiting the scattered Independent congregations. He became known, later, as *The Apostle of Carmarthenshire.* All this he did on horseback, riding through remote country districts to form his churches. He co-operated with Thomas Gouge who formed a Welsh Trust in London to provide funds for Welsh Bibles and for primary schools; this voluntary society did important work in the realm of Welsh education.

Though an undoubted Nonconformist and an independent in judgement, he was no extremist and was not averse to seeking the help of the Anglican clergy in bringing out his new cheap edition of the

Welsh New Testament in 1672. This was followed by a new and cheap edition of the Welsh Bible in 1677-78. In his appeal to the Welsh bishops for support in bringing out his new edition, Hughes wrote: 'An English Bible is useless in the hands of our people. The language is strange to them.'

With the support of Gouge and the Welsh Trust, Carmarthenshire received over 800 copies of Welsh Bibles, Testaments and other religious literature, while primary schools for poor children were also established in the county. At Carmarthen twenty-four children were catered for. Unfortunately, with the death of the philanthropist Thomas Gouge, in 1681, the schools came to an end although the distribution of religious books continued for a time.

Stephen Hughes' greatest service to Welsh literature was his work in collecting and publishing, in various editions, the poems of Vicar Prichard, the edition of 1681 being entitled *Canwyll y Cymru* (The Welsh People's Candle). Until Stephen Hughes collected, printed and published many of these verses, they remained in manuscript form and were therefore limited in their distribution. Hughes published many other books in the Welsh language, most being translations of religious and educational publications. At the end of most of them he added the Welsh alphabet in an effort to teach people to read.

By 1688, the year of his death, Stephen Hughes, with the assistance of friends, had completed a translation of John Bunyan's *Pilgrim's Progress*, which subsequently had a profound influence upon Welsh religious life.

He was a great encourager of young ministers and in one of his minor academies he trained to fruition some of the most powerful preachers of the Toleration period (i.e. post Toleration Act of 1689), including William Evans of Pencader, the new leader of Dissent after Hughes' death.

In the area over which his influence was felt, particular mention must be made of Carmarthen, Pencader, Llansteffan and the Llandeilo district, which were the main centres of his activity. Stephen Hughes' constant and varied labours at last impaired his health and on his death in 1688 he was buried at St. John's, Swansea.

DR. LEWIS BAYLY (died 1631)

The reasons for believing that Dr. Lewis Bayly, Bishop of Bangor, was a native of Carmarthen are threefold: in his will he gave 'towards the town of Carmarthen to buy a bell, five pounds'; Thomas Bayly, vicar of St. Peter's, one of the witnesses to Humphrey Toy's will, may have been his father and Anthony Wood in his *Athenae Oxonienses* 1691 states that he 'was born in the ancient borough of Carmarthen'. There is no definite evidence that Lewis Bayly was educated at the Queen Elizabeth Grammar School as so often is stated. After graduating from Exeter

College, Oxford, he became successively rector of Llanedi, Carms., in 1605, vicar of Evesham, treasurer of St. Paul's Cathedral and royal chaplain to James I. Consecrated Bishop of Bangor in 1616, he was often in trouble because of his puritanical leanings which he expressed forcibly.

Dr. Bayly's fame rests on his devotional treatise *The Practice of Piety,* published about 1613, which became so popular that by 1630 it was in its twenty-fifth edition. In the same year it was translated into Welsh by the poet and scholar, Rowland Vaughan. For three centuries it deeply influenced Puritan thought, not only in England and Wales, but also further afield, for it was translated into several languages. Some of this influence inspired John Bunyan, author of *The Pilgrim's Progress,* a classic of Puritan literature, and also Vicar Prichard, author of *Canwyll y Cymru* (The Welsh People's Candle).

Dr. Lewis Bayly was an ancestor of the Marquis of Anglesey of Plas Newydd.

GRIFFITH JONES of LLANDDOWROR (1683-1761)

Few men have conferred greater benefits on their country than Griffith Jones, Llanddowror, the founder of the Welsh Circulating Schools. He was a pioneer in Welsh education and vitally connected with the eighteenth century awakening of the Welsh people. He was born at Pant-yr-efel in the parish of Penboyr in 1683 and educated at the Queen Elizabeth Grammar School. Ordained at Abermarlais Church in 1708, he became a gifted and popular preacher, serving at Laugharne, Llandeilo-Abercywyn (1711) and Llanddowror (1716), where he remained until his death.

His fame rests on the efforts he made to spread literacy throughout Wales which began in 1731 with the establishment of the *Welsh Circulating Schools.* These schools, run by itinerant schoolmasters, taught both children and adults to read the Welsh Bible and to learn the Catechism of the Anglican Church. Where possible he would utilize the village church or other suitable buildings for three months at a time, holding classes in the evenings for those who could not attend in the daytime. Most of his subscriptions came from England, and Bibles, Testaments, Psalters and Church Catechisms were obtained from the Society for the Promotion of Christian Knowledge. Griffith Jones wrote an annual report of his work called Welsh Piety and he trained many of his teachers at Llanddowror. It has been calculated that at the time of his death

Griffith Jones
Drawn from his
reputed portrait.

over 8,000 persons were attending 210 existing schools, and that 158,000 between the ages of six and seventy years had learned to read in the twenty four years in which the schools functioned. Altogether 3,498 schools had been opened and they were an important factor in the spread of literacy in the Welsh language.

While at Laugharne Griffith Jones became master of the S.P.C.K. school founded by Sir John Philipps of Picton Castle, a leading figure in religious and educational matters, who became his friend, patron and later his brother-in-law. In 1720 Griffith Jones married Margaret Philipps, Sir John's sister. Another close associate was John Vaughan of Derllys Court, Carmarthen, a friend of Sir John Philipps and a prominent leader in the religious, social and educational life of the county. Moreover, John Vaughan's daughter, Bridget Vaughan, who married Arthur Bevan of Laugharne, later M.P. for Carmarthen, was also destined to become Griffith Jones' most valuable supporter and, as 'Madam Bevan', one of the most remarkable Welsh women of the eighteenth century. Her educational activities in Wales and her interest and help with the circulating schools of Griffith Jones, make her an outstanding figure in the history of this period. Madam Bevan was in close touch with the social, religious and political circles in London and Bath, and after the death of Griffith Jones she continued to superintend the schools, using her own personal fortune together with funds bequeathed to her for this purpose by Griffith Jones. On her death in 1779 she left most of her property for the use of the Schools, but her will was contested and remained in Chancery for thirty years. Consequently the schools were forced to close through lack of funds.

WILLIAM WILLIAMS (1717-1791) *Pantycelyn*

William Williams, Pantycelyn, reputed to be the greatest of all Welsh hymn writers, as well as poet and preacher, was born at Cefncoed, Llanfair-ar-y-bryn, Llandovery, in 1717. Originally intending to enter the medical profession, he experienced religious conversion on hearing Howel Harris preaching in Talgarth churchyard. In 1740 he became a deacon in the Established Church and until 1743 served as a curate at Llanwrtyd and Abergwesyn. Influenced by the growing Welsh Calvinistic Methodist revival, he became associated with evangelist Daniel Rowland and preached to congregations throughout the Principality.

William Williams

However, it was as a writer of inspiring Welsh hymns that William Williams became famous. As well as composing many hundreds of hymns in Welsh, he also wrote over one hundred in English. His first hymns, printed by Samuel Lewis in Carmarthen, appeared in 1744 under the title *Aleluia.* Further collections of hymns followed. His long poem *Bywyd a Marwolaeth Theomemphus* (Life and Death of Theomemphus) was printed at Carmarthen by John Ross in 1764, as well as his English volume of hymns *Gloria in Excelsis* in 1772. His most famous hymn is *Guide me, O Thou Great Jehovah.* He also wrote many books and pamphlets. He died on 11th January, 1791 at Pantycelyn, his farmhouse family home near Llandovery, and was buried at Llanfair-ar-y-bryn Church.

PETER WILLIAMS (1723-1796)

Peter Williams, annotator and commentator of the Welsh Bible and Welsh Methodist leader, was born near Laugharne in the parish of Llansadyrnin. He was educated at the Queen Elizabeth Grammar School and was greatly influenced by the preaching of George Whitefield who visited Carmarthen in April 1743. Peter Williams took Holy Orders in 1744, serving his first curacy at Eglwys Cymmin; later he joined the Methodist revivalists. His ministry was itinerant and he finally settled down at Gelli Lednais, in the parish of Llandyfaelog, about 1760.

Peter Williams is known best for his publication of the Welsh Bible with notes and comments at the end of each chapter. Because of the difficulty in obtaining printed Bibles in Welsh from English sources, he had the Scriptures printed in Wales and, by inserting his own Welsh notes and comments, circumvented the right of Oxford and Cambridge Universities to be the sole printers of Bibles. He published three editions during his lifetime, printed by John Ross at Carmarthen. His first edition was issued in parts at 1 shilling each. In 1770 he published his Welsh Bible in one volume, bringing it within the reach of the poorest people. No one can over-estimate the importance of his work, for written in simple, homely idiom, it did a great deal to preserve the Welsh language in the home. Today copies of *Beibl Peter Williams* can still be found in Welsh homes, where it is a valued family treasure. It is calculated that over eighteen thousand copies were published by various presses during his lifetime.

He came to live in the town while preparing his Bible for the printers, and his dwelling in Water Street was used as a preaching house, called the Tabernacle. In 1771 a second Tabernacle, now Heol Dwr Chapel, was built behind the first one, this building again being the property of Peter Williams, who then occupied the first building as a dwelling house. Although he had worked for the Methodist cause for many years, Peter Williams was expelled from the Calvinistic Methodist Association in 1791 for alleged Sabellian heresy (i.e. taking a heretical view of the nature of the Trinity).

A first edition of the Peter Williams' Bible, 1770, is preserved in Eglwys Cymmin Church and is inscribed by Madam Bevan of Laugharne who gave it to her god-daughter in 1779.

The Rev. Peter Williams is buried in Llandyfaelog parish churchyard where his grave is marked by a tablet commemorating his work, while in the church a plaque commemorates the bi-centenary of his birth.

THOMAS CHARLES (1755-1814)

Thomas Charles o'r Bala as he is known, was born at Longmoor Farm, Llanfihangel Abercywyn, St. Clears, in 1755. He was educated at the Presbyterian College, Carmarthen and at Jesus College, Oxford. His fame rests chiefly on his great work for the Sunday Schools in Wales. He was ordained in the Anglican Church in 1780 and held curacies in England and at Llanwddyn and Llanymawddwy. In 1783 he married Sally Jones of Bala and settled there, joining the Methodists in the following year. So began an active and distinguished life in the cause of Methodism which made him leader of the second generation of Welsh Methodists. He revived the Circulating Schools and initiated the Welsh development of the Sunday Schools, framing certain rules and preparing a catechism for the children. In 1799 he published, with Calvinistic Methodist preacher Thomas Jones, *Y Drysorfa Ysbrydol* (The Spiritual Treasury), a Methodist periodical, and 1805 to 1811 saw the publication, in four parts, of the famous Bible Dictionary, *Geiriadur Charles*, which was part of every Welsh Methodist home for nearly a century.

It has been calculated that more than 320,000 copies of his school books were printed during his lifetime. He helped to establish the British and Foreign Bible Society and frequently preached in London. In 1814 he edited one of the most accurate editions of the Welsh Bible ever produced. His brother was the hymn writer David Charles. Thomas died in 1814 and was buried at Llanycil. He has been described as 'the divine gift of South Wales to the North'.

DAVID CHARLES (1762-1834)

David Charles, the author of the well-loved Welsh hymns *O fryniau Caersalem* (From the Hills of Jerusalem) and *Rhagluniaeth fawr y nef* (Great Providence of Heaven) was born at Pant-dwfn, Llanfihangel Abercywyn, and was a younger brother of Thomas Charles of Bala. After an elementary education he was apprenticed to a ropemaker at Carmarthen. He became leader of the Methodist Society at Water Street Chapel and in 1811 he was ordained a minister with the Calvinistic Methodists. He had a natural gift of oratory and educated himself to such an extent that his published sermons in English and Welsh rank high in pulpit literature. But he is best-known for his hymns. He also became a successful businessman, owning a paper mill in Glannant

Road, a ropeyard and ropewalk between Glannant and Picton Terrace, land at Parcmaen and property in King Street (he lived at No. 60) and in Chapel Street. The ropewalk, with entrance off Picton Terrace, and paper-mill are shown on Wood's map of 1834. David Charles died in 1834 and was buried in Llangunnor churchyard.

David Charles

David Peter

DAVID PETER (1765-1837)

David Peter, the notable minister of Heol Awst (Lammas Street) Chapel, was born in Aberystwyth in 1765 and entered the Presbyterian Academy in August 1783, when it was located at Rhydygors, Johnstown. Here he studied for a short time at his own expense under the tutorship of Robert Gentleman. He then seems to have abandoned his ministerial plans and is next found keeping a school at St. Ishmael's, Pembrokeshire, for a period of twelve months. He returned in August 1786 to re-enter the Academy which had been temporarily removed to Swansea.

In October 1789 the Presbyterian Board appointed him to the Classical and Mathematical tutorship of the Academy at Swansea. In December 1792 'the members of the Protestant congregation assembling at Lammas Street, Carmarthen,' gave him a call to be their minister and he accepted the pastorate of Heol Awst Chapel. In 1795 the Presbyterian Academy was re-established at Carmarthen with David Peter as senior tutor (i.e. Principal). For forty years he remained in this post as well as being the head of the 'grammar' school which was run in connection with the Academy, until his retirement in 1835. At the same time he continued to be the minister of Lammas Street Chapel which he rebuilt and enlarged in 1802 and again in 1826. Classes for the Academy and the attached school were held in the chapel buildings.

In 1792 the Rev. David Peter was chosen by the Common Council Men of Carmarthen to be Master of Sir Thomas Powell's Charity School. Sir Thomas Powell had left the rents from three houses, in trust, for the education of six boys in reading, writing and arithmetic. In 1813, on the expiration of the leases, the rents increased from £22 per annum to £70 per annum, with the result that David Peter was able to increase the number of charity pupils from six to between twelve and fifteen.

A letter written by David Peter, and dated 13th May 1818, states that he then had under his superintendence twelve young men at the Presbyterian College, between forty and fifty boys at the 'grammar' school and between twelve and fifteen boys at the Charity school. All were located in the Heol Awst Chapel buildings.

In 1800 the Rev. David Peter was made a free burgess of the Borough. During his distinguished life he published a Welsh translation of Samuel Palmer's *Protestant Dissenter's Catechism* in 1803, but his most important literary work was *Hanes Crefydd yn Nghymru* (The History of Religion in Wales), published in 1816.

David Peter lived for a time in the house on the right of the entry into Quakers' Yard, Lammas Street. He also stayed for some time in 1795 in the house of John Ross, the printer. He died at Peterwell in 1837.

In the passageway to the old Quaker Meeting House in Quakers' Yard, Lammas Street, is an inscribed stone in a wall which reads:

This wall is the property of David Peter, 1831.

TOMOS GLYN COTHI (1764-1833)

The Rev. Thomas Evans, whose bardic name was Tomos Glyn Cothi, was born at Capel Sant Silyn, Gwernogle, near Brechfa. Self-educated, he became a radical thinker on theology and politics, eventually becoming a Unitarian minister and a champion of political reform. Two years after his ordination in 1794 he became minister of Ty Cwrdd Glyn Cothi, the first Unitarian chapel to be built in Wales. In 1795 he began the publication of a quarterly journal called *Y Drysorfa Gymysgedig* (The Miscellaneous Treasury) in which he attacked tyranny, the slave trade, the disabilities of dissenters and in which he extolled the principles of the French Revolution. It was suppressed by the government after three issues.

Tomos Glyn Cothi is said to have translated the *Marseillaise* into Welsh. In 1801 he was sentenced to two years' imprisonment for singing a seditious song, thought to have been written by his friend, Iolo Morgannwg. He served his sentence in Carmarthen Gaol and was twice put in the pillory where, it was related, 'of all the crowd a woman was the only one to throw a missile at him.'

Tomos Glyn Cothi was the author of several theological pamphlets and books; in addition, in 1809 he published an English-Welsh dictionary and in 1811 a collection of hymns. In the same year he moved to Aberdare to become the Unitarian minister of the Old Meeting House. Here he remained until his death.

TITUS LEWIS (1773-1811)

Titus Lewis, great preacher, orator and self-educated scholar, was born at Cilfowyr, Pembs., and in 1800 became minister of the Welsh Baptist Chapel when it was situated in Dark Gate (Eglwys y Porthtywyll). He produced a Welsh-English dictionary (1805), and *Hanes Wladol a Chrefyddol Prydain Fawr* (A History of the State and Religion of Great Britain) printed in Carmarthen in 1810. He made a translation of Dr. Gill's Commentary on the New Testament and issued a collection of hymns, including some of his own work. A prolific writer on theology, his great literary output is said to have been completed within a period of ten years. He died in 1811 at the age of thirty-eight and was buried in the field on which the present Tabernacle Chapel in Waterloo Terrace now stands. The first chapel on that site was built in 1812, largely as the result of the efforts of Titus Lewis.[1]

BISHOP CONNOP THIRLWALL (1797-1875)

Bishop Connop Thirlwall, whose mother was Welsh, was born in London in 1797 and became Bishop of St. Davids in 1840, an appointment he held for thirty-four years. He studied Welsh and became a fluent preacher in the language. He was one of the greatest Greek scholars of his age and he concluded his *History of Greece*, a standard work, after settling in Abergwili. Always a man of liberal principles, he advocated the admission of Dissenters to university degrees and he fought many battles single-handed for the broader view which ultimately prevailed. Among his many contributions to the educational and social advancement of Carmarthen were his efforts to bring into existence the South Wales and Monmouthshire Training College founded in 1848, the first teacher training college in Wales, now known as Trinity College, as well as the Carmarthenshire Infirmary founded in 1847. He also encouraged the restoration of churches and the building of schools. He was buried in Poets' Corner in Westminster Abbey. After his death a volume of his Welsh sermons was published in 1877.

Bishop Connop Thirlwall

DAVID ARCHARD WILLIAMS (1796-1879)

The Rev. David Archard Williams was essentially a Victorian, whose life was inseparably connected with the history of Carmarthen during most of the nineteenth century.[2] He held many prominent positions in both the civil and ecclesiastical affairs of the town.

Ven. Archard Williams

Born in 1796, the son of a curate of St. Peter's, he was left an orphan at four years old. He became a free scholar at the Queen Elizabeth Licensed Grammar School and from there he was ordained into the established church. He became an assistant master and later headmaster of the Grammar School (1824-1856), and in 1828 he was made rural dean. He was also perpetual curate of Llanfihangel-uwch-gwili, incumbent of St. David's Church, Carmarthen, rector of Merthyr and was deputised by the Diocese to deal with matters of probate in the Consistory Court. He was made Chancellor of the Diocese in 1857 and Archdeacon of Carmarthen in 1865.

His other appointments, at different times, included that of Chaplain at the Workhouse and the Asylum (now St. David's Hospital), editor of the *Journal*, director of the gasworks, county magistrate and vice-chairman of the Board of Guardians. He was instrumental in the building of the Model School, Bridge Street School and Christ Church. Probably he would like best to be remembered for his work at St. David's Church, which was built primarily for Welsh-speaking church people to worship in their own language, since this carried out the idea originated by his father. In the 1850's, when the church was found to be too small, he arranged for the building of the present clerestoried nave with aisles running west to east and at right angles to the old building. In the 1880's the original nave was converted into the present chancel as a memorial to Archdeacon Archard Williams.

MILITARY MEN

GENERAL SIR THOMAS PICTON (1758-1815)

General Sir Thomas Picton was born in 1758 at Poyston, Pembrokeshire and was killed on the field of Waterloo on 18th June, 1815. He lived for some time at Iscoed, Ferryside, to which place he had retired with honours gained in the Peninsular War, especially at the storming of Badajoz. After returning in triumph to Carmarthen he was summoned again to join the British and allied armies before Waterloo.

One of Wellington's ablest generals, Sir Thomas Picton distinguished himself in many battles and contributed much to the victory of Waterloo, a decisive factor being the charge of the 'Iron' 3rd Division which he commanded. Although he had been wounded two days previously at Quatre Bras - a musket ball had broken two of his ribs - Picton concealed

General Sir Thomas Picton

his injuries at Waterloo and, while leading the charge, was mortally wounded by a shot through his right temple. It is said, though it may be merely a legend, that the commission appointing him Commander-in-chief of the British army, in the event of Wellington being killed or disabled, was found in his coat pocket.

On no less than seven occasions Sir Thomas Picton received the thanks of the House of Commons on behalf of the nation. He was buried originally in St. George's, Hanover Square, but on June 8th, 1859, his remains were removed and placed in a vault prepared for them in the crypt of St. Paul's Cathedral, not far from the tomb of the Duke of Wellington. On the same day, Capt. Edwardes Gwynne of Rhydygors, one of the few Peninsular officers surviving at the time, presented to the Carmarthen Literary and Scientific Institute a cane, bearing on its metal mounting this inscription:

> This cane was in the hand of Sir Thomas Picton, G.C.B., when he gloriously fell at the battle of Waterloo, 18th June, 1815.

Other personal relics can be seen at the Carmarthen Museum and his full length portrait hangs in the Guildhall. Local recognition of his fame is marked by Picton's Monument at the top of Picton Terrace. The present obelisk is the second monument to be erected. The first, designed by John Nash, was a very elaborate column seventy-five feet high. A winding internal staircase led to the top of the column where there was a square gallery with small cannons at the corners and from which rose a pillar surmounted by a statue of Picton. The monument was decorated with bas-relief scenes of the general's triumphs and verbosely inscribed. The foundation stone was laid on August 16th, 1825, but the monument was allowed to deteriorate and was taken down in 1846. The foundation stone of the second monument, designed by architect Francis Fowler, was laid in 1847. In the autumn of 1984 the top section was removed as being unsafe, and in 1988 the whole monument was rebuilt

Iscoed, Ferryside

stone-by-stone on stronger foundations.[3]

General Picton's distinguished career was marred by an incident when he became governor of Trinidad in 1796. A Spanish magistrate applied for an order which involved the torture of a Mulatto slave, which Picton signed on being told that it was a customary practice. He was brought to trial for this in 1806 and was found guilty, but in a second trial he was acquitted of moral guilt. When he retired from the government of Trinidad, the sum of £5,000 was voted him by the inhabitants in token of their esteem. Some time afterwards, their chief town was burnt down and Picton gladly took the opportunity to devote the £5,000 to the relief of the sufferers.

GENERAL SIR WILLIAM NOTT (1782-1845)

General Sir William Nott can be claimed as Carmarthen's most famous soldier, for although born at Neath on 20th January, 1782, he counted Carmarthen as his home and was associated with it from youth. He returned to it twice during his career, the last time at the height of his fame in 1844, to die soon afterwards. He was the second son of Charles Nott a well-known English agriculturalist, of Shobdon in Hereford, who came to Wales at the invitation of Sir Herbert Mackworth of Neath. It was at Neath and Cowbridge Grammar School that William received his early education.

Charles Nott came to Carmarthen in 1794 to become the proprietor of the Ivy Bush Inn in King Street, where he was also a mail contractor. At the same time he took over Pont Garreg Farm, Johnstown, not far from Job's Well, which was later to become William's home.

In 1798 William enrolled in a volunteer corps at Carmarthen, formed as a result of the landing of the French at Fishguard. He entered the East India Company in 1800 and sailed for India with a Bengal cadetship. The voyage saw the beginning of his exciting life, for his ship, the East Indiaman *Kent*, was captured by a French privateer, the passengers being transferred to an Arab ship which eventually landed them safely. When William arrived at Calcutta he was appointed ensign and posted to the Bengal European Regiment at Berhampore; he was transferred to the 20th Native Infantry and promoted Lieutenant in February 1801.

General Sir William Nott

In 1804 Nott was in command of a detachment of the Bengal Volunteers sent against the tribes on the west coast of Sumatra, distinguishing himself in the capture of Moko.

A bitter quarrel with Captain Robertson, in command of the *Lord Castlereagh*, however, led to his being placed in strict confinement for four months on a breach of discipline charge. At the subsequent court-martial he was honourably acquitted whilst Captain Robertson was censured.

On October 5th, 1805, he married Letitia, second daughter of Henry Swinhoe; they had fourteen children, five of whom survived their father.

Nott was appointed Superintendent of Native Pensions and Paymaster of Family Pensions in March 1811, promoted Captain-lieutenant in June 1814, Captain in December 1814 and Major in 1823. Subsequently he returned to Carmarthen and settled down for a few years at Job's Well, which he bought as his home, but the failure of the Calcutta Bank made it necessary for him to sell the estate and again seek his fortune out East.

Having already made a name for himself as a brilliant administrator, his services were much in demand and in 1829 he was given the rank of Colonel.

It was not until the outbreak of the first Afghan war in 1838, however, that Nott began the active service which was to mark him as one of Britain's great military leaders. He was promoted Brigadier General and Major General in that year, the year in which his wife died at Delhi. In great grief after his loss, he proceeded to Karnal, sending his family back to Carmarthen. From their grandfather's home his sons penned him many letters while they were being educated at 'Mr. Williams' Academy.'

A deeply religious man of great moral courage, fearless and independent, he suffered from a sense of frustration at the general inefficiency he saw around him and, frequently superseded by other officers, he often clashed with his superiors. The dual system of military service saw the tried and experienced officers of the East India Company having to submit to the orders of 'silly scions of the aristocracy' (as Nott described them) and the campaign was undermined by professional jealousies and incompetence which brought about many disasters.

Nott was a blunt man and made many enemies with his outspoken, direct observations but his great moral character could not be pushed aside indefinitely. With the arrival of Sir John Keane as Commander-in-Chief, Nott was superseded by Willshire, but in October 1839 on Kean's departure, he was given the order to march and command at Kandahar, a place with which his name will always be associated. At Kandahar his work in forestalling and subduing rebellions soon earned him fame. Capturing the fortress of Kalat in November 1840, he was thanked by Parliament and the East India Company for his services. In June 1841 he was given command of the 2nd Infantry and in January 1842 of all troops in Lower Afghanistan. With the departure of General Cotton from Kabul, Nott was again denied the higher promotion due to him, which was given to Elphinstone of the Guards.

History records the murder of Macnaghten and the massacre of Elphinstone's army on the withdrawal from Kabul. Nott pressed upon the Government of India the necessity of holding on at Jalalabad and Kandahar - only to see Pollock given the command at Kabul.

In March 1842 the Afghan army, 12,000 strong, approached Kandahar and Nott marched out to meet them. In May 1842 he again defeated 8,000 Afghans gathered at the Babawali Pass to prevent any movement of his troops northwards. He did this with a force of 1,500 men, for which he received the congratulations of General Lord Ellenborough, who had favoured a policy of retreat following the loss of Ghazni and the repulse of General England.

In July 1842 Nott received orders to withdraw from Afghanistan and he decided to do so via Ghazni and Kabul, co-ordinating with Pollock's force through the Passes. Approaching about 40 miles from Ghazni on 20th August, he met Shamsh-ud-din, the Afghan chief, with 12,000 men and routed them. Shamsh-ud-din fled to Ghazni but then evacuated it on Nott's approach and here the British force, which included the 41st Welsh Regiment, liberated more than 300 Sepoys who had been sold into slavery when Palmer had capitulated.

Continuing his march to Kabul, Nott again met his old foe, Shamsh-ud-din, and other Afghan chiefs and again routed an army of 10,000. When he reached Kabul he found that Pollock had arrived there before him and the combined army eventually fought its way through the Passes to arrive on the banks of the Sutlej in December 1842.

Tributes now poured in upon him - but too late, for Nott's health had given way during his arduous service. He was appointed to the office of Resident at the Court of Lucknow with the title of Envoy to the King of Oude. 'I rejoice,' wrote Lord Ellenborough, 'in the opportunity afforded me of marking the high sense I entertain of the value of your military services.' He was invested with the Knight Grand Cross of the Order of the Bath and the Duke of Wellington in the House of Lords paid special tribute to Nott's merits. Sir Robert Peel said: 'During the whole of the time he was employed in these dangerous undertakings his gallant spirit never forsook him and he dreamt of nothing only vindicating his country's honour.'

In June 1843 he married Rose Wilson, daughter of Captain Dore of the 3rd Buffs. By 1844 he was a very sick man with an affliction of the heart which necessitated his retirement, and in the summer of that year he returned to England. The East India Company showed their gratitude by granting him an annuity for 'the foresight, judgement and courage evinced by him throughout the whole period of his command at Kandahar and during his brilliant and successful march to Ghazni and Kabul which so greatly contributed to the triumphant vindication of the army of the British nation and to the maintenance of its reputation.' London bestowed upon him the Freedom of the City.

General Nott was now too ill to attend the many functions and ceremonies arranged to fête him, but his journey home was a triumphant procession. A great reception awaited him in Carmarthen, when on 11th September, 1844, he was met by the Corporation and a large procession near Myrtle Hill, 'his carriage being drawn by St. Peter's Boys in their shirt sleeves, to his brother's house in Picton Terrace.'

He resided temporarily at 8 Nott Square (then called Market Street), while more than 100 workmen were employed in rebuilding his old home in Job's Well, Johnstown, which he had re-purchased. He never lived to see it finished, however, for he died on 1st January, 1845. He was buried at St. Peter's Church near the grave of his mother and father, his tomb being found on the north side of the churchyard. The funeral ceremony saw the town in mourning and representatives of all walks of life paid their last tributes. The date of birth on his tombstone is wrongly given as 1783.

His monument in Nott Square and his portrait in the Guildhall are the local tributes to a great soldier. The portrait is by T. Brigstocke, a notable Carmarthen artist, and the monument is the work of a Llandyfaelog sculptor, Edward Davis, the bronze figure being cast from the guns captured at the battle of Maharajpur and presented by the East India Company.

In 1955 General Nott's medals and insignia were presented to the town by his great grandsons, Sir John and Sir Guy Nott-Bower.

The following letter, written by Sir Robert Peel, and now in the possession of another descendant, is of interest:

to The Committee for Superintending the Erection of a Monument to General Sir William Nott.

Whitehall,
June 21, 1845.

Gentlemen,

I am commanded by the Queen to express her desire to contribute the sum of two hundred guineas towards the erection of a monument in honour of the late Sir William Nott. Her Majesty sends this contribution as a mark of her respect for the memory of that gallant officer, and of her high sense of the distinguished Services which he rendered to his Country.

I have the honour to be,
Gentlemen,
Your obedient Servant,
ROBERT PEEL.

POETS AND WRITERS

JOHN DYER (c.1700-1757)

No poet was more conscious of the beauty of the Towy valley than John Dyer who was born at Aberglasney, Llangathen. The son of a prosperous solicitor, it was intended that John should qualify as a lawyer but he preferred poetry and art. He spent some time in Italy studying painting but it was in poetry that he left his mark. Wordsworth praised him in a sonnet entitled *To the poet, John Dyer,* recognising his merit.

John Dyer

Dyer's best known poem, *Grongar Hill,* appeared in 1726 while two other poems, *The Ruins of Rome* and *The Fleece,* were both well-received in his lifetime. Dyer's name appears as a witness to the will of Sir Richard Steele, with whom he formed a great friendship at Steele's retreat of Tygwyn, Llangunnor. Having been persuaded by friends to take Holy Orders, Dyer was appointed to various livings, the last being at Coningsby, Lincolnshire, where he died. He was buried in Coningsby Church chancel.

John Dyer captured the beauty of the Towy valley in his poem *Grongar Hill,* the site of an ancient hill-fort near Aberglasney:

> Grongar! in whose mossy cells,
> Sweetly musing, Quiet dwells.

For here, he tells us, he often

> Sat upon a flowr'y bed,
> With my hand beneath my head,
> While stray'd my eyes o'er Towy's flood,
> Over mead and over wood,
> From house to house, from hill to hill,
> Till Contemplation had her fill . . . .

Contemplating Dryslwyn Castle he dwells upon this old ruin on the neighbouring hill that

> Holds and charms the wand'ring eye:
> Deep are his feet in Towy's flood,
> His sides are cloth'd with waving wood,
> And ancient towers crown his brow,
> That cast an awful look below . . . .

For time . . . .

> Has seen this broken pile complete,
> Big with the vanity of state;
> But transient is the smile of Fate!
> A little rule, a little sway,

A sunbeam in a winter's day,
Is all the proud and mighty have
Between the cradle and the grave ....

Painting the loveliness of the valley and soliloquising on the frailty of man, he adds:

O may I with myself agree,
And never covet what I see!
Content me with an humble shade
My passions tam'd my wishes laid ....

His work may seem more real to those who

.... by the murm'ring rill,
Hear the thrush, while all is still
Within the groves of Grongar Hill.

SIR LEWIS MORRIS (1833-1907)

Love took my heart and thrill'd it
 Through all its strings,
Play'd round my mind and fill'd it
 with sound of wings:
But to my heart he never came
To touch it with his golden flame.

Therefore it is that singing
 I do rejoice,
Nor heed the slow years bringing
 A harsher voice:
Because the songs which he has sung
Still leave the untouch'd singer young.

Sir Lewis Morris

Lewis Morris was born in Spilman Street in 1833. The son of Lewis Morris, a prominent solicitor and Town Clerk of Carmarthen, he received his early education at the Queen Elizabeth Grammar School. He achieved a 'double first' at Jesus College, Oxford, and choosing law as his profession, was called to the Bar in 1861. He was knighted for his services to higher education in Wales, having contributed substantially to the establishment of the University of Wales.

It was, however, as a poet that he made his name and this gift led to a close friendship with Alfred, Lord Tennyson, the Poet Laureate. Tennyson visited him at Penbryn, Mount Pleasant, his elegant mansion home in Llangunnor. In the late nineteenth century Sir Lewis Morris enjoyed a wide reputation for his poetry but after his death his poems fell into comparative oblivion. Yet 'considered sympathetically and without prejudice, they retain much of the charm they exerted over the late-Victorian public, and for those who cherish the scenic beauty of Carmarthenshire they are rich in local associations. *By the Sea, At Last,*

To my Motherland, Gwen, The Physicians of Myddfai, Between the Mountains and the Sea, By Towy-side, and *In Praise of Towy* - these are only a few of the poems in which he celebrates his deep affection for his native county, and all are well worth re-reading on their own merits, quite apart from their local interest.'[4]

In *Gwen, a Drama for Monologue* he expresses in words the beauty of the Towy valley seen from Llangunnor Churchyard:

How fair and fresh from this gray churchyard shows
The rich green vale beneath. Upon the deep
Lush meadows, where the black herd grazing seem
Like rooks upon the grass, a silvery gleam,
Now lost and now discovered, marks the place
Where winds the brimming river. Here, thick woods
Of oak and beech upon the sloping banks
Bend to the shadowy stream which glides beneath.
There, through the emerald meads, shallow or deep,
It hastes or loiters, till the tall dark elms,
Grouped by the distance, hide it. And above,
On either hand the eternal mountains rise,
Pine-clad below, upon whose upper heights
The unfenced heather purples. All the sky
Is flecked with soft white fleecy clouds which cast
Bewildering charms of shadow; and beyond
A shining sapphire drawn 'twixt earth and sky,
Glitters the summer sea.

Sir Lewis Morris also caught the loveliness and timelessness of vale and river in his poem *By Towy-side.* Few can be unmoved by his soliloquy when, one summer's day, he saw the river gliding, sinuous and silvery through the valley:

Nor shall a thousand centuries passing trace
One wrinkle on thy smooth unageing face.

. . . .

While thou, thro' those dim generations gone
Unchanged, unruffled, flow'dst serenely on.

. . . .

Thou in thy changing flow unchanging art,
As is the unchanging, changeful human heart.

. . . .

Glide on, O silent stream, I would a tongue
Were thine, to chant the mysteries of time.

Sir Lewis Morris' fame was such that at one time his name was mentioned for Poet Laureate. However, in addition to his poetical works, he also produced, in 1905, one volume of prose entitled *The New Rambler* - a selection of essays, addresses and recollections. '*The New Rambler* serves as an excellent corrective to the popular idea of Morris as a smooth, genteel, second-class Tennyson.'[5]

Sir Lewis Morris died on 12th November, 1907, at the age of

seventy-four and was buried with his forebears in Llangunnor churchyard, realising a wish he had expressed in verse in 1875:

Let me at last be laid
On that hillside I know, which scans the vale,
Beneath the thick yew's shade
For shelter, when the rains and winds prevail.

And here he rests in the ground on which he stood inspired as he looked down the Towy vale - a Carmarthen poet whose literary fame reached beyond the Welsh borders.

SIR RICHARD STEELE (1672-1729)

Richard Steele, born in Dublin, is renowned as the first publisher of the famous London magazine *The Tatler*, in 1709, which was itself the very first periodical publication. This was followed in 1711 by *The Spectator*, another famous periodical 'magazine'. To both these publications Steele contributed many lively essays and commentaries on the times. Another principal contributor was Joseph Addison, Steele's influential friend, who introduced him to the Whig political leaders of the day. On their behalf Steele wrote numerous political pamphlets. However, it is as an Essayist that Sir Richard Steele is chiefly remembered; for his essays on the characters, manners, style and dress of his contemporaries were the source of modern periodical literature - the Magazine.

Sir Richard Steele

Steele's association with Carmarthen came through his marriage in 1707 to Mary Scurlock of Tygwyn, Llangunnor. The only child of Johnathan Scurlock, she came of an influential and prosperous family, being connected by marriage to the Philipps family and they in turn with the Walpoles. Mary was his second wife and she inherited an income of £400 a year, a large sum in those days. It is probable that they met in political society. After the accession of George I in 1714, Steele was knighted and elected a Member of Parliament.

For the eleven years of their married life Steele remained Mary's devoted and 'happy slave'. He called her 'Dear Prue' and when his fortunes changed and he failed to succeed in his literary and stock-jobbing projects, it was to her home in Llangunnor that he retired. Here he wrote his greatest play *The Conscious Lovers* and here, too, he formed a close friendship with Dyer, the poet who wrote *Grongar Hill*, seen across the valley from Tygwyn.

Mary died in 1718 and she was buried in the south transept of

Westminster Abbey, opposite Dryden's monument, where a blue marble gravestone gives her age as forty.

Steele's last years were clouded by a paralytic stroke and he was moved to a house in King Street which belonged to the Scurlock family. Here he died in 1729. This house was later to become the Ivy Bush Inn. When the Ivy Bush moved to Spilman Street in 1803, the site became a timber yard and subsequently in 1854 the Assembly Rooms were built there. The Lyric cinema now stands on part of the site and a plaque commemorating Sir Richard Steele has been placed by the Civic Society on the building at the corner of King Street and Bank Lane.

Steele was buried on 4th September 1729 in the Scurlock family vault in St. Peter's Church. The vault was accidentally uncovered in 1876 when workmen were laying the present tessellated flooring and the decayed coffin and remains were seen. The skull on which was a peruke, tied at the back with a black bow, was in a very well preserved state.

In the Consistory Court, near the site of the vault, can be seen a brass plaque commemorating the famous essayist and contributor to *The Tatler, The Spectator* and *The Guardian,* 'the first chief promoter of the Periodical Press of England.' The date of his birth on this plaque is given as March 12th, 1671, which is one year earlier than that now generally accepted.

There is also a commemorative tablet in Llangunnor Church, placed there by a Mr. Williams of the Ivy Bush Inn.

Tygwyn was demolished and a new farmhouse, which later became the home of the Prosser family, was built in the early nineteenth century.

ARCHITECTS, ARTISTS AND MUSICIANS

JOHN NASH (1752-1835)

John Nash, the famous architect to the Prince Regent, later George IV, had his first commissions in Carmarthen. Subsequently he was to acquire fame for his design of many notable London buildings; for the construction of Regent Street, the Royal Pavilion at Brighton, Clarence House and for his reconstruction of Buckingham House into a royal palace. He was also responsible for the lay-out of Regent Street, Waterloo Place, Piccadilly Circus, Oxford Circus, the Church of All Souls (Langham Place), Portland Place and the many fine terraces and crescents encircling Regent's Park. Although the Regent Street project, stretching from Carlton House Terrace on the Mall as far as Langham Place, was an official building project of the Crown, it was not built by the government with government funds, but by a Commission under Act of Parliament with borrowed money. Since it was a commercial undertaking involving the acquisition of private sites, Nash was forced to build the Street piecemeal, thus sacrificing to some extent his ideal of

John Nash

blocks of architecture succeeding each other in a grand perspective.

Nash was also responsible for the lay-out of Regent's Park, with its famous Park Terraces, although the Park today is but a poor reflection of Nash's original conception - an ideal, self-contained garden city with a palace for the king, a church, secluded villas for the nobility, imposing terrace houses for the middle-classes and a working-class area fed by a canal. Outside London his work ranged from magnificent castles, country houses, villas, follies, cottages to public buildings, including bridges, theatres, hospitals and monuments. His Royal Pavilion at Brighton has come in for much criticism, but the classical Banqueting and Music rooms are worthy of admiration. Nash's last London undertaking, the enlargement and conversion of Buckingham House into a royal palace for George IV, was not very successful and, on the King's death in 1830, Nash was dismissed and the work was completed by Edward Blore. Nash's entrance gateway to Buckingham House, modelled on the Arch of Constantine in Rome and known as Marble Arch, was removed to its present site in 1851.

All this lay in the future, however, when as a young man John Nash came to Carmarthen. Born the son of a Lambeth engineer and mill-wright, who died when he was nine, Nash came of maternal ancestors who were Welsh; his mother is said to have had connections in Carmarthen and to have been buried in the town. It was in the wake of bankruptcy, however, that Nash came to Carmarthen in 1783. Having been trained under the London architect Sir Robert Taylor, he undertook as his first London project the building or remodelling of several houses in the vicinity of Bloomsbury Square as a speculation in 1777-78. He failed to sell the houses and was declared bankrupt in 1783.

One of his first commissions in Carmarthen, in partnership with a local builder named Saxon, was to provide a new roof and ceiling for St. Peter's Church in 1785, at a cost of 600 guineas. Donovan in his *Descriptive Excursion through South Wales*, 1804, describes how the workmen employed destroyed the old alabaster tomb of Hywel y Pedolau (Hywel of the Horseshoes) in order to provide plaster for the cornice work. [According to Welsh records, Hywel y Pedolau was foster brother to the first Prince of Wales, later King Edward II (1307-27), Sir Hywel's mother having been the young prince's nurse. Hywel's strength was such that he was able to break, or straighten, horse-shoes with his bare hands and this feat was portrayed on his tomb with the figure of a warrior holding in his clenched hands a large horse-shoe, as if in the act of breaking it asunder. The tomb was in the Chancel, but nothing of it remains today.]

Nash's ability in this local work was not conspicuously brilliant, for he was little more than a jobbing builder at that time. His ceiling at St. Peter's fell down in 1860. He designed the first Picton monument in 1825 but this was pulled down in 1846 because it had been allowed to fall into disrepair. He built at No.7, St. Peter's Street, an inn called *The Six Bells* (now demolished to make the car park entrance), which was a favourite dining place for the visiting clergy and, it is said, he forgot the staircase! This is hardly credible but there is evidence that at some time or other this oversight had to be put right, for the staircase was somewhat curious with a landing crossing a long window. Whether he forgot it or not, John Nash eventually became the greatest architect of his time.

While in Carmarthen he built a house for himself and it still exists as the caretaker's house of the former Pentrepoeth School. Known as 'Nolton House', it was formerly 'Green Gardens'. It is not exactly as he built it, having since been altered, but it is the only known Nash building still in existence in the town; it is marked with a Civic Society plaque.

Nash's most important work in the town was the building of the County Gaol. Whether he got the contract through competition or through the efforts of his local and influential friends is not known, but this formidable structure stood on the old castle site from 1792 to 1938, when it was demolished to make room for County Hall. Carmarthen Gaol was followed by two others at Cardigan and Hereford. All have certain resemblances to a design which was the work of his former employer, Sir Robert Taylor.

Nash's activities seem to have centred around Carmarthen for many years and while in the town he became a social figure of note, numbering among his friends John Vaughan of Golden Grove, one of his first and richest clients. He was also friendly with John George Philipps of Cwmgwili.

The high esteem in which he was held in the town is shown in an extract from Corporation minutes for the year 1828, when he was presented with an oak box ornamented with gold to the value of 30 guineas 'in consideration of valuable services rendered to the Corporation and the inhabitants at large.' This was the year of the completion of his Picton monument.

Among the country houses for the gentry which Nash designed at this period must be mentioned Dolaucothi, Ffynone, Llysnewydd, Foley House, Haverfordwest and Sion House, Tenby. For Hafod House in Cardiganshire Nash created a distinctive conservatory and an octagonal library. While in Wales Nash acquired his 'picturesque' approach to architecture, merging the latter into the landscape. In building or remodelling country mansions, he worked closely with the landscape gardener, Humphry Repton and one aspect of their work can be seen at Blaise Hamlet, near Bristol, a blue-print for rural village design.

It was in 1796 that John Nash moved back to London to begin that part of his career which was to make him famous. Towards the end of his life, however, he fell out of favour as an architect and his last days were spent at the home he designed for himself, East Cowes Castle, on the Isle of Wight. He is buried in East Cowes churchyard.

THOMAS BRIGSTOCKE (1809-1881)

In recent years renewed interest has been shown in the work of this Carmarthen artist, who was born at 61 King Street, on 17th April, 1809. He was the third son of David and Mary Brigstocke, his father being a well-respected painter, decorator, glazier and paperhanger, the founder of a well-known business family.[6]

A fluent Welsh speaker and writer, Thomas was educated at the Queen Elizabeth Grammar School but at sixteen, his artistic talents and interests being clearly evident, he was sent to the academy of Mr. Sass, R.A., in Bloomsbury, London. Eight months later he was admitted a student of the Royal Academy and subsequently he was awarded the silver medal of the Society of Arts on two occasions.

From the autumn of 1833 until the early 1840's Thomas Brigstocke studied at Paris, Florence, Rome and Naples. Much of this time was spent in painting copies of the great masters, and his copy of Raphael's *Transfiguration* was bought as an altar piece for Christ Church, Albany Street, London. While in Rome he painted the self-portrait now purchased by the National Library of Wales. At about this time too, he married a Mrs. Cridland; their only child died in infancy.

Having returned to England, Brigstocke exhibited his first painting at the Royal Academy in 1842. (In all, twenty five of his pictures were exhibited at the Royal Academy.) Soon afterwards the Oriental Club commissioned him to paint a portrait of his fellow townsman, General Sir William Nott, triumphant after his Afghan campaign. This portrait, which now hangs in the Guildhall, was submitted to Queen Victoria, the Court circular for 14th March, 1845 reading:

> Mr. Thomas Brigstocke had the honour by the Queen's Command of attending at the Palace yesterday to exhibit to Her Majesty and H.R.H. Prince Albert, the full length portrait of the late General Nott, G.C.B., painted by Mr. Brigstocke for the Town Hall, Carmarthen. Her Majesty was pleased to express her approval.

In 1847 Brigstocke was commissioned by Mohamet Ali Pasha, ruler of Egypt, to paint portraits of himself and his family, which resulted in the artist remaining in Egypt for sixteen months. Subsequently, until his death on 11th March, 1881 at Cavendish Square (he was buried at Kensal Green), he divided his time between painting portraits of famous men and of dogs, the latter being his favourite subject.

All accounts show that Thomas Brigstocke was highly intellectual, a good linguist, a charming companion, gentle and sensitive. In South Wales he painted portraits of many members of the landed gentry families. He had the ability to convey to canvas the natural expression of his sitters. In the Guildhall can be seen Brigstocke's portraits of General Sir William Nott, of John Jones of Ystrad, M.P. for the County and Chairman of the Quarter Sessions, and David Morris, M.P. for Carmarthen Borough for 27 years. A *Journal* report of the mid 1850's states: 'It is pleasing to know that Carmarthen has had the honour of giving birth to a gentleman of such undoubted talent.'

BRINLEY RICHARDS (1817-1885)[7]

Henry Brinley Richards was born on November 13th, 1817, in a house once standing in Lower Market Street, now called Hall Street, and baptised at St. Peter's Church on 10th December 1817. His father came originally from Llandovery but some time before 1816 he kept a music repository in Lower Market Street and in 1823 was appointed organist at St. Peter's Church - a post he held for nearly thirty years. He married Elizabeth Brinley of Swansea and they had six children of whom Henry Brinley, known as Brinley, was the eldest.

Brinley Richards

It soon became clear that Brinley's interests were artistic, his musical ability revealing itself at an early age. At the Cardiff Eisteddfod in 1834 sixteen-year-old Brinley, under the nom-de-plume *Merlin Tudor*, won the prize for variations on any Welsh air to be selected by the composer. This prize was the turning point in his career - from then on his one ambition was to be a musician. His achievement at the Eisteddfod brought him the patronage of the Duke of Newcastle and of the Earl of Westmorland who arranged for him to be enrolled as a student at the Royal Academy of Music. The following year he won the King's Scholarship and two years later repeated this success. Subsequently he was sent to Paris to study under French teachers, becoming a close friend of Chopin. On his return he was appointed first as an instructor at the Royal Academy, then a professor and finally a director.

Realising that the standard of music in Britain could only be raised by improving the standard of taste and appreciation, he established the Academy's local examination system which involved his travelling to all parts of the United Kingdom. By 1850 he had attained an international reputation as a composer, professor and an accomplished instrumentalist. Regarded as the finest piano player in Great Britain, he was 'a musician of great and varied attainments, and has written many things not unworthy of a Beethoven or a Mendelssohn.'

Nevertheless he was always prepared to encourage and to give practical help to aspiring young musicians and he never forgot his native Wales. Not only did he adjudicate at eisteddfodau, but he actively supported Welsh choirs and organised concerts in aid of Welsh charitable causes - all without any thought of payment. He remained in close touch with his Carmarthen friends, William Spurrell the printer and Dr. Henry Lawrence, a physician with interests in music. Among his numerous compositions his *Recollections of Wales* - the first collection of songs prepared for the piano - was published in 1852 and in 1873 his *Songs of Wales.* It was in 1862, however, that the anthem *God Bless The Prince of Wales* brought him to the height of his popularity.

While he was adjudicating at the national eisteddfod held in 1862 at Caernarvon Castle, Brinley Richards met by chance John Ceiriog Hughes, a well-known writer of Welsh lyric poetry and dedicated eisteddfodwr and adjudicator. For the 1862 eisteddfod *Ceiriog* had written the words for *The Prince of Wales' Cantata* - a choral work commemorating the birth of the first Prince of Wales at Caernarvon and also the coming-of-age of the then Prince of Wales, Prince Albert Edward. Since rumours of the Prince's forthcoming marriage to a Danish princess were rampant, Brinley Richards and *Ceiriog* decided there and then to compose a special anthem - the former to compose the music and the latter the verses. This was accordingly done, the Welsh verses being subsequently adapted into English by George Linley, a native of Leeds.

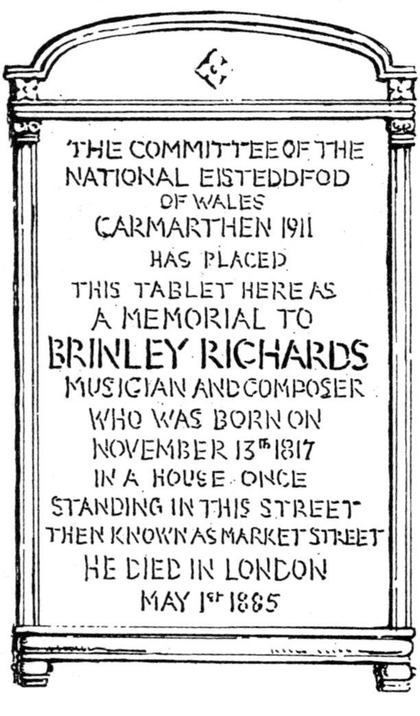

At its first performance in January 1863, which coincided with the announcement of the engagement of the Prince to Princess Alexandra of Denmark, the anthem was an immediate success. The royal wedding in March 1863 further ensured its nation-wide popularity, while press notices 'raved' at its haunting melody, referring to it as 'The Prince of Wales' Anthem' and our 'Second National Anthem'. Thus did Brinley Richards and *Ceiriog* make Welsh poems and melodies known to the outside world, contributing to the revival of interest in Celtic culture in the nineteenth century.

In one of his last letters Brinley Richards wrote: 'There is a glorious future for Wales; with such charming melodies Wales ought, and will, one day take a prominent position in the world of art.'

On May 1st 1885 he died in his sixty-seventh year and was buried in Brompton cemetery. A tablet to his memory can be found inset in the wall of a building in Hall Street, near the Guildhall. (The building marks the site of his birthplace).

LOCAL HISTORIANS

WILLIAM SPURRELL (1813-1889)

William Spurrell, printer, publisher and local historian, was born on 30th July 1813 at 13 Quay Street (demolished when Coracle Way was constructed). He was the third son of Richard Spurrell, Clerk to the Carmarthen Justices, and of Elizabeth Thomas of Frowen, near Llanboidy. John Spurrell, William's grandfather, had come to Carmarthen from Bath in the eighteenth century and settled in Lower Market Street (Hall Street) as an auctioneer and estate agent to the Mansel family. William was educated at the Queen Elizabeth Grammar School until, at the age of sixteen, he was apprenticed to John Powell Davies who had a printing establishment at 58 King Street. He remained there for five years and then went to the London office of Bradbury and Evans where he was employed on the production of the first editions of Dickens' *Pickwick Papers* and *Nicholas Nickleby* and of Disraeli's *Henrietta Temple.*

William returned to Carmarthen in 1839 and started his own business in 1840 in Spurrell's Court, Lower Market Street, where his family had some property. The following year he moved to 37, King Street and here the Spurrell printing business remained for nearly one hundred years. The site of this establishment is marked with a Civic Society plaque.

William Spurrell

William Spurrell became one of the best known Victorian printers, being also a Welsh scholar and an authority on local history and antiquarian matters.

In 1848 he issued the first edition of his *Welsh-English Dictionary* and in 1850 his *English-Welsh Dictionary.* Among his other productions were a Welsh Grammar, *Lessons in Welsh*, and an *English-Welsh Primer*. It must be remembered that William Spurrell was producing his dictionaries and cultivating the Welsh language at a time when it was being discriminated against and was regarded as unfashionable.

In 1857 he acquired *Yr Haul* (The Sun), the oldest of the Welsh Church magazines, which he edited and published monthly until 1884. In 1862 he started another church magazine, *Y Cyfaill Eglwysig* (The Ecclesiastical Friend).

From 1860 to about 1884 he printed a small two-page weekly pamphlet called *The Carmarthen Chronicle and Haul Advertiser* which consisted of local news and personal opinions showing his great antiquarian interests and advanced ideas. He was a noted writer to the Printers' Register and contributed a great deal to the improvement of the technical aspects of the printers' art. He revised the proofs of *Southward's Dictionary of Typography* and his design for the lay-out of the printing-case was adopted by most printing establishments of his day as a classic in design.

Always ready to further education, especially among the working classes, William Spurrell was one of the founders of the Carmarthen Mechanics' Institute in 1839 which later became the Literary and Scientific Institution housed in the Assembly Rooms. However, he is best known for his book *Carmarthen and its Neighbourhood* which was first published in 1860 with a second enlarged edition in 1879. There was also a shortened *Guide* in paper covers (1882). The contents of the book were the first published record of the town's history in easily accessible form, as distinct from learned journals or newspaper reports, and its record of contemporary events provides a valuable source of local history. Some of its historical data cannot be regarded as completely accurate, however, since it was produced when historical research was in its infancy.

In 1875 William Spurrell was made a Justice of the Peace for the Borough; he was also prominent on administrative and educational committees in the town. He died in 1889 at the age of seventy-five and was buried in St. David's churchyard, the business passing to one of his sons, Walter, who became a J.P. and Mayor in 1899, 1902 and again in 1926. On Walter's death in 1934 the printing business left the Spurrell family.

ALCWYN C. EVANS (1828-1902)

Alcwyn Caryni Evans spent a good deal of his time in researching local history and historical documents. The son of Donnard Evans who kept an academy at the Quakers' House in Quakers' Yard, Lammas Street, Alcwyn also kept a school for forty years, at first situated where Lammas Street Chapel school-room now stands and afterwards at the

Quakers' House. In 1867 he submitted to the Welsh National Eisteddfod, held in Carmarthen, a history of the town and county which was awarded the first prize and a gold medal by the adjudicators, Archdeacon Archard Williams and William Spurrell.

It was through 'a desire expressed by Mr. A. C. Evans' that J. R. Daniel-Tyssen, procured the *Royal Charters and Historical Documents Relating to the Town and County of Carmarthen* from the Public Record and other Offices. Alcwyn Evans then edited and annotated these Charters and Documents which were printed by Spurrell in 1878. He compiled a mass of material from old town records and his voluminous manuscripts are now kept in the National Library at Aberystwyth.

Alcwyn Evans

GEORGE EYRE EVANS (1857-1939)[8]

A fascinating book could be written about the life and work of George Eyre Evans, Honorary Secretary of the Carmarthenshire Antiquarian Society and Field Club from 1906 until his death in 1939 and chief creator of the County Museum. A man of many and varied interests, he was an enthusiastic local historian who was chiefly responsible for collecting together a vast range of items of historical interest which formed the foundation of the present Museum.

With his gracious, somewhat eccentric character, his intense Victorian personality made him an outstanding picturesque figure in the life of Carmarthen.

It was as a young boy that he first came to the town, when his father, the Rev. David Lewis Evans, a Unitarian minister, became Professor of Hebrew and Mathematics at the Presbyterian College. George was born on 8th September, 1857 at Colyton Parsonage in Devon. His mother was the daughter of Captain George Eyre Powell, R.N. of Colyton, whose father had served on Nelson's flagship. From his mother he inherited the traditions and values of Victorian county society: respect, loyalty, service, good manners and correct behaviour. From his father he inherited more unorthodox, progressive views on religion, science and social conditions.

He was educated at the Queen Elizabeth Grammar School with its classical tradition and John Ashbridge's School, sometimes called the 'Carmarthen Collegiate School', where, in the words of George Eyre Evans: 'Mr. Ashbridge was in many ways abreast of the educational methods of his day, never letting a pupil pass from a subject until he was assured the boy had mastered it.' Subsequently his education

George Eyre Evans

followed Unitarian lines at the Academy of Gwilym Marles, Llandysul, to be followed by study at Liverpool University. Destined for the Unitarian ministry, he held pastorates at Whitchurch (Shropshire) and Aberystwyth, during which time he published a long list of material mainly referring to these localities.

In 1906 Mr. Evans became Honorary Secretary of the Carmarthenshire Antiquarian Society and Field Club, founded in the previous year, and until his death in 1939, he carried it on his shoulders, helped by the literary and financial contributions of its members. About the time that he became secretary, the idea was born of a County Museum. Although he must be regarded as its creator, he was helped in his work by others, chief of whom was Ernest Vale Collier, also a member of the Antiquarian Society and its director from 1920 to 1932.

The first museum was established at the rear of Messrs. Spurrell's printing works at 37 King Street and in 1908 was moved to a larger room on the premises of Messrs. Brigstocke at 54 King Street. The growing collection of antiquities owed much to the gracious powers of persuasion of the museum's founder who could coax people from all walks of life to contribute interesting articles and documents. It must be remembered that the museum was built up in the years when prehistory, archaeology and folk-culture were sciences in their infancy; when the amateur, not the professional archaeologist or historian was the norm and when public interest had to be awakened in the remains of the past. This, in itself, was a great achievement. In 1920 the museum moved to 5 Quay Street and in 1935 it expanded into the premises next door at No. 4.

In 1910 George Eyre Evans was appointed Inspecting Officer of the Royal Commission on Ancient Monuments in Wales and Monmouthshire. The work took him to visit nearly every ancient monument or site in the Principality and continued until 1928, by which time seven volumes were published, each volume being an inventory for an individual county. Unfortunately, the Inventory for Carmarthenshire cannot now be regarded as sufficiently accurate in the light of more recent scientific archaeological investigations.

He was also a member of the editorial board of the Cambrian Archaeological Association, of the Court of Governors of Aberystwyth University College and of the Council of the National Museum of Wales. In 1924 he became a member of the Council of the National Library of Wales. Always physically active, he had an enquiring mind, an observant eye and an inquisitive nature, especially when collecting items for the museum!

At the age of sixty-seven the indefatigable, ever-youthful Mr. Evans joined the Boy Scout movement and soon became County Scout Commissioner for Carmarthenshire and in 1928 Deputy Scout Commissioner for Wales. It was at this period that he could often be seen walking around Carmarthen in his short-trousered scouting uniform. His boundless energy continued in his work for the Carmarthenshire Antiquarian Society both as its Honorary Secretary and as Editor of its Transactions, which contained articles, reviews, reports and notes of historical interest. He also organised the Society's Field Days until the year of his death. A prolific writer, he made numerous contributions to prestigious historical journals as well as articles for the local press, always distinguishable by the green ink in which they were written! He, too, was a distinctive figure with his short, goatee beard, gold-rimmed spectacles and well-cut, tweed knickerbocker suits.

Recognition of his services came in July 1937 when George Eyre Evans was made a Freeman of the Ancient Borough of Carmarthen. Unmarried, he died suddenly on 9th November, 1939, still in full harness, at his home at No. 4 The Parade. He was cremated, rather unusual at that time, and his ashes were placed near those of his father in the burial ground of Alltyblacca Unitarian Chapel, near the river Teifi on the border of Carmarthenshire and Cardiganshire.

ERNEST VALE COLLIER (1859-1932)

Ernest Vale Collier was one of the founders of the Carmarthenshire Antiquarian Society and of the County Museum, although much of his pioneering work has been overshadowed by that of his colleague, George Eyre Evans. He helped to assemble some of the museum's early collections, especially of Roman coins, and he was the director of the Antiquarian Society from 1920-32, being present at every one of its field days, most of which he had planned and arranged. His interests were many and varied: an architect by profession, he was also a talented amateur artist, a producer and performer of the Carmarthen Operatic Society, a recognised authority on ecclesiastical subjects and he also served on the Borough Council from 1906 to 1921. The son of Canon Charles Collier, Principal of King Alfred's College, Winchester, Ernest Vale Collier had spent over forty years in Carmarthen when he died at 15, Picton Place in 1932.

Ernest Vale Collier

1 See *Eighteenth and Nineteenth Centuries - Religious Revival, Tabernacle Chapel.*
2 Unpublished notes supplied by the late Mr. T. L. Evans.
3 See *Highways and Byways - Monuments.*
4 David E. Painting, *Sir Lewis Morris* in *The Carmarthen Antiquary,* 1961.
5 *Ibid.*
6 See *Trade and Industry - Family Businesses.*
7 Francis Jones, *God Bless the Prince of Wales,* 1969.
8 E. Vernon Jones, *Carmarthenshire Historian,* 1985. See also *18th and 19th Centuries - Town Development, Antiquarian Society and Museum.*

Royal Welsh Fusiliers Monument, c. 1860

Picton's Monument, 1861

- 21 -

HIGHWAYS AND BYWAYS

Although many of Carmarthen's old lanes, alleyways and courts have disappeared over the years through redevelopment schemes, the area that was enclosed within the town walls still retains its basic street lay-out : this is the legacy left by medieval Carmarthen. But there is an even older legacy, going back nearly 2,000 years, dating from Roman Carmarthen: Moridunum's boundary defences, marked by a rampart and ditch, can still be traced today along the line of The Esplanade, The Parade, Parade Road, Little Water Street, Richmond Terrace, Old Oak Lane and Llwbr-yr-Ardd. These all run around the Roman ramparts. Priory Street is probably the oldest street in Carmarthen, its origins going back to the Roman east-west street running through Moridunum.

Some of the town's streets and their origins are given below. This is followed by a list of places which have now disappeared. Translations from the Welsh street names which have no English version displayed on the street signs are indicated by *(tr.)*.

Abergwili Road: Mouth of the (river) Gwili *(tr.)*
Aelybryn: Brow of the hill. *(tr.)*
Alltycnap: Hillside mound. *(tr.)*
Argel: A refuge. *(tr.)*
Awel Tywi: Towy breeze. *(tr.)*
Abbey Mead: A reference to the meadow near to the site of the medieval Priory.
Avenue (The): Developed at the end of the nineteenth century.
Bank Lane: Named after Morris' Bank which stood at the Spilman Street end of the lane in 1834 and subsequently on the King Street end. Originally it was called Prickett's Lane after a crockery dealer who lived there.
Barn Road: Formerly Barn Row, from a tithe barn that stood thereabouts. A field situated to the west of Penlan Road (now Waterloo Terrace) in 1786 was called Barnsfield. **Barnsfield Terrace** was later built in the locality.
Belvedere Avenue: A belvedere is a look-out point.
Blue Street: In 1797 called Golden Grove Street. Originated in 1796 when the Wynveth Stream was covered over to form a wagon road from the Quay. Takes its name from the political colour of the Whig party in Carmarthen, *The Blues.*
Bridge Street: Narrow medieval street leading down to where the Bridge

Gate once stood, one of the gateways in the town walls.

Bronwydd: Hillside of trees. *(tr.)*

Bro Hedydd: The land, or region, of the lark. *(tr.)*

Bro Myrddin: The land, or region, of Merlin. *(tr.)*

Bronydre: The hillside of the town. *(tr.)*

Bryngorwel: The hill on the horizon. *(tr.)*

Brynderwen: Oak tree hill. *(tr.)*

Brynhaul Street: Sunny hill street. *(tr.)*

Brynteg: Fair hill. *(tr.)*

Bryntywi: Towy hill. *(tr.)*

Brewery Road: The remains of Norton's Brewery, now used as warehousing, still stand half-way up the hill.

Bull Lane: Connects Blue Street and Quay Street. Ran to the rear of the Bull Inn, later the Old Bull Café.

Cae Bryndrain: Thorn Hill field *(tr.)*. Once part of Thorn Hill Farm.

Cae Celyn: Holly field. *(tr.)*

Cae Eithin: Gorse field. *(tr.)*

Cae Grug: Heather field. *(tr.)*

Cadifor Street: A modern street named after Cadifor, a medieval Prior of St. John's Priory.

Capel Evan Road: The fields hereabout are recorded as having belonged to the Priory of St. John. Evan or Ifan from the Latin Iohannes (colloquially Iovannes), a form of John.

Chamberlain's Lane: Entrance to Castle Gatehouse, Nott Square. Called after the Chamberlain's Hall above the gate.

Chapel Street: Slaughter House Lane in 1819. Subsequently renamed after the English Wesleyan Chapel

Chapel Yard: Between 22 and 23 Priory Street; continues into the lane **Llwybr-yr-ardd** [garden path *(tr.)*] which leads onto the Esplanade.

Church Lane: Once a narrow lane skirting St. Peter's churchyard wall. It was widened to its present extent when the old Art School was built and the end houses in Spilman Street and King Street were removed.

Church Street: Recorded as St. Peter's Street on John Speed's map of 1610.

Cilddewi Park: David's shelter. *(tr.)*

Clos Mawr: Big Yard *(tr.)* The yard adjacent to the present No.1 Guildhall Square, the entrance being through a passageway adjoining No.1. In 1766 it was the site of the meat market. Later it was called Spurrell's Yard, where William Spurrell started as a printer on family property, 1840. Also designated as the Welsh name for Guildhall Square.

Clos-y-deri: Oak trees close. *(tr.)* A Housing Association development in

Priory Street.

Conduit Lane: From a conduit (public water supply) at the King Street end of the lane. Runs alongside the foundations of the 1415 town wall.

Coronation Road: The houses were built at the time of the Coronation of Elizabeth II in 1953.

Courtlands Park: Named by the developer who lived in a house called Courtlands.

Crispin Avenue: Built on a circular eminence, called Castle Crispin, which may have been an Iron Age fort. St. Crispin, the patron saint of shoemakers, is not known to have any associations with this place.

Cwmoernant: The valley of the cold stream *(tr.).* Recorded in the *Cartulary of the Priory* in 1369.

Cwm Ystrad Park: Wide vale *(tr.).* Ystrad is the name of a mansion that stands nearby.

Dan-y-banc: Under the bank *(tr.).* The lane between Castle Hill and Parade Road, beneath the town walls. In 1873 called Steam Street. The adjacent area near the old station was known as Kidwelly Fach *(Little Kidwelly).*

Dark Gate: The site of the medieval gate, also called the Wynveth Gate after the Wynveth Stream which ran to the north and west of it. The Gate was demolished in 1796. In 1797 Dark Gate was called Union Place.

Dolgwili: Gwili meadow. *(tr.)*

Devereux Drive: Named after the Devereux family, notably represented by Walter Devereux, chief founder of the Queen Elizabeth Grammar School, who is buried in St. Peter's Church. *(see Some Carmarthen Personalities)*

Esplanade (The): This name means a level piece of ground used for promenading. Formerly called East Parade.

Ferrar Street: A commemoration of Bishop Ferrar, the Protestant Martyr, who was burnt at the stake in 1555. *(see Some Carmarthen Personalities)*

Francis Terrace: Built by a Mr. Francis, landlord of the Six Bells Inn in St. Peter's Street.

Furnace Road: Sometimes called Furnace Gardens, as it was built on the extensive gardens of Furnace House (now the library) which at one time belonged to the Morgan family, the proprietors of the ironworks.

Ger-y-llan: By the church. *(tr.)* Housing for retired clergy built in the grounds of St. Peter's vicarage.

Glan Tawelan: Tawelan bank *(tr.).* The Tawelan is the stream running through Johnstown.

Glan yr Ystrad: Wide valley bank. *(tr.)*

Glannant: Stream bank *(tr.)*. At one time the stream flowing this way was uncovered and visible .

Glantowy: Towy bank. *(tr.)*

Glynderi: Glen of oak trees. *(tr.)*

Gors Court: A name preserved in a block of flats in St. Catherine Street after an enclosed court which formerly stood here. Gors means marsh, an old name for this area.

Groesfordd fach: Little cross-roads. *(tr.)*

Guildhall Square: The present Guildhall was completed in 1777 on the site of an earlier Tudor Guildhall. On John Speed's map of 1610 the square is called 'St. Maries Stret' (St. Mary's Street).

Hafod Cwnin: Rabbit pasture or dwelling. *(tr.)* This road was built on the land of Cwnin farm.

Hafod Elfed: Elfed's dwelling. *(tr.)*. A tribute to the Rev. Elfed Lewis (1860-1953). Archdruid Elfed was a great Christian leader, poet, hymnologist and eisteddfodwr. He was born at *Y Gangell,* a cottage in Cynwyl Elfed which has now been restored in his memory.

Hall Street: Originally called Lower Market Street. The name was changed by the Town Council in 1881.

Heol Arfryn: The road on the hill. *(tr.)*

Heol Disgwylfa: Disgwylfa means a watching place; a look-out. *(tr.)*

Heol Drindod: Trinity road. *(tr.)*

Heol Dyfnallt: A tribute to the Rev. Dyfnallt Owen, pastor of Heol Awst Chapel, eisteddfodwr and Archdruid.

Heol Morfa Brenin: King's sea-marsh road *(tr.)*. Fields near the river in this vicinity are known by the old name of King's Marsh.

Heol Rudd: Named after the Rt. Rev. Anthony Rudd, Bishop of St. Davids (1594-1615) and founder of Rudd's charity and Rudd's almshouses in Carmarthen.

Heol Salem: Formerly part of Alltycnap Road, now named after the chapel which stands there.

Heol Spurrell: A tribute to the distinguished Carmarthen printer. *(see Some Carmarthen Personalities)*

Heol-y-Delyn: Harp road. *(tr.)* See Parcydelyn.

Heol-y-Felin: Mill road. *(tr.)* Now the entrance to Parc Hinds and formerly a lane to the old tinworks or tin-mills.

Heol-y-Wawr: Road of the dawn. *(tr.)*

Jackson's Lane: Called after a barber, named Jackson, who lived there.

Job's Well: In 1740 the Borough Corporation owned a form of public bathing place called 'Job's Well and Bathing House.' In 1741 repairs to 'the bathing place of Job's Well amounted to £1. 4s. 4d.' and 'the Chamberlain to pay said sum out of the town rates.' A record of 1776 states: 'A certain cold bath or well, called Job's Well, being part of the Corporation Estate, is greatly out of repair, same is ordered to be repaired.' The poet Dyer mentions having fallen into Job's Well. In the early nineteenth century General Sir William Nott lived at a house in Job's Well and on his return from India and Afghanistan he repurchased the property. The house was being rebuilt at the time of his death in 1845. The property is now part of St. David's Hospital.

John Street: Called after houses built by a John Daniel.

Jolly Tar Lane: Alongside the Jolly Tar Inn (now the Boat Club) on the Quay.

Jubilee Place: A row of houses in Little Water Street converted from an old brewery malthouse. The Old Playhouse Theatre may have stood here or, according to other reports, it adjoined No. 20 opposite.

Justice's Lane: The lane between The Quay and Coracle Way, east of Jolly Tar Lane; called after a corn merchant named Justice who had a storehouse nearby.

King Street: Probably named after the Kyng family who acquired a large number of burgages or land-holdings in Carmarthen in the thirteenth century. Together with the Spilmans, the Kyng family are the earliest recorded burgess family. A William Kyng is first recorded in about 1197. King Street originated as a trackway between the Norman town centred on the castle and Old Carmarthen which included St. Peter's Church and the Priory. The 'street' was not enclosed within the first town walls of 1233. However, the later walls of 1415 enclosed King Street with a Gateway, called the White Gate, at the St. Peter's end of the street, by Conduit Lane. The 1415 wall ran along the eastern side of the present Conduit Lane. The first documentary reference to King Street occurs in 1355, in the *Cartulary of the Priory,* when it is called 'Sutternistret.'

Knoll Gardens: A knoll is a small hill or eminence.

Lammas Street: The Welsh name is Heol Awst - August Street. Lammas, literally 'loaf-mass' (bread-feast), was celebrated on August 1st, which is still known as Lammas Day. In the early Church Lammas Day was a harvest festival at which loaves of bread, made from the first ripe corn, were consecrated. In medieval times August 1st was the day when the town's 'open fields' were thrown open for common pasture until planting time in the following spring. Some of Carmarthen's 'open fields' lay on either side of Lammas Street.

Lime Grove Avenue: Named after Lime Grove House nearby, as was **The Grove** which adjoins.

Llanllwch: The Church of swamp or lake. *(tr.)* *(see below)*

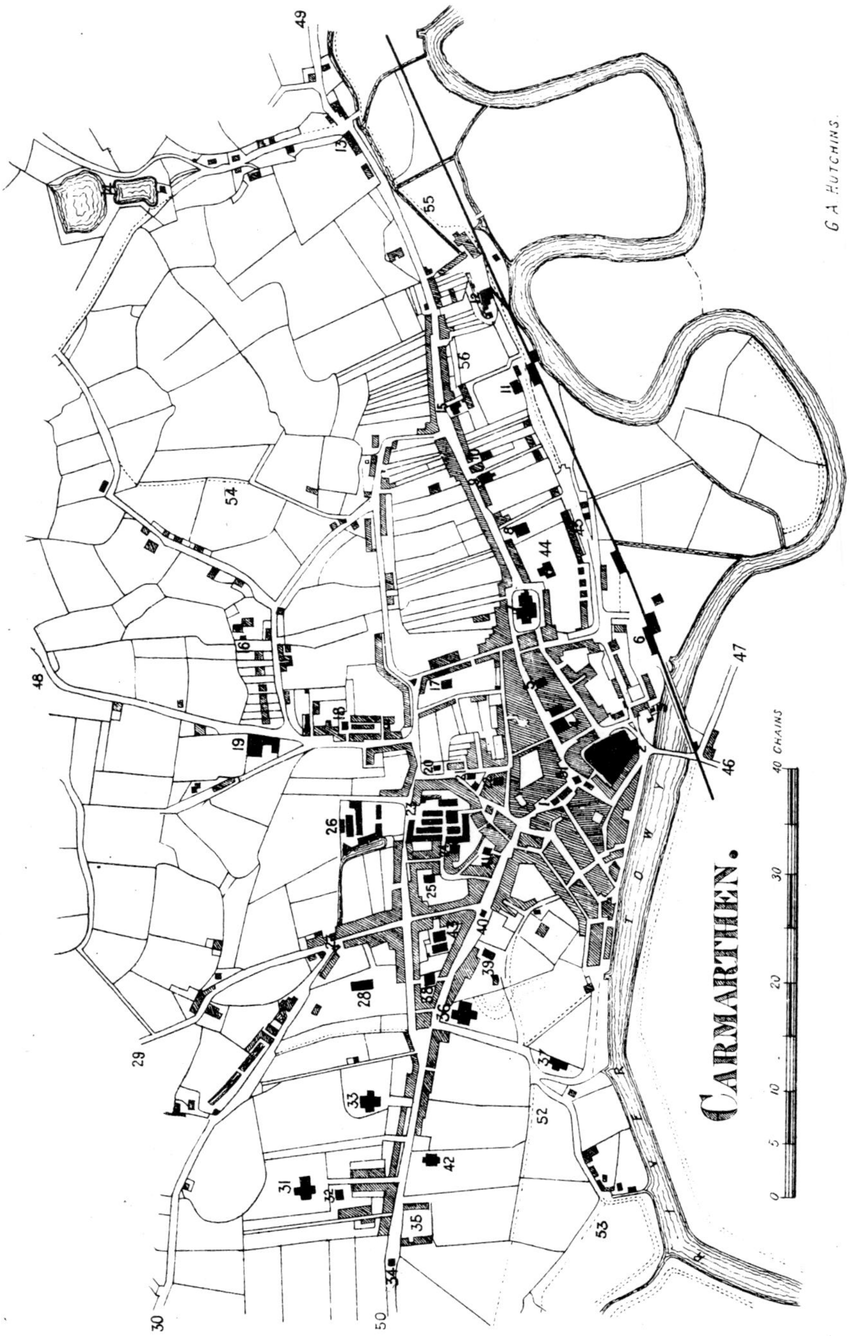
CARMARTHEN.
G A HUTCHINS.
0 5 10 20 30 40 CHAINS

KEY TO THE REFERENCES IN THE MAP.

1. Town Hall, Guildhall-square
2. Gaol and Castle remains, north; Bridge, south; Quay, west
3. Towyside School-Chapel
4. Public Rooms; Post Office
5. Probate Office & County Court Office, King-street
6. Railway Station
7. St. Peter's Church; St.-Peter-street
8. Infirmary, Priory-street
9. St. Peter's School-Church, do.
10. Penuel Chapel, do.
11. Grammar School
12. Tinworks
13. Tanerdy
14. Cwmoernant Reservoirs
15. Priory-street Congregational Chapel
16. Wellfield Reservoir
17. Pentrepoth Board School
18. Tabernacle
19. Workhouse
20. Welsh Wesleyan Chapel
21. Station-house, Cambrian-place
22. English Wesleyan Chapel
23. Market-place
24. Unitarian Chapel, Mansel-street
25. Zion Chapel, do.
26. Slaughter-house and Cattle-market
27. Water-street Turnpike Gate
28. Model Schools
29. Road to Cemetery and Llan Newydd
30. Road to Training College and Asylum
31. Roman Catholic Chapel
32. Union-street Chapel
33. St. David's Church
34. Picton's Monument
35. Barracks
36. Christ Church, Lammas-street
37. Gasworks
38. Congregational Chapel
39. Lammas-street Chapel
40. Fusiliers' Monument, Lammas-street.
41. English Baptist Chapel, do.
42. St. David's Parsonage
43. Water-street Chapel
44. Vicarage
45. Parade
46. Road to Carmarthen Junction
47. Road to Llangunnor
48. Penlan
49. Road to Abergwili, Glangwili, and Conwil
50. Road to St. Clears and Llanstephan
51. Nott-square
52. Five Fields
53. Brickyard Fields
54. Capel Ifan Fields
55. Pond Side
56. Nuns' Walk

Plan of the town published by Spurrell in 1879

Little Water Street: On John Speed's map of 1610 the northern end is called Water Street, from a stream which ran through there and then turned to cross what is now Pentrepoeth and John Street car park.

Little Bridge Street: This was partly demolished in 1963 for the making of Coracle Way. It ran outside the town walls between Bridge Street and the bottom of Quay Street. A portion of the town wall can still be seen in what remains of the street.

Long Acre Road: A modern road recalling arable land of Old Carmarthen mentioned in the *Cartulary of the Priory.*

Lôn Hir: Long lane. *(tr.)*

Llwynmeredydd: Meredith's grove *(tr.)*. The entire estate is built on land belonging to a farm of this name, now demolished.

Maes Llewelyn: Llewelyn's field. *(tr.)*

Maes-y-dderwen: Oak tree field. *(tr.)*

Mansel Street: Called after Richard Mansel Philipps who owned the ground.

Merlin Street: A modern street named after the legendary character.

Mill Street: Originally Dam Street, later Dame Street; from a mill dam once at the north end of the street, near Dark Gate.

Millbrook Crescent: The open stream that once flowed down Glannant Road from Trevaughan fed wool and paper mills that stood near here.

Morley Street: Named after cabinet-makers David Morley and his son, also David, who occupied extensive premises in the area.

Morfa Lane: Sea-marsh lane. *(tr.)*

Mostyn Avenue: Named after Mostyn in North Wales on the suggestion of a Town Councillor who came from there.

Myrddin Crescent: The first houses were built in the 1920's; the name is the Welsh version of Merlin. **Myrddin Court** was developed in the 1960's on the site of some houses called Tabernacle Row, which were demolished.

Nant-yr-Arian: Silver stream *(tr.)*, referring to the stream nearby.

Nash Avenue: Named after John Nash, the architect. *(see Some Carmarthen Personalities)*

Navigation Lane: This lane at one time ran from Friars' Park to Mill Street, but is now only recognisable as the rear entrance to Tesco's store.

North Parade: True Lovers' Lane in 1850.

Nott Square: The site of the original market place outside the main gateway of the royal castle which was constructed in 1109. From this nucleus of traders and artisans the Norman town of Carmarthen gradually evolved. The medieval market cross stood here until it was taken down in 1783 when a covered market was built. The latter was removed in 1846 and General Nott's monument was erected on the site in 1851 *(see Some Carmarthen Personalities)*. On John Speed's map of 1610 it was called High Street; later called Upper Market Street.

Old Oak Lane: Broad Oak Lane in 1834. Follows the line of Roman Moridunum's defensive ditch.

Old Priory Road: The road leading to the site of the Priory. At the beginning of this century the upper part was called Priordy Ucha (upper Prior's house) and the lower part Priordy Issa (lower Prior's house). Priordy Chapel stands on the corner of Priory Street and Old Priory Road.

Orchard Street: This street originally ran from Woods Row to Francis Terrace and was severed when Pentrepoeth School was demolished and the car-park extended in 1990. The orchard was between Orchard Street and John Street.

Pantglas: Green hollow or valley. *(tr.)*

Parade (The): Was constucted by public subscription in 1782 as a pleasant walk and planted with trees in 1800.

Parc Bagnall: Named after George and James Bagnall who were businessmen and public figures in the nineteenth century. *(see Family Businesses in Trade and Industry.)*

Parc Thomas: Built on a field of that name.

Parcmaen Street: Stone field street *(tr.)*. This street may possibly follow the line of medieval open-field strips.

Parcyrafon: Field by the river or stream. *(tr.)*

Parcyronnen: Ash tree field. *(tr.)*

Park Hall: The first housing estate built by the Borough Council after 1939-45 war.

Park Hinds: Land given to the town as a playing field by John Hinds, M.P.

Park Lane: From Friars Park to Morfa Lane. Once called Friars Lane.

Park Terrace: Formally called Magazine Row after the ammunition store, or magazine as it was called, established at the Barracks near Picton's monument. Re-named Park Terrace, referring to the park which adjoins the rear of the houses.

Parcydelyn: Field of the harp. *(tr.)* Parcydelyn is the name of the farm which owned this land.

Penbryn Avenue: Hill-top. *(tr.)*

Penlan Road: Top of the slope or ascent *(tr.)*. The name of the prominent hill above the town with a farm of the same name on top.

Penlan-ffos Road: Hill-top ditch *(tr.)*. This road leads to the farm of the same name.

Pentrefelin: Mill village *(tr.)*. Here was a field called Parc-y-felin in 1834. St. Catherine's Mill was nearby.

Pentremeurig Road: Meurig's (Meyrick's) village *(tr.)*. The name of the farm at the end of College Road.

Pentrepoeth: Originally 'Pentrepoth'. Said to be from 'Village of the Gate' because of its close proximity to the town wall's eastern gate. Original name of Orchard Street area.

Penuel Street: Named after the chapel at the Priory Street end.

Penybanc: Top of the bank. *(tr.)*

Picton Court: At one time called the Rope Walk. An avenue of trees in 1834.

Picton Place: Bailey Street in 1834 as on John Wood's map. Also called Picton Terrace North.

Picton Terrace: Built about the time of the foundation of the first Picton Monument in 1825. Where the monument now stands was known as Pen Llwyn-y-witch (now Penllwyn Park). The area was used as a recreation ground before the opening of the present Carmarthen Park in 1900.

Penllwyn Park: Top of the grove. *(tr.)*

Pond Street: Here was the pond that fed St. Catherine's Mill.

Pontgarreg: Stone bridge.*(tr.)*The name of the mill nearby.

Priory Row: A row of houses built on part of the Priory site.

Priory Street: Probably the oldest street in Carmarthen, roughly following the line of the Roman east-west street in Moridunum. Named from the medieval Priory of St. John the Evangelist sited nearby.

Printers' Cottages (off Priory Streeet): Built on the site of the printing works of J. R. Lewis and afterwards Mervyn Lewis.

Prospect Place: Sited in Lammas Street. Originally called Yard Fawr.

Prosser Close: In memory of the Rt. Rev. David Prosser, Bishop of St. Davids (1927-1950) and Archbishop of Wales (1944-1949).

Quakers' Yard: Sited in Lammas Street. Sometimes called The Retreat. A passage-way near the Water Street/Lammas Street corner leads to the yard where the Quakers had their meeting-house and burial ground.

Quay Street: Originating in the Norman town, it was a busy thoroughfare in the Middle Ages for traffic from the medieval quay at Island Wharf to the town centre. Merchants had their houses here and in the eighteenth and nineteenth centuries it became a fashionable quarter of the town. In 1963 the lower end of the street was demolished for the construction of Coracle Way.

Red Lion Yard: Now it is more of a passage than a yard, leading from Guildhall Square to Chapel Street. The archway seen in the sketch (in chapter on *Political Strife*) was demolished in 1952. The yard was at the rear of the Red Lion Inn which figured prominently in the Whig and Tory riots in 1755 when it became the Tory headquarters. The front of the inn faced Guildhall Square. Later in the eighteenth century the English Wesleyans met in a room in Red Lion Yard, which became known as 'Wesley's Room'. In 1804 the first Wesleyan Chapel was built nearby in Chapel Street.

Red Street: Takes its name from the colour of the Tory party, *The Reds*, in the political conflicts with the Whigs, *The Blues*, in the eighteenth and nineteenth centuries.

Reservoir Road: Leads to Cwmoernant and the 'amenity pools' which were originally constructed in 1841 and 1858 as reservoirs to provide the town with its first piped water supply conveyed by iron pipes.

Richmond Terrace: Originally Richmead Terrace, from Waun Dew (Rich meadow), part of the Commons of Old Carmarthen. Follows the line of Moridunum's rampart and ditch defences.

Ross Avenue: A tribute to John Ross the printer. *(see Printing Pioneers)*

Russell Terrace: Named after Sir John Russell, eminent chemist and soil scientist, a former President of the British Association for the Advancement of Science, who was trained at Carmarthen Presbyterian College.

Shaw's Lane: A cooper named Shaw lived here.

Spilman Street: The first documentary reference to the street occurs in 1355, in the *Cartulary of the Priory*, when 'Spylmanstret' is recorded. Named after the Spilman family who acquired a number of burgages or land-holdings in Carmarthen in the thirteenth century. The Spilmans, like the Kyngs, are the earliest recorded burgess families. Richard 'Spilmon' is first mentioned in the late twelfth century. Robert, son of Richard, was witness to a document in about 1197. In the 1360's John Andrew Spilman is referred to as Mayor in the *Cartulary of the Priory* - one of the earliest recorded holders of the office.

Springfield Road: Takes its name from the many springs in that area.

St. Catherine Street: From the chapel of St. Catherine which, it is thought, stood near the site of the present cattle mart. St. Catherine's Mill was also situated here. The lower part of the street was called Felen Saint in 1819. The upper half (Water Street to Parcmaen Street) was called Goose Street in 1874.

St. Mary's Lane: Constructed in 1862 and named after the medieval Church of St. Mary which stood here, and which also gives its name to St. Mary Street.

St. Non's Avenue: St. Non was the reputed mother of St. David. The area was developed in the 1920's and 30's.

St. Peter's Street: A name recorded on Speed's map of 1610.

Steele Avenue: A tribute to Sir Richard Steele, author and essayist. *(see Some Carmarthen Personalities)*

Tanerdy: Tannery house. *(tr.)* A tannery is recorded in the vicinity.

Tawelan: The stream that flows through Johnstown.

Temple Gardens: The houses and yard reached by the passage between 11 and 12 Lammas Street. Named after the Temple Bar Inn (formerly The Tin Jug).

Thomas Court: Between 94 and 95 Lammas Street.

Towyside: Originally called Golden Grove.

Towy Mews: A redeveloped close near Old Priory Road.

Trem y bedol: Horseshoe view. *(tr.)* The horseshoe bend in the river is visible from here.

Trem y dref: Town view. *(tr.)*

Trevaughan: First recorded c.1270-80 in the *Cartulary of the Priory.* Possibly named after Meilyr Vychan, a Welsh burgess and reeve of Carmarthen.

Trinity Fields: At one time the grounds of Ystrad Mansion and latterly part of the sports fields used by Trinity College. The developers have named the roadways to show the association with the mansion which was once the home of John Jones, M.P. for the Borough. The roads developed include: **Coed-y-plas** - Mansion Wood. *(tr.)* **Lôn-y-plas** - Mansion Lane. *(tr.)* **Plas-y-ddol** - Mansion on the meadow. *(tr.)* **Porth-y-plas** - Mansion Gateway. *(tr.)* **Plas Penwern** - Mansion at the head of the marsh or alders. *(tr.)*

Union Street: Union Buildings (a few houses) in 1834.

Water Street: From a stream which ran beneath. The aqueduct built to supply water to the Friary may have run this way from the slopes of Trevaughan. In 1874 the street was divided into Upper and Lower Water Street.

Waterloo Terrace: Originally Tabernacle Row, called after the Tabernacle Baptist Chapel built in 1812. Re-named in honour of the battle of Waterloo, 1815, when further development took place.

Wauniago: James' Meadow. *(tr.)* The name of the estate between Job's Well Road and Penbryn Avenue. In medieval times an area of common land; later a farm of that name.

Wellfield Road: Takes its name from the numerous wells and springs in the area.

Woods Row: Named after an attorney called Thomas Woods who died in 1811.

Ystrad Drive: Wide valley or vale. *(tr.)*

PLACES WHICH HAVE DISAPPEARED

Several yards, rows and lanes have disappeared over the years, including the following:

Alma Row: In Cambrian Place, behind former brewery malthouse.

Arthur's Yard: In St. Catherine Street.

Bluefield Row: In Waundew.

Broad Street: Mentioned in a Poor Rate survey of 1819. Area of John Street and Barn Road.

Buckingham Place: Named after the Duke of Buckingham which was a tavern at No. 13. Near the Pothouse, now demolished.

Chequers Alley: Now the roadway where buses exit from the bus station into Blue Street. Probably named after an inn of that name

Cotterill's Lane: In Blue Street.

Crown Yard: In Woods Row. Demolished 1970

Davies' Yard: On the Quay.

Duke Yard: At 108 Priory Street. Named after a tavern called the Duke of Cumberland situated there.

Fishpond Row: In Richmond Terrace. Probably called after the fishponds which once belonged to the Priory.

Gell Street: In the 17th century the lower part of Lammas Street was known as Gell Street. Named after Sir William Gell who lived in Gellingham House on the corner of Mill Street and Lammas Street.

Gibraltar Steps: These were on the site of the present Towy Works.

Globe Yard: In Priory Street. Called after the Globe Inn.

Goose Lane: A short, narrow lane between Lammas Street and St. Catherine Street, opposite Morfa Lane. Now a pathway alongside No. 57 Lammas Street. The upper part of St. Catherine Street (Water Street to Parcmaen Street) was once called Goose Street. The story goes that in bygone times, when stock was driven to market on foot, there was the practice of driving geese through warm tar, spread in Goose Lane, in order to provide temporary 'soles' for their feet. The site is now marked by a Civic Society plaque

Pentre Cyrill: At the Quay end of Mill Street. Demolished in 1969 for the bus station.

Island Row: A row of houses on Island Wharf, the medieval Quay. A tract of land that was surrounded by water when the tide came in.

Joshua's Yard: In Priory Street.

Knight's Buildings: A lane between 66 and 67 Lammas Street.

Love Lane: A lane of steep steps at one time leading from Little Bridge Street to the Quay. Originally called Waterloo Steps after the Waterloo Inn on the Quay end. Then called Jones' Place and from about 1880 Love Lane. The lane was partly demolished and closed in 1963 and finally obliterated some years later.

Lynch's Buildings: In Water Street. After a hat-maker named Lynch.

Mansion Yard: In St. Catherine Street.

Masons' Yard: In Lammas Street. Named after the Masons' Arms originally on this site.

Moss Lane: In Blue Street.

Merlin's Lane: This is now the passageway leading from Cambrian Place to the market entrance in Red Street. The old Borough Council Offices once stood here.

Maesycrugiau Court: Next to the Infirmary, now built over by a garage.

Pump Row: In Mill Street.

The Pothouse: This was a building, now demolished, standing near the river to the west of Sawmill Terrace, which may originally have been a pottery works. Later it was used as a pottery storehouse. The river frontage at this point was known as Pothouse Wharf and is now adjacent to the Boat Club slipway

Sawmill Terrace: Named from the sawmills once working in the vicinity, near the Pothouse. Now demolished.

Scott Terrace: In Water Street, where Walter Scott (the son-in-law of John Ross, the printer) kept a nursery garden.

Speedwell Yard: In Lammas Street between Nos. 97 and 98. Called after the Speedwell Inn which stood there.

Square Court: Between 82 and 83 St. Catherine Street.

St. Catherine's Court: An old enclosed court off St. Catherine Street, near the present Gors Court.

Temperance Yard: Between 29 and 30 Lammas Street.

BRIDGING THE CENTURIES - THE TOWN BRIDGE

The present town bridge, which replaced the old stone bridge with its seven arches, was opened by the Rt. Hon. Leslie Burgin, then Minister of Transport, on 4th April 1938. The stone bridge was demolished in 1936, a temporary wooden structure having been previously erected alongside. Coupled with the construction of the present bridge, was the making of a new road from Penymorfa and the setting back of Castle Hill wall a distance of thirty feet.

Protracted discussions took place over the antiquity of the old stone bridge, which had been claimed, erroneously, to be of Roman origin.

The position of the Roman bridging point is unknown. However, it is known from records that a bridge has stood on the present site since the Middle Ages. Professor John Lloyd[1] records a bridge in 1220, 1223 and 1233 when fighting took place to capture the castle. At these dates the bridge was a wooden structure. After the destruction of the timber bridge in 1233, a new bridge was built of stone and, at the same time, the first stone town wall was commenced. During the reign of Edward II, in 1326, pontage (i.e. a bridge toll) was charged on various merchandise at Carmarthen 'to aid in the repair of Carmarthen bridge, which has been destroyed and for the repair of which a large outlay is necessary.' For three years the burgesses were to have pontage and to have a boat on the Towy for the passage of those who wished to pass over. They were to

The Old Bridge (demolished 1936)

The New Bridge
(Illustration from the souvenir programme of the official opening ceremony on 4th April, 1938)

appoint men to collect the profits from such passage and devote them to the building of the bridge. (T.C.A.S. Vol. 18)

John Speed's map of 1610, which cannot be relied upon for complete accuracy, shows a bridge with six arches and a parapet with six triangular recesses for foot passengers. The bridge was widened by six feet in 1777. In 1828 the bridge was widened for a second time and the recesses or rest-holes, to enable foot passengers to get out of the way of horses and carriages, taken down and a parapet with iron railings erected. It was this stone bridge which was demolished to be replaced by the present one.

Records of the seventeenth century speak of very harsh winters at that time with the Towy being frozen over for several months. In 1683 there was such a hard frost that 'people did play football under the bridge and a coach went over the ice upon the river below the bridge.'

A diary kept by a resident of Carmarthen in 1855 recorded that from 12th February to 20th March the Towy was frozen over and 'some slided from the bridge to the Gas Quay.'

BY-PASSING THE TOWN

Increasing motor traffic has necessitated several schemes for by-passing the town. The first scheme involved the demolition of Sawmill Terrace, Buckingham Place, Little Bridge Street, Lower Quay Street and parts of the Quay and created the stretch of road known as Coracle Way in 1963. This scheme was completed in 1970 when the lower end of Morfa Lane was connected with Travellers Rest via Llansteffan Road.

More recently a major southern by-pass has been completed taking traffic around the town from Nant-y-caws to Pensarn and then across the Towy on a new road-bridge linking with the existing by-pass to the west of the town. The new road-bridge is called *Pont Lesneven* in honour of Carmarthen's twin town in Brittany. (Twinned in 1982.)

A further scheme for an eastern by-pass is also envisaged.

MONUMENTS

PICTON'S MONUMENT

This was erected in memory of General Sir Thomas Picton who was killed at the battle of Waterloo on 18th June, 1815. One of Wellington's ablest and most distinguished generals, Sir Thomas Picton lived for a time at Iscoed, Ferryside. The present monument replaces an earlier one designed by John Nash and built by Daniel Mainwaring, a highly-respected Carmarthen stone and marble mason. The first monument was very elaborate, being 75 feet high, with an internal winding staircase leading to the top of the column where there was a square gallery. Small cannons were placed at the corners of the gallery from which rose a pillar surmounted with a statue of Picton. Costing £3,000, realised by public subscription, the monument was decorated with bas-relief scenes of the general's triumphs and verbosely inscribed. The foundation stone was laid on 16th August, 1825 and the monument was dedicated on 29th July, 1828. Unfortunately, the ornamental bas-reliefs which had been sculpted in Roman cement by a young London sculptor, Edward Hodges Baily, were unable to withstand Carmarthen's inclement weather and within a few years were in a dilapidated state. Replacements in stone were made by Baily and sent from London but these were never erected on the monument. It would seem that they were forgotten and lay neglected for years in a nearby close. Eventually, in the 1970's, they were rescued from a garden in Johnstown and are now in the Museum.[2] In 1846 the first Picton Monument was taken down, since it had been allowed to fall into a state of disrepair.

The foundation stone of the second monument, designed by architect Francis Fowler, was laid in 1847. On July 25th, 1854 this monument was struck by lightning which displaced the top stone. In more recent years there were reports that it was unsafe and in the Autumn of 1984, following a report that it was in danger of collapse, the top section was removed.

In 1988 the whole monument was rebuilt stone-by-stone on new stronger foundations. In the process of excavating the foundations a 'time capsule' was found, consisting of a glass cup containing Sir Thomas Picton's Waterloo medal and a selection of gold, silver and copper coins dated 1799-1825; there was also a set of Maundy money. The cup was discovered under a silver-plated metal square inscribed with the information that the first stone of the 1825 monument was laid by the Rt. Hon. Frances Baroness Dynevor, assisted by Sir Christopher Cole, Royal Navy, and M.P. for Glamorgan. The medal and coins are now kept at the County Museum together with other Picton memorabilia. A full set of 1988 coins and a plaque bearing the coat-of-arms of Carmarthen District Council were placed under the foundations of the restored monument.

THE ROYAL WELCH FUSILIERS' MONUMENT

This monument was erected in Lammas Street in August 1858 in memory of the men of the 23rd Royal Welch Fusiliers who died in the Crimean War against Russia in 1854-55. It is a neat little obelisk surrounded by cast iron railings in the form of crossed muskets. The 23rd was first formed by William III (of Orange) to oppose James II in 1689, and it is said that the first man to join came from Friars' Park, Carmarthen.

A Russian cannon brought from the Crimea was placed in front of the monument, but this was melted down for scrap metal during the Second World War.

The first Picton Monument

Picton's Monument

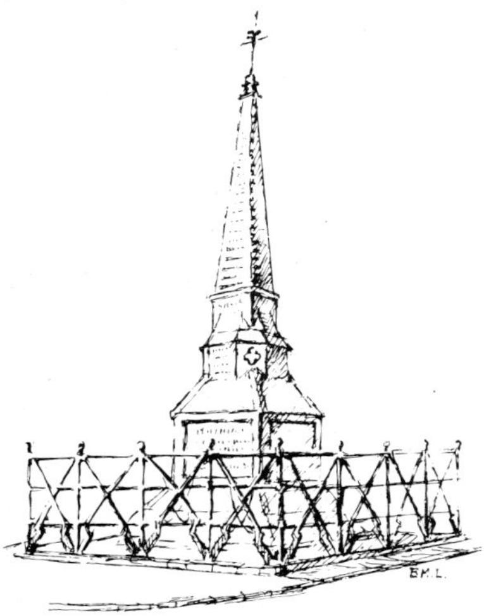

The Fusiliers' Monument

The Boer War Monument

NOTT'S MONUMENT

Nott's Monument, in Nott Square, formerly Upper Market Street, was erected in March 1851 on the site of the covered Market Place, the latter having been erected in 1783 on the site of the medieval Market Cross. General Sir William Nott, often claimed as Carmarthen's most famous soldier, was the son of Charles Nott, proprietor of the Ivy Bush Inn in King Street. After a distinguished military career in India and Afghanistan he returned to his old home at Job's Well, Johnstown. He died in January 1854 and was buried in St. Peter's churchyard, near the grave of his parents. Nott's monument, to which Queen Victoria gave 200 guineas, is the work of an accomplished sculptor, Edward Davis, the bronze statue being cast from guns captured at the battle of Maharajpur and presented by the East India Company. Edward Davis was the son of Dr. David Davis of Llandyfaelog who became a celebrated London physician and who was in attendance at Queen Victoria's birth.

At the base of the monument is a plaque commemorating the martyrdom of Dr. Robert Ferrar, Protestant Bishop of St. Davids, who was burnt at the stake in the old Market Place on March 30th, 1555.

THE BOER WAR MONUMENT

In front of the Guildhall stands the Boer War memorial which is in memory of the men of Carmarthenshire who fell in the South African War of 1899-1902. Its erection was promoted by the *Carmarthen Journal* and it was unveiled by Major General MacKinnon on 27th April, 1906. The contractors were John Lewis and Sons, marble masons of Carmarthen and the honorary architects were E. V. Collier and W. D. Jenkins.

THE CENOTAPH

The Cenotaph stands in front of the Infirmary in Priory Street and commemorates the men of Carmarthenshire who fell in the two World Wars, 1914-18 and 1939-45. It is to this monument that parades of ex-servicemen and others converge on Remembrance Day and similar occasions. The Cenotaph is the work of Sir William Goscombe John.

The Cenotaph

THE PARISH OF LLANLLWCH

The Parish of Llanllwch was originally part of the historic Parish of St. Peter. Since the boundaries of St. Peter's Parish formed the boundaries of the Borough of Carmarthen, Llanllwch lay within the Borough. By an Order of the Queen in Council, dated November 10th, 1843, the old parish of St. Peter was divided into three districts: St. Peter's, St. David's and Llanllwch. Subsequently, in July 1857, these were formed into separate parishes. In 1974, under local government reorganisation, the Borough of Carmarthen ceased to exist as such, but since its boundaries were retained, Llanllwch still remained within the authority of Carmarthen Town Council.

From Norman times the Llanllwch area formed part of the royal demesne lands attached to Carmarthen castle, supplying the latter with food and produce. In the fourteenth century, however, the demesne lands, sometimes referred to as the Manor of Llanllwch, ceased to be worked directly from the castle and were farmed out for rent to customary tenants called gablers or gafol-men. They paid six-pence an acre for their holdings.

When the Black Death reached Llanllwch in 1349-50 all of the tenants except one died and the lands were left waste and uncultivated. Over fifty years later, during the rebellion of Owain Glyn Dwr, the hamlet was 'totally destroyed and devastated,' according to the castle Chamberlain's accounts of 1407-1409.

The first reference to a mill at Llanllwch appears in 1300, but in the 'Minister's Accounts' for 1412-1413 the mill is referred to as being 'totally destroyed'.[3] This destruction was also the result of the Owain Glyn Dwr revolt.

The name Llanllwch presumably recalls a lake or pool which is known to have existed in the vicinity in earlier times. Today the area is still marshy and a large tract of boggy land further to the west of Llanllwch is known as Llanllwch Bog.

St. Mary's Church, Llanllwch

ST. MARY'S CHURCH, LLANLLWCH

St. Mary's Parish Church was originally a chapel attached to St. Peter's Church and, like St. Peter's, was conferred on the Priory of St. John the Evangelist at Carmarthen in the early Middle Ages. Little is known of the church's history, but its tower, probably dating from the fifteenth century, still remains standing, although the rest of the church has undergone much restoration.

In his Visitation of 1710 Archdeacon Tenison reported the roof of St. Mary's to be 'intirely destroy'd' and the edifice to be 'disus'd'. The Vaughans of Derllys were closely associated with the church and were generous benefactors, and one of the monuments in the church is in memory of John Vaughan of Court Derllys (died 1722) who 'in his lifetime contributed largely towards the building of this Chapel, and industriously promoted the same charitable disposition in others.' The church was again restored in 1862 and 1865 when eisteddfodau in aid of the restoration fund were held in Carmarthen's market place.

Another monument is dedicated to the memory of several members of the Edwardes family who lived at Rhydygors.

RHYDYGORS HOUSE

The house of this name, now demolished, stood near the river in Johnstown on the site of an earlier medieval dwelling. Little is known of this medieval dwelling apart from the fact that it was occupied by the Wynter family who held a substantial amount of land in Carmarthen; one Walter Wynter was Archdeacon of Carmarthen about 1329. A south wing was added late in the seventeenth century; the main portion of the later house was erected in the mid eighteenth century. During the Tudor period the children of the owner, Edward ap John, adopted his Christian name as their family name, with it eventually taking the form of 'Edwardes'. For several generations this family gave distinguished service in town and county; one David Edwardes, who was Borough Sheriff in 1680, being largely responsible for the manuscripts known as the *Golden Grove Books,* while in the eighteenth century another David Edwardes became an admiral.

Rhydygors House shortly before demolition

From 1779-1785 the Carmarthen Presbyterian College, a dissenting academy, was housed at Rhydygors, where the men were to 'live in' under strict rules. During the First World War several families of Belgian refugees were accommodated at the house. The Edwardes family left

Rhydygors at the beginning of this century, but several members are buried in Llanllwch church. The house was demolished in 1972.

1 Sir John Lloyd, *A History of Carmarthenshire*, Vol. 1.
2 Edna Dale-Jones, *Daniel Mainwaring, builder of the Picton Monument* in *The Carmarthenshire Antiquary*, Vol. XXV, 1989.
3 Terrence James, *Carmarthen: An Archaeological and Topographical Survey*, 1980.

Nott's Monument, 1861
with the Angel Vaults behind

- 22 -

INNS AND TAVERNS

Wine was an important trade commodity in medieval Carmarthen with considerable quantities being consumed by the castle garrison. Ships sailed up the Towy bringing wine mainly from Gascony (France) and between 1302 and 1313 at least twenty-six ships brought wine to the town for the use of the castle; by 1324 the number had risen to forty-four and by 1335 the number was fifty-two.

Apart from wine, home-made ale was in general use during the Middle Ages, especially by the poorer classes who could not afford imported wine. Towards the end of the fourteenth century it is probable that beer became popular and also came into general use. Brew-houses became part of monastic establishments, but when in the sixteenth century the monasteries were dissolved, together with their guest-houses, this vacuum encouraged the establishment of an increasing number of inns and taverns.

The first inns mentioned in Carmarthen appear in a Rent Roll of 1573 when there is reference to 'ye Nagg's Head' and to the 'Angell or Exchange'. A report of 1577 shows that there were then 4 or 5 inns, 2 taverns and 31 ale-houses.[1] In 1657 there are references to the Angell, Black Lion, Blue Bell House, Bull Inn and Nagg's Head House. When the Duke of Beaufort visited the town in 1684 it is recorded that 'the publick conduit ran with wine'. In the will of John Oakley, dated 1688 (he was Mayor in 1662) the following taverns, at which he had left goods, are listed: Sun, Moon, Starr, Globe, Flower-de-Luce, Prince's Arms, Spread Eagle, Rose, Greyhound, Crown, Anchor.

The 'Six Bells Inn', close to St. Peter's Church in St. Peter's Street, probably took its name from the church's six bells which were cast in 1722. (There are now eight bells - two being added in 1904). Down to the end of the nineteenth century it was the inn to which 'the rural clergy drove on Visitation Days and where the students of the Presbyterian College often dined on their yearly Prize Day.'

In 1802 there were 64 inns or ale-houses in Carmarthen, in 1822 there were 82, while in 1829 there were 84 (excluding Johnstown, Abergwili, Pensarn and all outlying districts).

The following list includes all the names, past and present, that we have been able to find. The same name may apply to inns in different localities, the name having been given to different premises at various times. e.g. A 'Nagg's Head' is recorded in both St. Mary Street (where Cromwell is said to have stayed; now Nos. 3-4) and in Dark Gate.

Abergwili: Wheaten Sheaf; Black Ox; Drovers' Arms.

Barn Road: Butchers' Arms (number 12); Tanners' Arms (13) - *a tannery stood on the site of the present Capitol building.*

Blue Street: Blue Bell; Jolly Sailor; Lark (32); Prince of Wales; Ship (29); Shipwrights' Arms; White Hart; Ship and Castle; Shakespeare - *recorded as a Masonic meeting place in 1766.*

Brewery Road: Inn on the Hill.

Brickyard: Railway Inn - *between the old railway station (L.M.S.) and the river. Licence revoked when the station moved to its present site.*

Bridge Street: The Baulkwood (3); Curriers' Arms; Buffalo (20); Dial; Hare (3); Horse and Jockey (17); King's Head (18); Pelican (31); Three Sewins; Y Rar; Wheat Sheaf; Greyhound (37); King David; Red Cow (28); Unicorn (14); Three Tuns - *Spurrell refers to an old inhabitant who remembered being in the Three Tuns from where he witnessed the departure of Lord Nelson, with Sir William and Lady Hamilton, from the town in 1802. There was a Three Tuns in Priory Street in 1875. A rate book of 1836 also locates an inn by this name in Lammas Street.*

Buckingham Place: Duke of Buckingham (13) - *a site at the west end of Spring Gardens.*

Cambrian Place: Cambrian Arms (9) - *now* Coracle Tavern; Glamorgan Arms (1); Falcon House.

Chapel Street: White Horse (8) - *opposite the rear of Barclay's Bank.*

Dark Gate: Morgan's Arms; Nagg's Head - *on the corner of Dark Gate and Blue Street.* The Half Moon Hotel, *established 1806, absorbed the Nagg's Head and a large house next to this in Blue Street. It continued for many years as a coaching hotel using the Nagg's Head as a bar and a wine and spirit stores. The business was run by Mr. William Bright and then continued by Mrs. Bright until her retirement in 1884. Her son-in-law Henry Cadle then took over. It was used as a Y.M.C.A. during the 1914-18 war.*

The Half Moon Hotel
(corner of Blue Street and Dark Gate)

Guildhall Square: Black Lion; Bull (17) - *later the Old Bull Café;* Red Lion (6 & 7) - *a favourite place for dining and for social events. Masonic meetings in 1772 and 1788. Red Lion Inn was headquarters of the Tory party in the eighteenth century. 'Red Lion Yard' may have been the inn yard and stabling with coaching facilities. Nearly all demolished by modern shops;* Talbot Inn (15 & 16); Number 7 or The Hole in the Wall; Coffee Pot.

Johnstown: Royal Oak; Ystrad Arms; Friends' Arms; The Poplars.

John Street: Black Swan - *'in the meat market';* Bird in Hand (18); Bunch of Grapes (16) - *the Freemasons met here in 1733;* Gloucester Arms (15); Grey Cow (9) - later Tally Ho; Stag's Head (19) - *now to be found as the* New Stag's Head *in the town centre service area.*

King Street: Bacchus (25); Black Lion; Coach and Horses; Cresselly Arms (34); Elephant (11) - *'good stabling in 1820';* Seren Cymru (24); Green Post (23) - *a reference to the posting green from which the mail coaches started. Later a shop of the same name stood on the site;* King's Arms (37 & 38) - *Lord Nelson stayed here;* Mackworth Arms (10); Marquis of Granby (32); Glue Pot (58); Number 31; Cock and Hen (14); Crown; Old Ivy Bush (12 & 13) - *a large coaching inn. The archway between Nos.12 & 13, still existing, led to the stables of the inn;* The Ivy Bush - *as well as the Old Ivy Bush, there was also a later inn, called the Ivy Bush, on the site of the present Lyric cinema and neighbouring properties. In 1729 Sir Richard Steele died in a house on this site, which later became the Ivy Bush Inn. In 1794 Charles Nott, father of General Sir William Nott, became proprietor of this inn. In 1803 the Ivy Bush moved to Spilman Street.*

The Marquis of Granby

Lammas Street: Angel (15); Barley Mow (33); Black Horse - *on site of English Baptist Church;* Boar's Head (120) - *a story is told that the landlord of this hotel was killed by a bull during the usual practice of bull-baiting in Carmarthen streets: the accident put an end to this practice;* Boot and Shoe; Bremenda Arms - site now taken by the Golden Lion; Carpenter's Arms; Cawdor Arms (114);

Coopers' Arms (19); Drovers' Arms (106); Falcon (111); Farmers' Arms; Golden Lion (formerly 23, then 102); Harp (110); Live and Let Live; Masons' Arms (Masons' Yard, 34); Mermaid (101); Milford Arms (99); New Inn (108); Old Queen's Arms (99); Plough (112 & 113); Railway Tavern (75); Red Cow - *on site of English Congregational Church;* Rising Sun; Rose and Crown (117); Temple Bar - *in passage between 11 & 12, formerly called* Tin Jug. *Area now called Temple Gardens;* Smiths' Arms (88); Speedwell (96 & 97 Speedwell Yard); Three Compasses (107); Sugar Loaf; Vine - *corner of Water Street, now site of Midland Bank;* Volunteers' Stores (41) - *probably an off-licence, formerly called* King William; The Three Tuns; White Lion (23).

Little Bridge Street: Cross Hands.

Llangunnor Road: The Queen's; The Star.

Llanllwch: Travellers' Rest.

Lower Market Street (Hall Street): Devil Tavern - *recorded in 1773;* Bumper Tavern - *recorded in 1773;* The Falcon.

Mansel Street: Mansel Arms (1); New Vine (21).

Mill Street: Albion (52) - *now part of Albion Arcade;* Chequers - *probably near Chequers Alley;* Pirate (34); Lord Nelson (32).

Mount Pleasant, Llangunnor: Penbryn Manor Hotel - *once the home of Sir Lewis Morris.*

Nott Square (Upper Market Street): Angel Vaults (10); Sun - *the Carmarthen Journal records in 1833 that the proprietor died 'by the bite of a fox';* Swan (11) - *on site of former Three Crowns. It was demolished to improve the view of Castle Gateway;* Three Crowns - *a Masonic Lodge met here in 1753.*

Park Terrace (Magazine Row): Three Horseshoes (7).

Pensarn: Square and Compass - *demolished for by-pass.*

Picton Terrace: Antelope (2) - *formerly known as* The Golden Key.

Priory Street: Boot and Anchor (82); Cart and Horses (127); Castle (137); Duke of Cumberland (108) - *near Duke's Yard;* Eagle (131) - *now the Association Football Club;* Emlyn Arms (50); Globe (133) - *near Globe Yard;* King's Arms (103); Maesycrugiau Arms (9); Masons' Arms (88); New King George (123); Old King George (5); Printers' Arms (6); Three Cranes - *east of Priordy Chapel;* Three Crowns - *between the White Horse and King's Arms;* White Horse (112); Three Tuns - *also in Bridge Street and Lammas Street;* Red Lion (2); Ropemakers' Arms (61); Sawyers' Arms; Royal Oak.

Quay Street: Ship and Castle (16) - *in Lower Quay Street;* Union Hall (34).

The Quay: Hope and Anchor - *later called* The Jubilee; Ship Aground; Sloop (22); Jolly Tar (14) - *now the Boat Club;* Waterloo (7) - *adjacent to Waterloo Steps;* Three Mariners.

The Nelson Hotel and Bunch of Grapes

The Three Tuns Inn, Priory Street, 1875

Queen Street: Alma (1); Elephant (4); Spread Eagle (8); Royal George (19); Prince of Saxe-Coburg; Old White Lion (5) - *where a Masonic Lodge met in 1812;* Lamb and Flag (11) - *demolished when frontage set back in 1865, when it was incorporated into the* Queen's Hotel (10 & 11); Carmarthen Arms; Coach and Horses.

Red Street: Curriers' Arms; Fountain (7); Market House (12) - *adjoining the Merlin Brewery;* Lamb - *known from the late 1860's as* The Nelson (6); Old Fountain; The Salutation.

Spilman Street: Black Ox (25); Coach and Horses (14); Elephant and Castle (26); George and Dragon; Golden Lion (24) - *on corner of Spilman Street and Church Lane;* Lion Royal - *between County Hall and Queen Street. Took the title Royal after a visit of George IV in 1821;* Saracen's Head (37); Stag and Pheasant (35); Star and Garter (14 or 15) - *during riots in 1832 a mob attacked this inn and 'the landlord defended himself with powder and shot';* Victoria (29); Ivy Bush Royal - *which moved in 1803 from King Street to Spilman Street.*

St. Catherine Street: Apple Tree (4); Plough (8); Sunnyside - *on site of the entrance to Model School (now sheltered housing).*

St. Mary Street: Plume of Feathers (7); Nagg's Head (3-4).

St. Peter's Street: The Angel (9) - *afterwards the* Royal Exchange; Six Bells (7) - *said to have been built by John Nash;* Forest Arms (3) - *afterwards* Jeremy's Hotel, *now the Registry Office.*

Tanerdy: Farmers' Arms - *opposite Reservoir Road;* Crossroads - *on Abergwili Road/Bronwydd Road junction;* Francis Well - *on Bronwydd Road/Glangwili junction;* Welsh Guardsman - *formerly Cwnin Farm.*

Woods Row: Green Dragon (15).

Water Street: Bakers' Arms; Barley Sheaf; Bay's Head and Star; Bear Fawr - *between Water Street Chapel and Farmers' Arms;* Black Bull; Black Horse (25); Blue Boar (3); Cardigan Arms (52 & 53);

Farmers' Arms (72); Fox and Terrier; Fox and Hounds; Friends' Arms (69); Hatters' Arms - *near 'Water Street Gate';* Holly Bush - *near 'Water Street Gate';* Morgan Arms (37) - *built on property of Charles Morgan, Furnace House, now* The Dairies Club; Swansea Castle (80) - *licence revoked in 1930;* Red Cow - *next to Swansea Castle;* Saddlers' Arms (4); Square and Compass (43); Three Salmons (5); Weavers' Arms (62).

COACHING INNS

With the building of new turnpike roads and the improvement of old roads towards the close of the eighteenth century, Carmarthen found itself at the centre of a network of roads radiating from the town. Its importance as a market town and trading centre increased and with improved communications and transport, Carmarthen became an important coaching centre.

In the early decades of the nineteenth century stage coaches were connecting Carmarthen with London and all the major towns of England and Wales, although journeys were long and tedious and often involved staying over-night at various coaching-inns which had sprung up all over the country. With good weather the run between London and Carmarthen took about two days but it could take much longer in the winter. In the severe winter of 1814 the last coach to get through, before Carmarthen was cut off by snow, arrived four days late. By the 1830's Carmarthen's most famous coaching inns, the Ivy Bush and the Boar's Head, were doing brisk business with passenger coaches coming and going daily to all parts of the Kingdom.

The Picton Coach ran daily, Sundays excepted, from the Ivy Bush to Swansea, via Kidwelly and Llanelli, taking five and a half hours.

The Regulator Coach ran three times a week to Tenby and Haverfordwest, while the Collegian Coach ran three times a week to Lampeter and Aberystwyth. Another Collegian Coach ran three times a week to Brecon, Hereford, Worcester and Birmingham. All left from the Ivy Bush Hotel. For passengers wishing to go to London, the Paul Pry (4-inside Post Coach) left the Ivy Bush every morning at 5 o'clock except Sunday, and arrived at Cheltenham at 7 p.m. the same evening. Passengers could then either proceed to London immediately, arriving at 6 a.m. the following morning or spend the night at the Royal Hotel in Cheltenham departing at 8 a.m. the next morning.[2]

Besides the Ivy Bush and the Boar's Head, there were other notable coaching inns in the town such as the Red Lion in Guildhall Square, with its Red Lion Yard where the horses were stabled; the King's Arms in King Street; the Lion Royal (corner of Spilman Street and Queen Street); the Greyhound in Bridge Street; the Half-Moon Hotel (formerly Nagg's Head) in Dark Gate; and the Talbot in Guildhall Square. (Trades

associated with horses flourished e.g. harness makers, curriers, shoe smiths, coach builders and stabling).

By 1850 when the railway from London reached Swansea, coaching services were integrated with train services and London was not much more than twelve hours from Carmarthen. However, the coming of the South Wales Railway to Carmarthen in 1852 heralded the approaching end of the coaching days, although even in 1869 coaches were still running daily to Aberaeron, Aberystwyth, Cardigan, Lampeter, Llandeilo, Llandovery, Llangadog and Newcastle Emlyn.

A SONG ABOUT INN SIGNS, 1794

The following song, which names several old inns in the town, is taken from a book entitled *Comic Songs* by Thomas Merchant, published in 1794 by Daniel Ross of Carmarthen. Written in the days of the French Revolution, when Britain was at war with France, the song illustrates the loyalty of the common people to King and country.[3]

Carmarthen Loyalty: Or, A Song about Signs.

When to please you the Lyre of my Muse has been strung,
Of Potatoes, of Dyers, of Frenchmen I sung;
But Potatoes, and Frenchmen, and Dyers she resigns,
And I'm going to sing you a Song about Signs.

When Folks meet together Dissension to sow,
And by breeding Contentions encourage the Foe;
While false Motives and Colours they hold to our View,
'Tis a *Sign* they might find something better to do.

But in *Britain,* thank Heaven, we're rather too wise,
For our Neighbours in *France* have now opened our Eyes;
And however mad People together combine,
Of Disloyalty *here* we sha'n't find the least Sign.

Then let the Convention attempt to come here,
To eat up our Beef, or to drink our strong Beer;
Of that they'd be short, but if Fighting they wish,
At each Sign in the Town they would meet a full Dish.

But rough entertainment they'd find at the *Buck*,
And they'd meet at the *Ivy-Bush* no better Luck;
They'd get their Heads comb'd if they call'd at the *Fleece*,
And they'd run from the *Swan* like a Parcel of Geese.

They'd have little to boast of Success to their Cause,
If the *Buffalo* once got them fast in his Paws;
From the *Cock* they'd get Plenty of Spurs and of Pegs,
From the *Freemason's-Arms* they'd soon take to their Legs.

The *Lions*, no matter if black, white, or red,
Would prove that they good British Lions were bred;
The *Castle* to *Frenchmen* would scarcely be civil,
And they'd get from the *Angel* all kick'd to the *Devil*.

May the Sign of the *King* ever meet with Respect,
And our good Constitution each *Briton* protect;
And may he who first caus'd all the Troubles in *France*,
Be hung on a *Sign-Post*, on Nothing to Dance.

1 Terrence James, *Carmarthen: An Archaeological and Topographical Survey*, 1980.
2 Pat Molloy, *Four Cheers for Carmarthen*, 1981.
3 We are indebted to Elizabeth Twist, formerly of the County Record Office, for a copy of this song.

Appendix I

Mayors of Carmarthen

This list is taken from the list of Mayors-Escheator as given in *The Principality of Wales in the Later Middle Ages* 1972 (R. A. Griffiths) and from 1536 to 1900 the list is taken from *A History of Carmarthenshire* Vol. II (ed. Sir John E. Lloyd).

The earliest holders of office, which might compare with that of the mayoralty, were called Reeves; these were not elected representatives but officials responsible to the Crown. The earliest reeves are recorded in the late 13th century. Carmarthen's early Mayors were mayors-escheator, i.e. officials who had the duty of dealing with escheats - land and property lapsing to the Crown through lack of heirs or forfeiture. The Mayoralty is discussed more fully in the Chapter on *Civic Dignity.*

A manuscript entitled *Kalendar of All ye Names of Mayors . . . . of Carmarthen from ye year of our Lord 1400* is kept in the National Library of Wales. The Kalendar is written on pieces of parchment sewn together, $11^1/_2$ yds. long and $4^1/_4$ ins. wide. Unfortunately, nothing is known of its history or authorship. According to George Eyre Evans (*Yr Encilion:* Vol. 1, Part 1, 1912), 'the principal hand ends with the year 1700'. *The Kalendar* begins with a Mayor named David Lloyd in 1400 and ends with a Mayor of the same name who died in office in 1718.

However, there are also in existence three other parchment rolls, bearing similar titles and covering the periods 1400-1726, 1400-1732 and 1400-1744. They appear to have been compiled by different hands and though similar in content, they show some slight variations. Nothing is known of their origin. These three rolls are kept in the Carmarthen Record Office.

The list of Mayors-Escheator, as given by Professor Ralph A. Griffiths, commences in the mid 14th century, before the Kalendar list, and is more comprehensive, filling in the gaps in the Kalendar manuscript, particularly in the early 15th century. Apart from these additions, and some variations of spelling, the lists are the same.

1356 John Laurence (Lawrence)
1368-69 John Andrew Coubrigge (Cowbridge)
1369? John Andrew Spilman
1375-76 Thomas ap Dafydd ap Gruffydd
1376-77 John Banov (Banow, Bannowe)
1377-78 Dafydd Llwyd
1378-79 John Hancock
1379-80 Thomas Japh
1380-81 Thomas Rede
1381-82 John Laurence
1382-83 John Banov (Banow, Bannowe)
1383-84 John Iorwerth
1384-85 John Roger

1385-86 Dafydd Llwyd
1393-95 John Hugon (Higon)
1395-96 William Roger
1397-98 John Hugon (Higon)
1398-99 William Roger
1399-1400 John More
1400-01 Dafydd Llwyd
1407-08 John Hugon (Higon)
1408-09 John ap Hywel
1409-10 William Roger
1410-11 John More
1411-12 Thomas Walter
1412-13 John Willy Fisher
1413-14 John More
1414-15 Nicholas Bluet
1415-17 John More
1417-19 William Rede
1420-21 William Rede
1422-23 William Rede
1423-24 John Bernard Bola
1424-26 Nicholas Bluet
1426-27 John Willy Fisher
1428-29 John More
1429-31 William Rede
1431-32 John Willy Fisher
1432-33 Nicholas Bluet
1433-35 John More, Snr.
1435-36 Nicholas Bluet
1437-38 Nicholas Bluet
1438-39 John Willy Fisher
1439-40 Nicholas Bluet
1440-41 Stephen ap Gruffydd
1441-42 Maredudd Tailor
1442-44 William Fisher, Snr.
1444-45 Nicholas Bluet
1445-46 Thomas Higon (Hugon)
1447-48 Nicholas Bluet
1448-50 Lewis ap Rhys Gethin
1451-52 Thomas Hugon (Higon)
1452-53 Nicholas Bluet
1453-54 Philip Gravell
1456-57 Gruffydd ap Nicholas
1457-58 Rhys ap Hywel
1461-62 John Wardebek
1462-63 John More, Jnr.
1463-64 John Wardebek
1464-65 William Tawk
1465-68 John Higon (Hugon)
1468-69 Rhys ap Hywel
1470-71 Thomas Clerk
1471-72 Thomas Gethin
1472-73 Gwilym ap Gwilym Wehydd
1473-75 John Wardebek
1476-77 John Higon (Hugon)
1478-79 Gwilym ap Gwilym Wehydd
1480-81 Rhys ap Hywel
1481-82 John Higon (or Hugon)
1482-83 Jankyn Llwyd Hir
1485-86 Thomas Gethin
1486-87 Dafydd ap Rhys ap Robert
1487-88 John Higon (or Hugon)
1488-89 Sir Rhys ap Thomas
1489-90 Rhys ap Ieuan ab Einion
1490-91 John Tucker
1491-92 Stephen Gravell
1492-93 Maurice Rede
1493-94 Richard Owen (ab Owain)
1494-95 Sir Rhys ap Thomas
1496-97 Rhys ap Ieuan ab Einion
1497-98 Stephen Gravell
1498-1500 Hugh Higon (Hugon)
1500-01 Sir Rhys ap Thomas
1503-04 Geoffrey Dier
1504-06 Sir Gruffydd ap Rhys
1506-08 Richard Rede
1509-10 William Morris (Morys)
1510-11 Philip Rhys ap Thomas Fychan
1511-12 Sir Gruffydd ap Rhys
1512-13 William (or Gwilym) ap Gwilym Wehydd
1513-14 Sir Gruffydd ap Rhys
1514-15 Gwallter (or Geoffrey) Dier
1515-16 Philip David
1516-17 Sir Rhys ap Thomas
1517-18 John ap Thomas ap Gwilym
1519-20 John Hir
1521-22 Richard ap Dafydd Gwallter
1522-23 Gruffydd Higon (Hugon)
1523-24 Dafydd ap Dafydd
1524-25 John Jenyns
1525-26 Thomas ab Owain
1526-27 John ap Rhys ab Ieuan ab Einion
1527-28 Philip David
1529-30 Dafydd (ap) Llywelyn
1530-31 Gruffydd Higon (Hugon)

1531-32 Sir Walter Devereux, Lord Ferrers
1532 Sir Walter Devereux
1533 John David Lloyd
1534 Sir Walter Devereux
1535 Sir Walter Devereux
1536 Richard Devereux
1537 Martin David
1538 Thomas Brine
1539 David Rees
1540 David Rees
1541 William Read
1542 Thomas Hancock
1543 Thomas Walter
1544 Morgan ap David
1545 John Jennins
1546 Martin David *died in office;* David Richard *completed term.*
1547 Richard ap Ievan
1548 Griffith William
1549 Griffith Donne
1550 David Nash
1551 Griffith Higgon
1552 Thomas Morgan
1553 Jenkin David ap John
1554 John Vaughan
1555 John Griffith
1556 Griffith Donne
1557 Humphrey Toy
1558 Thomas Beynon
1559 Rees Penry
1560 William Davies
1561 Jenkin David ap Ievan Philip
1562 David William Read
1563 John Vaughan
1564 Robert Birt(t)
1565 Griffith John David Lloyd
1566 Thomas Lewis
1567 Griffith ap Eynon
1568 Lodovici (Lewis) Davies
1569 Richard Lewis
1570 Lewis William
1571 Griffith Rhys
1572 Richard Philipps
1573 Richard Philipps
1574 Walter Vaughan
1575 Griffith ap Ievan
1576 Lewis David ap David
1577 David ap Ievan
1578 William Philipps
1579 William Philipps
1580 Walter Vaughan
1581 Griffith ap Ievan
1582 Robert Toy(e)
1583 Edward Middleton
1584 David Edwards
1585 Thomas Nothed
1586 Thomas Atkins
1587 Philip William
1588 Griffith Howell
1589 John Morris
1590 Henry Owen
1591 John Birt(t)
1592 Thomas David
1593 Robert Birt(t)
1594 John Fisher
1595 Morris Lloyd
1596 William Thomas Morris *died in office;* David Edwards *completed term.*
1597 Walter Vaughan *died in office;* Philip William *completed term.*
1598 Henry Vaughan
1599 Henry Philipps
1600 Thomas Rees
1601 William Thomas
1602 Ievan Thomas
1603 Sir John Vaughan (afterwards Earl of Carbery)
1604 Thomas Parry
1605 Thomas Atkins
1606 Ievan Long
1607 John Griffith John
1608 Thomas Vaughan
1609 Martin Beynon
1610 William Lewis
1611 Thomas Higgs
1612 Thomas Davids (Davies)
1613 Edward Atkins *died in office* Martin Beynon *completed term*
1614 Richard Jeanes
1615 David Edwards
1616 John Bowen
1617 Griffith Davids
1618 Griffith Lewis
1619 Thomas Atkins

Signatures of Mayors of Carmarthen

Robert Toye 1582
Edward Myddleton 1583
David Edwardes 1615
Thomas Woode 1633
William Gower 1656
John Scurlocke 1665

Henry Vaughan 1598
Dawkin Gove 1677
John Hughes 1650
Charles de Lancy 1685
Sir Sackville Crow 1686
William Brigstocke 1705

Henry Vaughan 1700

1620 Morgan David
1621 David Bevan
1622 Richard Barret
1623 Henry Vaughan
1624 Thomas Muggall (Muggull, Muggle) *died in office* William Thomas *completed term*
1625 Griffith Beynon
1626 Anthony Jones
1627 Griffith Read
1628 William Lewis
1629 Richard Jeanes
1630 John Bowen
1631 Griffith Lewis
1632 Thomas Atkins
1633 Thomas Woode
1634 Thomas Jones
1635 Richard Thomas
1636 Robert Lewis
1637 Atwill Taylor
1638 Lewis Jones
1639 Rowland Phillips
1640 Morris James
1641 George Oakley
1642 David Bevan
1643 Thomas Philipps
1644 Thomas Philipps
1645 Thomas Griffith
1646 George Jeanes
1647 Thomas Jones
1648 Dawkin Gove
1649 Robert Brend
1650 John Hughes, senior
1651 David Edwards
1652 Richard Thomas
1653 Edward Jones
1654 John Vaughan
1655 Robert Birt
1656 William Gower
1657 Griffith Beynon
1658 Walter Thomas
1659 John Hughes, junior *died in office;* Anthony Jones *completed term.*
1660 Anthony Jones
1661 George Lewis
1662 John Oakley
1663 Robert Lewis
1664 Thomas Beynon
1665 John Scurlocke
1666 Richard Leigh
1667 John Muggall
1668 John Vaughan
1669 William Brigstocke
1670 Sir Henry Vaughan
1671 Robert Lewis, junior
1672 Altham Vaughan
1673 John Vaughan
1674 John Williams
1675 Thomas Griffith
1676 Thomas Jones
1677 Dawkin Gove
1678 Thomas Newsham
1679 David Jones
1680 Edward Gower
1681 Edward Jones
1682 Owen Brigstocke
1683 William Jones
1684 John Philipps
1685 Charles de Lancy
1686 Sir Sackville Crow
1687 Rowland Gwynne
1688 Sir Rice Williams *replaced by* Martin Beynon, Oct. 29, 1688
1689 John Rider
1690 Thomas Rogers
1691 George Catchmaid
1692 Howell David
1693 Thomas Powell
1694 Griffith Lewis
1695 Morris James
1696 John Davies
1697 Theophilus Bevan
1698 Griffith Williams *died in office;* William Brigstocke *completed term.*
1699 John Williams
1700 Henry Vaughan
1701 Sir Anthony Rudd
1702 John Scurlocke
1703 Thomas Manwaring
1704 Anthony Jones
1705 William Brigstocke *died in office;* William Jones *completed term.*
1706 Anthony Jones
1707 John Newsham
1708 James Phillips

1709 William Gower
1710 John Vaughan
1711 Nathan Morgan
1712 John Morgan
1713 Rees Thomas
1714 Francis Lloyd
1715 John Thomas
1716 Thomas Jones
1717 Thomas Lloyd
1718 David Lloyd *died in office;*
Benjamin Davies *completed term.*
1719 Benjamin Davies
1720 Morgan Davies
1721 William Thomas
1722 Arnold Bowen
1723 Peter Chetle
1724 John Lewis
1725 John Roberts
1726 John Williams
1727 Thomas Rees
1728 George Davies
1729 John Philipps
1730 Henry Price
1731 John Leigh
1732 Robert Rees
1733 James Johnson
1734 William Rees
1735 David Lewes
1736 Edward Davies
1737 John Newsham
1738 Charles Morgan
1739 John Lloyd
1740 John Philipps
1741 John Williams
1742 William Thomas
1743 John Morgan
1744 John Philipps
1745 Evan Williams (At this period there were great irregularities, with the Whig and Tory parties each electing their own Mayor amd sometimes the 'mob' choosing a third.) 'Admiral' Thomas Jones elected by the mob.
1746 William Thomas
Anthony Rogers
1747 John Philipps
1748 Evan Williams
1749 David Lloyd
D. Thomas
John Newsham
1750 John Jones
1751 John Lewis
1752 Francis Morgan
1753 David Edwards
John Adams
1754 Roger Philipps
1755 William Leigh
Evan Davies
1756 John Evans
Charles Webb
1757 William Leigh
1758 Arthur Jones
Robert Morgan
Thomas Lloyd
1759 Woodford Rice
Richard Wilson
1760 James Evans
James Williams
1761 Edward Read
William Morgan
1762 John Evans
Vaughan Horton
James Williams
1763 *No elections*
1764 Albert Davids *sworn* 6th August (first Mayor under new Charter)
Edward Parry *sworn* October
1765 Francis Morgan *died in office;*
Edward Parry *completed term*
1766 Vaughan Horton
1767 George Rice
1768 Arthur Jones
1769 Morris Howell
1770 Henry Morris
1771 David Edwards
1772 William Williams
1773 George Philipps
1774 Richard Le Davids
1775 David Williams
1776 Walter George
1777 George Evans
1778 George Lewis
1779 John Morgan
1780 John Lloyd
1781 Thomas Howell

1782 John Williams
1783 John George Philipps
1784 Thomas Blome
1785 Morgan Lewis
1786 Jeremiah Owen
1787 Richard Howell
1788 William Price
1789 George Talbot Rice
1790 Herbert Pryse Ball
1791 Thomas Williams
1792 William Lewes
1793 William Bonnell
1794 John Morgan *died in office;* William Price *completed term.*
1795 Josiah Llewelyn
1796 David John Edwards
1797 Charles Morgan
1798 Richard Mansel Phillips
1799 William Morris
1800 John Morgan
1801 James Hughes
1802 Sir William Paxton
1803 Thomas Morris
1804 William Morgan
1805 Dr. Charles Morgan
1806 John Hughes
1807 John Williams Hughes
1808 Lord Cawdor
1809 John Jones
1810 John George Philipps
1811 Mark Roch
1812 David Morris
1813 Sir George Griffies Williams
1814 Dr. Charles Morgan
1815 Charles Morgan
1816 John George Philipps
1817 John Hughes
1818 John Williams Hughes
1819 Charles Morgan
1820 John Williams Hughes
1821 Thomas Morris
1822 Charles Morgan
1823 David John Edwards
1824 Daniel Prytherch
1825 Robert Waters
1826 Grismond Philipps
1827 Aaron Timmins
1828 Dr. John Bowen
1829 David Jones
1830 David John Edwards
1831 Daniel Prytherch
1832 Grismond Philipps
1833 Aaron Timmins
1834 David Davies
1835 Capt. John George Philipps (First mayor under Municipal Corporations Act)
1836 Thomas Morris
1837 Thomas Morris
1838 William Philipps
1839 Charles Jones
1840 Thomas Taylor Webb
1841 William Morris
1842 Edmund Hills Stacey
1843 William Morris
1844 George Davies
1845 Thomas Charles Morris
1846 Samuel Tardrew
1847 William George Thomas
1848 John Lewis
1849 Valentine Davis
1850 Valentine Davis
1851 William Morris
1852 William Morris
1853 Lewis Morris
1854 Lewis Morris
1855 Thomas Charles Morris
1856 John Lewis Philipps
1857 James Rowlands
1858 Henry Norton
1859 John Thomas
1860 John Thomas
1861 William de Grouchy Warren
1862 William de Grouchy Warren
1863 Valentine Davis
1864 John Adams
1865 Robert Brodie
1866 Edward Bowen Jones
1867 David Davies
1868 John Lewis
1869 John Lewis
1870 Henry Norton
1871 John Thomas
1872 William de Grouchy Warren
1873 David Lewis
1874 David M. Morgan

1875 David Bonnell Edwards
1876 Thomas Mostyn Davies
1877 Thomas Thomas
1878 Richard William Richards
1879 Charles William Jones
1880 John Morris
1881 James Jenkyn Jones
1882 James Jenkyn Jones
1883 James Jenkyn Jones
1884 John Lewis
1885 Thomas Mostyn Davies
1886 William Richard Edwards
1887 Edward Alfred Rogers
1888 Howell Howells
1889 Thomas Davies
1890 Thomas Jenkins
1891 Thomas Jenkins
1892 James Davies
1893 Henry Cadle
1894 Henry Brunel White
1895 Henry Brunel White
1896 Henry Brunel White
1897 Henry Brunel White
1898 John Lewis
1899 Walter Spurrell
1900 Edward Colby Evans
1901 Edward Colby Evans
1902 Walter Spurrell
1903 Edward Alfred Rogers
1904 Edward Alfred Rogers
1905 Henry Evan Blagdon-Richards
1906 Joseph Nicholas Williams
1907 John Lewis
1908 John Crossman
1909 Walter Lloyd
1910 William Thomas
1911 John Beynon Arthur
1912 John Beynon Arthur
1913 John Lewis
1914 John Lewis
1915 John Lewis
1916 John Lewis
1917 William Evans
1918 William Evans
1919 Andrew Fuller Mills
1920 Andrew Fuller Mills
1921 Lewis David Thomas
1922 John Richards
1923 Andrew Fuller Mills
1924 John Hinds
1925 Andrew Fuller Mills
1926 Walter Spurrell
1927 David John Davies
1928 David John Davies
1929 William Jones
1930 William Jones
1931 William Jones
1932 Thomas Lloyd
1933 Thomas Lloyd
1934 Thomas Lloyd
1935 John Owen Morgans
1936 John Owen Morgans
1937 John Owen Morgans
1938 James Islwyn Davies
1939 James Islwyn Davies
1940 James Islwyn Davies
1941 Philip William Trefor Thomas
1942 Philip William Trefor Thomas
1943 Philip William Trefor Thomas
1944 John Russell Lewis Jones
1945 John Jenkins
1946 John Jenkins
1947 Enoch Davies
1948 Enoch Davies
1949 Enoch Davies
1950 William David Jones
1951 William David Jones
1952 Charles Wright Griffiths
1953 Charles Wright Griffiths
1954 James John Lewis
1955 James John Lewis
1956 Caron Clifford Jones
1957 Caron Clifford Jones
1958 Thomas John Thomas *died in office*
1959 Mark Ernest Clifford Jones
1960 Mark Ernest Clifford Jones
1961 Mrs. Alice Kate White *died in office* (first woman mayor); Thomas Idwal Jones *completed term.*
1962 Thomas Idwal Jones
1963 Ellis James Powell
1964 Sidney Jeremy
1965 David Denzil Harries
1966 William Wynford Francis Davies

1967 Charles Wright Griffiths
1968 Leslie Hyde Howells
1969 David Jones Howells
1970 William Colvin
1971 Ronald Byles Evans
1972 Lawrence Victor Rice
1973 Roy Nicholl
1974 Ivor Morgan Morris (first Town Mayor after Local Government reorganisation)
1975 Thomas James Hurley
1976 Samuel David Thomas
1977 Thomas Henry Gwynne Davies
1978 Gwynne Morris Williams
1979 Mrs. Joyce Lodwick
1980 Mrs. Helen Margaret Thomas
1981 Peter Hughes Griffiths
1982 Samuel David Thomas
1983 Mrs. June Williams
1984 John Elfed Williams
1985 Kenneth Bryan Maynard
1986 Malcolm Morgan Jones
1987 Miss Mary Kathleen Davies
1988 Mrs. Siân Morris
1989 William Gwynoro Jones
1990 Peter Hughes Griffiths
1991 John Elfed Williams
1992 Mrs. S. M. Lorraine Maynard
1993 Richard J. Goodridge
1994 Mrs. Agnes M. Dunbar

Picton Terrace

Appendix II

Members of Parliament, 1536-1992

The list of Members of Parliament for Carmarthen Borough is extracted from *A History of Carmarthenshire* (Sir John E. Lloyd) up to 1900 and from *British Parliamentary Election Results* by F. W. S. Craig. Previous to the Reform Act of 1832 there was one member for the Borough and one for the County. The Act gave two members to the County, while Llanelly was added to the Carmarthen Borough Constituency. In 1885 the County was divided into the two districts of East and West Carmarthenshire, each returning one member. In 1918 Carmarthen was incorporated into West Carmarthenshire and Llanelly into East Carmarthenshire, to be called the Carmarthen and Llanelly constituencies respectively. Prior to 1900 a blank date before the year indicates a By-election.

Parliament summoned to meet	
June 8, 1536	Returns lost
April 28, 1539	Returns lost.
January 16,1542	Griffith Williams
November 23, 1545	Griffith Williams
November 4,1547	Thomas Phayer, Forest
March 1, 1553	William Parry, Carmarthen
October 5, 1553	Griffith Higgon, Carmarthen
April 2, 1554	William Awbrey, Cantref (Brecon)
November 12, 1554	John Parry, Carmarthen
October 21, 1555	William Wightman
January 20, 1558	John Vaughan, Golden Grove
January 23, 1559	John Parry (as 1554)
January 11, 1563	John Morgan
April 2, 1571	John Morgan
May 8, 1572	Thomas Wigmore, Wigmore Castle (Hereford)
November 23, 1584	John Puckering[1]
1584	Edward Don Lee, Abercyfor
October 15, 1586	Edward Don Lee
February 4, 1589	Gelly Meyrick, Gladestry (Radnor)
February 19, 1593	Sir Thomas Baskerville
October 24, 1597	Sir Thomas Baskerville
October 27, 1601	Walter Rice, Newton

March 19, 1604	Walter Rice
April 5, 1614	No return made.
January 16, 1621	Henry Vaughan, Derwydd
February 12, 1624	Henry Vaughan
May 17, 1625	Sir Francis Annesley, Newport Pagnell (Bucks)
February 6, 1626	Henry Vaughan (as 1621)
March 17, 1628	Henry Vaughan
April 13, 1640	Sir Francis Lloyd, Maesyfelin (Cardigan)
November 3, 1640	Sir Francis Lloyd[2]
1646	William Davids
July 4, 1653	'Barebones Parliament'. No elections held.
September 3, 1654	No member summoned for the Borough
January 27,1659	David Morgan, Carmarthen
April 25, 1660	Arthur Annesley, Newport Pagnell (Bucks)
May 8, 1661	John Vaughan, Golden Grove
March 6, 1679	Altham Vaughan, Golden Grove
October 17, 1679	Altham Vaughan
March 21, 1681	Altham Vaughan
May 19, 1685	Richard Vaughan, Derllys
January 22, 1689	Richard Vaughan
March 20, 1690	Richard Vaughan
November 22, 1695	Richard Vaughan
August 24, 1698	Richard Vaughan
February 6, 1701	Richard Vaughan
December 30, 1701	Richard Vaughan
August 20, 1702	Richard Vaughan
June 14, 1705	Richard Vaughan
July 8, 1708	Richard Vaughan
November 25, 1710	Richard Vaughan
November 12, 1713	Richard Vaughan
March 17, 1715	Richard Vaughan
May 10, 1722	Richard Vaughan*
1725	James Philipps, Pentyparc
November 28, 1727	Arthur Bevan, Laugharne[3]
June 13, 1734	Arthur Bevan
June 25, 1741	John Philipps, Kilgetty
1745	Sir John Philipps, Picton (as 1741)
August 13, 1747	Thomas Mathews, Llandaff*
1751	Griffith Philipps, Cwmgwili
May 31,1754	Griffith Philipps
May 19,1761	Ralph, Earl Verney
May 10, 1768	Griffith Philipps (as 1751)

November 29, 1774	John Adams, Peterwell (Cardigan)
October 31, 1780	George Philipps, Coedgain
May 18, 1784	John George Philipps, Cwmgwili
August 10, 1790	John George Philipps
July 12, 1796	John George Philipps[4]
August 31, 1802	John George Philipps#
1803	Sir William Paxton, Middleton Hall
December 13, 1806	George Campbell
June 22, 1807	George Campbell
November 24, 1812	George Campbell#
1813	John Frederick Campbell
August 4, 1818	John Frederick Campbell
April 21, 1820	John Frederick Campbell[5]
1821	John Jones, Ystrad
July 25, 1826	John Jones
September 14, 1830	John Jones
June 14, 1831	John Jones[6]
December 18, 1832	William Henry Yelverton, Whitland Abbey
February 19, 1835	David Lewis, Stradey
September 11, 1837	David Morris, Carmarthen
August 19, 1841	David Morris
September 21, 1847	David Morris
August 20, 1852	David Morris
April 30, 1857	David Morris
May 31, 1859	David Morris*
1864	William Morris, Carmarthen
August 15, 1865	William Morris
December 10, 1868	John Stepney Cowell-Stepney, Llanelly
March 5, 1874	Charles William Nevill, Llanelly#
1876	Arthur Keppel Cowell-Stepney, Llanelly#
1878	Benjamin Thomas Williams, Narberth
April 29, 1880	Benjamin Thomas Williams#
1882	John Jones Jenkins, Swansea
January 12, 1886	Sir John Jones Jenkins
August 5, 1886	Sir A. K. Cowell-Stepney, Llanelly (as 1876)
August 4, 1892	Evan Rowland Jones, London
August 12, 1895	Sir John Jones Jenkins (as 1886)

Election date	
October 8, 1900 G.E.	Alfred Davies (Lib) 2,837
	Sir John Jones Jenkins (Unionist) 2,047

January 17, 1906 G.E.	W. Llewellyn Williams (Lib) 3,902
	Hon. Vere B. Ponsonby (Unionist) 1,808
January 19, 1910 G.E.	W. Llewellyn Williams (Lib) 4,197
	Lord Tiverton (Unionist) 1,965
December 3, 1910 G.E.	W. Llewellyn Williams (Lib) unopposed
January 24, 1912 By	W. Llewellyn Williams (Lib) 3,836
	H. C. Bond (Unionist) 2,555
	F. G. Vivian (Ind Lab) 149
March 17, 1915 By	W. Llewellyn Williams (Lib) unopposed

CARMARTHEN CONSTITUENCY

December 14, 1918 G.E.	John Hinds (Coalition Lib) unopposed
November 15, 1922 G.E.	John Hinds (Nat Lib) 12,530
	Hon. G. W. R. V. Coventry (Unionist) 8,805
	D. Johns (Agric Ind) 4,775
	H. Llewellyn Williams (Lib) 3,874
December 6, 1923 G.E.	Sir E. J. Ellis-Griffith (Lib) 12,988
	Sir Alfred Stephens (Con) 8,677
	Rowland Williams (Lab) 7,132
August 14, 1924 By	Sir Alfred M. Mond (Lib) 12,760
	Rev. E. T. Owen (Lab) 8,351
	Sir Alfred Stephens (Con) 7,896
October 29, 1924 G.E.	Sir Alfred M. Mond[7] (Lib later Con) 17,281
	Rev. E. T. Owen (Lab) 7,953
June 28, 1928 By	W. N. Jones (Lib) 10,201
	Daniel Hopkin (Lab) 10,154
	Sir C. C. Mansel (Con) 8,361
May 30, 1929 G.E.	Daniel Hopkin (Lab) 15,130
	W. N. Jones (Lib) 14,477
	Hon. J. B. Coventry (Con) 9,961

October 27, 1931 G.E.	R. T. Evans (Lib) 15,532 Daniel Hopkin (Lab) 14,318 Delme W. C. Davies-Evans (Con) 9,434
November 14, 1935 G.E.	Daniel Hopkin# (Lab) 18,146 R. T. Evans (Lib) 12,911 E. O. Kellett (Con) 7,177
March 26, 1941 By	R. Moelwyn Hughes (Lab) unopposed
July 5, 1945 G.E.	R. Hopkin Morris (Lib) 19,783 R. Moelwyn Hughes (Lab) 18,504
February 23, 1950 G.E.	R. Hopkin Morris (Lib) 24,472 A. L. Ungoed-Thomas (Lab) 24,285
October 25, 1951 G.E.	R. Hopkin Morris (Lib) 25,632 David Owen (Lab) 25,165
May 26, 1955 G.E.	Sir R. Hopkin Morris* (Lib) 24,410 J. Evans (Lab) 21,077 Mrs. Jennie E. Davies (Plaid Cymru) 3,835
February 28, 1957 By	Lady Megan Lloyd George (Lab) 23,679 J. Morgan Davies (Lib) 20,610 Mrs. J. E. Davies (Plaid Cymru) 5,741
October 8, 1959 G.E.	Lady Megan Lloyd George (Lab) 23,399 A. Talfan Davies (Lib) 16,766 J. B. Evans (Con) 6,147 Hywel H. Roberts (Plaid Cymru) 2,545
October 15, 1964 G.E.	Lady Megan Lloyd George (Lab) 21,424 A. Talfan Davies (Lib) 15,210 Gwynfor R. Evans (Plaid Cymru) 5,495 Mrs. H. E. Protheroe-Beynon (Con) 4,996
March 31,1966 G.E.	Lady Megan Lloyd George* (Lab) 21,221 D. Hywel Davies (Lib) 11,988 Gwynfor R. Evans (Plaid Cymru) 7,416 Simon J. Day (Con) 5,338

July 14, 1966 By	Gwynfor R. Evans (Plaid Cymru) 16,179 Gwilym Prys Davies (Lab) 13,743 D. Hywel Davies (Lib) 8,650 Simon J. Day (Con) 2,934
June 18, 1970 G.E.	Gwynoro G. Jones (Lab) 18,719 Gwynfor R. Evans (Plaid Cymru) 14,812 Huw G. E. Thomas (Lib) 10,707 L. H. Davies (Con) 4,975
February 28, 1974 G.E.	Gwynoro G. Jones (Lab) 17,165 Gwynfor R. Evans (Plaid Cymru) 17,162 D. R. Owen-Jones (Lib) 9,698 W. F. Newton Dunn (Con) 6,037
October 10, 1974 G.E.	Gwynfor R. Evans (Plaid Cymru) 23,325 Gwynoro G. Jones (Lab) 19,685 D. R. Owen-Jones (Lib) 5,393 R. A. Hayward (Con) 2,962 E. Brisbane Jones (Ind B C) 342
May 3, 1979 G.E.	Roger G. Thomas (Lab) 18,667 Gwynfor R. Evans (Plaid Cymru) 16,689 Nigel M. Thomas (Con) 12,272 R. C. C. Thomas (Lib) 4,186 Colin D. Grice (Nat Front) 149 E. J. J. Clarke (Ind K B U) 126
June 9, 1983 G.E.	Roger G. Thomas (Lab) 16,459 Nigel M. Thomas (Con) 15,305 Gwynfor R. Evans (Plaid Cymru) 14,099 Mrs. Joan R. Colin (Alln S D P) 5,737 Brian Kingzett (Ecol) 374 Colin D. Grice (Brit Nat) 154
June 11, 1987 G.E.	Alan W. Williams (Lab) 19,128 Roderick Richards (Con) 14,811 Hywel T. Edwards (Plaid Cymru) 12,457 Gwynoro G. Jones (S D P) 7,203 G. E. Oubridge (Green) 481

April 9, 1992 G.E.	Alan W. Williams (Lab) 20,879 H. Rhodri G. Thomas (Plaid Cymru) 17,957 Stephen J. Cavenagh (Con) 12,782 Juliana M-J. Hughes (Lib Dem) 5,353

Abbreviations (Party affiliations) and notes:

Agric Ind -	Agriculturist Independent
Alln S D P -	Alliance - Social Democratic Party
Brit Nat -	British National Party
Con -	Conservative Party
Ecol -	Ecology Party
Green -	Green Party
Ind -	Independent
Ind B C -	Independent British Candidate
Ind K B U-	Independent Keep Britain United
Ind Lab -	Independent Labour
Lib -	Liberal Party
Lib Dem -	Liberal Democratic Party
Lab -	Labour Party
Nat Front -	National Front Party
Nat Lib -	National Liberal
Plaid Cymru -	Welsh (Nationalist) Party
S D P -	Social Democratic Party
Unionist -	(Conservative and) Unionist Party

G.E.- General Election * - Died in office
By - By-Election # - Resigned

1 Elected to sit for Bedford.
2 Disabled to sit.
3 Husband of 'Madam Bevan'.
4 M. D. Magens elected but disqualified on petition.
5 Elevated to the peerage as Lord Cawdor.
6 No return due to rioting. Election held later in Aug. 1831.
7 Elevated to the peerage as Lord Melchett.

Appendix III

Roll of Honorary Freemen of Carmarthen

Date of Presentation	
May 31, 1910	Lt.-Gen. Sir James Hills-Johnes, V.C., G.C.B.
January 14, 1918	Capt. (Dr.) Ernest Emrys Isaac, M.C., Royal Army Medical Corps [. . . for conspicuous gallantry and devotion to duty while tending the wounded . . .]
January 29, 1918	Sgt. William Archard Morris, D.C.M., 2nd Battn. The Welch Regiment [. . . for conspicuous gallantry and devotion to duty in action . . . fine leadership . . . against hostile attacks]
January 29, 1918	C.S.M. Howard Vincent Burnhill, M.M., 15th Battn. The Welch Regiment [. . . for rescuing seven wounded men at Mametz Wood]
January 29, 1918	Sgt. Harry Evans, M.M., 6th Battn. The Welch Regiment [. . . for conspicuous gallantry and devotion to duty . . . repulsed three attacks and held a position against great odds]
April 8, 1918	Major Arthur Rowland Davies, M.C., Royal Engineers
July 17, 1918	Capt. Edward Theophilus Davies, M.C., Royal Artillery
October 3, 1918	Cpl. David Jones, M.M., Royal Engineers
April 29, 1919	Pte. David John Jeremy, M.M., 1st 4th Battn. The Welch Regiment
April 29, 1919	Sgt. John Williams, M.M., 15th Battn. The Welch Regiment
April 29, 1919	Pte. John Davies, D.C.M., 24th Battn. The Welch Regiment
April 29, 1919	Cpl. Edward John Williams, M.M., 436th Welsh Field Coy. Royal Engineers

April 29, 1919	Gnr. Thomas Davies, Royal Garrison Artillery [for transfusion of blood to a wounded comrade]
September 23, 1919	Lt.-Col. Arthur Evans, O.B.E., M.C., Royal Engineers
September 23, 1919	Capt. Howard Belmont White, M.C., 1st 4th Battn. The Welch Regiment
September 23, 1919	C.S.M. William Henry Williams, D.C.M., Royal Engineers
May 18, 1920	R.S.M Albert Owen James, M.S.M., Army Cyclist Corps [for valuable services with the forces in Italy]
May 18, 1920	Sapper John Samuel Jones, M.M., Cable Section Royal Engineers [. . . for maintaining communications under heavy shell-fire until wounded (Ypres)]
May 18, 1920	Pte. William Llewelyn, M.M., 14th Battn. Royal Welsh Fusiliers [. . . a company runner . . . he went back on five occasions under heavy shell-fire with messages]
May 18, 1920	S.Q.M.S. Sigebert Frederick John Thompson, M.M., Royal Army Service Corps [. . . for continuous devotion to duty]
May 18, 1920	Cpl. Dewi Aeron Evans, M.M., 15th Battn. The Welch Regiment [. . . for rescuing wounded during an attack on Mametz Wood]
May 18, 1920	Cpl. David John Jones, M.M., Royal Air Force
May 18, 1920	Sgt. John William Kettley, M.S.M., 81st Labour Company
September 8, 1923	Rt. Hon. David Lloyd George, O.M., M.P.
December 12, 1923	Major John Francis, D.S.O., M.C., 437th Welsh Field Coy. Royal Engineers [. . . for services rendered in the advance from Beersheba to Jerusalem]
December 12, 1923	Capt. Christopher Gwynne Lewis, M.C., 6th Battn. The Welch Regiment
September 10, 1925	John Hinds, Esq., Lord Lieutenant,
June 7, 1926	Major Charles Edward Williams, O.B.E.(Mil.), Royal Engineers

June 7, 1926	Capt. Thomas Witheredge Langman, O.B.E.(Mil.), 5th Battn. The Welch Regiment
June 7, 1926	Lt. Hugh William Spurrell, M.C., Machine Gun Corps
June 7, 1926	Capt. Harold Baskerville Williams, O.B.E.(Mil.), Royal Army Veterinary Corps
August 26, 1930	Henry Brunel White, Esq.
July 22, 1937	George Eyre Evans, Esq.
October 4, 1945	The Welch Regiment
May 30, 1950	Major David Hugh Davies, M.C., Royal Armoured Corps
May 30, 1950	Stoker P/O Enoch Davies, D.S.M., Royal Navy [. . . for outstanding courage and devotion to duty in attempting to rescue ratings from a steam-filled boiler room in H.M.S. Sumarez . . . during an engagement in the sinking of the Scharnhorst]
May 30, 1950	Sgt. Ernest Edward Duckfield, M.M., Royal Army Service Corps
May 30, 1950	Cpl. Gwyn Evans, M.M., The Welch Regiment [. . . for carrying urgent messages under enemy fire at Reasel, Holland]
May 30, 1950	Sgt. Stanley Rupert Edwards, D.F.M., Royal Air Force
May 30, 1950	Acting Sgt. Edward Hurley, M.M., Royal Engineers
May 30, 1950	L/Cpl. Powell James, M.M., The Welch Regiment
May 30, 1950	Cpl. Arthur Leonard Lewis, D.C.M., Lincolnshire Regiment
May 30, 1950	L/Cpl. William Richard John Lloyd, D.C.M., Sherwood Foresters [. . . while a POW he made eleven attempts to escape . . . as an example of sustained determination . . . it is unsurpassed]
May 30, 1950	Pte. William John Oliver, M.M., 1st Battn. The Welch Regiment
May 30, 1950	Brinley Parry Richards, Croix de Guerre, Friends' Ambulance Unit

May 30, 1950	Sgt. Hubert Woodward, Croix de Guerre, Royal Army Ordnance Corps
July 22, 1953	Ald. John Owen Morgans
July 10, 1969	The Royal Regiment of Wales
March 14, 1980	Theodore Frederick Rogers, Esq.
April 30, 1982	Her Majesty's Welsh Regiment of Foot Guards

Note: Following the two World Wars of 1914-18 and 1939-45 the Honorary Freedom was conferred upon those men of the Borough who had been awarded decorations or commended for valour or distinguished conduct. Where it is available an extract from the citation that accompanied the award has been included above.

Sgt. James Orman, D.C.M. who was due to receive the Honorary Freedom for his distinguished conduct in the Dardanelles campaign in 1915, for which he was awarded the Distinguished Conduct Medal, was killed in Palestine on March 9th, 1918, before the honour could be bestowed upon him.

Houses on the Parade

Appendix IV

Population Figures

The Census figures for Carmarthen from 1801 to 1991 are as follows:

Date	Population
1801	5,548
1811	7,275
1821	8,906
1831	9,995
1841	9,526
1851	10,462
1861	9,993
1871	10,499
1881	10,514
1891	10,338
1901	10,025
1911	10,221
1921	10,011
1931	10,310
1951	12,114 (Males 5,636 - Females 6,478)
1961	13,247 (Males 6,263 - Females 6,984)
1971	13,081 (Males 5,999 - Females 7,082)
1981	11,890 (Males 5,523 - Females 6,367)
1991	12,240 (Males 5,604 - Females 6,636)

Select Bibliography

Archaeology in Dyfed 1976-1986, A review by Dyfed Archaeological Trust (Carmarthen, 1986)

Bevan, W. L., *Diocesan Histories: St. David's*. (London: S. P. C. K., 1888)

Brigstock, T. E., *St. Peter's Church, Carmarthen, Notes for Visitors*. (Carmarthen, 1934)

Carmarthenshire Antiquary (The), This is the present title of the Journal of the Carmarthenshire Antiquarian Society and Field Club, founded in 1905. First published as *The Transactions* (referred to as T.C.A.S. in the text), in 1941 its title became *The Carmarthen Antiquary* and from 1970 *The Carmarthenshire Antiquary*.

Carmarthenshire Historian (The), First two volumes published as *The Carmarthenshire Local History Magazine* (Published successively by Carmarthenshire Community Council, Dyfed Rural Council and Dyfed Association of Voluntary Services, 20 Volumes from 1964 to 1985.)

Carmarthenshire Studies, Essays presented to Major Francis Jones, eds. Tudor Barnes and Nigel Yates. (Carmarthenshire County Council, 1974)

Craig, F. W. S., *British Parliamentary Election Results*. (Colchester: Political Reference Publications and London: Macmillan) several consecutive volumes

Daniel-Tyssen, J. R., *Royal Charters and Historical Documents relating to the Town and County of Carmarthen, etc.* (Carmarthen: Spurrell, 1878)

Etheridge, Ken, *Welsh Costume* (Ammanford, 1958)

Evans, J. G., *The Black Book of Carmarthen*. Facsimile. (Oxford, 1888)

Evans, K. M., *A Book of Welsh Saints* (Penarth: Church in Wales Publications, 1967)

Evans, Martin, *An Early History of Queen Elizabeth Grammar School Carmarthen 1576-1800* (Carmarthen)

Encilion (Yr), A Journal of the Carmarthenshire Antiquarian Society and Field Club, 2 volumes only (Carmarthen, 1912)

Famous Welshmen, (Cardiff: University of Wales Press, 1947)

Griffiths, R. A., *The Principality of Wales in the Later Middle Ages, I - South Wales, 1277-1536*. (Cardiff: University of Wales Press, 1972)

Inventory of The Ancient Monuments (An), V - County of Carmarthen, Royal Commission on Ancient and Historical Monuments in Wales and Monmouthshire. (H.M.S.O., 1917)

James, Heather, *Roman West Wales*. (Carmarthen: Rampart Press, 1982)

James, Terrence, *Carmarthen: An Archaeological and Topographical Survey*. (Carmarthen: Dyfed Archaeological Trust, 1980)

Jarman, A. O. H., *The Legend of Merlin*. (Cardiff: University of Wales Press, 1970)

Jenkins, J. Geraint, *Nets and Coracles*. (Newton Abbot: David and Charles, 1974)

Jones, Francis, *God Bless the Prince of Wales*. (Carmarthenshire Community Council, 1963)

Lewis, E. A., *The Welsh Port Books*, 1550-1603. (London, 1927)

Lloyd, D. M. and E. M., *A Book of Wales*. (London: Collins, 1953)

Lloyd, Sir J. E., *A History of Carmarthenshire*, 2 volumes. Cardiff, Vol. 1 (1935) and Vol. 2 (1939)

Lower, M. A., *Chronicle of Battle Abbey*, 1060-1176. (London: John Russell Smith, 1851)

Molloy, Pat, *A Shilling for Carmarthen*. (Llandysul: Gomer, 1980)

Four Cheers for Carmarthen. (Gomer, 1981)

And They Blessed Rebecca. (Gomer, 1983)

Newell, E. J., *A History of the Welsh Church*. (London, 1895)

Parry-Jones, D., *Welsh Country Upbringing*. (London: Batsford, 1948)

Payne, F. G., *Welsh Peasant Costume*. (Cardiff: Welsh Folk Museum, 1969)

Phillips, T., *Cartularium S. Johannis de Caermarthen*. (Cheltenham, 1865)

Prys-Jones, A. G., *The Story of Carmarthenshire*, Vol. 1. (1959) and Vol. 2 (1972). (Llandybie: Christopher Davies)

Randall, Alan, *The Passionists at Carmarthen 1889-1986*. (Carmarthen, 1986)

Rivet, A. L. F. and Smith, Colin, *The Place Names of Roman Britain*. (London: Batsford, 1979)

Spurrell, William, *Carmarthen and its Neighbourhood*. (Carmarthen, 1879)

Temple, Nigel, *John Nash and the Village Picturesque*. (Gloucester: Alan Sutton, 1979)

Wacher, John, *The Towns of Roman Britain*. (London: Batsford, 1974)

Wesley Church Carmarthen, 1861-1961, Centenary Handbook. (Carmarthen, 1960)

Williams, Glanmor, *The Welsh Church from Conquest to Reformation*. (Cardiff: University of Wales Press, 1976 revised edition)

Jackson's Lane, 1970

Glossary

As an aid for students and others we include a short glossary of abbreviations and of those technical and obscure words whose meanings are not explained or readily accessible in the text.

Abbreviations:

A.D. : In the year of our Lord (from the Latin *Anno Domini*) meaning dates after the Birth of Christ.

B.C. : Before Christ (dates before the Birth of Christ)

c. : about (from the Latin *circa*)

e.g. : for example (from the Latin *exempli gratia*)

ibid. : in the same place (from the Latin *ibidem*)

i.e. : that is (from the Latin *id est*)

viz. : namely (from the Latin *videlicet*)

* * * * * * * * *

Acre: Originally as much land as a yoke of oxen could plough in a day. Now 4,840 sq. yards.

Ap or Ab: son of (from the Welsh *map* or *mab*).

Archdruid: The chief druid; president of the Gorsedd of Bards formed in 1792, whose pageantry and ceremonial functions at the National Eisteddfod run in conjunction with its work of preserving and fostering the Welsh language. Not to be confused with the ancient Celtic druids recorded by Julius Caesar.

Balinger: A small boat.

Barque: A three mast sailing ship with the fore and main masts square rigged and the rear or mizzen mast with fore-and-aft rigging.

Bascule bridge: A draw bridge with the raising part counterbalanced with weights. In a **rolling bascule bridge** the balancing point is a curved rocking-type pivot.

Battlement: An indented parapet at the top of a wall or tower (also described as **crenellated**).

Brig: A two mast sailing ship with square rigging but with an additional fore-and-aft sail on her main mast.

Cantref: In the Middle Ages the land under the rule of a single Welsh prince was called a *gwlad*. This was divided into areas called *cantrefi* (hundreds) which may have been the area originally occupied by a hundred families. Later the *cantref* became a district containing a hundred *trefi*, a *tref* being the area of land occupied by a clan which was based on kinship. Each *cantref* was divided into smaller units called *cymydau* (commotes). Each commote or *cwmwd* contained a number of *trefi*.

Cartulary: A collection of records of a monastery or similar place.

Chamberlain: An official who received rents and revenues.

Cog: An early form of ship, broadly built with roundish prow and stern.

Commote: A division of a cantref (Welsh *cwmwd*). See above.

Court of Star Chamber: A criminal court sitting in the Star Chamber in Westminster (so-called because of its decoration) which was abolished in 1641 having become arbitrary and oppressive.

Croft: A piece of enclosed ground for agriculture.

Debtors: In this case, those who were imprisoned for debts. Imprisonment for debt in general was abolished in 1867.

Demesne: The part of a manor (landed estate) reserved for the lord's use and worked by tenants in return for their own land-holdings. At Carmarthen the demesne (pronounced de-main) belonged to the Crown and was supervised from the royal castle. See Manor below.

Eisteddfodwr: One who frequents eisteddfodau (eisteddfods).

Elegy: A song or poem of lamentation or meditation.

Entrepôt: A commercial centre for distribution or temporary deposit of goods.

Esquire: A title of dignity immediately below knight, formerly a young attendant to a knight.

Eulogy: A writing or speech in honour of a deceased person.

Fitz: son of (from the Anglo-french *fiz*, modern French *fils*)

Flavian: During the time of the Flavian dynasty. Flavius was the family name of the Roman emperors beginning with Vespasian in AD 69 and ending with Domitian in AD 96.

Folly: A building or structure of no apparent usefulness and said to have shown the folly of the builder.

Fuller: A finisher who cleaned and thickened cloth.

Fustian: A coarse cloth of cotton and flax.

Gaol: This spelling of jail is used since, during the lifetime of the buildings referred to, it was the accepted and official variant in common use.

Genealogy: The study of the descent, lineage or pedigree of families.

Heraldry: The art of designing or describing armorial bearings, coats-of-arms.

Holland: Coarse unbleached linen, first made in Holland.

Hundred: A subdivision of a shire into an area of 100 hides. A hide was originally the amount of land necessary to sustain a peasant household. Therefore a Hundred was originally an area of land supporting one hundred peasant households. (The hide varied according to locality and date.)

League: A measure of distance, usually taken as 3 miles.

Leat: A water-course.

Maltster: A person who made malt, which was grain prepared for brewing by being allowed to germinate and then dried.

Manor: After the Norman Conquest the land, especially in England, was divided up into estates called manors. The lord of the manor had jurisdiction over tenants who held their strips of land in return for working on the lord's land. Later, tenants paid rent for their holdings.

Maundy money: Silver money (coins) distributed to deserving people on Maundy Thursday (the Thursday before Easter) by the royal Almoner. A symbolic ceremony which is now usually performed personally by the Sovereign using specially minted silver coins.

Michaelmas: The feast of St. Michael (29th September).

Murage: A toll or tax levied for building or repairing the walls of a town.

Née: Born. Used in indicating a woman's maiden name.

Peruke: A wig.

Ordinance: An authoritative direction, decree or command.

Pillory: An instrument of punishment comprising a wooden frame, supported on a pillar, pierced with holes through which the head and hands of a person were put so as to subject him to public ridicule or abuse. This punishment was abolished in 1837.

Ploughland or carucate: Originally the amount of land that could be tilled by one plough-team of oxen in one year. On average roughly 100 acres depending on the type of soil.

Poet Laureate: An eminent poet appointed as an officer of the Royal Household to write poetry for special national occasions.

Pontage: A tax or toll for the use or maintenance of a bridge.

Press Gang: A body of men under the command of an officer employed to press (i.e. capture or kidnap) men for service in the army or more usually the navy. Conditions in those days were harsh enough to deter all but the most desperate from volunteering.

Privateer: Literally a private man-of-war. An armed vessel, owned and crewed by private persons, authorised to capture enemy shipping.

Recorder: A magistrate or judge. Originally a person with legal knowledge appointed by the Mayor and Aldermen to record or keep in mind the proceedings of their courts and the customs of their borough.

Reeve: An official appointed by a landowner, e.g. the Lord of the Manor, to supervise his estates and tenants.

Samian: A fine red pottery (tableware) found extensively on Roman sites.

Schooner: A sailing ship with two or more masts all with fore-and-aft rigging.

Seditious: Inciting revolt or rebellion against a government.

Sepoy: A (native) Indian soldier under British command.

Shearman: One who cuts or shears woollen cloth.

Sheriff: (Shire Reeve) Chief officer of the Crown in charge of a shire or county.

Stocks: An instrument of punishment. The offender sat with his ankles locked between two planks or stocks of wood.

Tinker: A craftsman who mended metal pots, kettles and other metal household articles. The modern usage implying a clumsy mender or jack-of-all-trades is not applicable.

Tuckers (Guild of): Fullers or cloth-finishers who cleaned and thickened cloth.

Score: Twenty (20).

Spelt wheat: A variety of wheat, common in southern Europe.

Turnpike: Historically, a spiked barrier (made of pikes) across a road to prevent a sudden attack by horsemen; later the term came to be used for a toll-gate. Hence turnpike road.

Vicus: In the case of Carmarthen a settlement of traders and artisans outside the East gate of the Roman military fort. A term denoting a settlement subordinate to a higher authority either civil or military.

ye: Properly pronounced as *the* - the y being a way of writing the Anglo-saxon letter þ (the thorn) pronounced as *th.*

Ecclesiastical terms:

Archdeacon: A church official next in rank to a Bishop who superintends part of a diocese called an archdeaconry and has the power of spiritual censure.

Canon: A member of the cathedral chapter (with a seat in the cathedral). Originally a clergyman living within the cathedral and ordering his life according to the church canons or laws.

Catechism: An instruction in the Christian religion in the form of question and answer.

Chancel: The eastern part of a church, usually for clergy or choir.

Chancellor: One of the chief dignitaries of a cathedral whose ceremonial duties include applying the seal and presiding at a consistory court.

Charnel: A house or vault for the bones of the dead which were placed there because of repeated burials in a small area.

Clerestory: The upper part of a church nave containing windows, above the roofs of any side aisles, lighting the central part of the building.

Consistory court: The place where a diocesan (church) court would be held by the Chancellor of the diocese to administer church law.

Curate: An assistant to a beneficed clergyman (i.e. a clergyman with a parish). A **perpetual curate** was an incumbent of a parish, ranking as a vicar, who was appointed by the patron of the parish and licensed by the Bishop.

Excommunicate: To cut off from communion or religious rites.

Heresy: Theological opinion in opposition to what is considered orthodox or accepted.

Lay: Non-clerical, belonging to the people as opposed to the clergy. Hence **laity** (= the people).

Nave: The main body of a church.

Piety: Being pious, reverential to God.

Prebendary: The holder of a paid office in a cathedral.

Precentor: One of the chief dignitaries of a cathedral whose nominal duties of directing the singing were normally undertaken by a lesser official.

Prior: The superior officer of a Priory.

Psalter: The Book of Psalms, part of the Bible.

Rector: Historically a parson or incumbent who received the tithes of his parish. Since the abolition of tithes the office is identical with that of Vicar. In Roman Catholic use the head priest of a parish is called the Rector.

Rood: A cross or crucifix, now an obsolete term.

Rural dean: A clergyman who superintends part of an archdeaconry called a rural-deanery.

Sacristy: The place in a church for keeping vestments, sacred vessels and valuable property.

See: The diocese or place of authority of (in this case) a Bishop.

Sepulchral: A description of a place serving as a tomb or a place for burial.

Surrogate: A deputy. Now normally applied to a clergyman who is deputised to perform marriages.

Tessellated: Composed of variously coloured tiles arranged in patterns.

Testament: Each of the two divisions of the Bible: the Old and New (Christian) Testaments.

Transept: Either of the transverse arms extending north and south in a cross-shaped church.

Vestry: A room or part of a church or chapel where clergy robe and where vestments and records are kept.

Vicar: Historically a priest acting in the place of a rector. Unlike a rector, a vicar did not receive tithes. Since the abolition of tithes the status of vicar is identical with that of rector.

Pre-decimal Money

Each £1 was divided into 20 shillings (s.), each shilling into 12 pence (d.) and each penny into 2 half-pence or 4 farthings.

Common coins in circulation at various times were:

Gold: Sovereign (£1) and half-sovereign (10s.)

Silver: Crown (5s.), half-crown (2s. 6d.), florin (2s.), shilling (1s.), six-pence (6d.), three-pence (3d.) and before 1856 the groat (4d.).

Copper: Penny (1d.), half-penny (1/2d.), farthing (1/4d.)

The Guinea (worth £1. 1s.) was not seen as a coin after 1816 but the term and value were commonly used when money was contributed to funds and for certain specialised transactions.

Before the advent of Treasury notes in 1914, when £1 and 10s. notes appeared, paper money usually consisted of notes issued by private banks for large amounts, with limited circulation. The use of gold coins for domestic purposes ceased after 1915.

The seemingly odd amounts of 6s. 8d. and 13s. 4d., often quoted in historical documents, were conveniently one-third and two-thirds of a £. The *Noble* was a coin usually valued at 6s. 8d. and the *Mark* was the term used for the value of 13s. 4d.

Woods Row during demolition 1973

Index

Quay Street

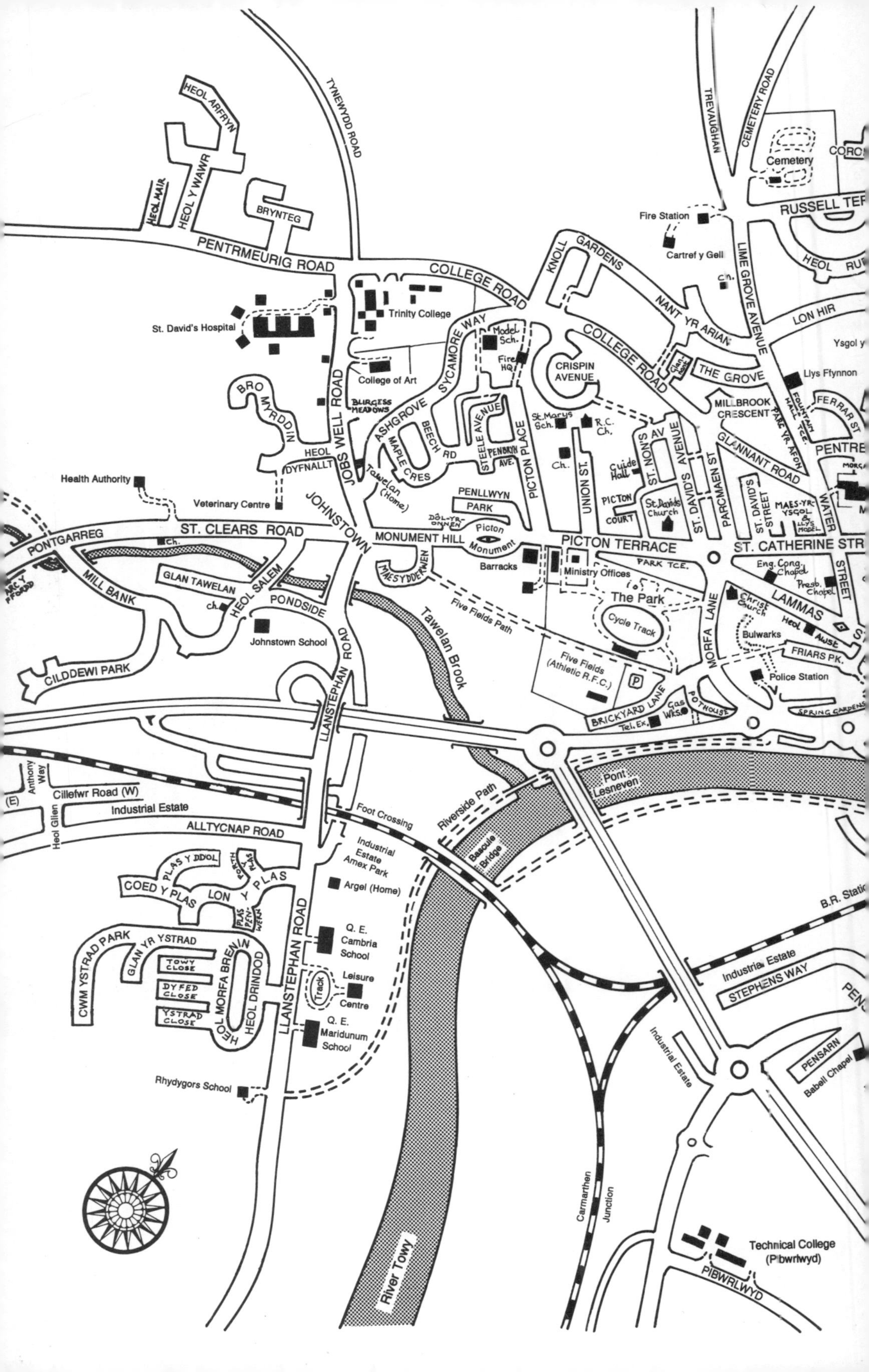
TYNEWYDD ROAD
HEOL ARFFRYN
HEOL Y WAWR
HEOL MAIR
BRYNTEG
PENTRMEURIG ROAD
COLLEGE ROAD
St. David's Hospital
Trinity College
College of Art
SYCAMORE WAY
Model Sch.
Fire HQ
CRISPIN AVENUE
KNOLL GARDENS
NANT YR ARIAN
TREVAUGHAN
CEMETERY ROAD
Cemetery
Fire Station
Cartref y Gell
RUSSELL TER
LIME GROVE AVENUE
HEOL
LON HIR
Ysgol y
THE GROVE
Llys Ffynnon
MILLBROOK CRESCENT
FERRAR ST
PENTRE
GLANNANT ROAD
BRO MYRDDIN
JOBS WELL ROAD
BURGESS MEADOWS
ASHGROVE
MAPLE CRES
BEECH RD
STEELE AVENUE
PENBRYN AVE.
PICTON PLACE
St. Marys Sch.
R.C. Ch.
Ch.
UNION ST.
Guide Hall
ST. NON'S AV
ST. DAVID'S AVENUE
PARCMAEN ST
ST. DAVID'S STREET
MAES-YR-YSGOL
WATER STREET
HEOL DYFNALLT
Health Authority
Veterinary Centre
Tawelan (Home)
PENLLWYN PARK
PICTON COURT
St. Davids Church
JOHNSTOWN
ST. CLEARS ROAD
PONTGARREG
MONUMENT HILL
Picton Monument
PICTON TERRACE
ST. CATHERINE STR
MILL BANK
GLAN TAWELAN
HEOL SALEM
MAESYDDERWEN
Barracks
Ministry Offices
PARK TCE.
The Park
Cycle Track
Eng. Cong. Chapel
Presb. Chapel
Christ Church
LAMMAS
Ch.
PONDSIDE
Johnstown School
Five Fields Path
Tawelan Brook
MORFA LANE
Bulwarks
FRIARS PK.
Police Station
CILDDEWI PARK
LLANSTEPHAN ROAD
Five Fields (Athletic R.F.C.)
P
BRICKYARD LANE
Tel. Ex.
Gas Wks.
POTHOUSE
SPRING GARDENS
Anthony Way
Cilefwr Road (W)
(E)
Industrial Estate
Heol Glien
ALLTYCNAP ROAD
Foot Crossing
Riverside Path
Pont Lesneven
Bascule Bridge
Industrial Estate Amex Park
PLAS Y DDOL
COED Y PLAS
LON Y PLAS
Argel (Home)
B.R. Station
Industrial Estate
STEPHENS WAY
CWM YSTRAD PARK
GLAN YR YSTRAD
TOWY CLOSE
DYFED CLOSE
YSTRAD CLOSE
HEOL MORFA BRENIN
HEOL DRINDOD
Q. E. Cambria School
Track
Leisure Centre
Q. E. Maridunum School
Industrial Estate
PENSARN
Babell Chapel
Rhydygors School
Carmarthen Junction
River Towy
Technical College (Pibwrlwyd)
PIBWRLWYD